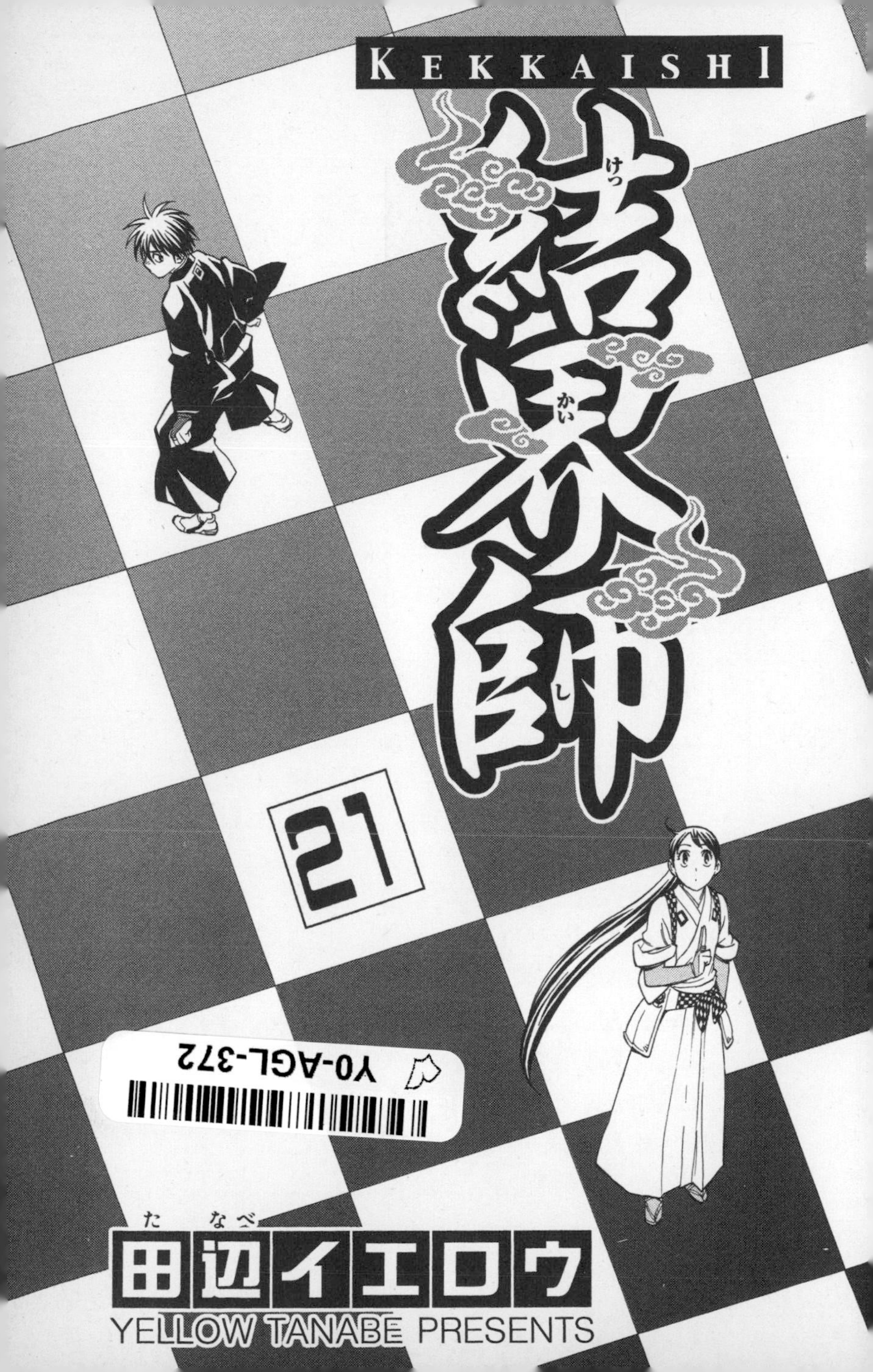
KEKKAISHI
結界師
けっ かい し
21
たなべ
田辺イエロウ
YELLOW TANABE PRESENTS

The Story Thus Far

Yoshimori Sumimura and Tokine Yukimura have an ancestral duty to protect the Karasumori Forest from supernatural beings called ayakashi. People with their gift for terminating ayakashi are called kekkaishi, or "barrier masters."

When Ichiro Ogi, the archrival of Yoshimori's brother Masamori, causes the deaths of several of his Night Troops, Masamori challenges him. Their battle is fierce, but Masamori eventually triumphs—or so it seems. Instead of Ichiro, it is his little brother Rokuro who lies dying at the scene. It turns out that Ichiro is an entity composed of all the Ogi brothers—brothers who have abandoned their youngest to save themselves.

Masamori asks Okuni, a powerful member of the Council of Twelve, to save Rokuro. In exchange, he agrees to form an alliance with her...

KEKKAISHI VOL. 21
TABLE OF CONTENTS

ADAIR, Sam

Patron

8767

Patron#

Check one:

☒ Email sent

☐ Spoke with patron

☐ Left message with family member

☐ Left message on machine

☐ Patron called in request for hold

☐ SMS/Text

Notes:

ADAIR, Sam

Person

Telephone

Conditions
Left sent
Spoke with patient

☐ Left message with family member

☐ Left message on machine

☐ Patient called in request to hold

Date
2/8/22

Day
Th

Chapter 195: Descent from the Heavens

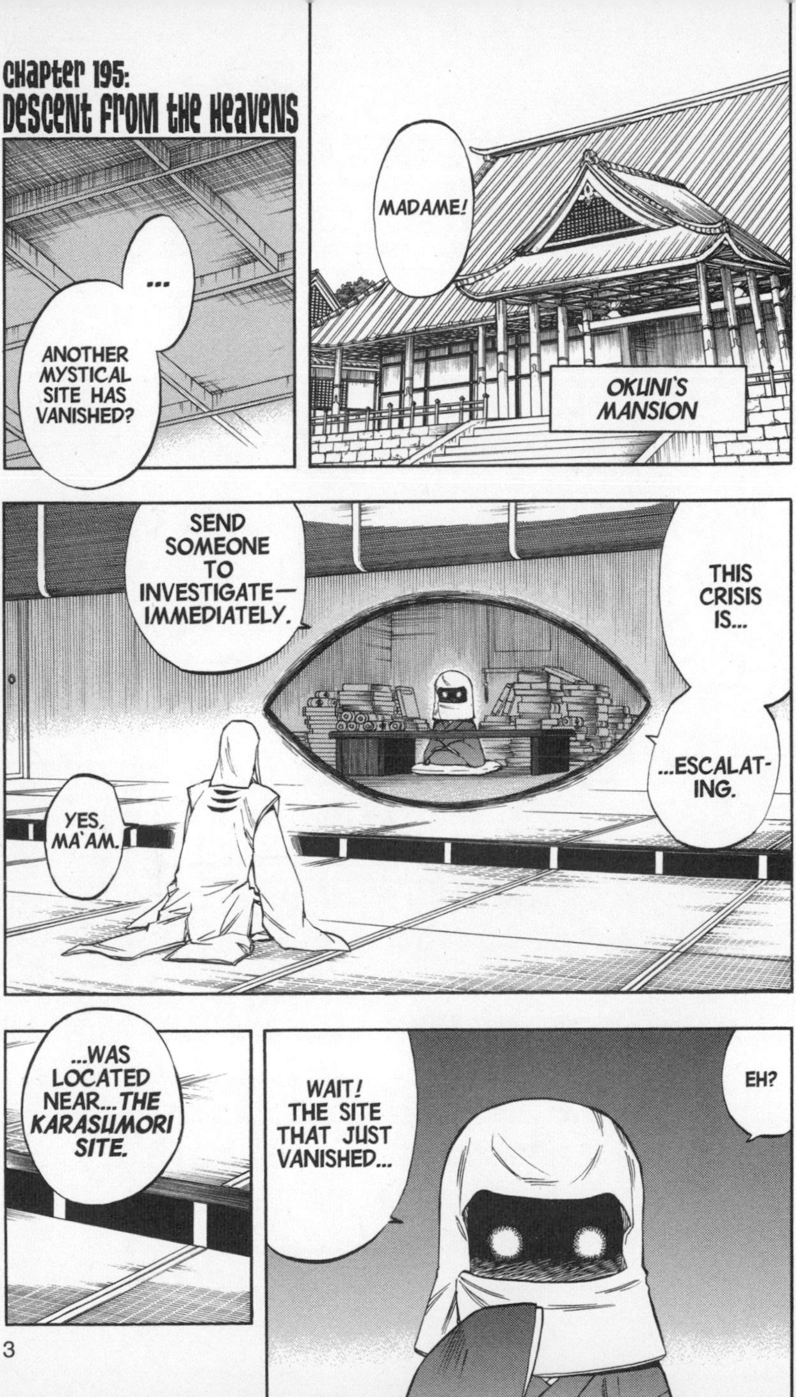
MADAME!
OKUNI'S MANSION
...
ANOTHER MYSTICAL SITE HAS VANISHED?
THIS CRISIS IS...
...ESCALAT-ING.
SEND SOMEONE TO INVESTIGATE—IMMEDIATELY.
YES, MA'AM.
EH?
WAIT! THE SITE THAT JUST VANISHED...
...WAS LOCATED NEAR...THE KARASUMORI SITE.

Chapter 195: Descent from the Heavens

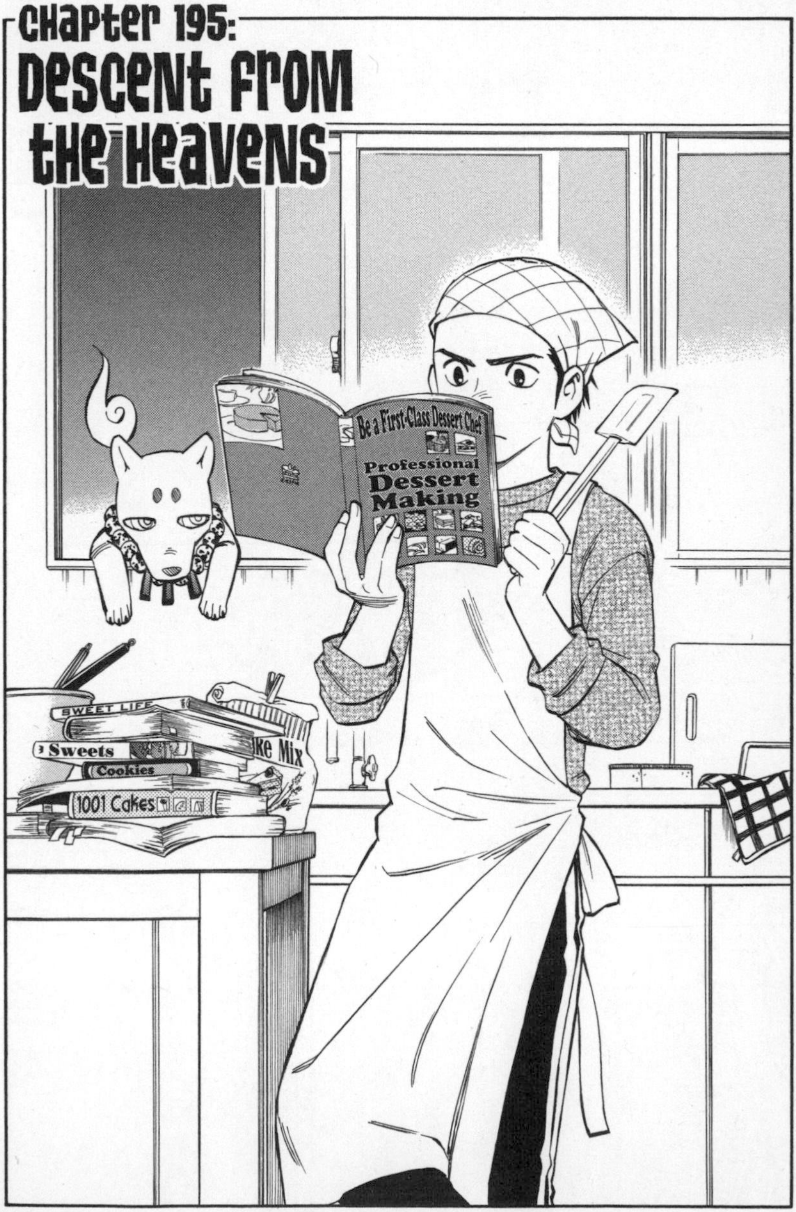
Be a First-Class Dessert Chef
Professional Dessert Making
SWEET LIFE
Sweets
Cookies
1001 Cakes
ke Mix

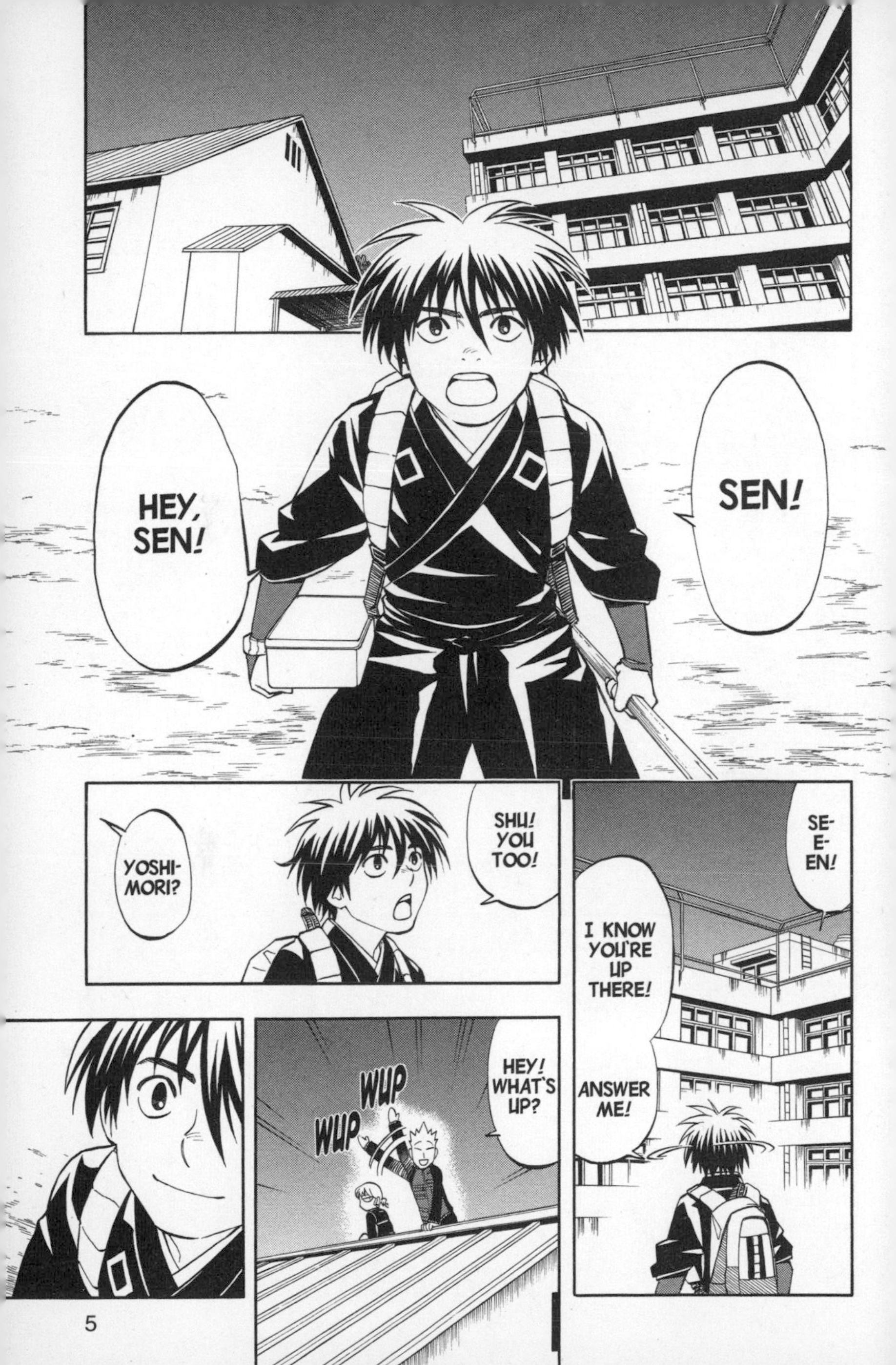
SEN!
HEY, SEN!
SE-E-EN!
I KNOW YOU'RE UP THERE!
ANSWER ME!
SHU! YOU TOO!
YOSHIMORI?
HEY! WHAT'S UP?
WUP WUP

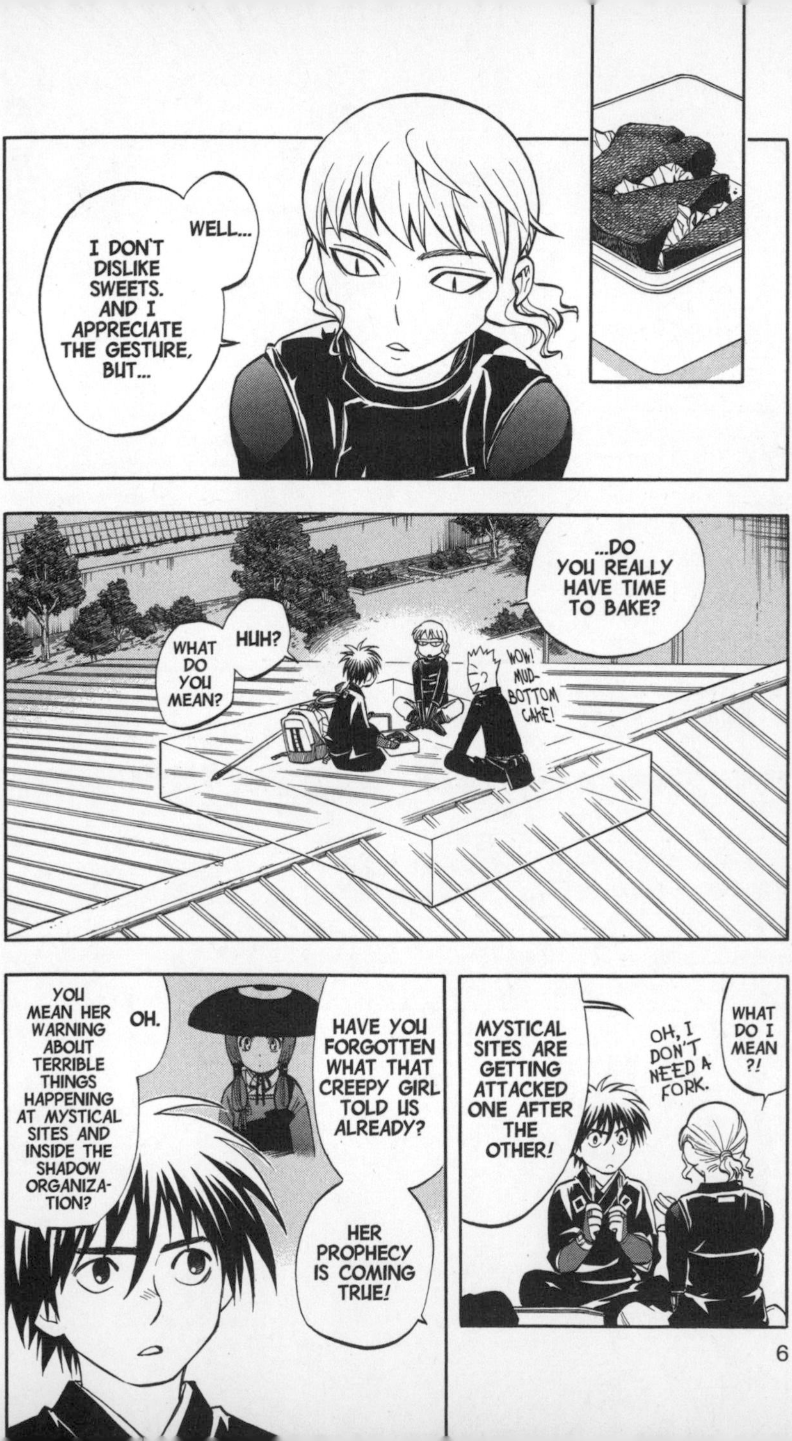
WELL... I DON'T DISLIKE SWEETS. AND I APPRECIATE THE GESTURE, BUT...
...DO YOU REALLY HAVE TIME TO BAKE?
WOW! MUD-BOTTOM CAKE!
HUH?
WHAT DO YOU MEAN?
WHAT DO I MEAN ?!
OH, I DON'T NEED A FORK.
MYSTICAL SITES ARE GETTING ATTACKED ONE AFTER THE OTHER!
HAVE YOU FORGOTTEN WHAT THAT CREEPY GIRL TOLD US ALREADY?
HER PROPHECY IS COMING TRUE!
OH.
YOU MEAN HER WARNING ABOUT TERRIBLE THINGS HAPPENING AT MYSTICAL SITES AND INSIDE THE SHADOW ORGANIZA-TION?

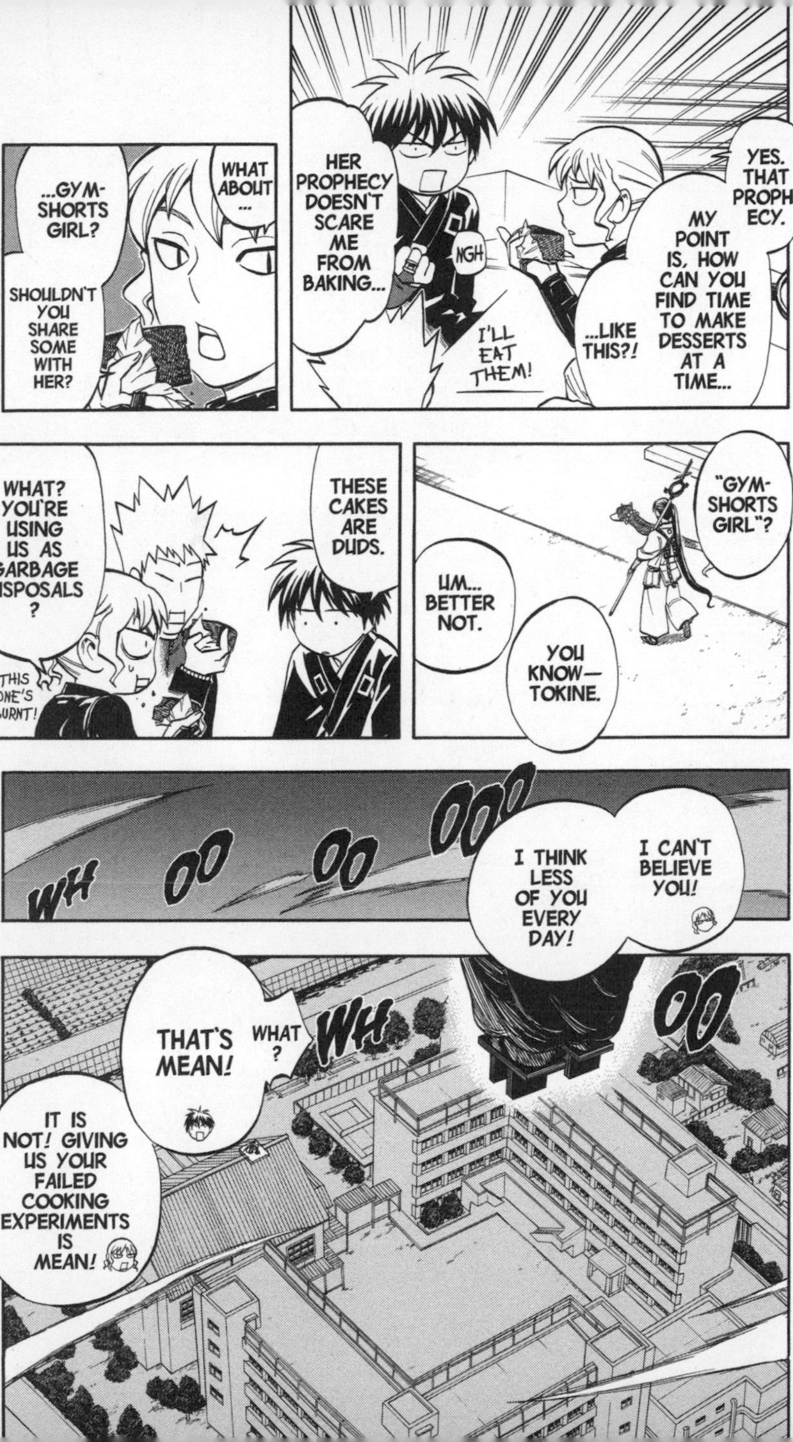
YES. THAT PROPHECY.
MY POINT IS, HOW CAN YOU FIND TIME TO MAKE DESSERTS AT A TIME...
...LIKE THIS?!
I'LL EAT THEM!
NGH
HER PROPHECY DOESN'T SCARE ME FROM BAKING...
WHAT ABOUT...
...GYM-SHORTS GIRL?
SHOULDN'T YOU SHARE SOME WITH HER?
"GYM-SHORTS GIRL"?
YOU KNOW—TOKINE.
UM... BETTER NOT.
THESE CAKES ARE DUDS.
WHAT? YOU'RE USING US AS GARBAGE DISPOSALS?
THIS ONE'S BURNT!
I CAN'T BELIEVE YOU!
I THINK LESS OF YOU EVERY DAY!
WHOOOOOOO
WHOO
WHAT?
THAT'S MEAN!
IT IS NOT! GIVING US YOUR FAILED COOKING EXPERIMENTS IS MEAN!

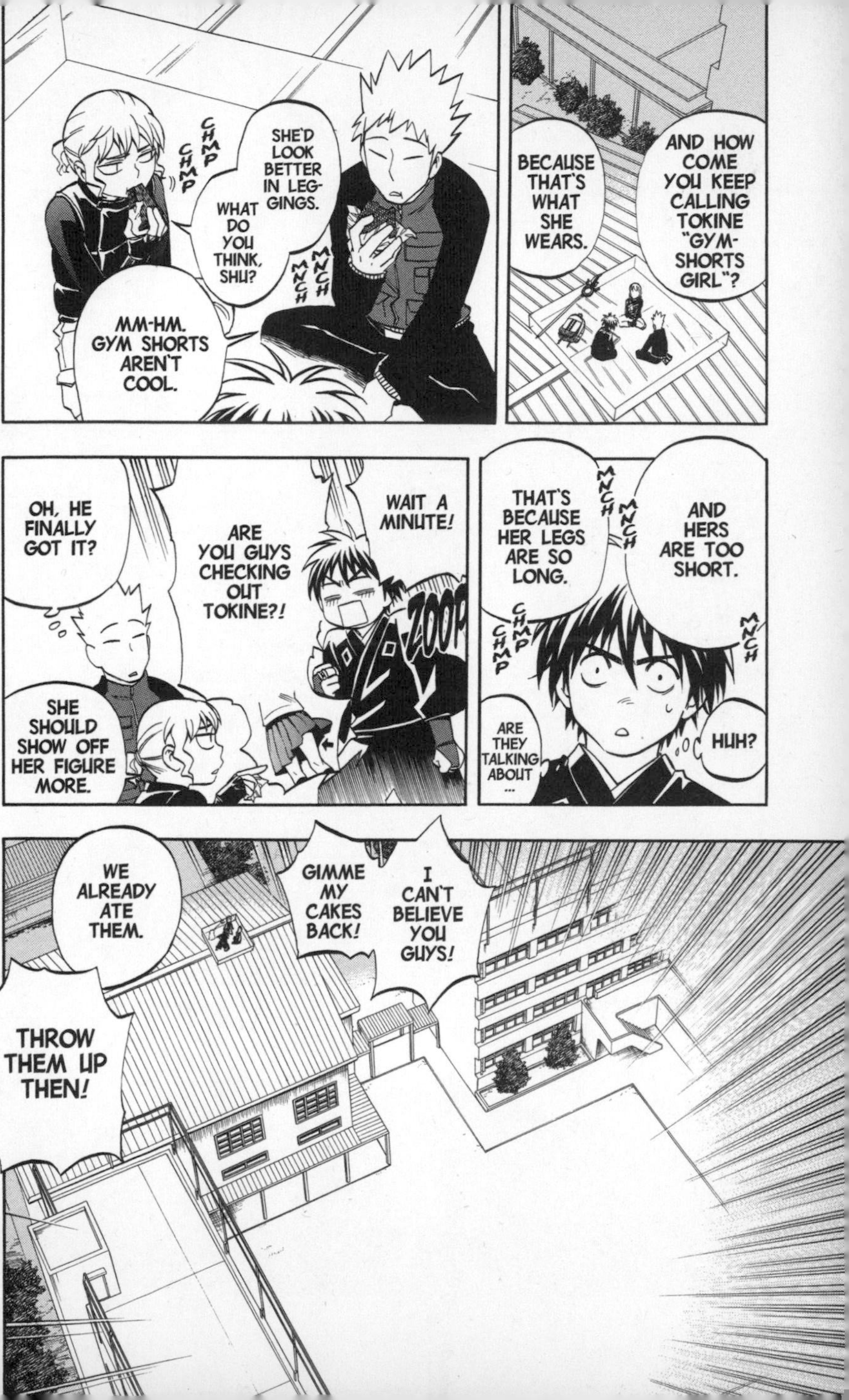
AND HOW COME YOU KEEP CALLING TOKINE "GYM-SHORTS GIRL"?
BECAUSE THAT'S WHAT SHE WEARS.
SHE'D LOOK BETTER IN LEG-GINGS.
CHMP CHMP
WHAT DO YOU THINK, SHU?
MNCH MNCH
MM-HM. GYM SHORTS AREN'T COOL.
AND HERS ARE TOO SHORT.
MNCH MNCH
THAT'S BECAUSE HER LEGS ARE SO LONG.
CHMP CHMP
MNCH
HUH?
ARE THEY TALKING ABOUT ...
WAIT A MINUTE!
ZOOP
ARE YOU GUYS CHECKING OUT TOKINE?!
OH, HE FINALLY GOT IT?
SHE SHOULD SHOW OFF HER FIGURE MORE.
I CAN'T BELIEVE YOU GUYS!
GIMME MY CAKES BACK!
WE ALREADY ATE THEM.
THROW THEM UP THEN!

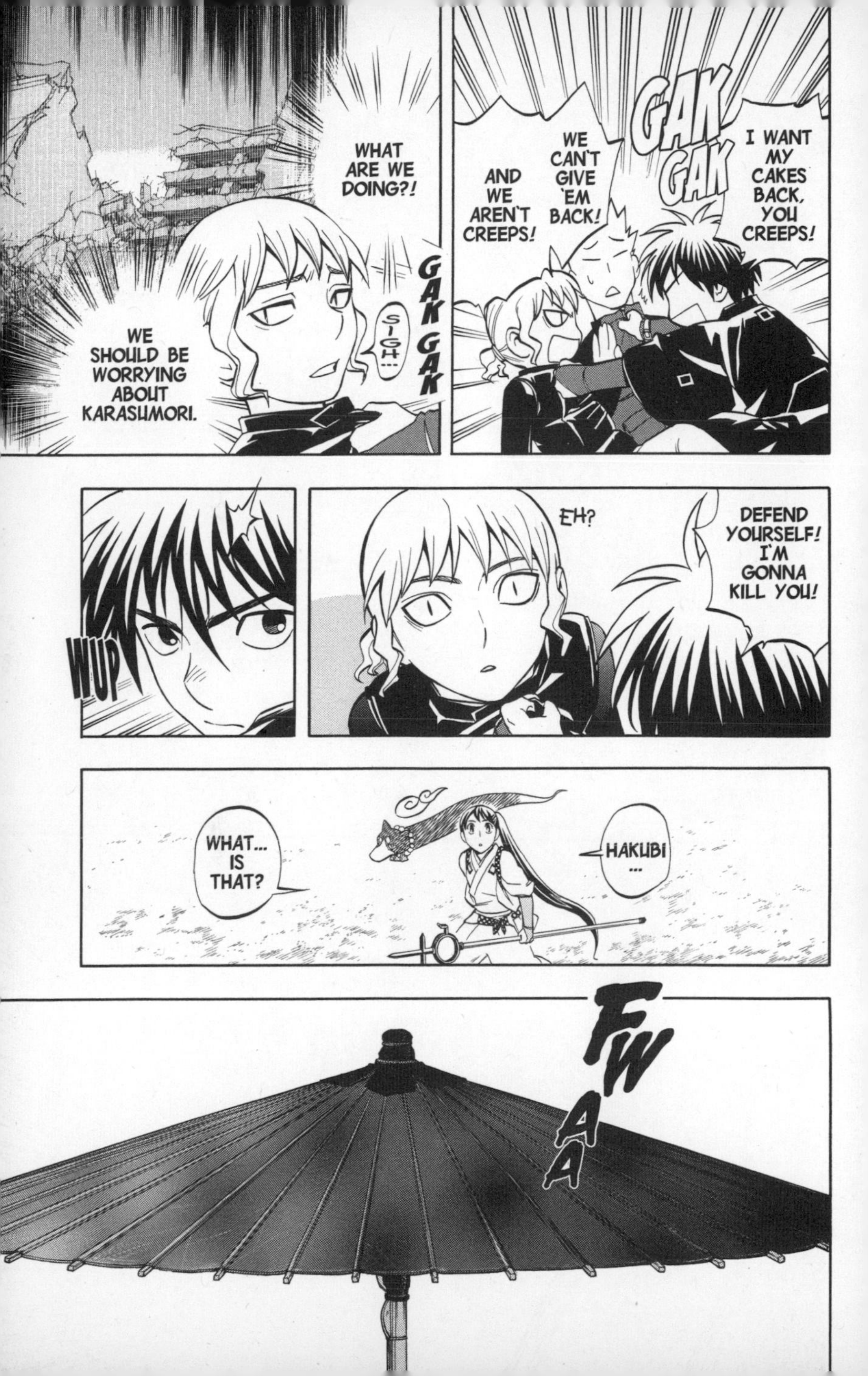
GAK GAK
I WANT MY CAKES BACK, YOU CREEPS!
WE CAN'T GIVE 'EM BACK!
AND WE AREN'T CREEPS!
WHAT ARE WE DOING?!
GAK GAK GAK
SIGH...
WE SHOULD BE WORRYING ABOUT KARASUMORI.
DEFEND YOURSELF! I'M GONNA KILL YOU!
EH?
WUP
HAKUBI...
WHAT... IS THAT?
FWAA

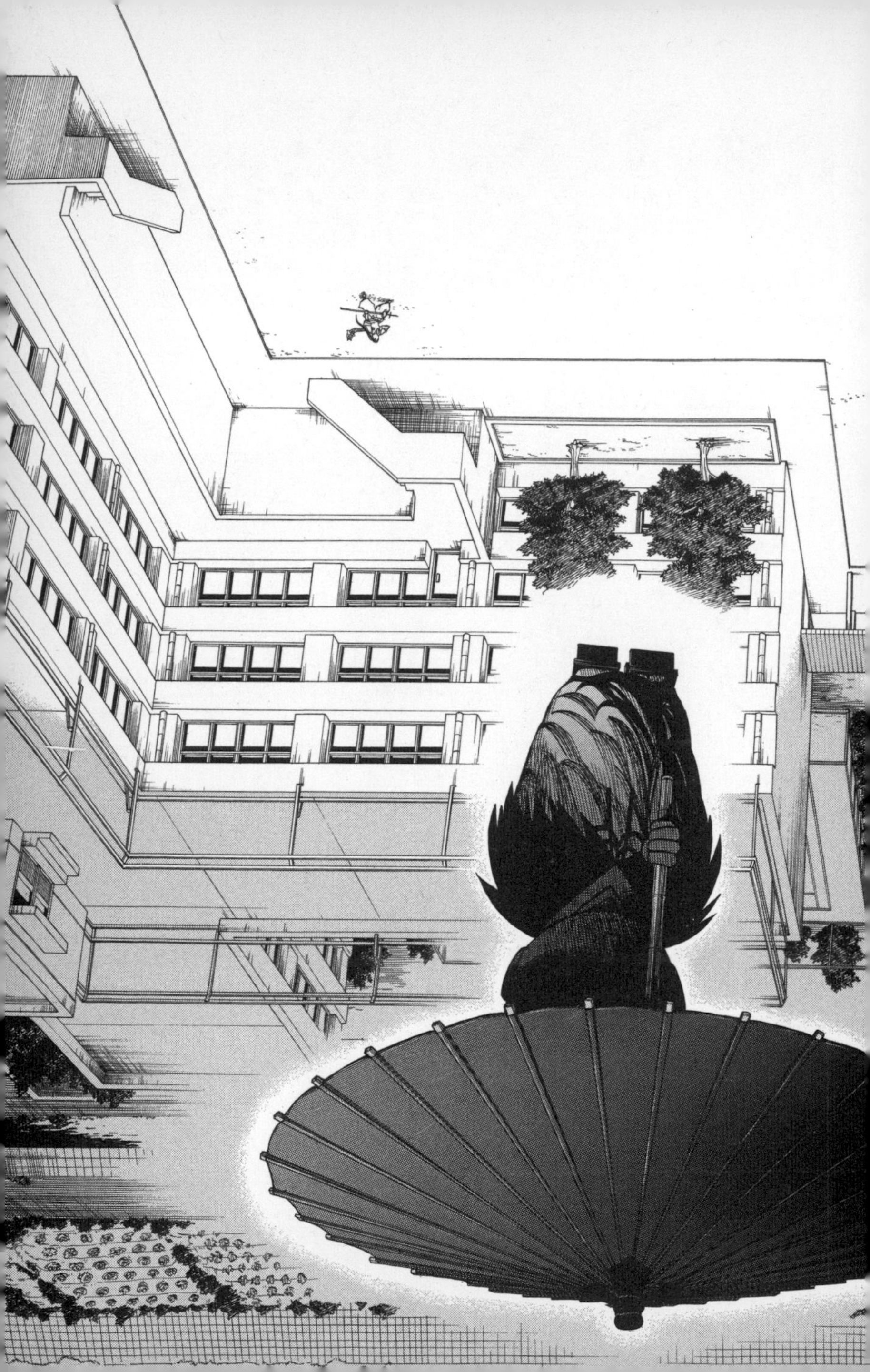

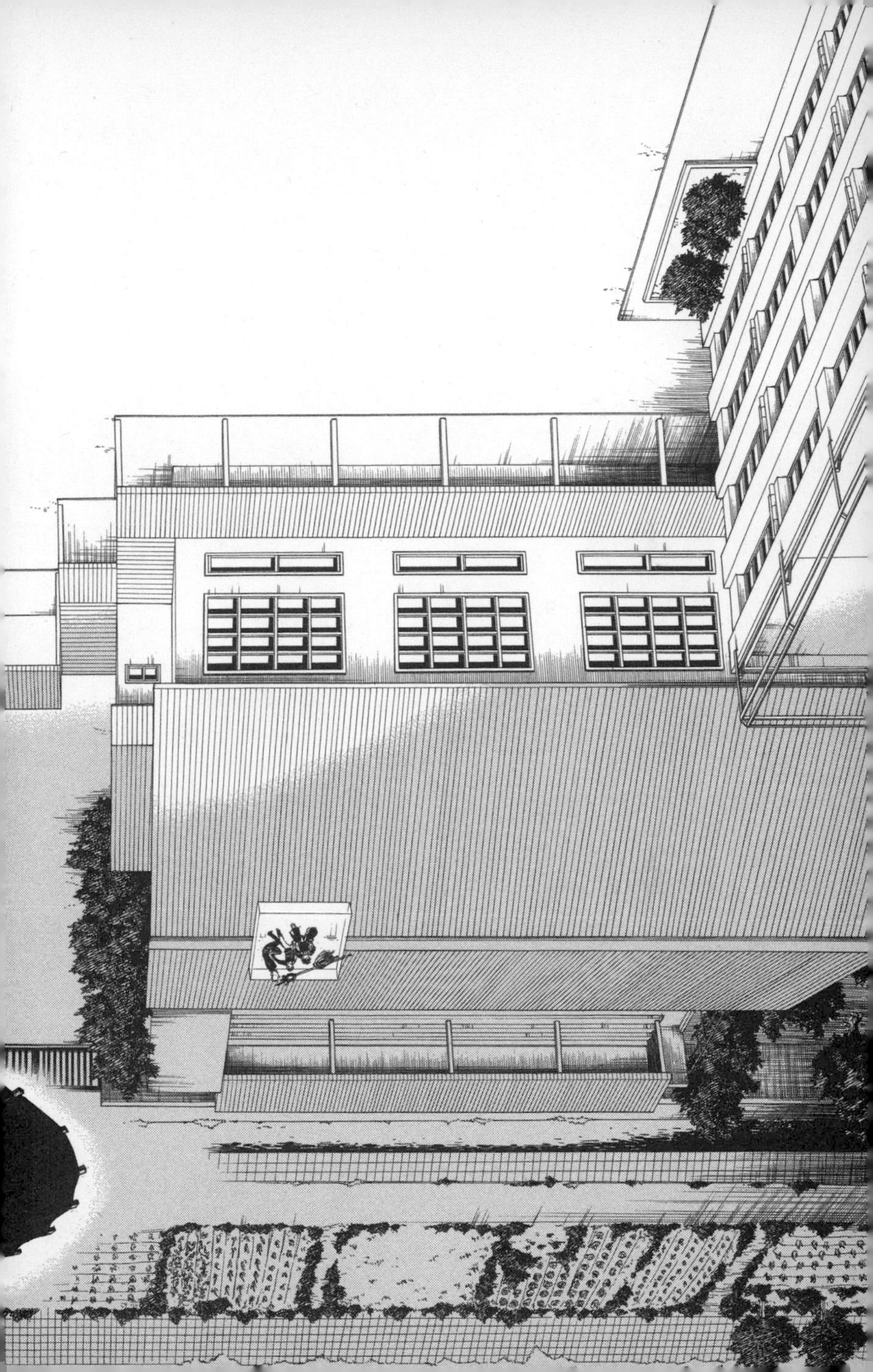

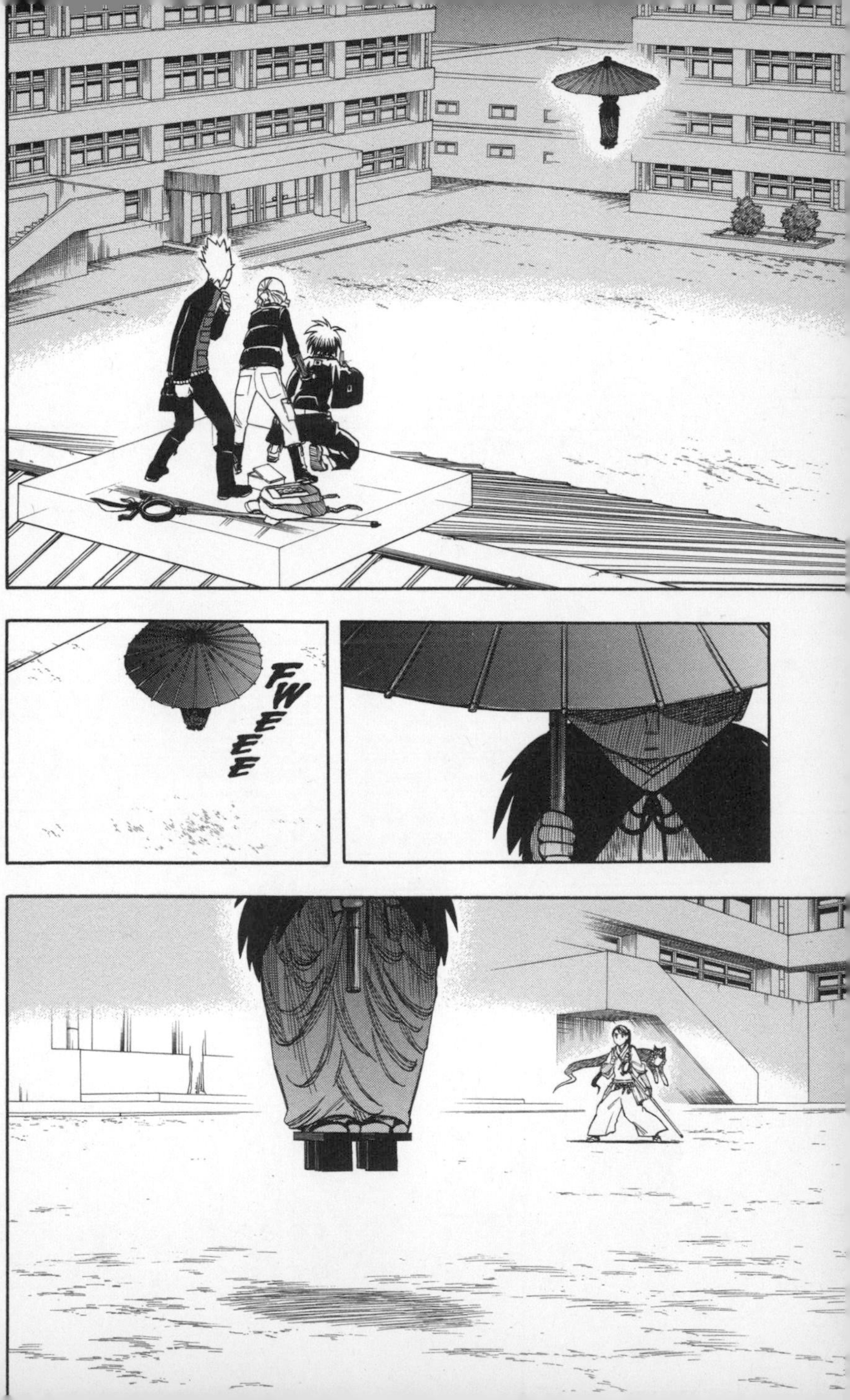
FWEEEE

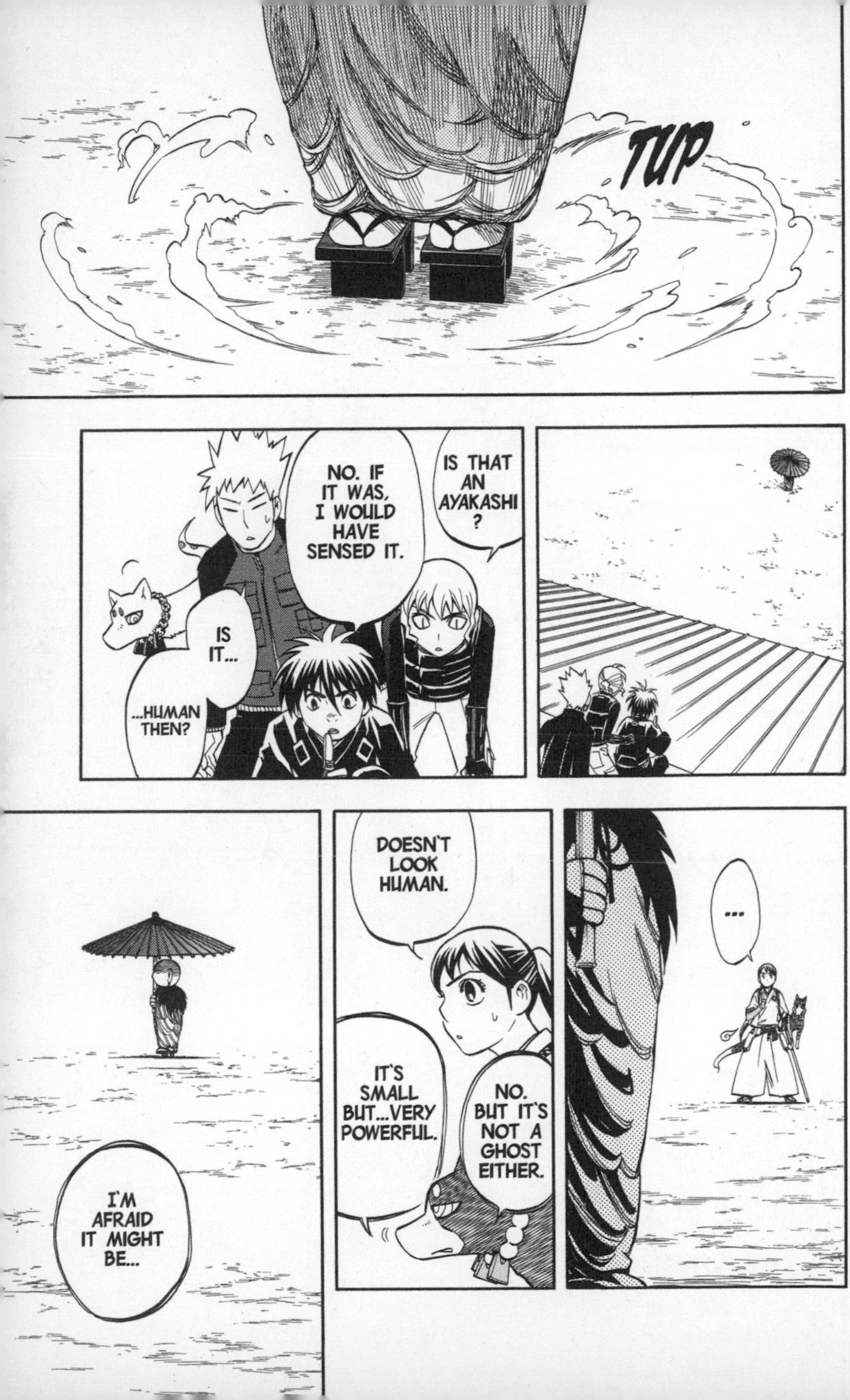
TUP
IS THAT AN AYAKASHI?
NO. IF IT WAS, I WOULD HAVE SENSED IT.
IS IT...
...HUMAN THEN?
...
DOESN'T LOOK HUMAN.
NO. BUT IT'S NOT A GHOST EITHER.
IT'S SMALL BUT...VERY POWERFUL.
I'M AFRAID IT MIGHT BE...

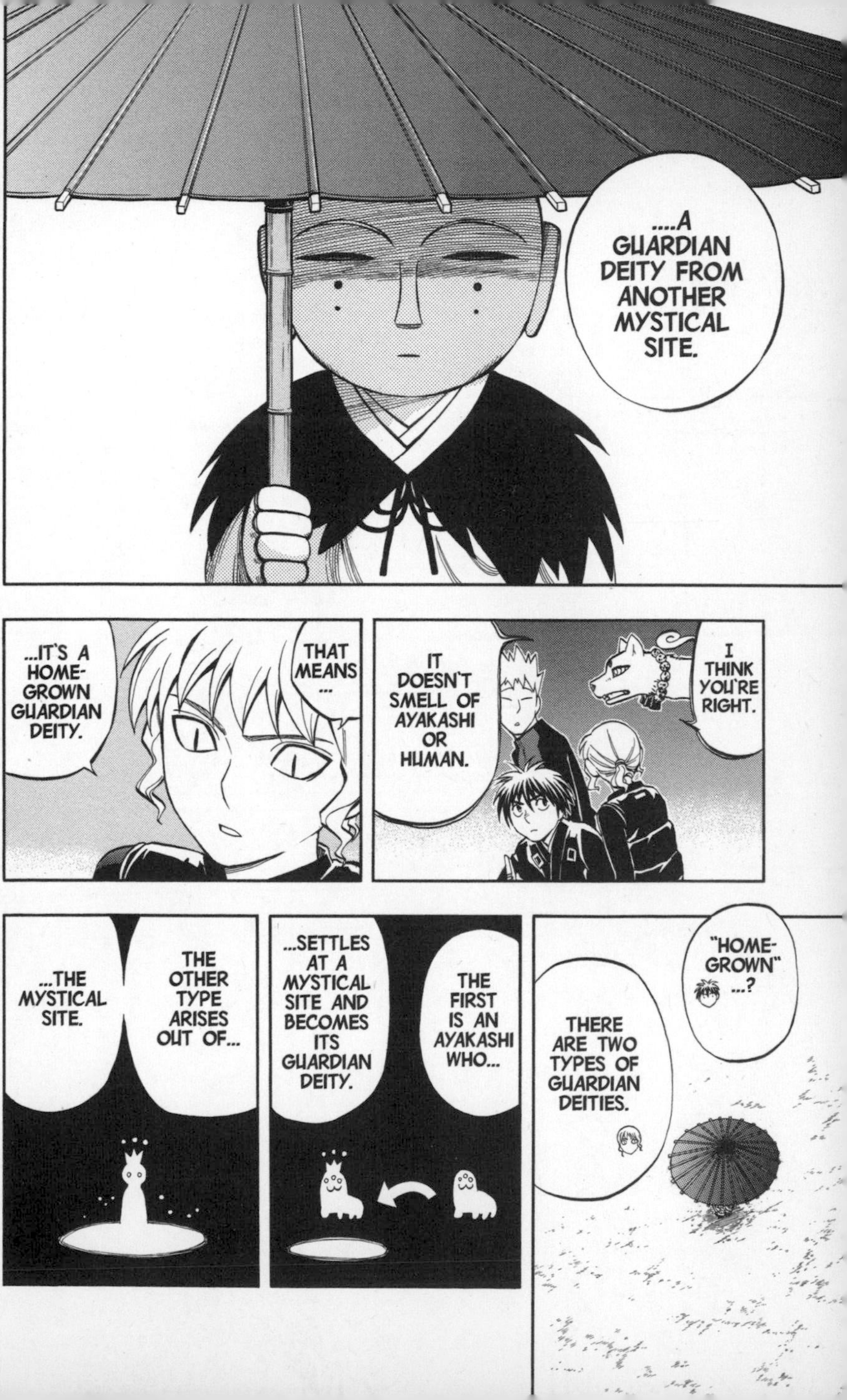
....A GUARDIAN DEITY FROM ANOTHER MYSTICAL SITE.
I THINK YOU'RE RIGHT.
IT DOESN'T SMELL OF AYAKASHI OR HUMAN.
THAT MEANS ...
...IT'S A HOME-GROWN GUARDIAN DEITY.
"HOME-GROWN" ...?
THERE ARE TWO TYPES OF GUARDIAN DEITIES.
THE FIRST IS AN AYAKASHI WHO...
...SETTLES AT A MYSTICAL SITE AND BECOMES ITS GUARDIAN DEITY.
THE OTHER TYPE ARISES OUT OF...
...THE MYSTICAL SITE.

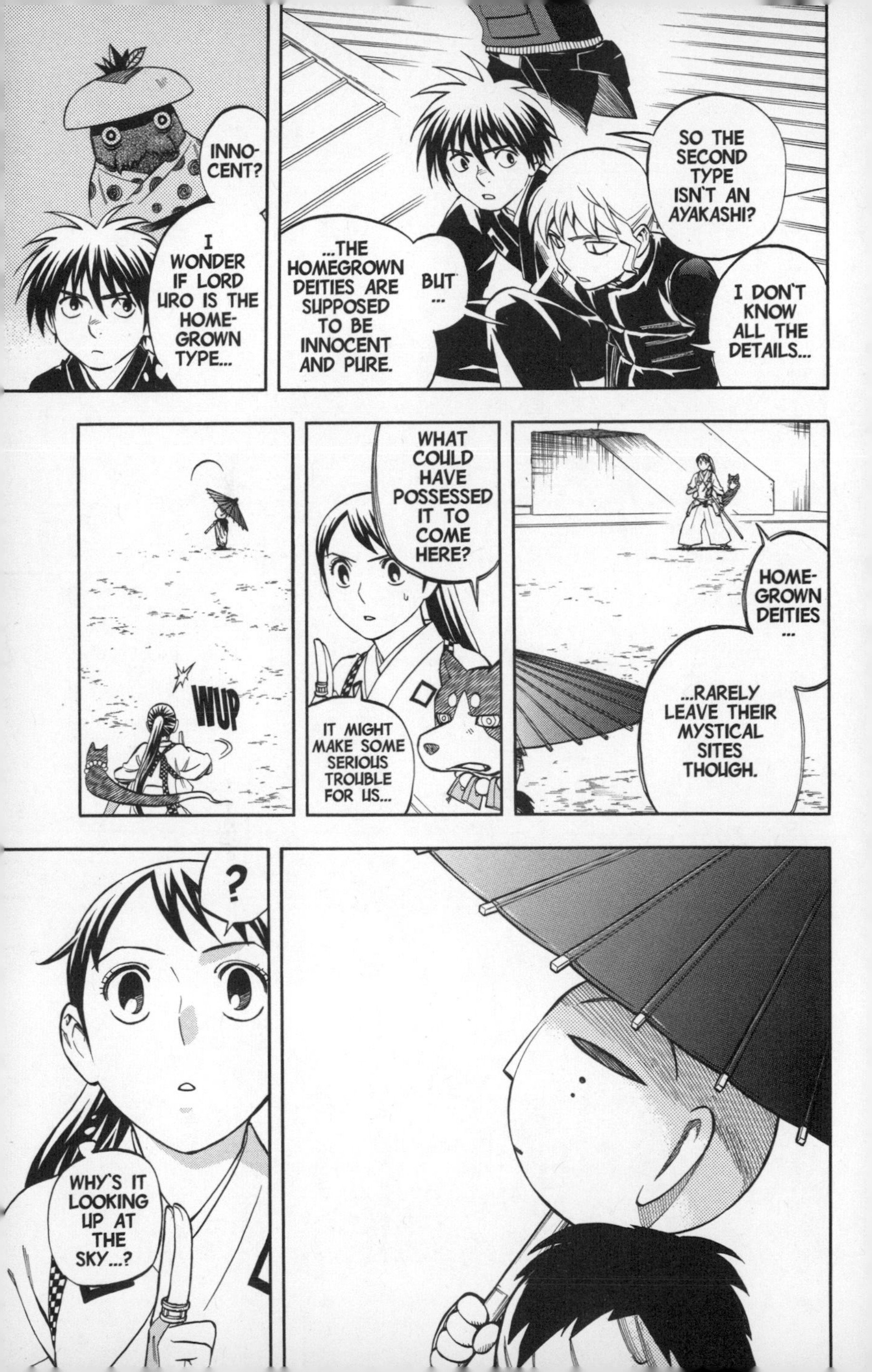
SO THE SECOND TYPE ISN'T AN AYAKASHI?
I DON'T KNOW ALL THE DETAILS...
BUT...
...THE HOMEGROWN DEITIES ARE SUPPOSED TO BE INNOCENT AND PURE.
INNO-CENT?
I WONDER IF LORD URO IS THE HOME-GROWN TYPE...
HOME-GROWN DEITIES...
...RARELY LEAVE THEIR MYSTICAL SITES THOUGH.
WHAT COULD HAVE POSSESSED IT TO COME HERE?
IT MIGHT MAKE SOME SERIOUS TROUBLE FOR US...
WUP
?
WHY'S IT LOOKING UP AT THE SKY...?

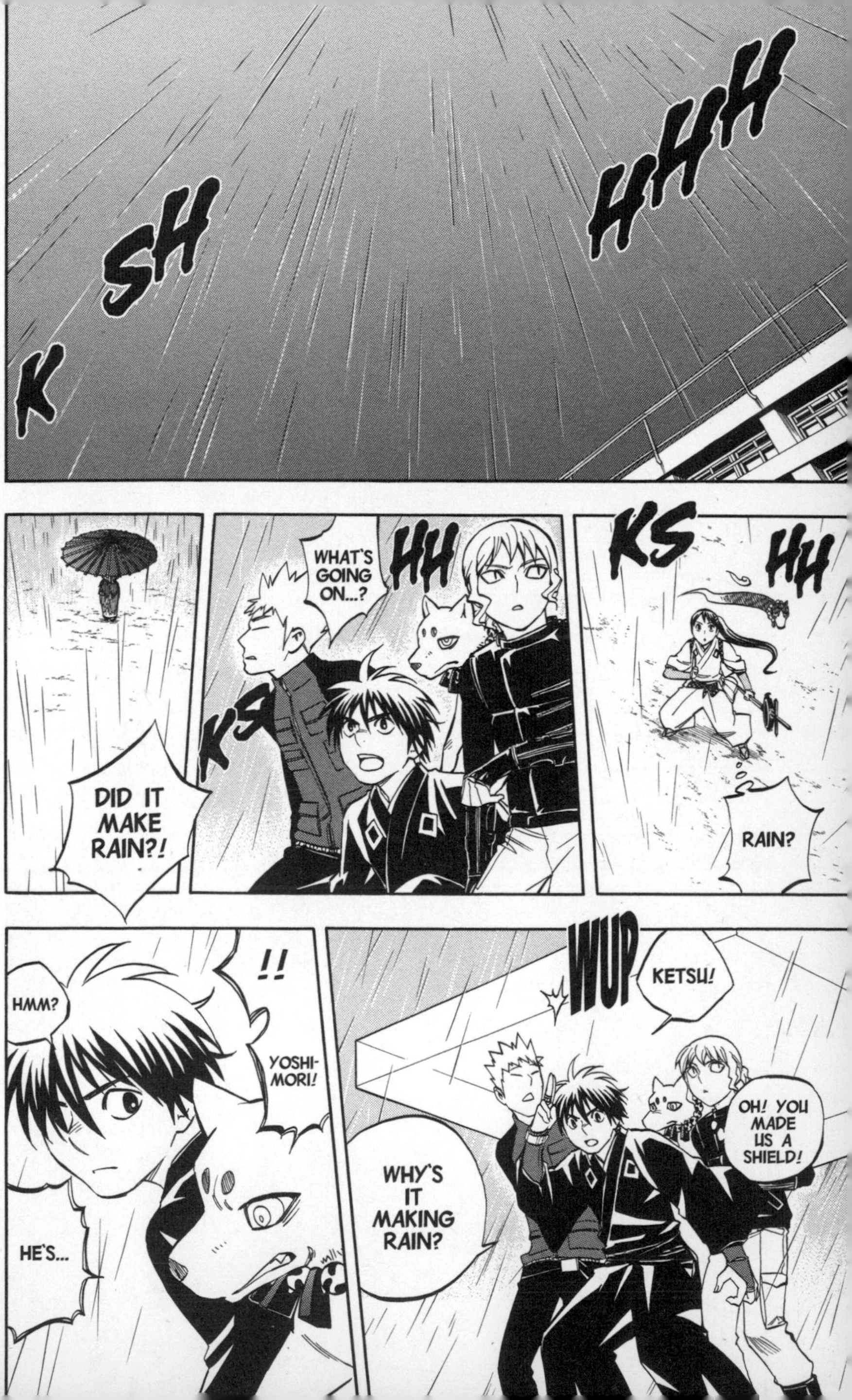
K SH HHH
KS HH
RAIN?
HH
WHAT'S GOING ON...?
KS
DID IT MAKE RAIN?!
WUP
KETSU!
OH! YOU MADE US A SHIELD!
WHY'S IT MAKING RAIN?
!!
HMM?
YOSHI-MORI!
HE'S...

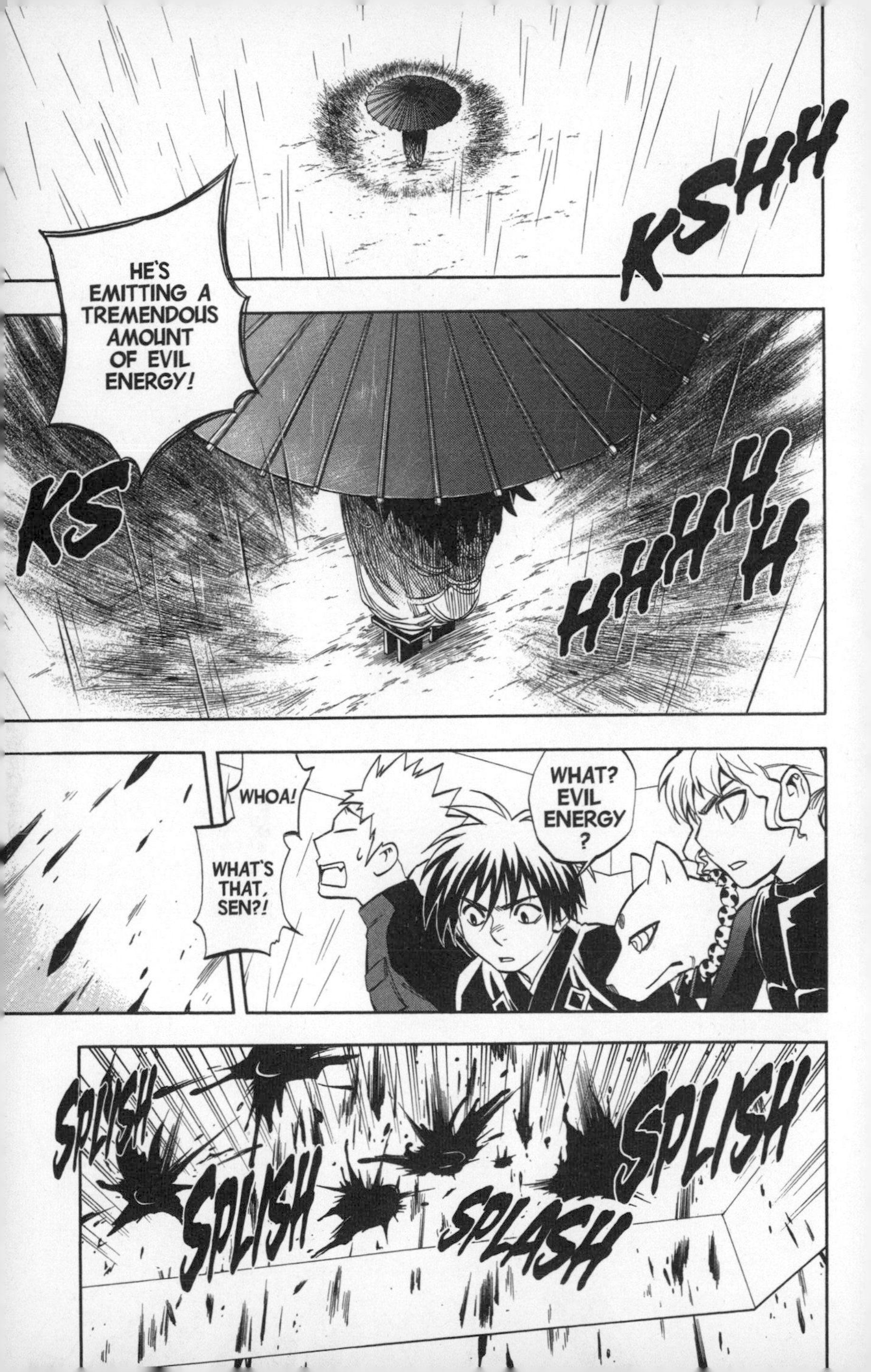
KSHH
HE'S EMITTING A TREMENDOUS AMOUNT OF EVIL ENERGY!
KS
HHHHH
WHAT? EVIL ENERGY?
WHOA!
WHAT'S THAT, SEN?!
SPLISH
SPLASH
SPLISH
SPLISH

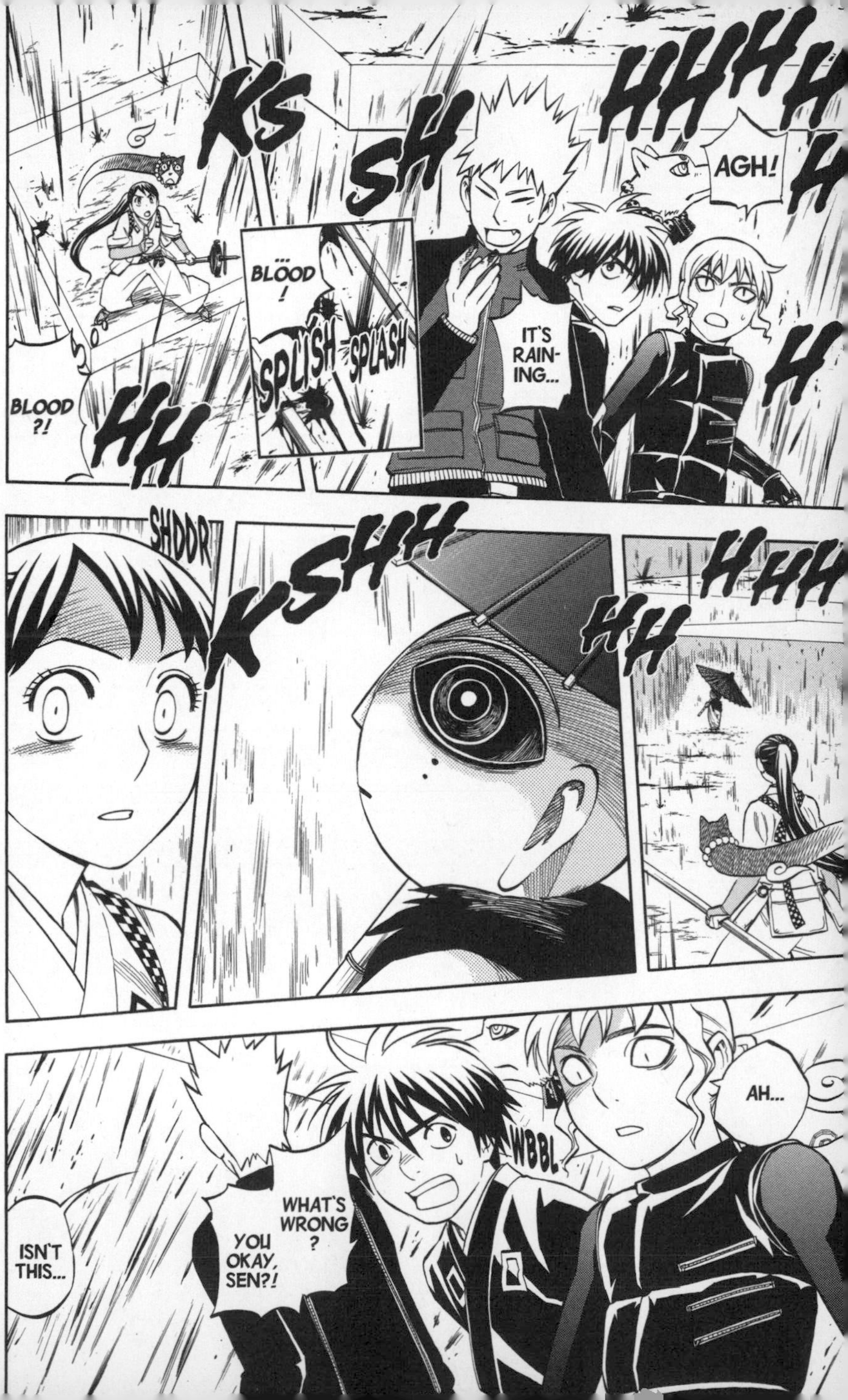
AGH!
HHHHH
KSSH
IT'S RAINING...
...BLOOD!
SPLISH SPLASH
BLOOD?!
HH
HHHHH
KSHH
SHDDR
AH...
WBBL
WHAT'S WRONG?
YOU OKAY, SEN?!
ISN'T THIS...

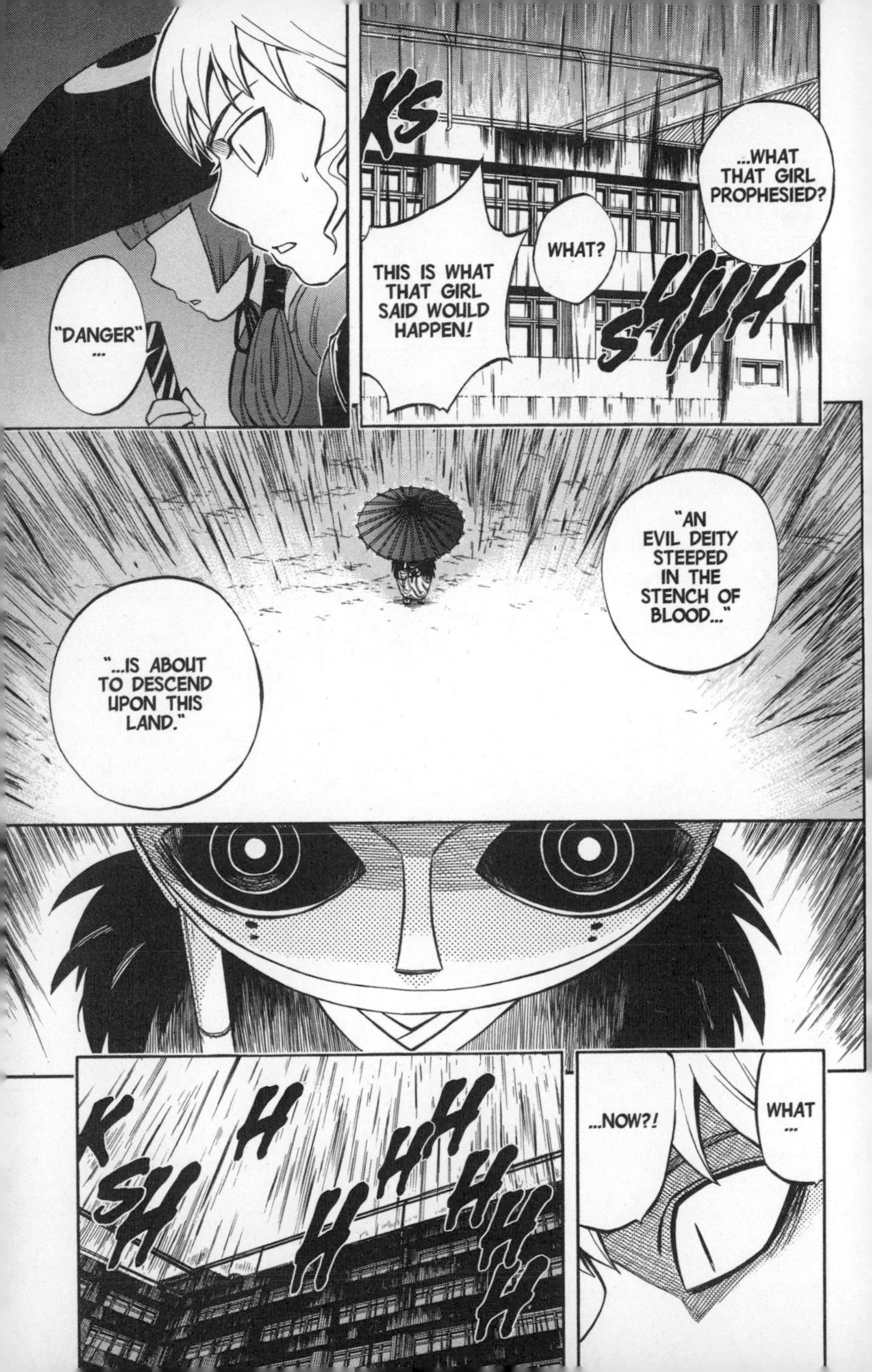
...WHAT THAT GIRL PROPHESIED?
SHHH
WHAT?
THIS IS WHAT THAT GIRL SAID WOULD HAPPEN!
KS
"DANGER" ...
"AN EVIL DEITY STEEPED IN THE STENCH OF BLOOD..."
"...IS ABOUT TO DESCEND UPON THIS LAND."
WHAT ...
...NOW?!
KSHHHHHHHHHH

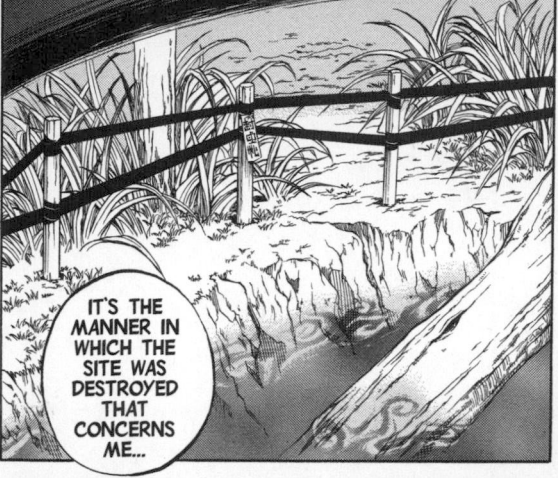

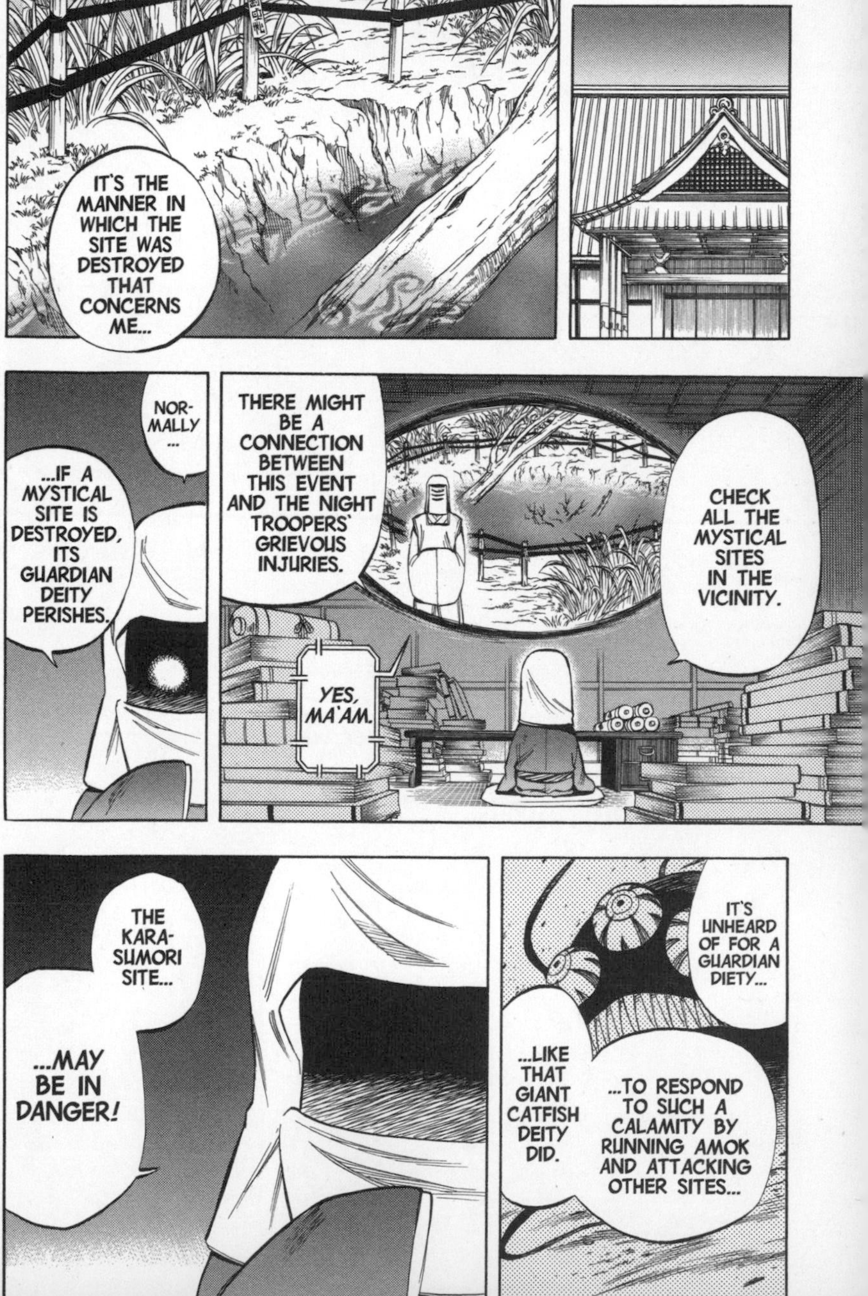
IT'S THE MANNER IN WHICH THE SITE WAS DESTROYED THAT CONCERNS ME...
CHECK ALL THE MYSTICAL SITES IN THE VICINITY.
THERE MIGHT BE A CONNECTION BETWEEN THIS EVENT AND THE NIGHT TROOPERS' GRIEVOUS INJURIES.
YES, MA'AM.
NOR-MALLY ...
...IF A MYSTICAL SITE IS DESTROYED, ITS GUARDIAN DEITY PERISHES.
IT'S UNHEARD OF FOR A GUARDIAN DIETY...
...TO RESPOND TO SUCH A CALAMITY BY RUNNING AMOK AND ATTACKING OTHER SITES...
...LIKE THAT GIANT CATFISH DEITY DID.
THE KARA-SUMORI SITE...
...MAY BE IN DANGER!

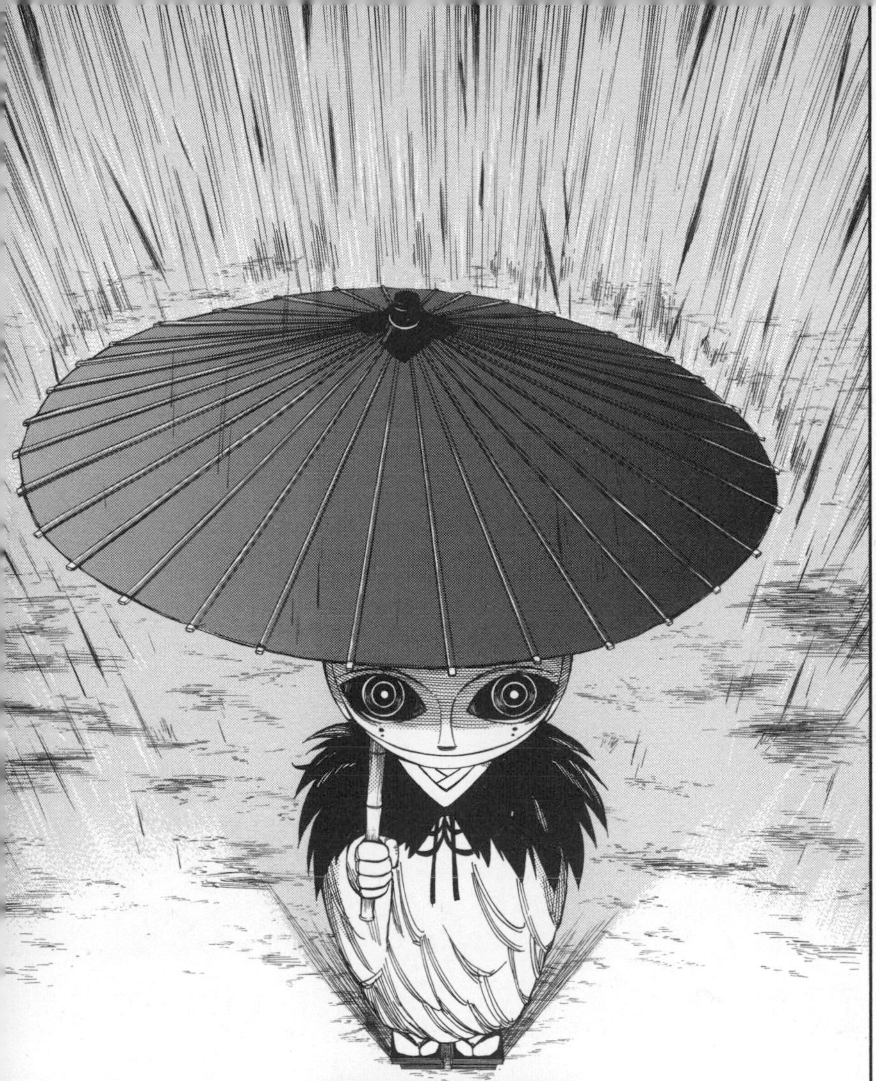

Chapter 196: Rain

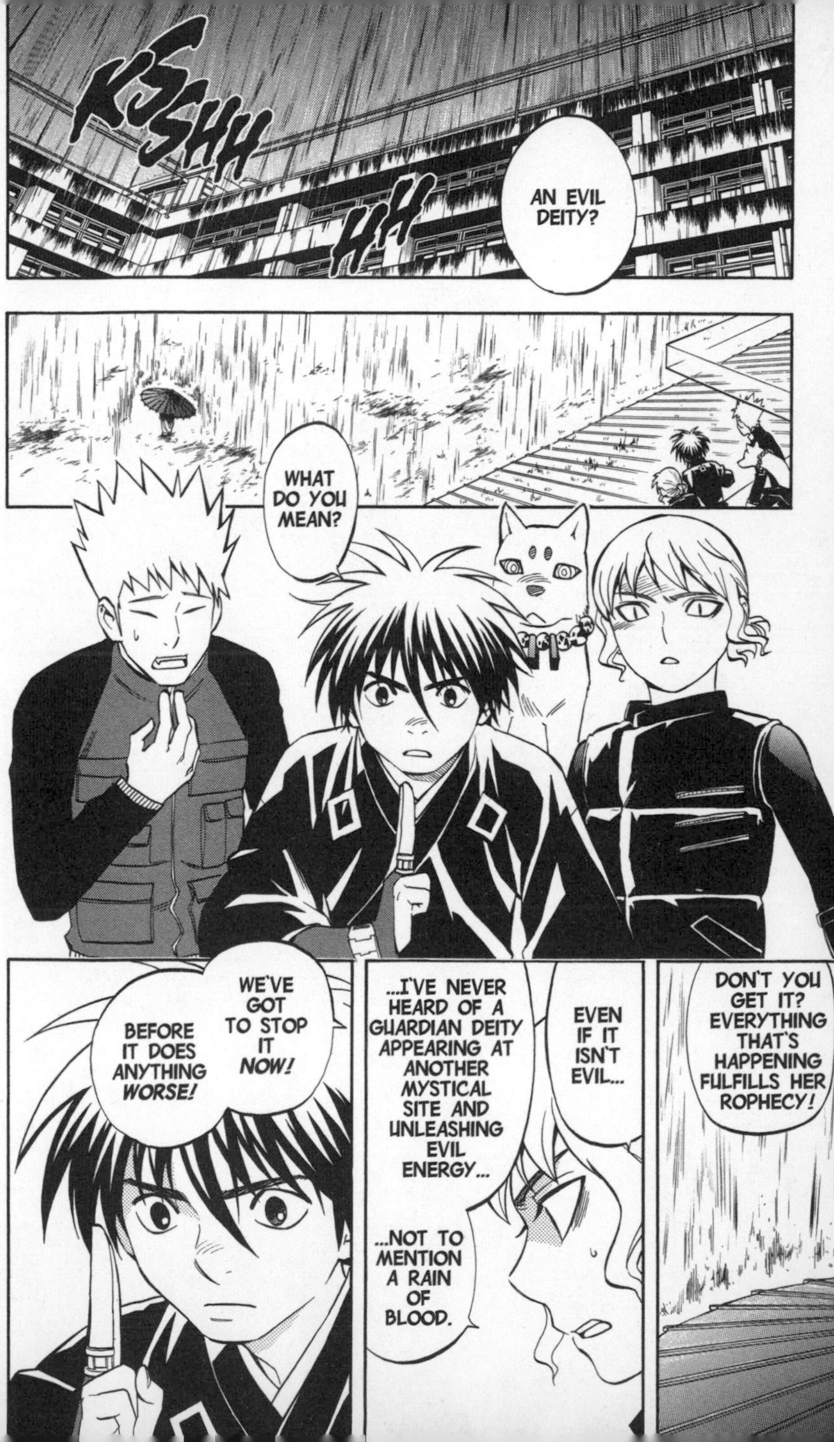
KSHH
HH
AN EVIL DEITY?
WHAT DO YOU MEAN?
DON'T YOU GET IT? EVERYTHING THAT'S HAPPENING FULFILLS HER ROPHECY!
EVEN IF IT ISN'T EVIL...
...I'VE NEVER HEARD OF A GUARDIAN DEITY APPEARING AT ANOTHER MYSTICAL SITE AND UNLEASHING EVIL ENERGY...
...NOT TO MENTION A RAIN OF BLOOD.
WE'VE GOT TO STOP IT NOW!
BEFORE IT DOES ANYTHING WORSE!

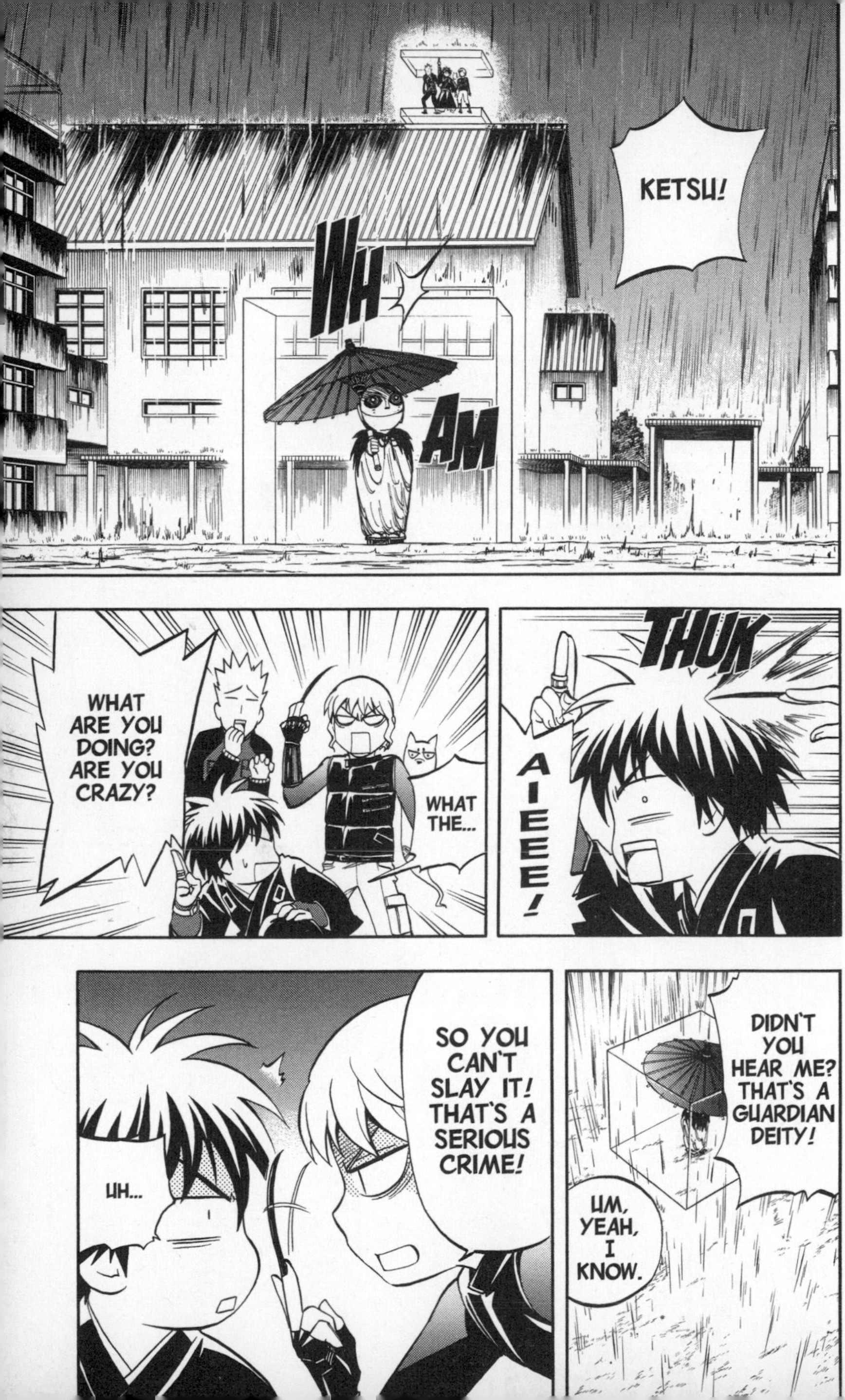
KETSU!
WH
AM
THUK
AIEEE!
WHAT ARE YOU DOING? ARE YOU CRAZY?
WHAT THE...
DIDN'T YOU HEAR ME? THAT'S A GUARDIAN DEITY!
UM, YEAH, I KNOW.
SO YOU CAN'T SLAY IT! THAT'S A SERIOUS CRIME!
UH...

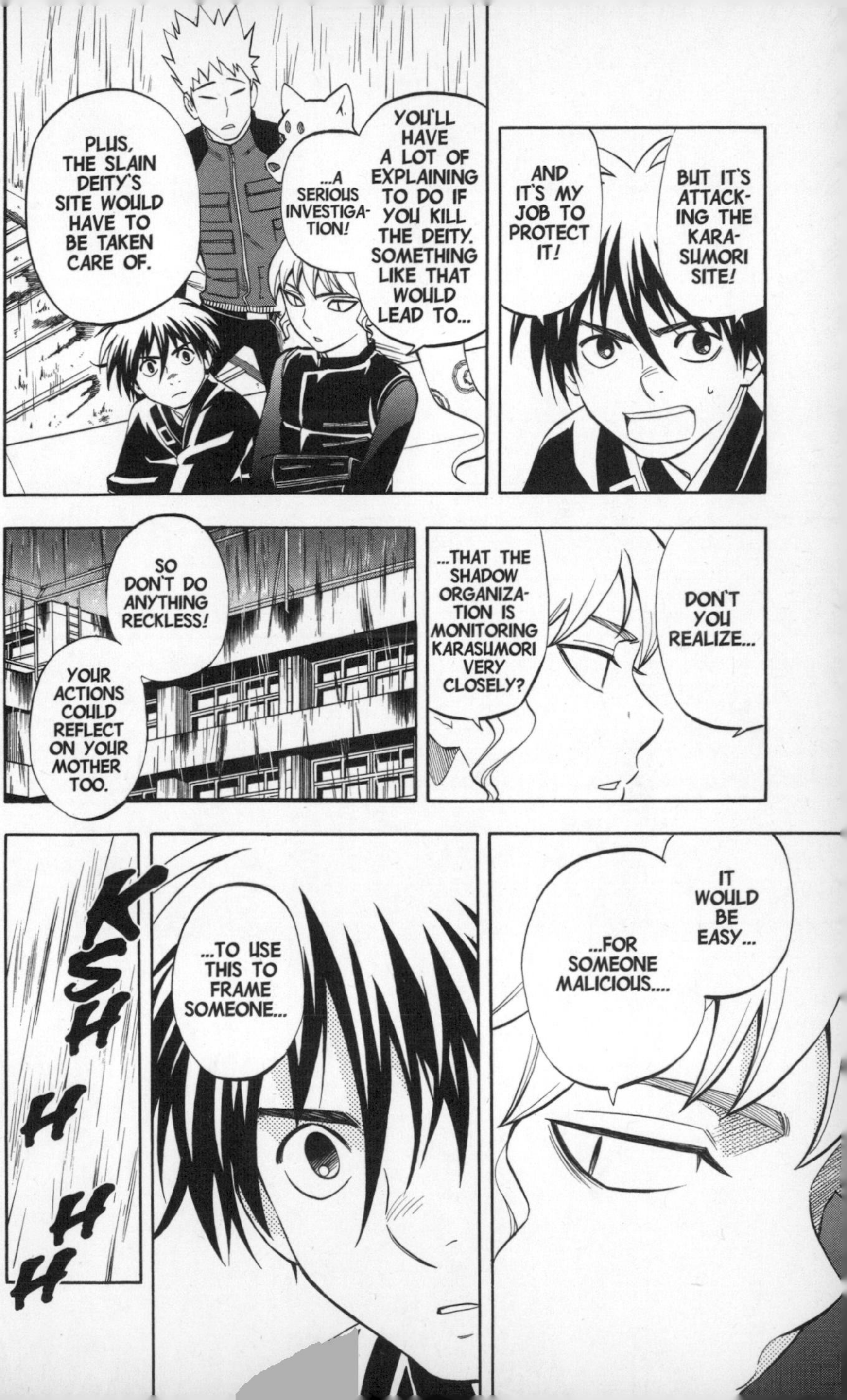
BUT IT'S ATTACKING THE KARASUMORI SITE!
AND IT'S MY JOB TO PROTECT IT!
YOU'LL HAVE A LOT OF EXPLAINING TO DO IF YOU KILL THE DEITY. SOMETHING LIKE THAT WOULD LEAD TO...
...A SERIOUS INVESTIGATION!
PLUS, THE SLAIN DEITY'S SITE WOULD HAVE TO BE TAKEN CARE OF.
DON'T YOU REALIZE...
...THAT THE SHADOW ORGANIZATION IS MONITORING KARASUMORI VERY CLOSELY?
SO DON'T DO ANYTHING RECKLESS!
YOUR ACTIONS COULD REFLECT ON YOUR MOTHER TOO.
IT WOULD BE EASY...
...FOR SOMEONE MALICIOUS....
...TO USE THIS TO FRAME SOMEONE...
KSHHHHH

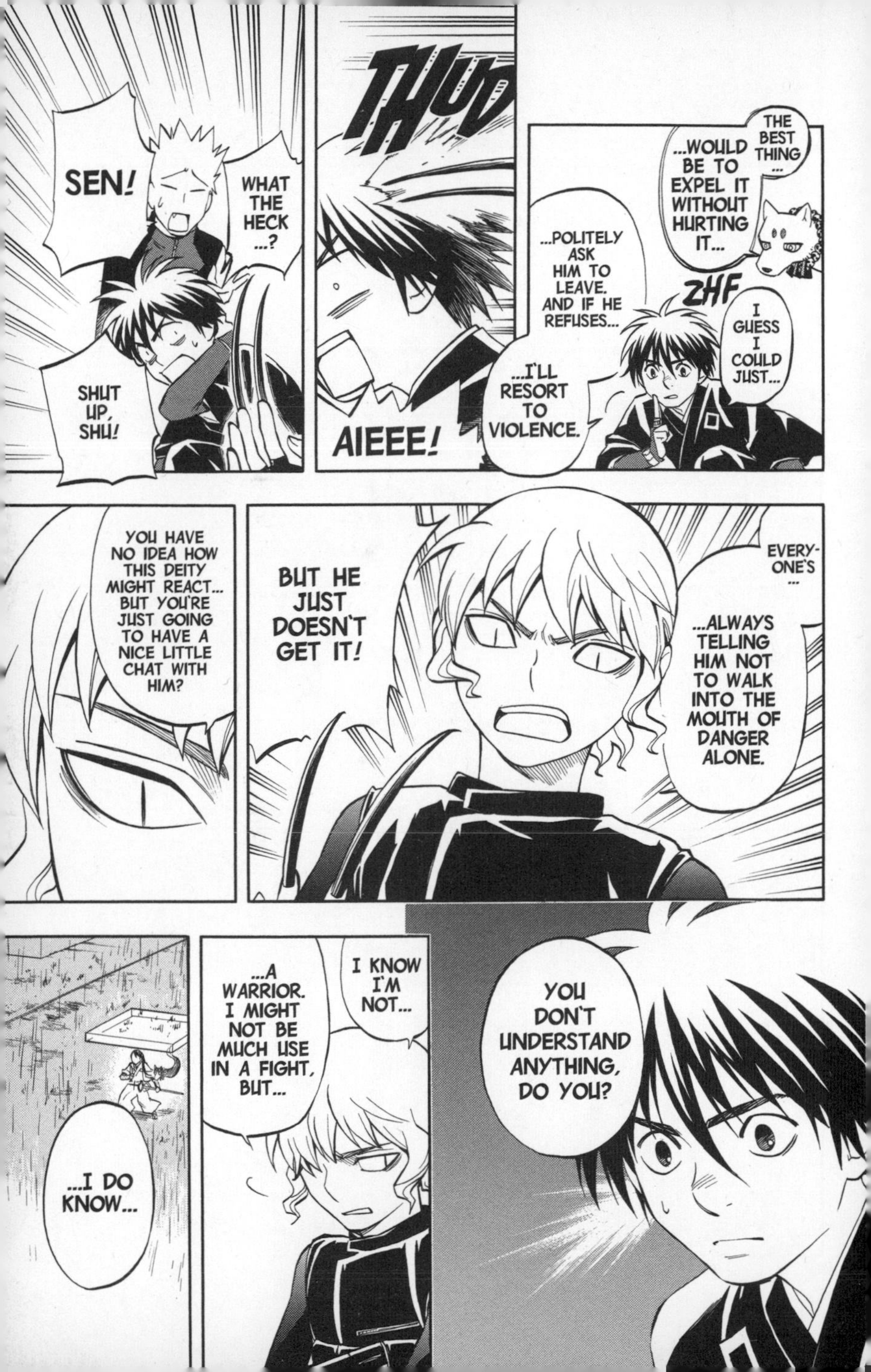
THE BEST THING ...
...WOULD BE TO EXPEL IT WITHOUT HURTING IT...
ZHF
I GUESS I COULD JUST...
...POLITELY ASK HIM TO LEAVE. AND IF HE REFUSES...
...I'LL RESORT TO VIOLENCE.
THUD
AIEEE!
SEN!
WHAT THE HECK ...?
SHUT UP, SHU!
EVERY-ONE'S ...
...ALWAYS TELLING HIM NOT TO WALK INTO THE MOUTH OF DANGER ALONE.
BUT HE JUST DOESN'T GET IT!
YOU HAVE NO IDEA HOW THIS DEITY MIGHT REACT... BUT YOU'RE JUST GOING TO HAVE A NICE LITTLE CHAT WITH HIM?
YOU DON'T UNDERSTAND ANYTHING, DO YOU?
I KNOW I'M NOT...
...A WARRIOR. I MIGHT NOT BE MUCH USE IN A FIGHT, BUT...
...I DO KNOW...

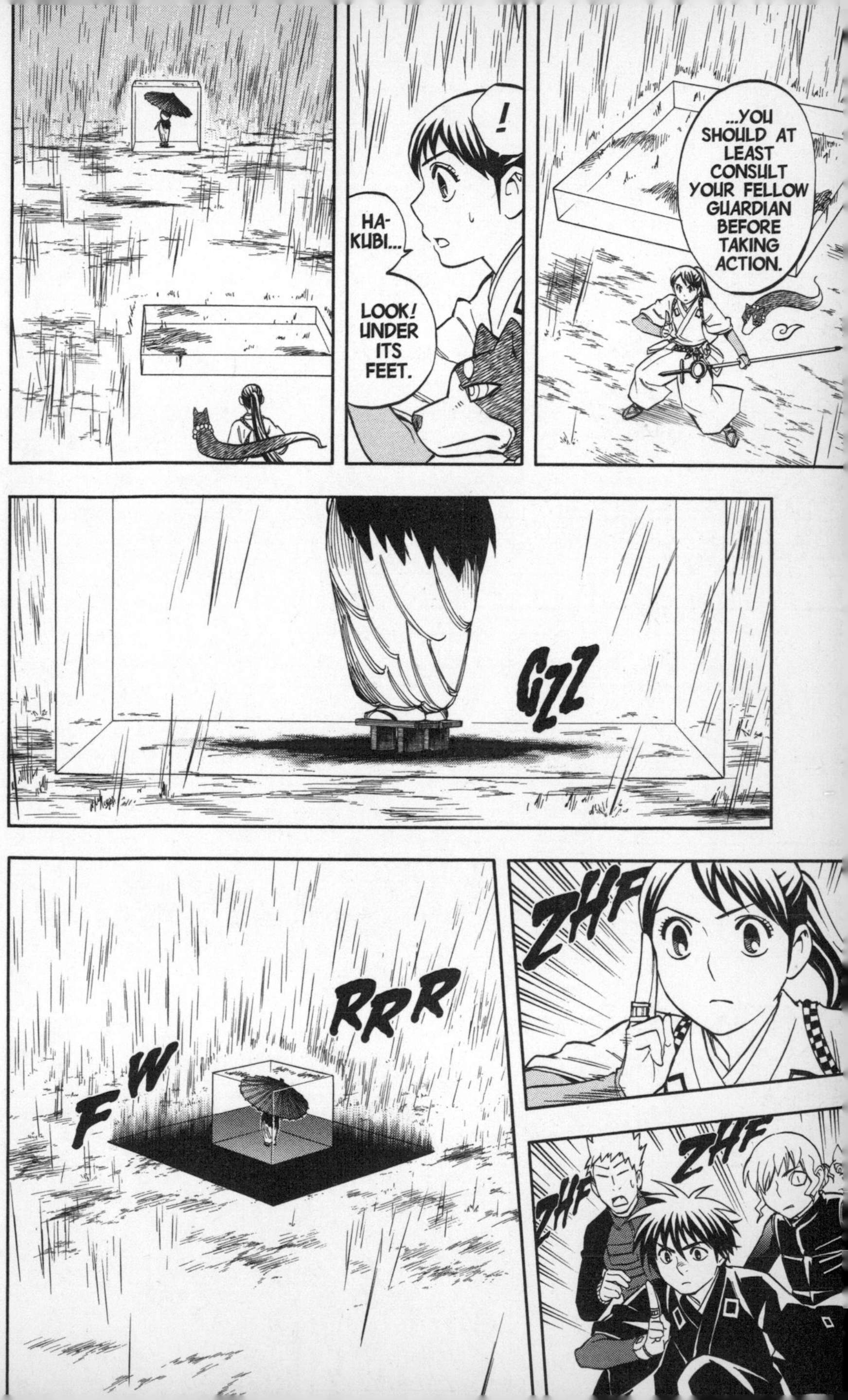
...YOU SHOULD AT LEAST CONSULT YOUR FELLOW GUARDIAN BEFORE TAKING ACTION.
!
HA-KUBI...
LOOK! UNDER ITS FEET.
GZZ
ZHF
ZHF
ZHF
RRR
FW

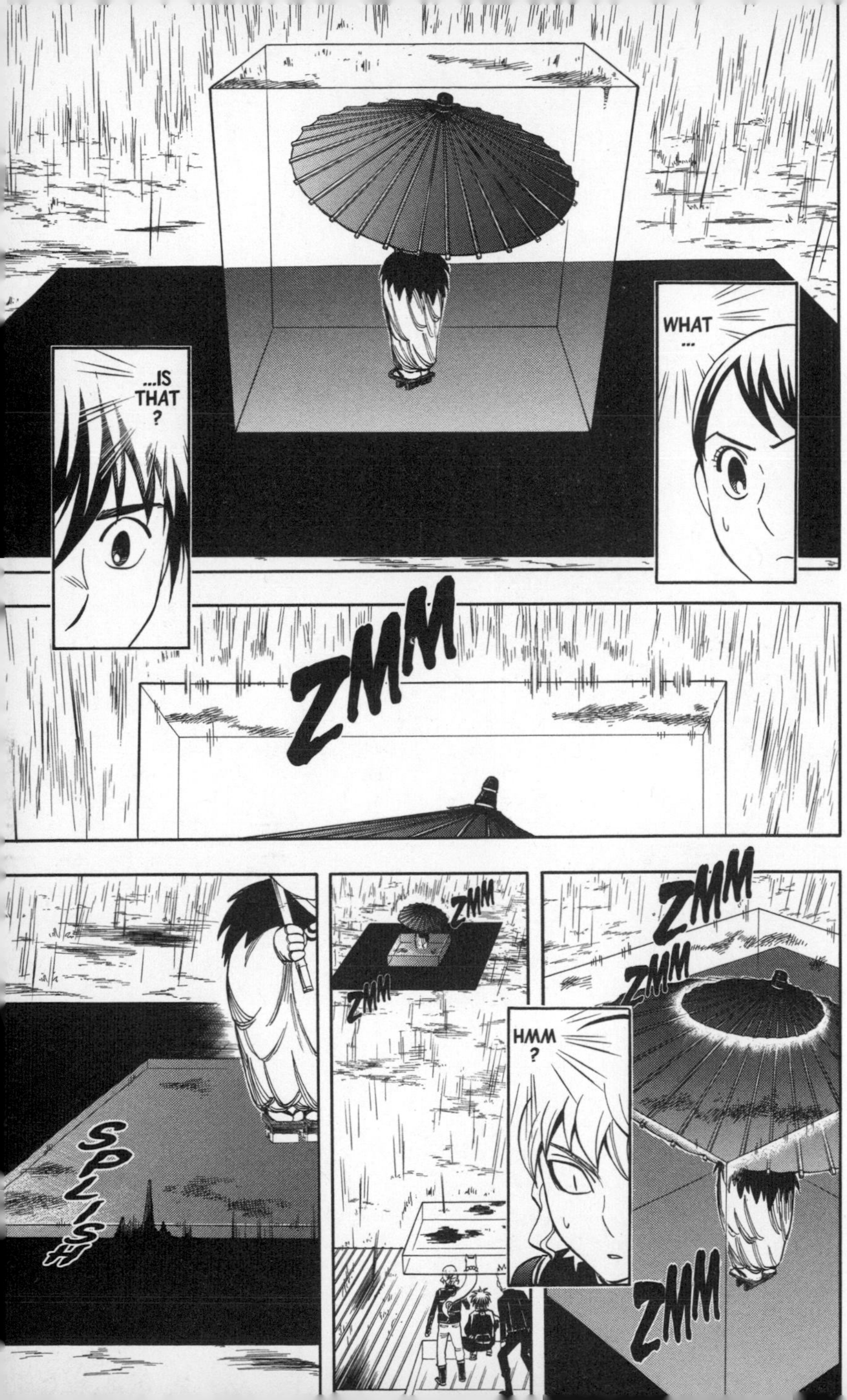
WHAT ...
...IS THAT ?
ZMM
ZMM
ZMM
ZMM
HMM ?
ZMM
ZMM
SPLISH

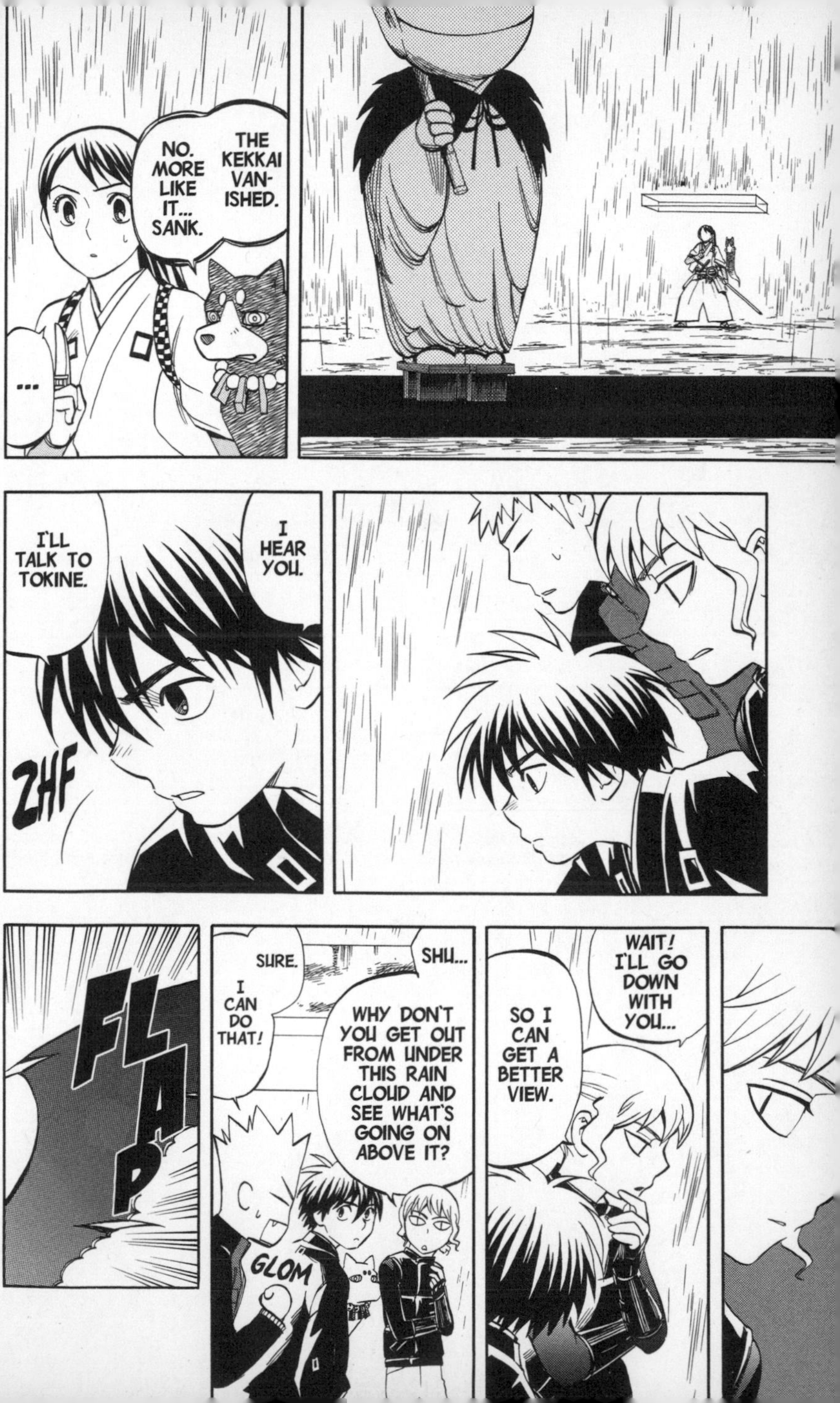
THE KEKKAI VANISHED.
NO. MORE LIKE IT... SANK.
...
I HEAR YOU.
I'LL TALK TO TOKINE.
ZHF
WAIT! I'LL GO DOWN WITH YOU...
SO I CAN GET A BETTER VIEW.
SHU...
WHY DON'T YOU GET OUT FROM UNDER THIS RAIN CLOUD AND SEE WHAT'S GOING ON ABOVE IT?
SURE.
I CAN DO THAT!
GLOM
FLAP

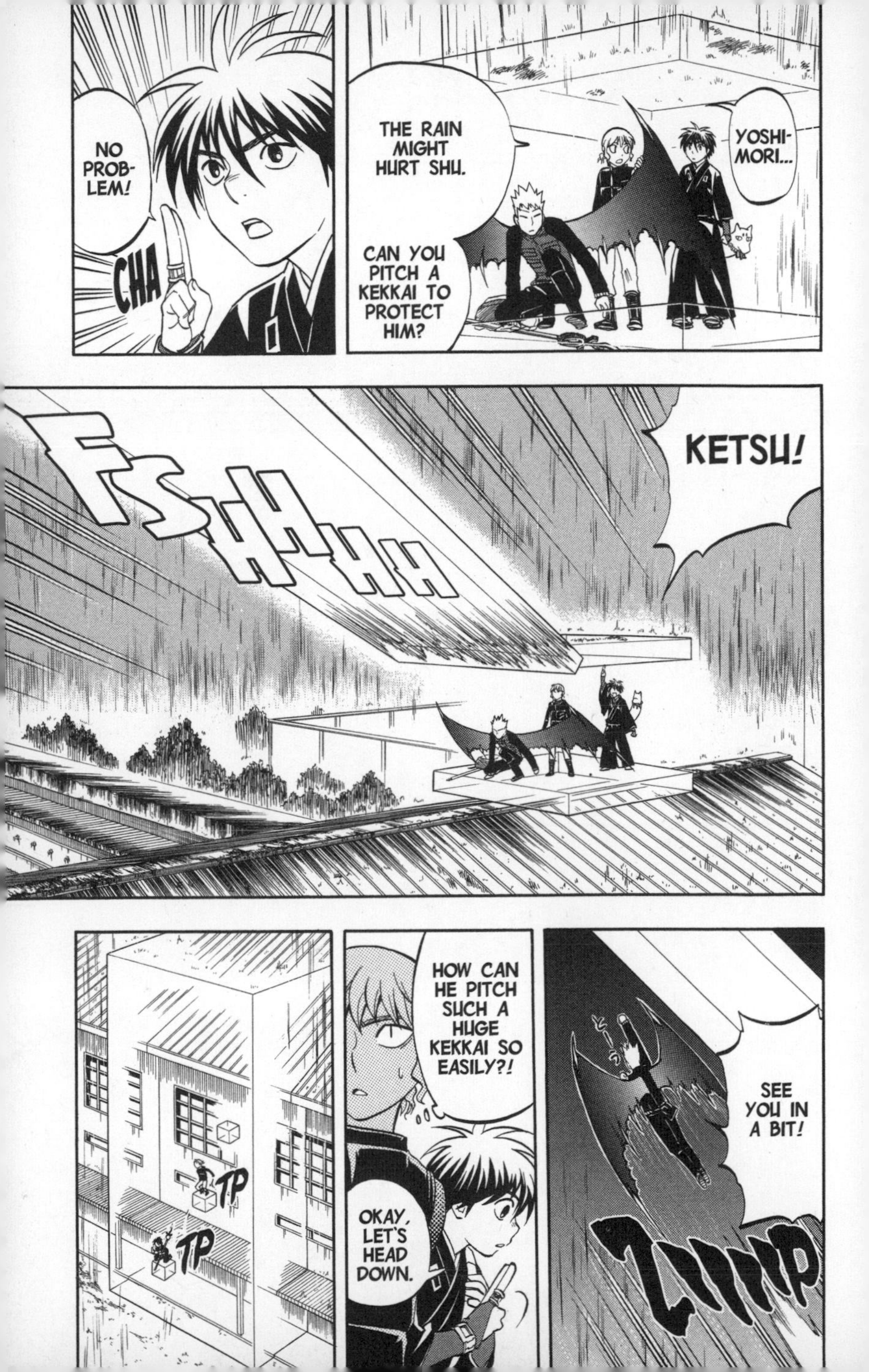
YOSHI-MORI...
THE RAIN MIGHT HURT SHU.
CAN YOU PITCH A KEKKAI TO PROTECT HIM?
NO PROB-LEM!
CHA
KETSU!
FSSHHHH
SEE YOU IN A BIT!
ZIIIP
HOW CAN HE PITCH SUCH A HUGE KEKKAI SO EASILY?!
OKAY, LET'S HEAD DOWN.
TP
TP

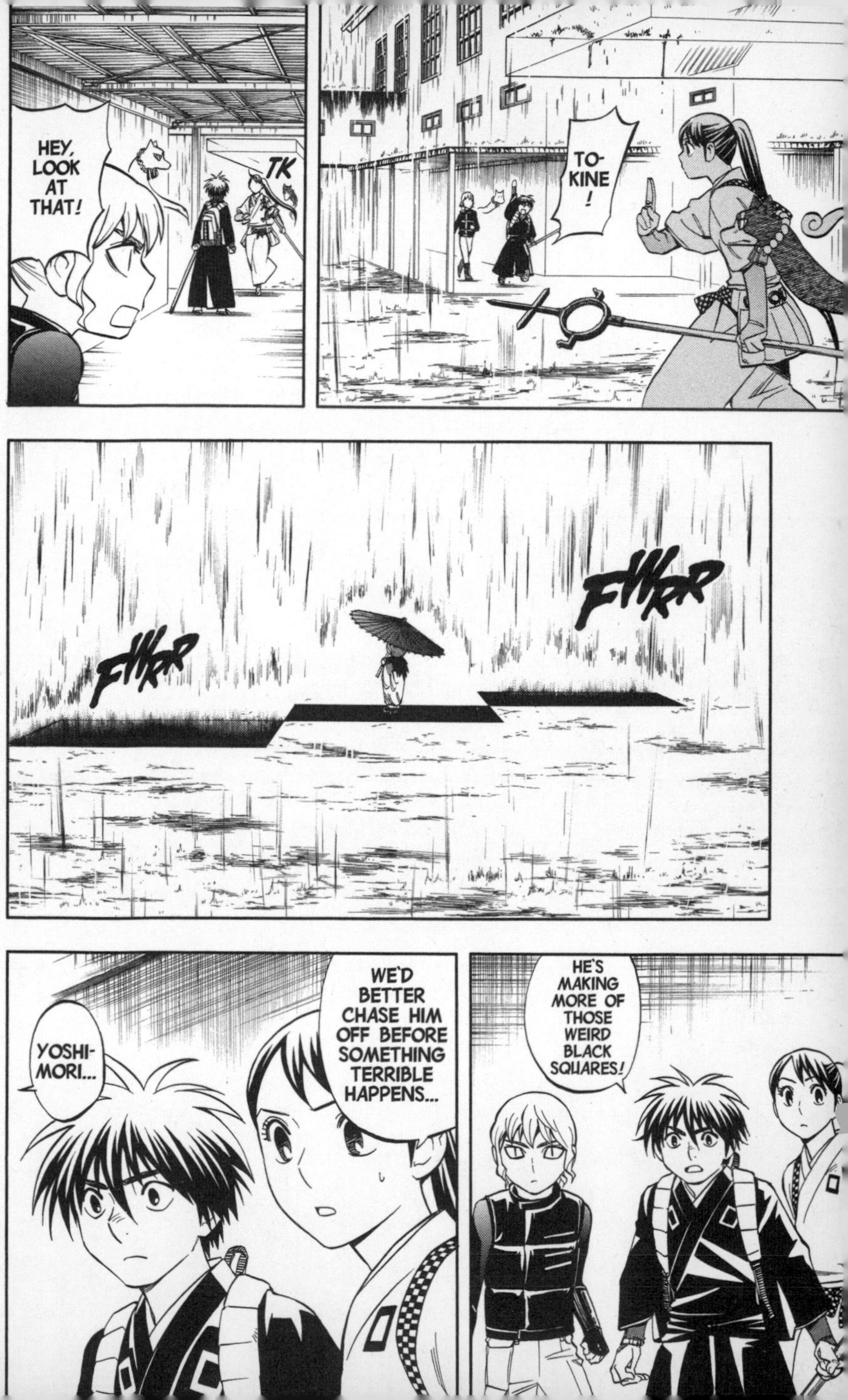
TO-KINE!
HEY, LOOK AT THAT!
TK
FWRR
FWRR
HE'S MAKING MORE OF THOSE WEIRD BLACK SQUARES!
WE'D BETTER CHASE HIM OFF BEFORE SOMETHING TERRIBLE HAPPENS...
YOSHI-MORI...

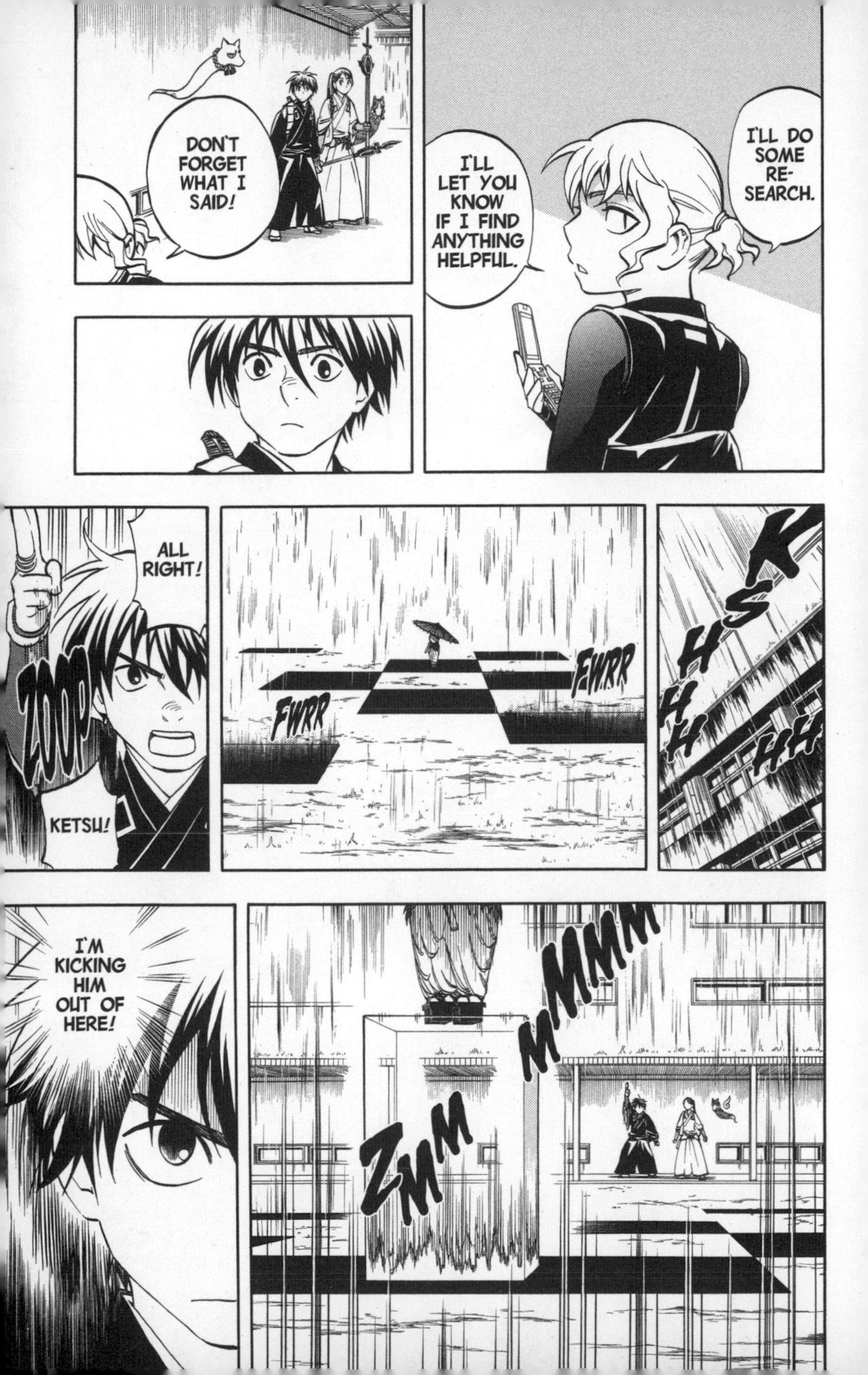
I'LL DO SOME RE-SEARCH.
I'LL LET YOU KNOW IF I FIND ANYTHING HELPFUL.
DON'T FORGET WHAT I SAID!
KSHHHHHH
FWRR
FWRR
ALL RIGHT!
ZOOP
KETSU!
ZMMMMMMM
I'M KICKING HIM OUT OF HERE!

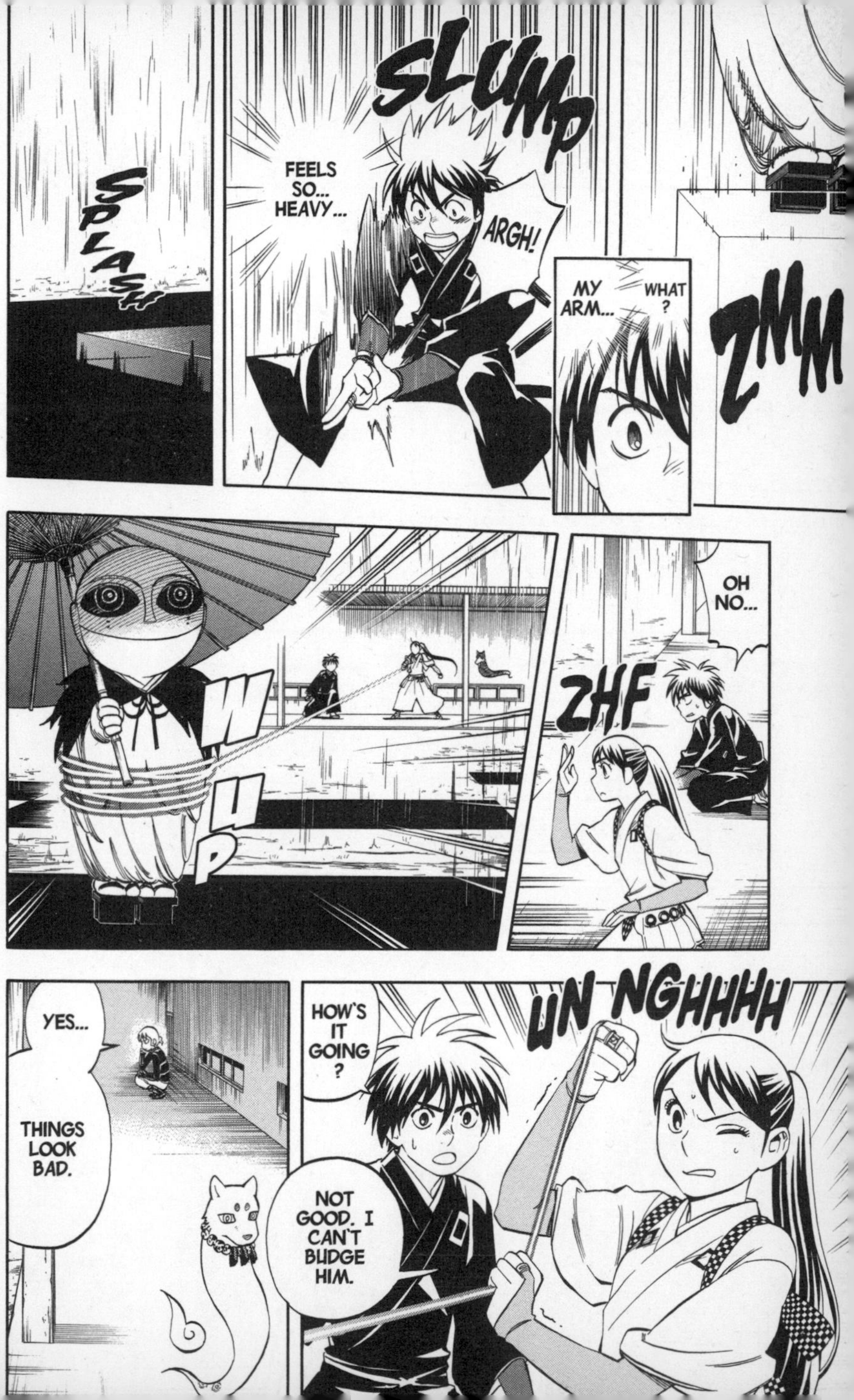
ZMM
WHAT?
MY ARM...
SLUMP
ARGH!
FEELS SO... HEAVY...
SPLASH
OH NO...
ZHF
WUP
UN NGHHHH
HOW'S IT GOING?
NOT GOOD. I CAN'T BUDGE HIM.
YES...
THINGS LOOK BAD.

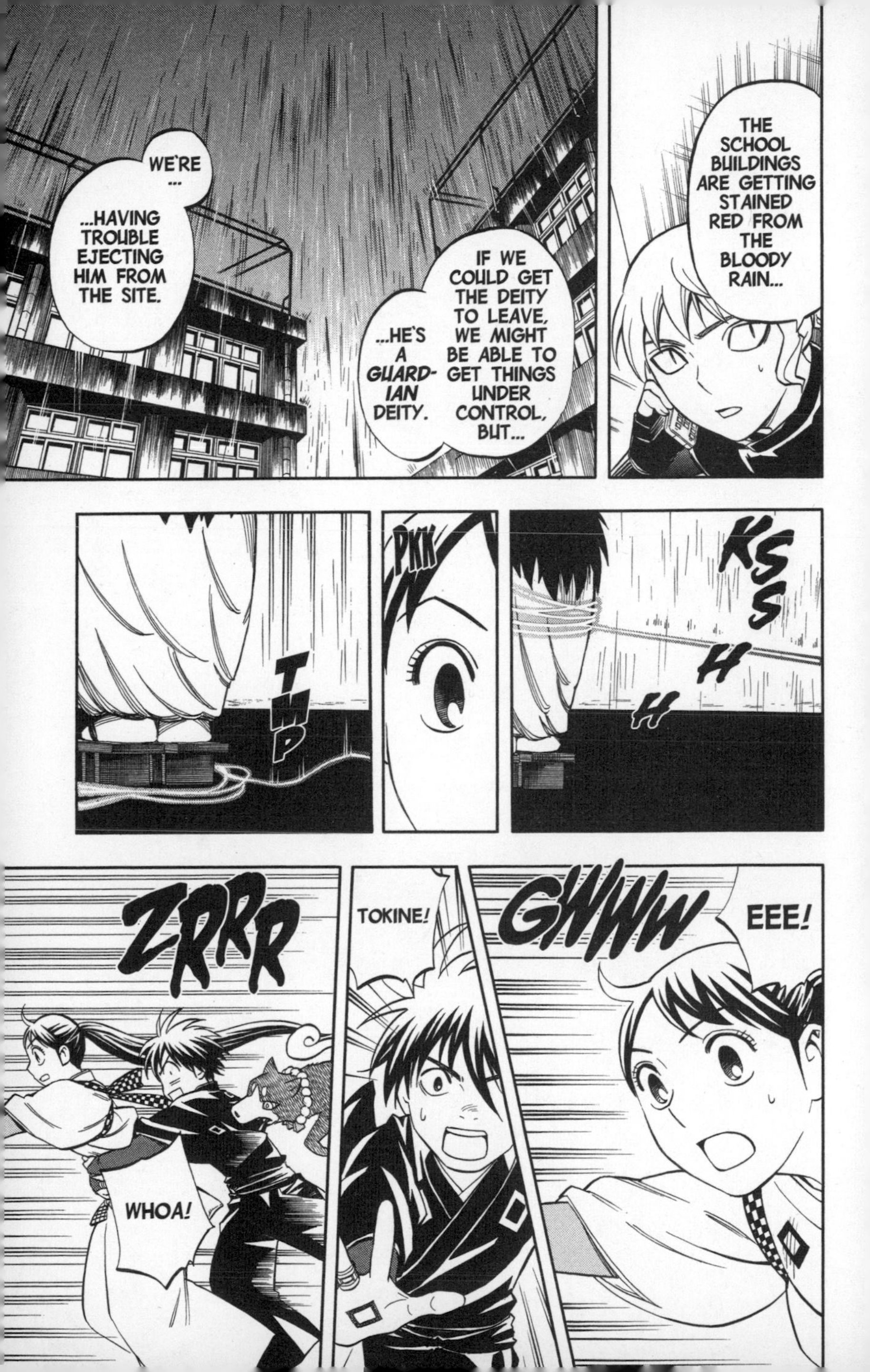
THE SCHOOL BUILDINGS ARE GETTING STAINED RED FROM THE BLOODY RAIN...
IF WE COULD GET THE DEITY TO LEAVE, WE MIGHT BE ABLE TO GET THINGS UNDER CONTROL, BUT...
...HE'S A GUARDIAN DEITY.
WE'RE ...
...HAVING TROUBLE EJECTING HIM FROM THE SITE.
KSSHH
PKK
TMP
EEE!
GWWW
TOKINE!
ZRRR
WHOA!

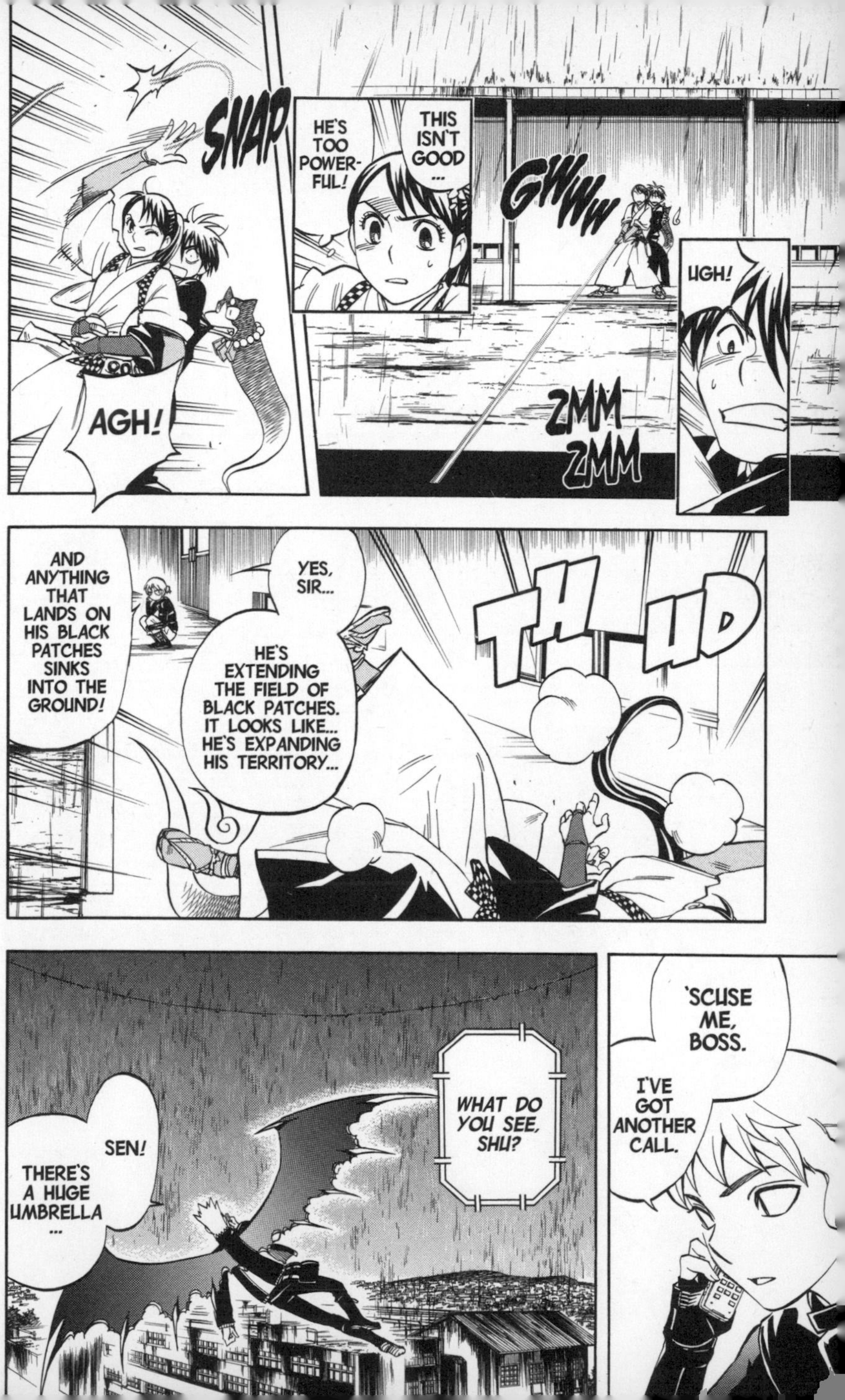
UGH!
ZMM ZMM
GWWW
THIS ISN'T GOOD...
HE'S TOO POWER-FUL!
SNAP
AGH!
TH-UD
YES, SIR...
HE'S EXTENDING THE FIELD OF BLACK PATCHES. IT LOOKS LIKE... HE'S EXPANDING HIS TERRITORY...
AND ANYTHING THAT LANDS ON HIS BLACK PATCHES SINKS INTO THE GROUND!
'SCUSE ME, BOSS.
I'VE GOT ANOTHER CALL.
WHAT DO YOU SEE, SHU?
SEN!
THERE'S A HUGE UMBRELLA...

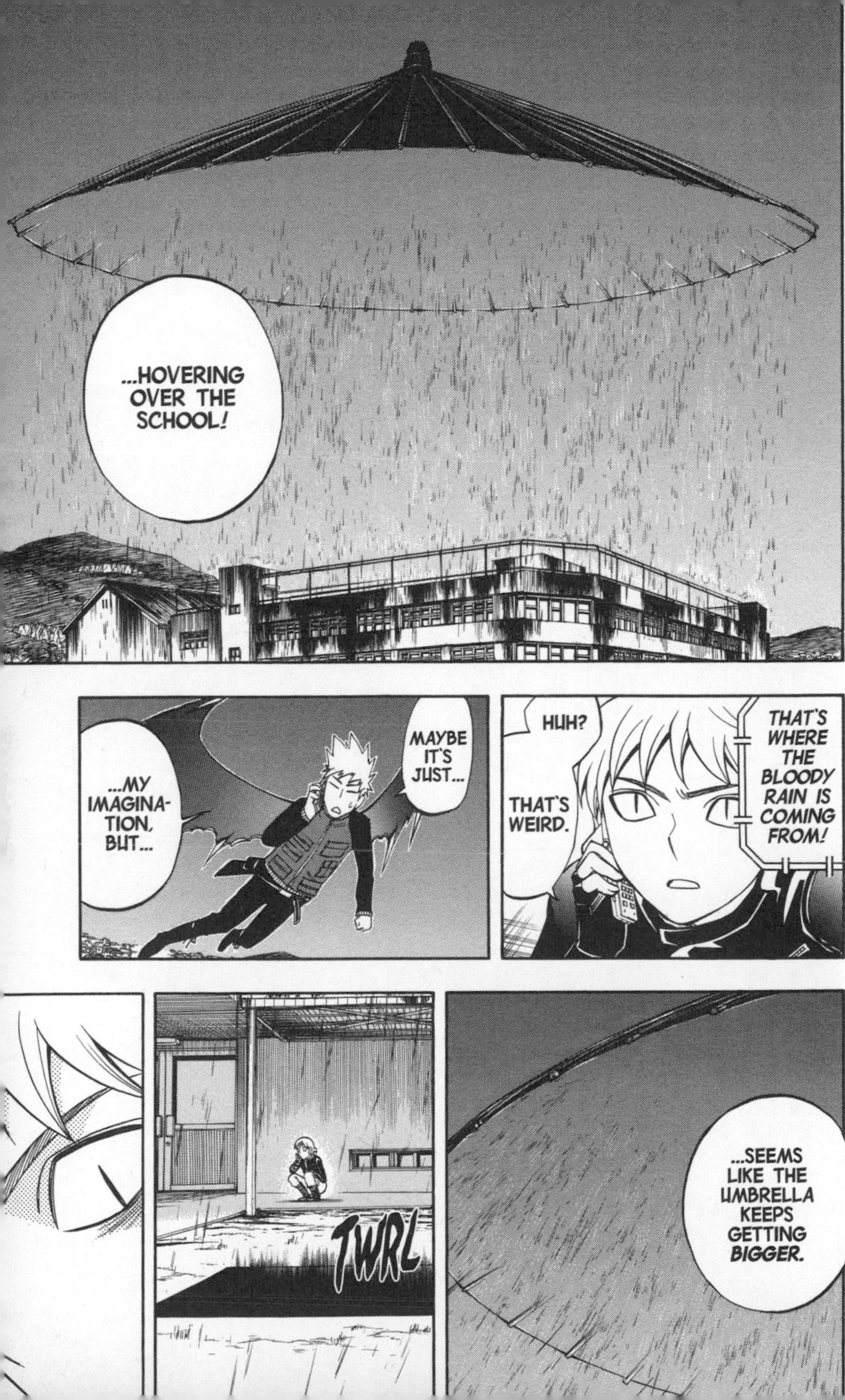
...HOVERING OVER THE SCHOOL!
THAT'S WHERE THE BLOODY RAIN IS COMING FROM!
HUH?
THAT'S WEIRD.
MAYBE IT'S JUST...
...MY IMAGINATION, BUT...
...SEEMS LIKE THE UMBRELLA KEEPS GETTING BIGGER.
TWRL

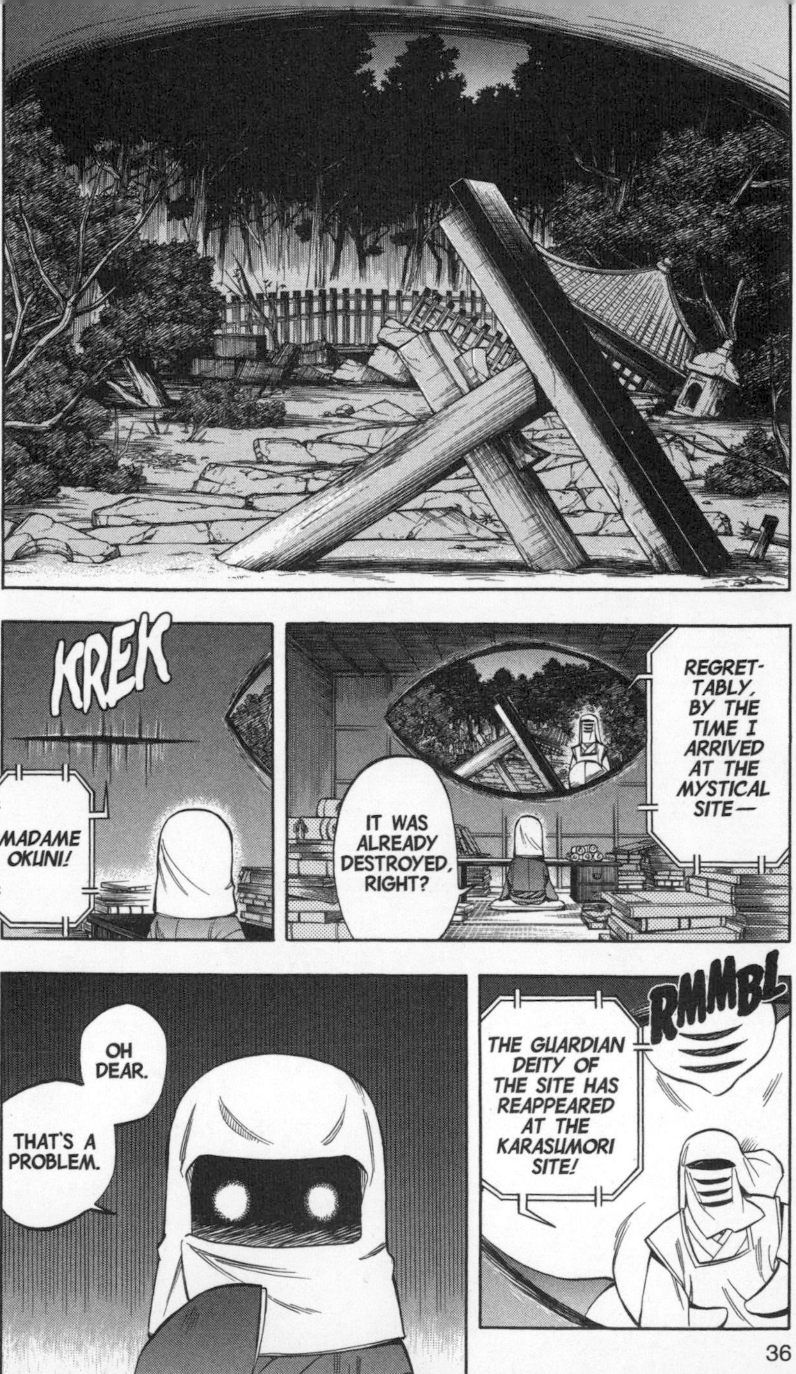
REGRET-TABLY, BY THE TIME I ARRIVED AT THE MYSTICAL SITE—
IT WAS ALREADY DESTROYED, RIGHT?
KREK
MADAME OKUNI!
RMMBL
THE GUARDIAN DEITY OF THE SITE HAS REAPPEARED AT THE KARASUMORI SITE!
OH DEAR.
THAT'S A PROBLEM.

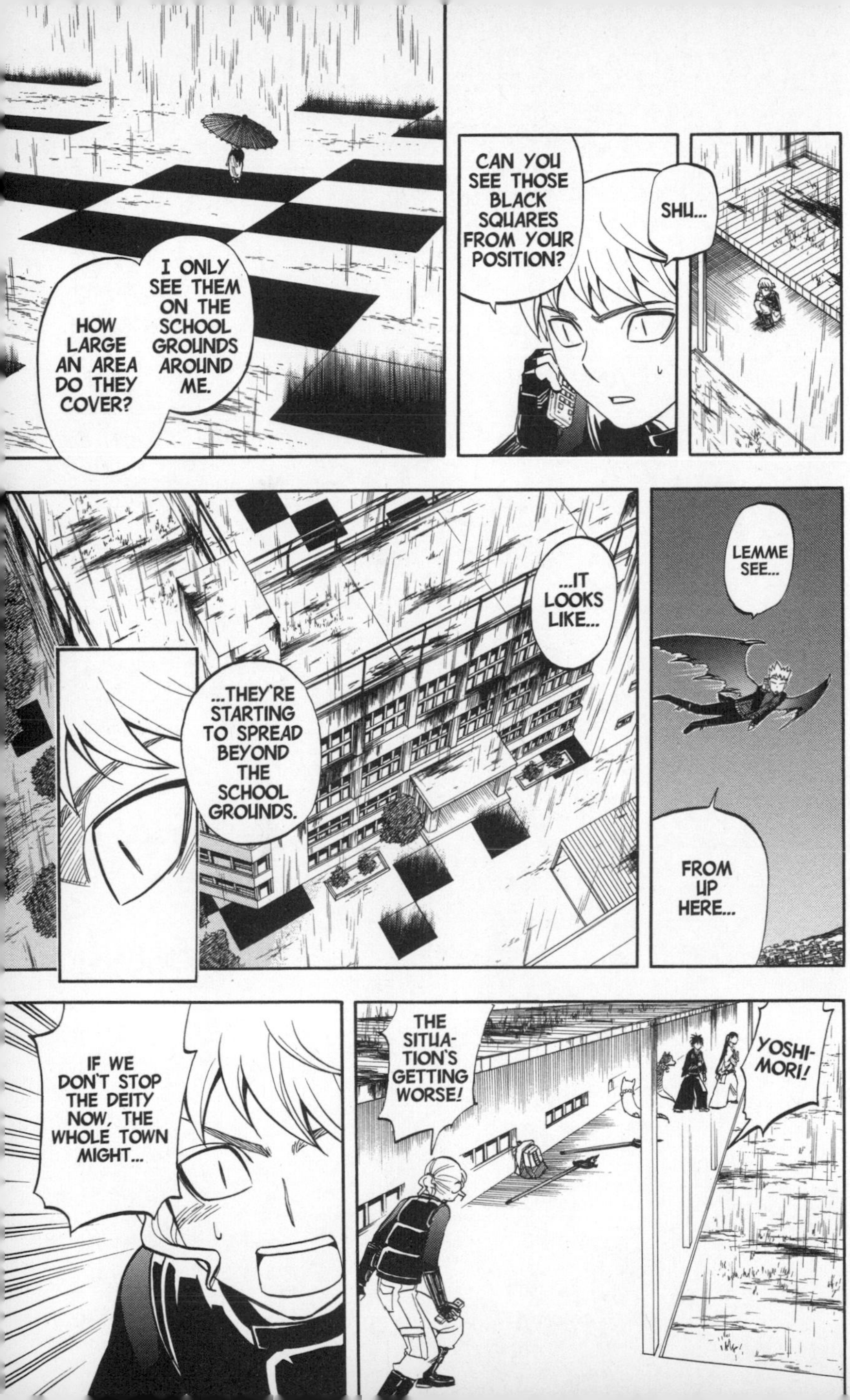
SHU...
CAN YOU SEE THOSE BLACK SQUARES FROM YOUR POSITION?
I ONLY SEE THEM ON THE SCHOOL GROUNDS AROUND ME.
HOW LARGE AN AREA DO THEY COVER?
LEMME SEE...
FROM UP HERE...
...IT LOOKS LIKE...
...THEY'RE STARTING TO SPREAD BEYOND THE SCHOOL GROUNDS.
YOSHI-MORI!
THE SITUA-TION'S GETTING WORSE!
IF WE DON'T STOP THE DEITY NOW, THE WHOLE TOWN MIGHT...

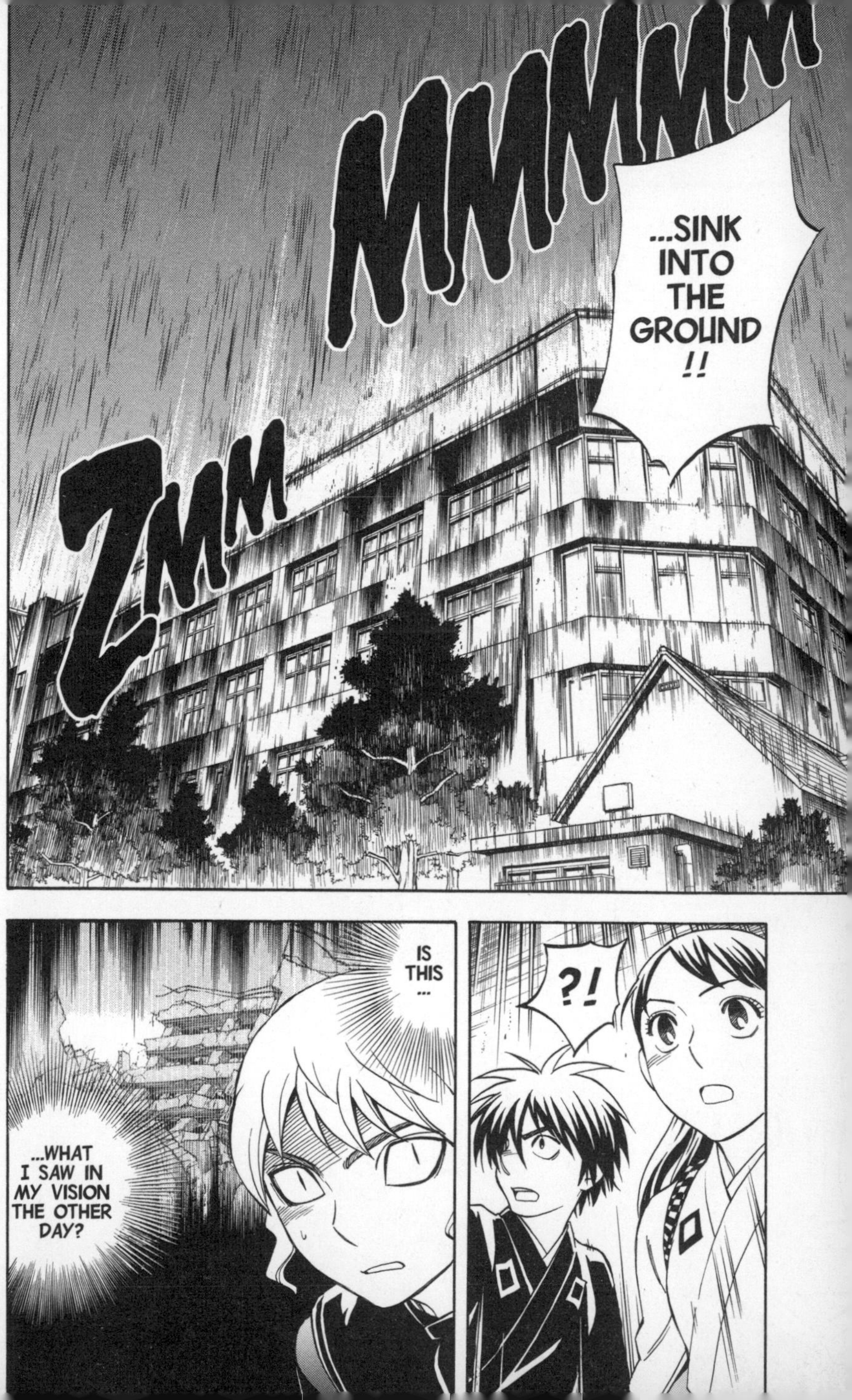
...SINK INTO THE GROUND !!
ZMM MMMMMM
?!
IS THIS ...
...WHAT I SAW IN MY VISION THE OTHER DAY?

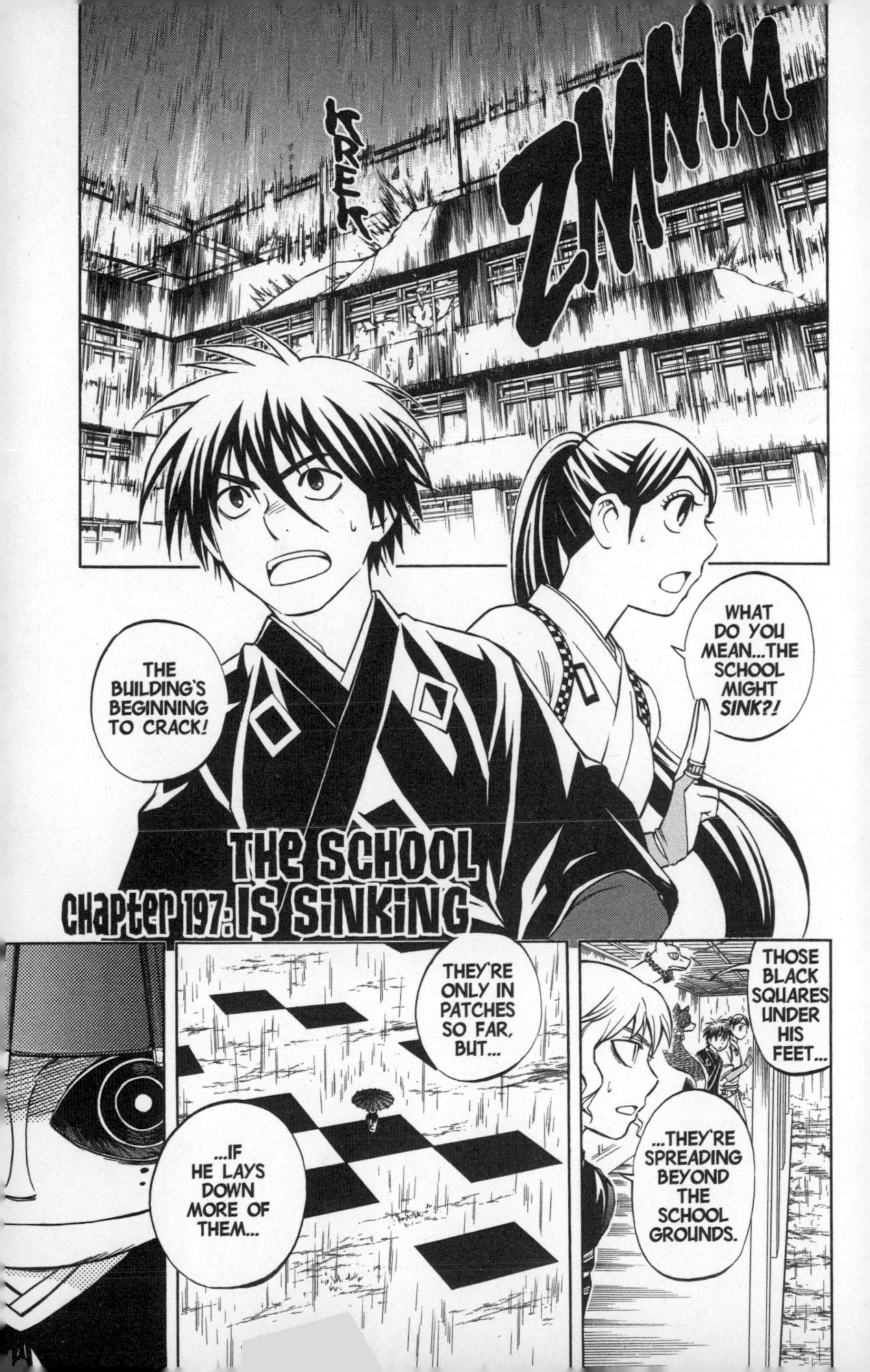
ZMMM
KREK
THE BUILDING'S BEGINNING TO CRACK!
WHAT DO YOU MEAN...THE SCHOOL MIGHT SINK?!
Chapter 197: THE SCHOOL IS SINKING
THOSE BLACK SQUARES UNDER HIS FEET...
...THEY'RE SPREADING BEYOND THE SCHOOL GROUNDS.
THEY'RE ONLY IN PATCHES SO FAR, BUT...
...IF HE LAYS DOWN MORE OF THEM...

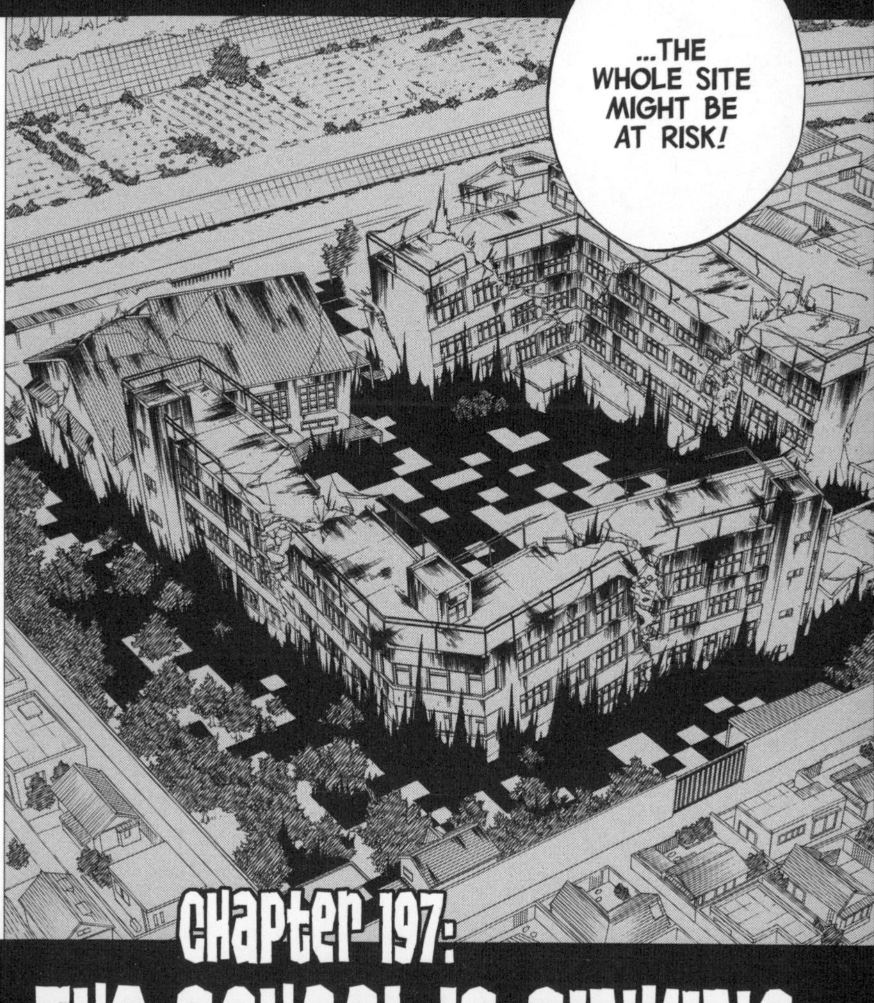
...THE WHOLE SITE MIGHT BE AT RISK!

Chapter 197: The School Is Sinking

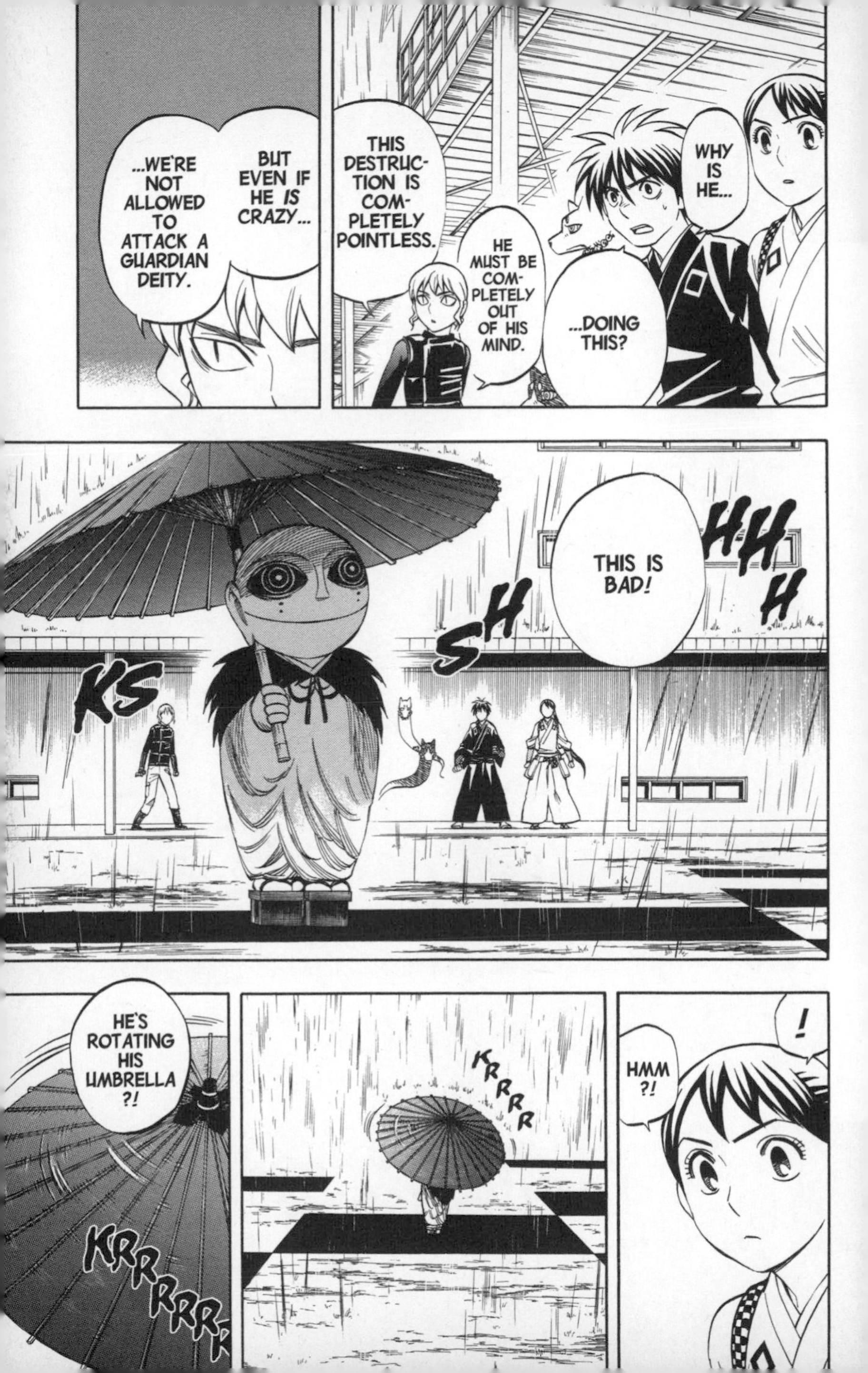
WHY IS HE...
...DOING THIS?
HE MUST BE COMPLETELY OUT OF HIS MIND.
THIS DESTRUCTION IS COMPLETELY POINTLESS.
BUT EVEN IF HE *IS* CRAZY...
...WE'RE NOT ALLOWED TO ATTACK A GUARDIAN DEITY.
HHHH
THIS IS BAD!
SH
KS
!
HMM ?!
KRRRR
HE'S ROTATING HIS UMBRELLA ?!
KRRRRRR

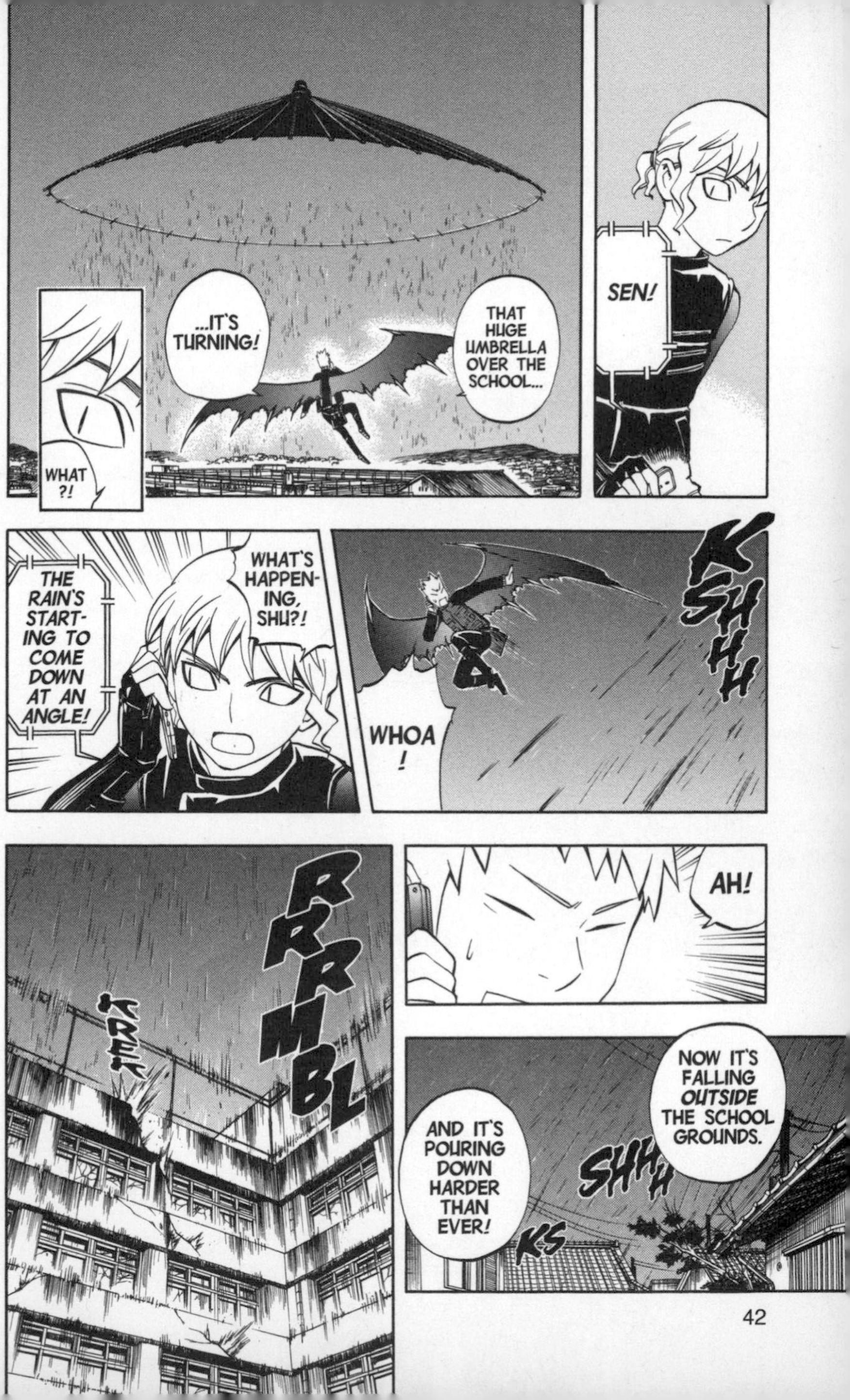
SEN!
THAT HUGE UMBRELLA OVER THE SCHOOL...
...IT'S TURNING!
WHAT ?!
KSHHH
WHOA !
WHAT'S HAPPENING, SHU?!
THE RAIN'S STARTING TO COME DOWN AT AN ANGLE!
AH!
RRRMBL
KREK
NOW IT'S FALLING OUTSIDE THE SCHOOL GROUNDS.
SHHH
AND IT'S POURING DOWN HARDER THAN EVER!
KS

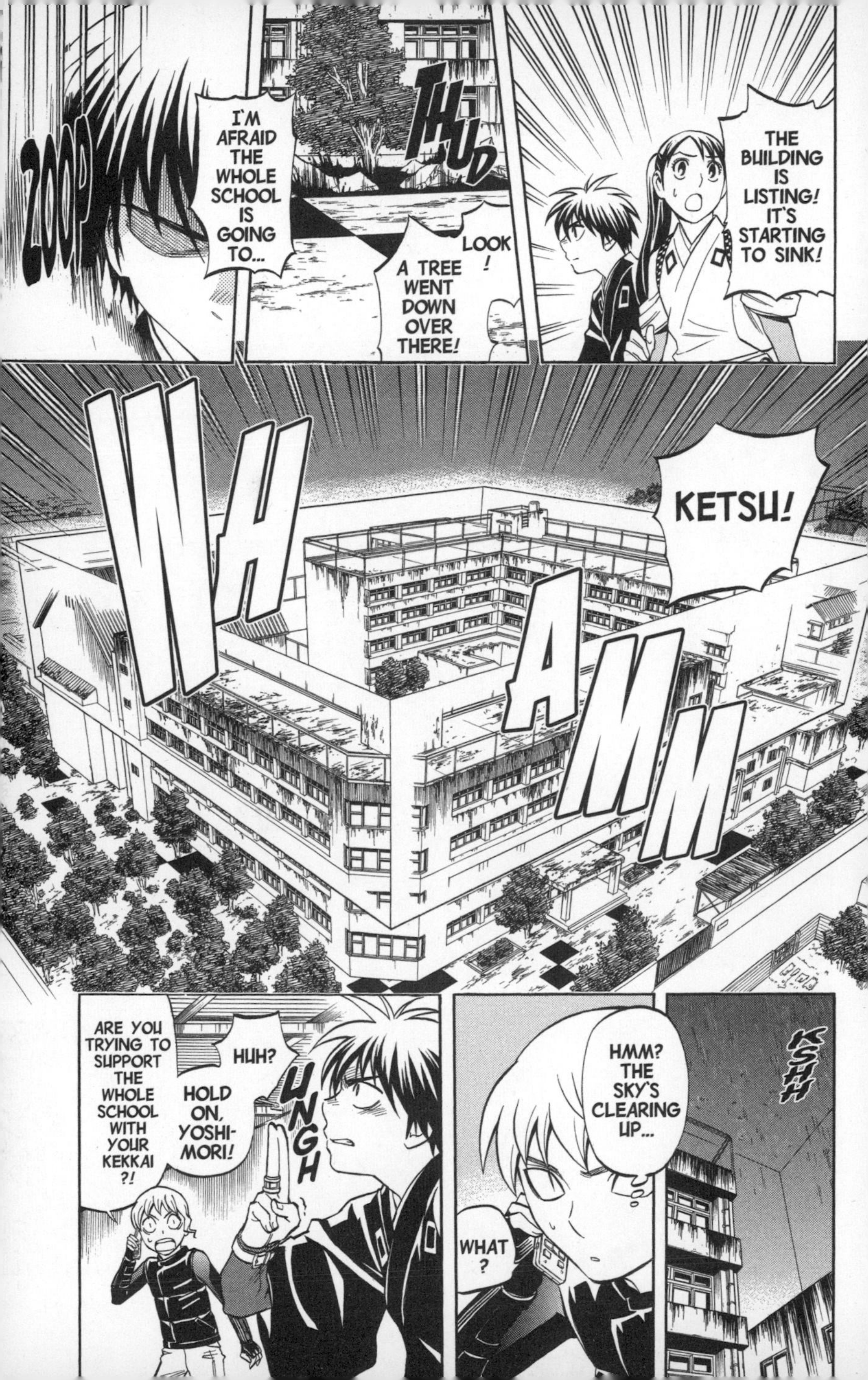
THE BUILDING IS LISTING! IT'S STARTING TO SINK!
THUD
LOOK!
A TREE WENT DOWN OVER THERE!
I'M AFRAID THE WHOLE SCHOOL IS GOING TO...
ZOOP
KETSU!
WHAMM
KSHH
HMM? THE SKY'S CLEARING UP...
WHAT?
UNGH
HUH?
HOLD ON, YOSHI-MORI!
ARE YOU TRYING TO SUPPORT THE WHOLE SCHOOL WITH YOUR KEKKAI?!

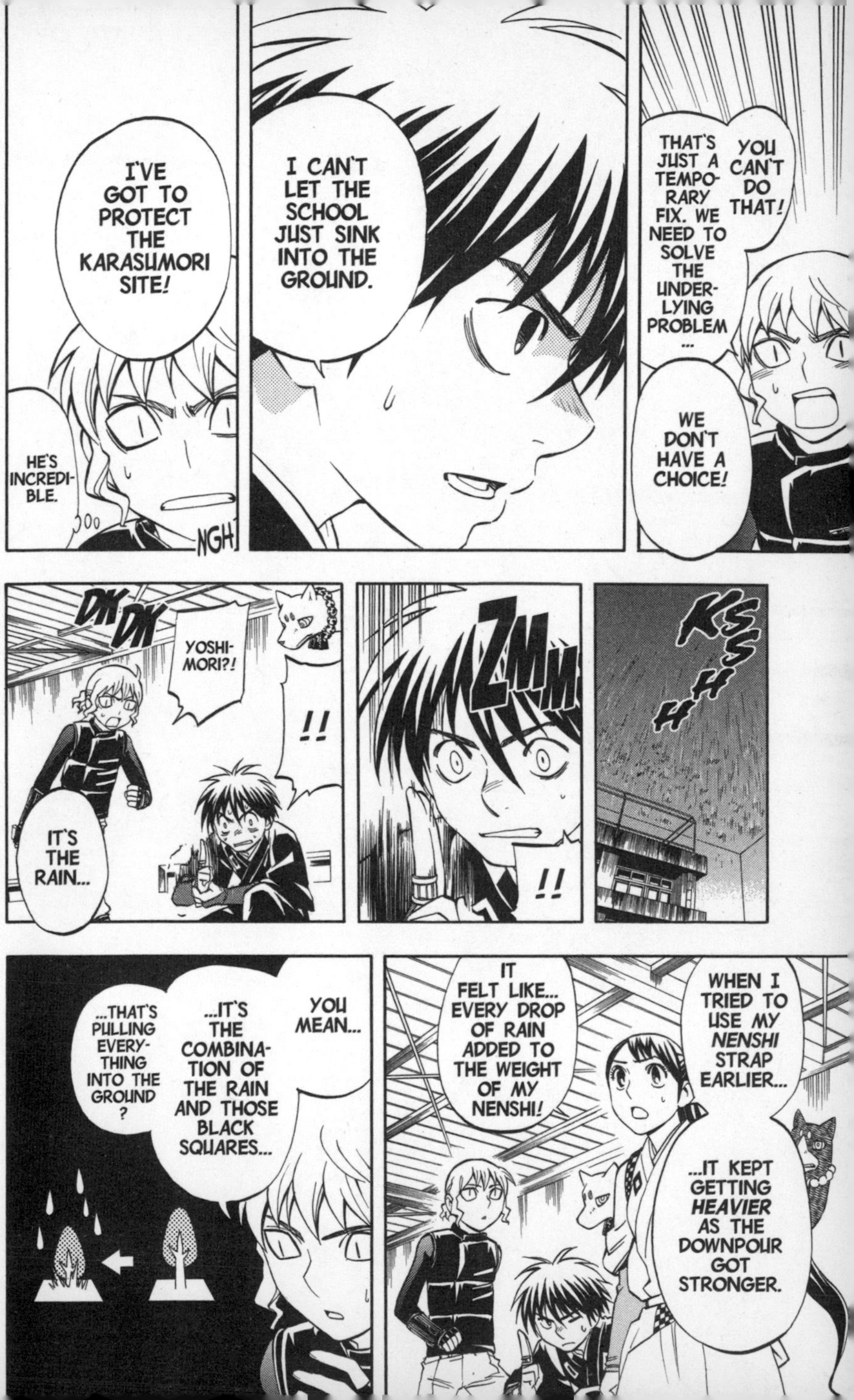
YOU CAN'T DO THAT!
THAT'S JUST A TEMPORARY FIX. WE NEED TO SOLVE THE UNDERLYING PROBLEM...
WE DON'T HAVE A CHOICE!
I CAN'T LET THE SCHOOL JUST SINK INTO THE GROUND.
I'VE GOT TO PROTECT THE KARASUMORI SITE!
HE'S INCREDIBLE.
NGH
KSSHHH
ZMM
!!
!!
YOSHIMORI?!
DK DK
IT'S THE RAIN...
WHEN I TRIED TO USE MY NENSHI STRAP EARLIER...
...IT KEPT GETTING HEAVIER AS THE DOWNPOUR GOT STRONGER.
IT FELT LIKE... EVERY DROP OF RAIN ADDED TO THE WEIGHT OF MY NENSHI!
YOU MEAN...
...IT'S THE COMBINATION OF THE RAIN AND THOSE BLACK SQUARES...
...THAT'S PULLING EVERYTHING INTO THE GROUND?

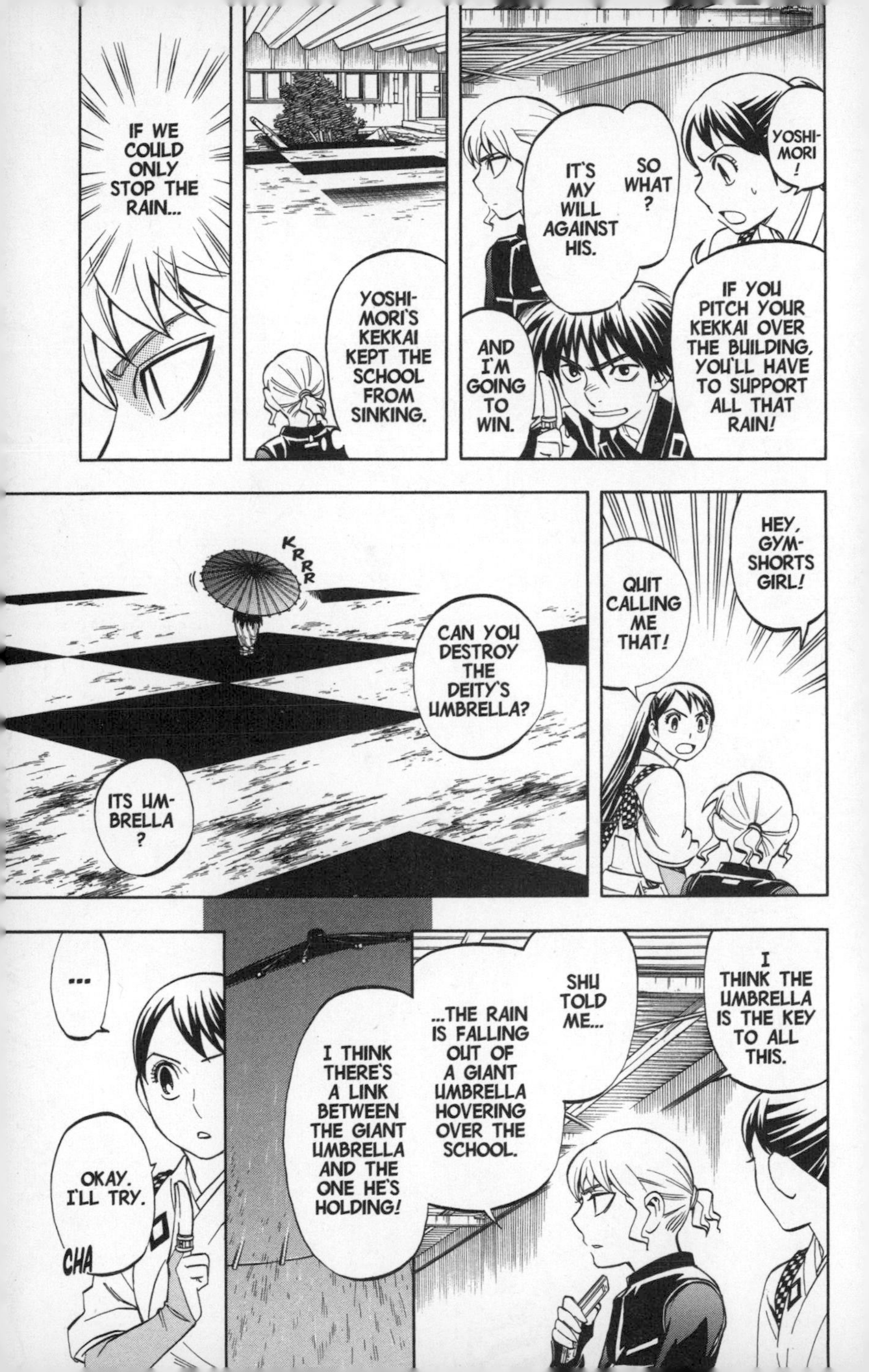
YOSHI-MORI!
IF YOU PITCH YOUR KEKKAI OVER THE BUILDING, YOU'LL HAVE TO SUPPORT ALL THAT RAIN!
SO WHAT?
IT'S MY WILL AGAINST HIS.
AND I'M GOING TO WIN.
YOSHI-MORI'S KEKKAI KEPT THE SCHOOL FROM SINKING.
IF WE COULD ONLY STOP THE RAIN...
HEY, GYM-SHORTS GIRL!
QUIT CALLING ME THAT!
CAN YOU DESTROY THE DEITY'S UMBRELLA?
KRRR
ITS UM-BRELLA?
I THINK THE UMBRELLA IS THE KEY TO ALL THIS.
SHU TOLD ME...
...THE RAIN IS FALLING OUT OF A GIANT UMBRELLA HOVERING OVER THE SCHOOL.
I THINK THERE'S A LINK BETWEEN THE GIANT UMBRELLA AND THE ONE HE'S HOLDING!
...
OKAY. I'LL TRY.
CHA

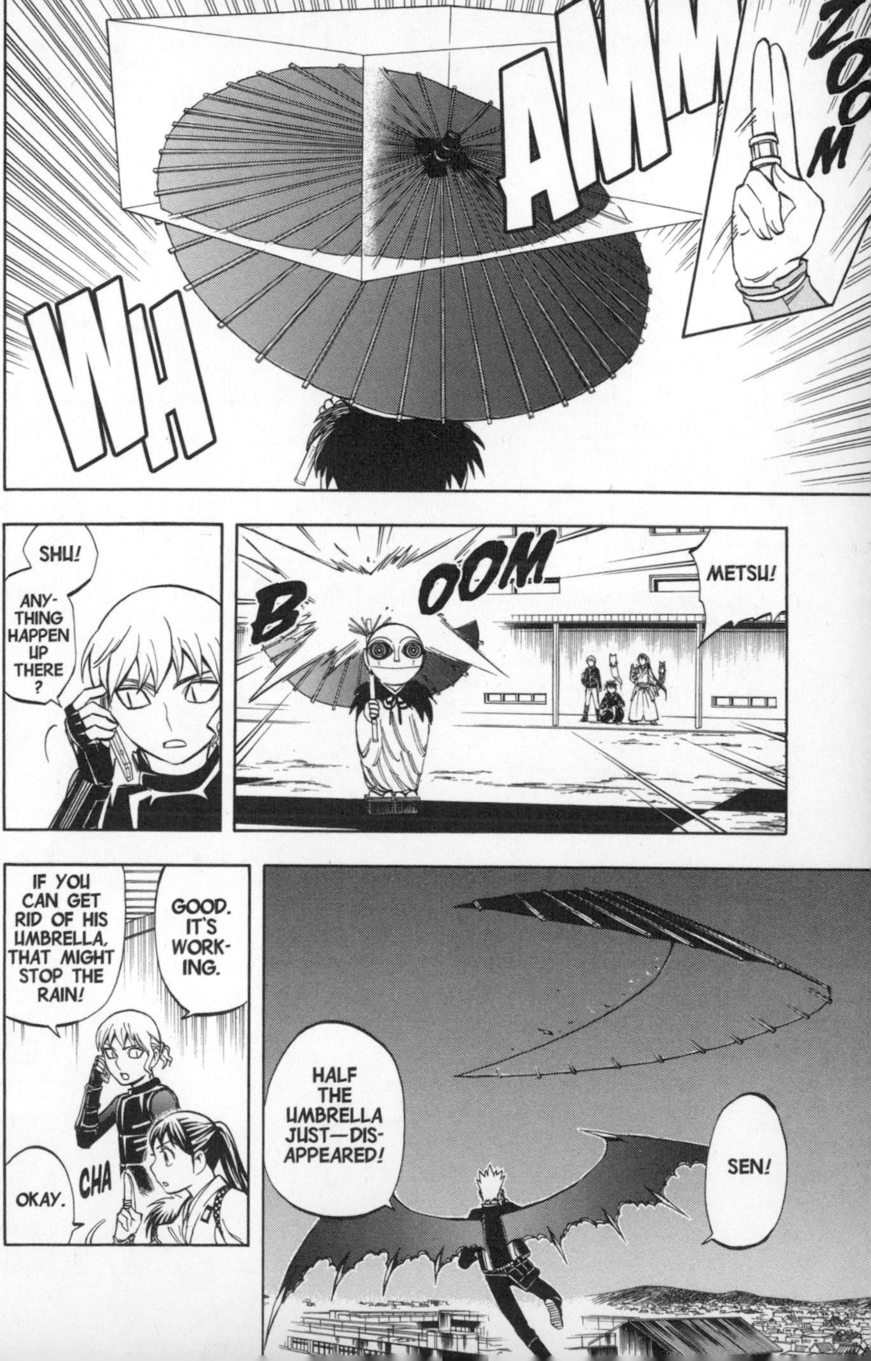
ZOOM
WHAMM
METSU!
BOOM
SHU!
ANYTHING HAPPEN UP THERE?
SEN!
HALF THE UMBRELLA JUST—DISAPPEARED!
GOOD. IT'S WORKING.
IF YOU CAN GET RID OF HIS UMBRELLA, THAT MIGHT STOP THE RAIN!
CHA
OKAY.

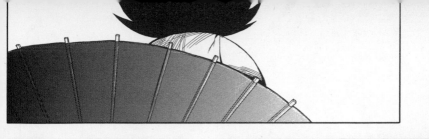

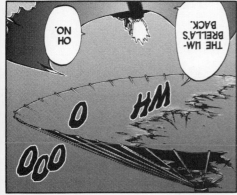

ZRR
KHRP
KHRP
KHRP
KHRP
KHRP
KHRP
KRHP KRHP KRHP
IT'S REGENER-ATING...
WHOOOO
THE UM-BRELLA'S BACK.
OH NO.
CREAK

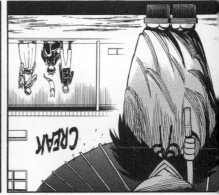

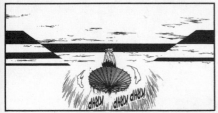

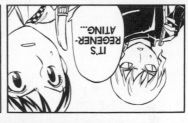

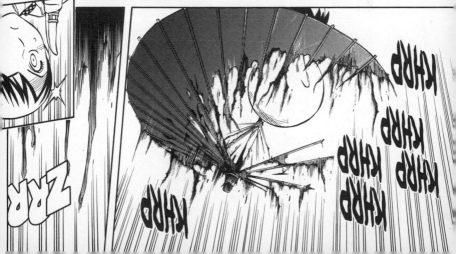

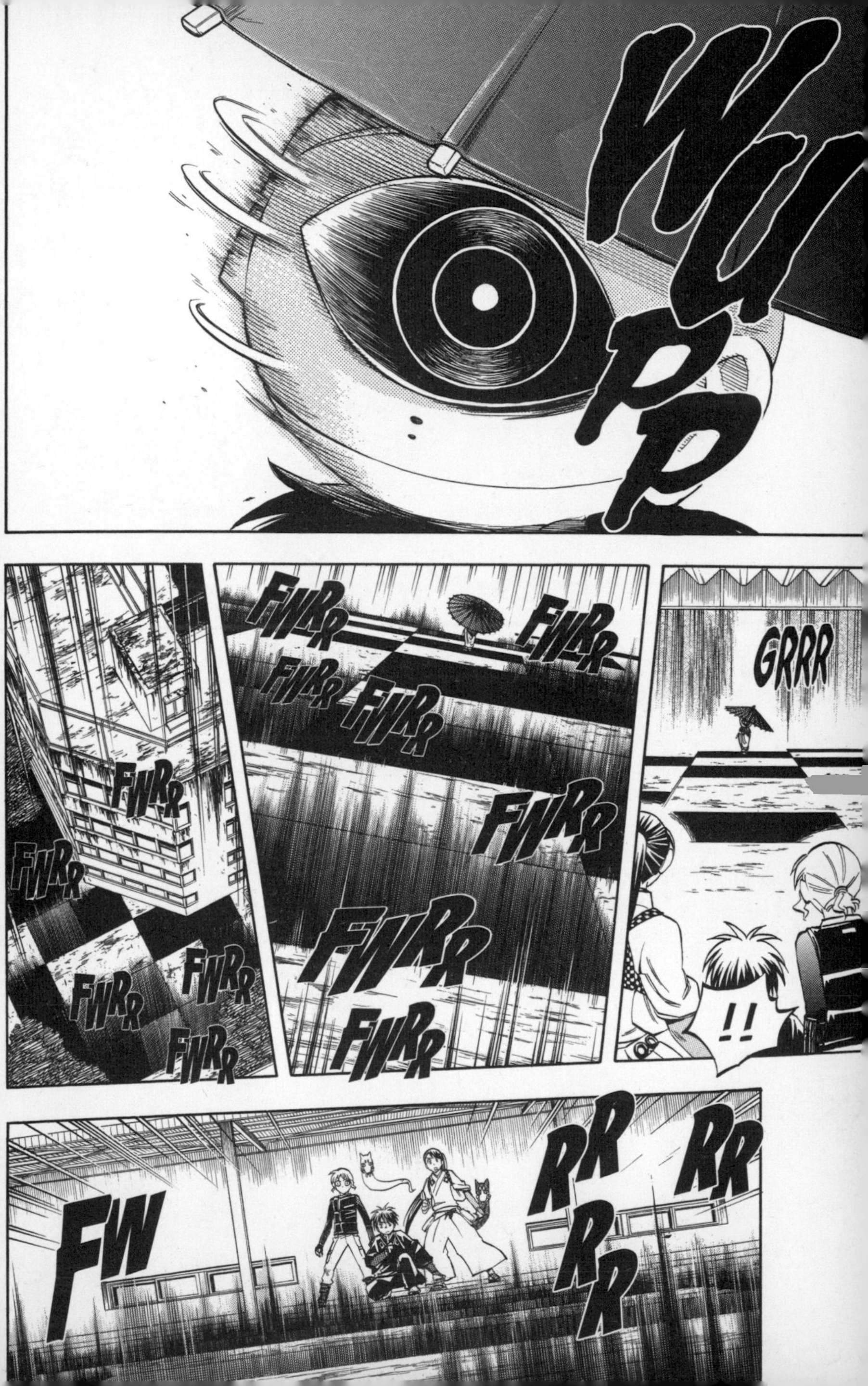
WHIPP
GRRR
!!
FWRR
FWRR
FWRR
FWRR
FWRR
FWRR
FWRR
FWRR
FWRR
FWRR
FWRR
RR
RR
RR
FW

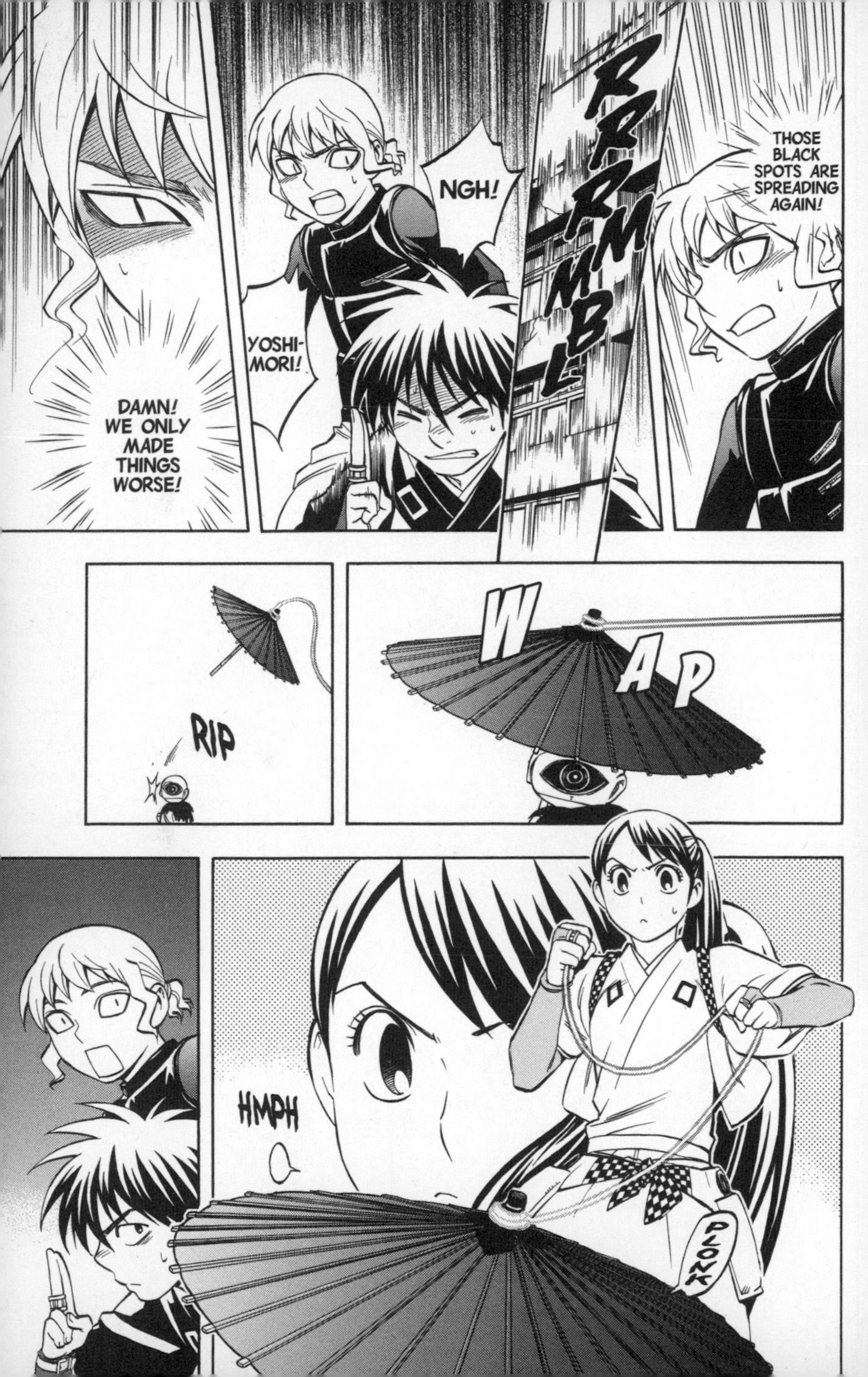
THOSE BLACK SPOTS ARE SPREADING AGAIN!
RRRMMBL
NGH!
YOSHI-MORI!
DAMN! WE ONLY MADE THINGS WORSE!
WAP
RIP
HMPH
PLONK

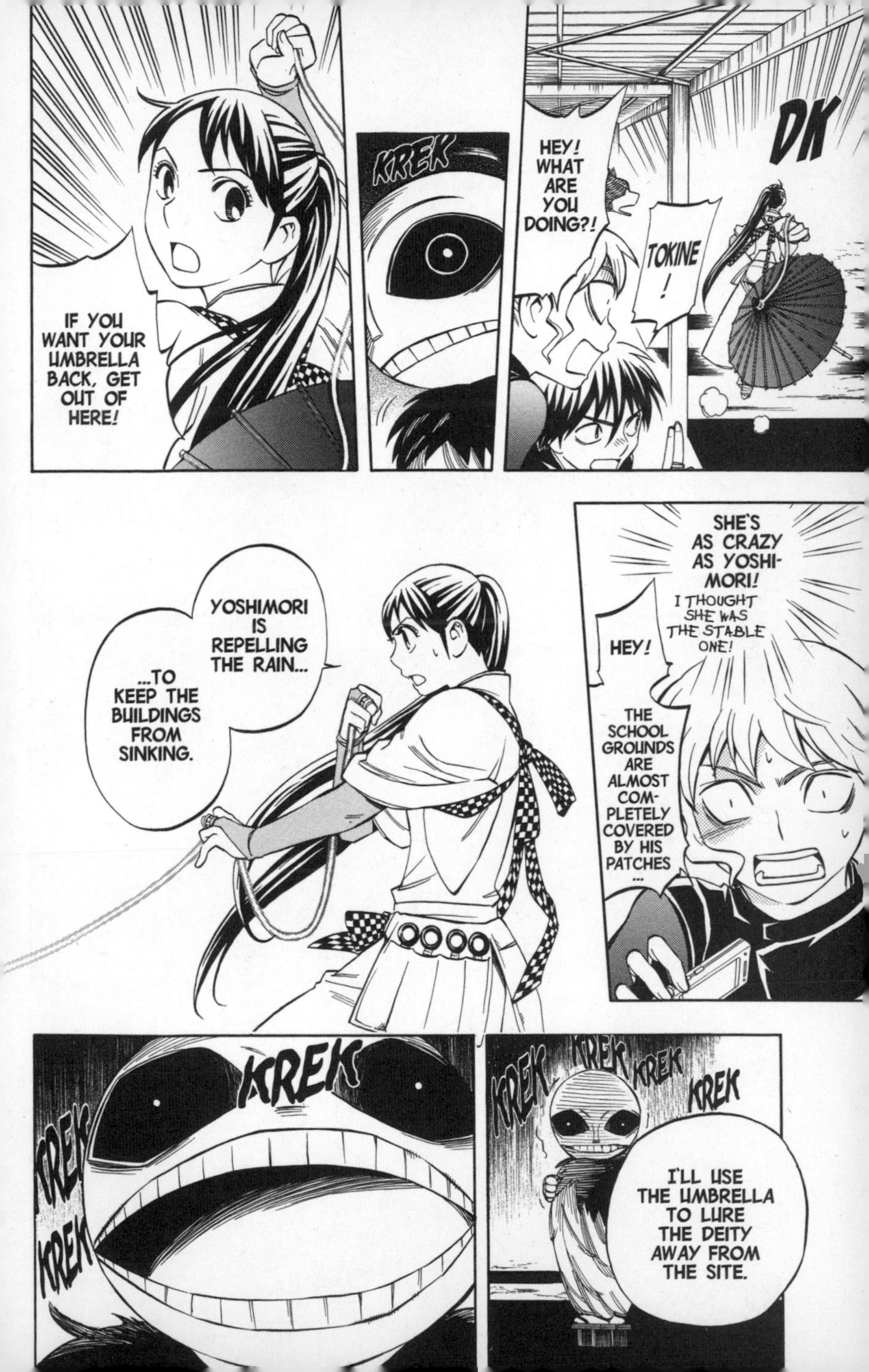
DK
TOKINE!
HEY! WHAT ARE YOU DOING?!
KREK
IF YOU WANT YOUR UMBRELLA BACK, GET OUT OF HERE!
SHE'S AS CRAZY AS YOSHI-MORI!
I THOUGHT SHE WAS THE STABLE ONE!
HEY!
THE SCHOOL GROUNDS ARE ALMOST COM-PLETELY COVERED BY HIS PATCHES ...
YOSHIMORI IS REPELLING THE RAIN...
...TO KEEP THE BUILDINGS FROM SINKING.
KREK KREK KREK
KREK
I'LL USE THE UMBRELLA TO LURE THE DEITY AWAY FROM THE SITE.
KREK
KREK

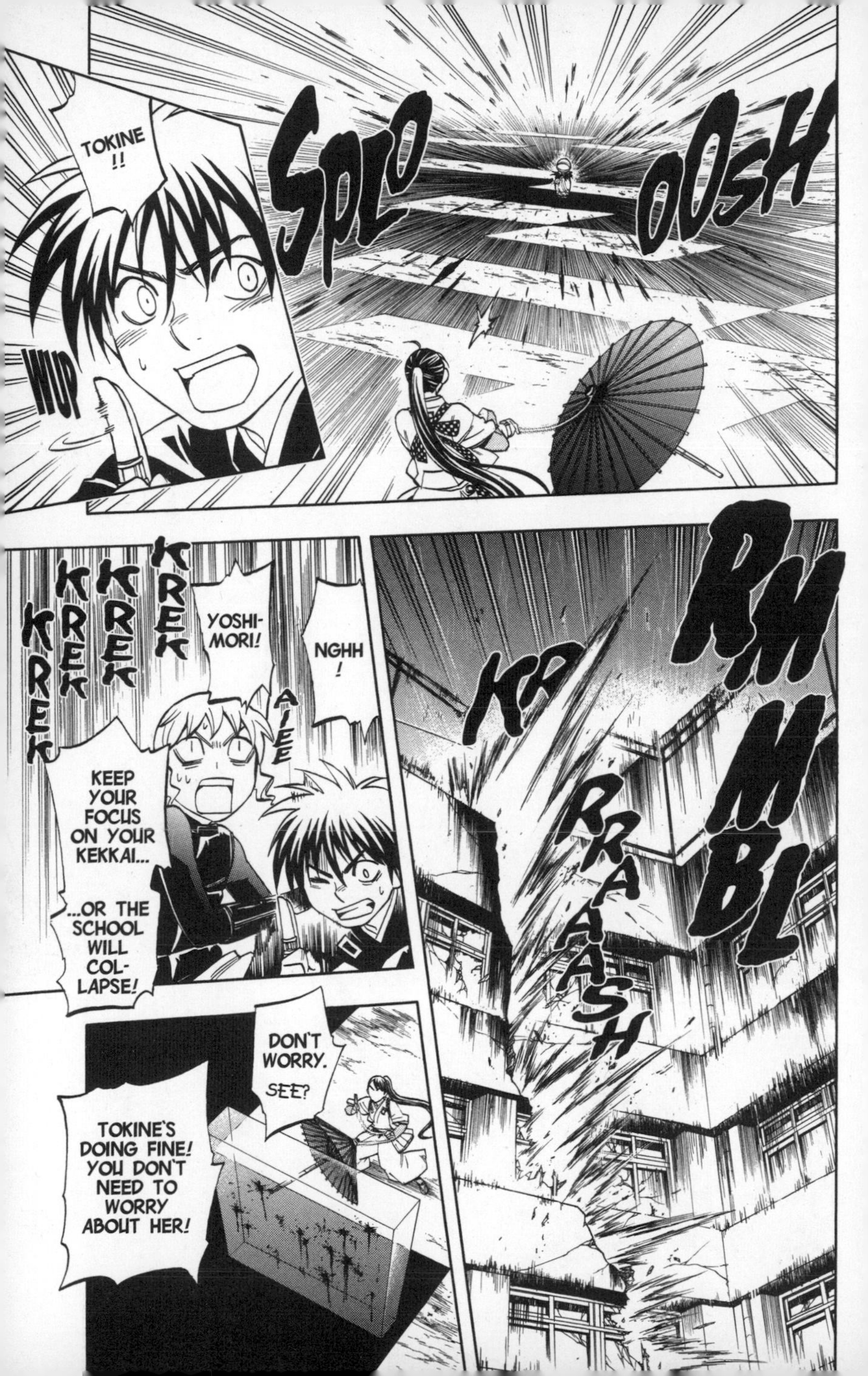
SPLOOOSH
TOKINE!!
WUP
RMMBL
KRRAASH
KREK KREK KREK KREK
YOSHIMORI!
NGHH!
AIEE
KEEP YOUR FOCUS ON YOUR KEKKAI...
...OR THE SCHOOL WILL COLLAPSE!
DON'T WORRY.
SEE?
TOKINE'S DOING FINE! YOU DON'T NEED TO WORRY ABOUT HER!

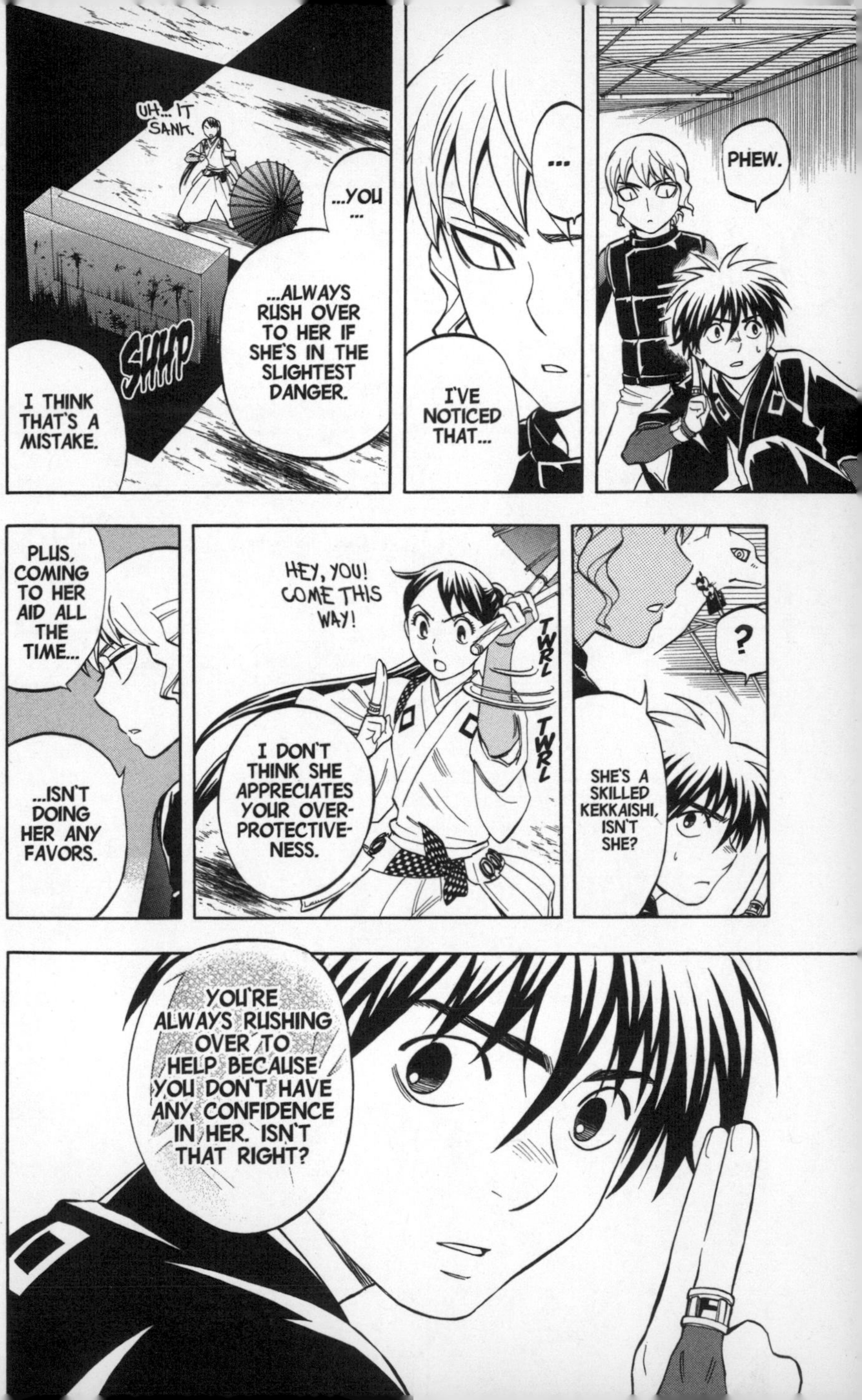
PHEW.
...
I'VE NOTICED THAT...
...YOU ...
...ALWAYS RUSH OVER TO HER IF SHE'S IN THE SLIGHTEST DANGER.
UH... IT SANK.
SHHP
I THINK THAT'S A MISTAKE.
?
SHE'S A SKILLED KEKKAISHI, ISN'T SHE?
HEY, YOU! COME THIS WAY!
TWRL
TWRL
I DON'T THINK SHE APPRECIATES YOUR OVER-PROTECTIVE-NESS.
PLUS, COMING TO HER AID ALL THE TIME...
...ISN'T DOING HER ANY FAVORS.
YOU'RE ALWAYS RUSHING OVER TO HELP BECAUSE YOU DON'T HAVE ANY CONFIDENCE IN HER. ISN'T THAT RIGHT?

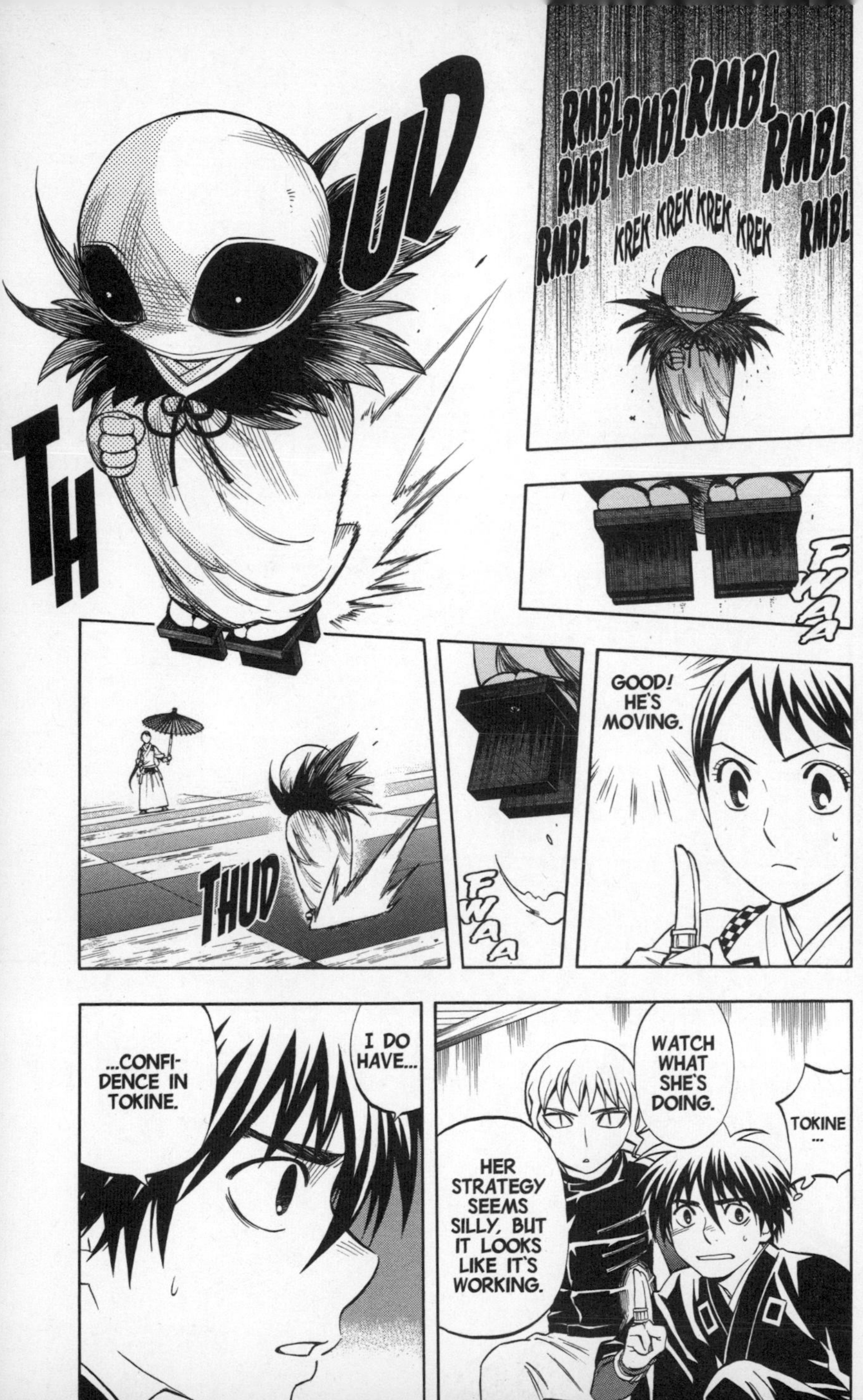
RMBL RMBL RMBL RMBL RMBL RMBL RMBL RMBL
KREK KREK KREK KREK
FWAA
THUD
GOOD! HE'S MOVING.
FWAA
THUD
TOKINE ...
WATCH WHAT SHE'S DOING.
HER STRATEGY SEEMS SILLY, BUT IT LOOKS LIKE IT'S WORKING.
I DO HAVE...
...CONFI-DENCE IN TOKINE.

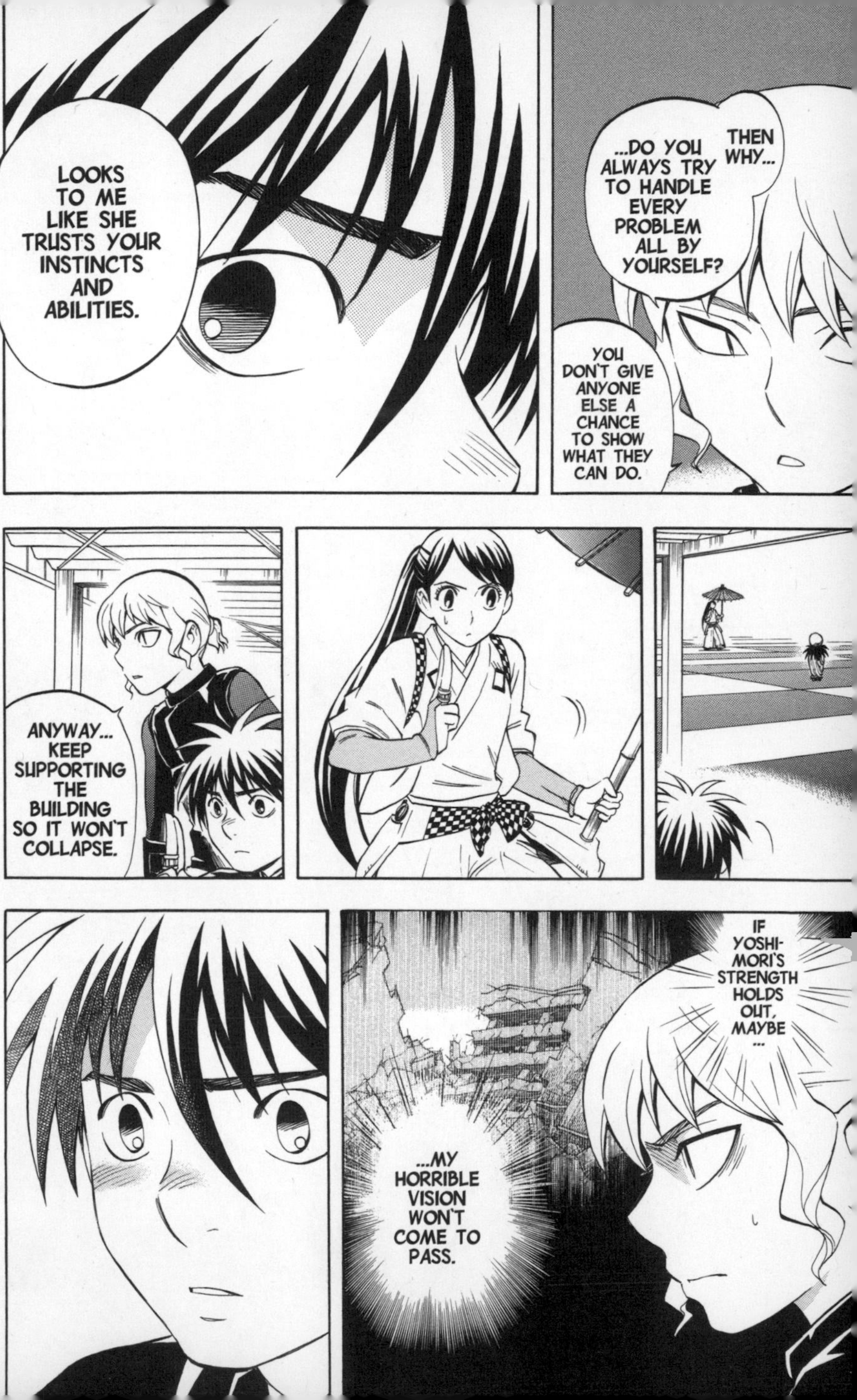
THEN WHY...
...DO YOU ALWAYS TRY TO HANDLE EVERY PROBLEM ALL BY YOURSELF?
YOU DON'T GIVE ANYONE ELSE A CHANCE TO SHOW WHAT THEY CAN DO.
LOOKS TO ME LIKE SHE TRUSTS YOUR INSTINCTS AND ABILITIES.
ANYWAY... KEEP SUPPORTING THE BUILDING SO IT WON'T COLLAPSE.
IF YOSHI-MORI'S STRENGTH HOLDS OUT, MAYBE ...
...MY HORRIBLE VISION WON'T COME TO PASS.

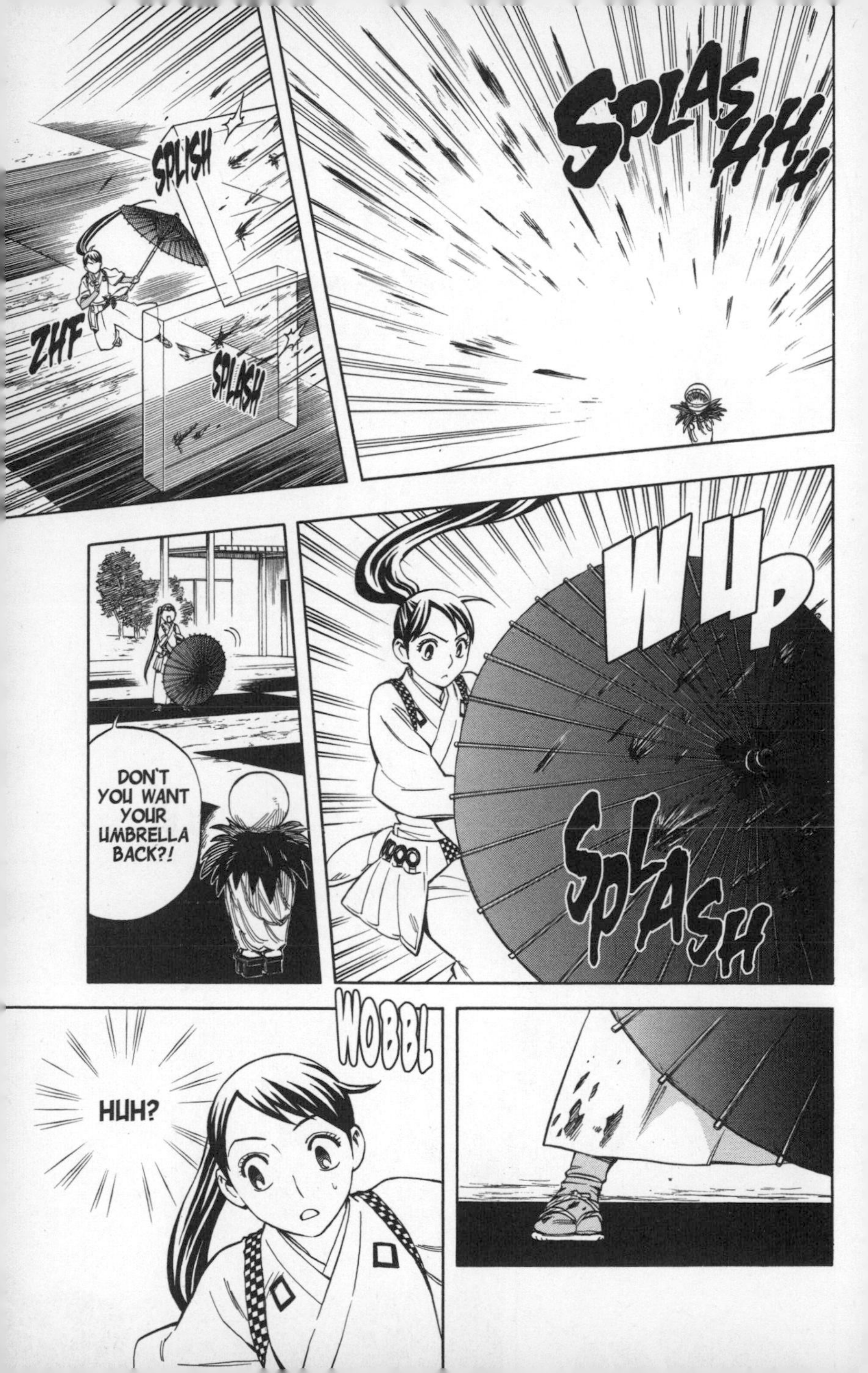
SPLASHHH
SPLISH
ZHF
SPLASH
WHUP
SPLASH
DON'T YOU WANT YOUR UMBRELLA BACK?!
WOBBL
HUH?

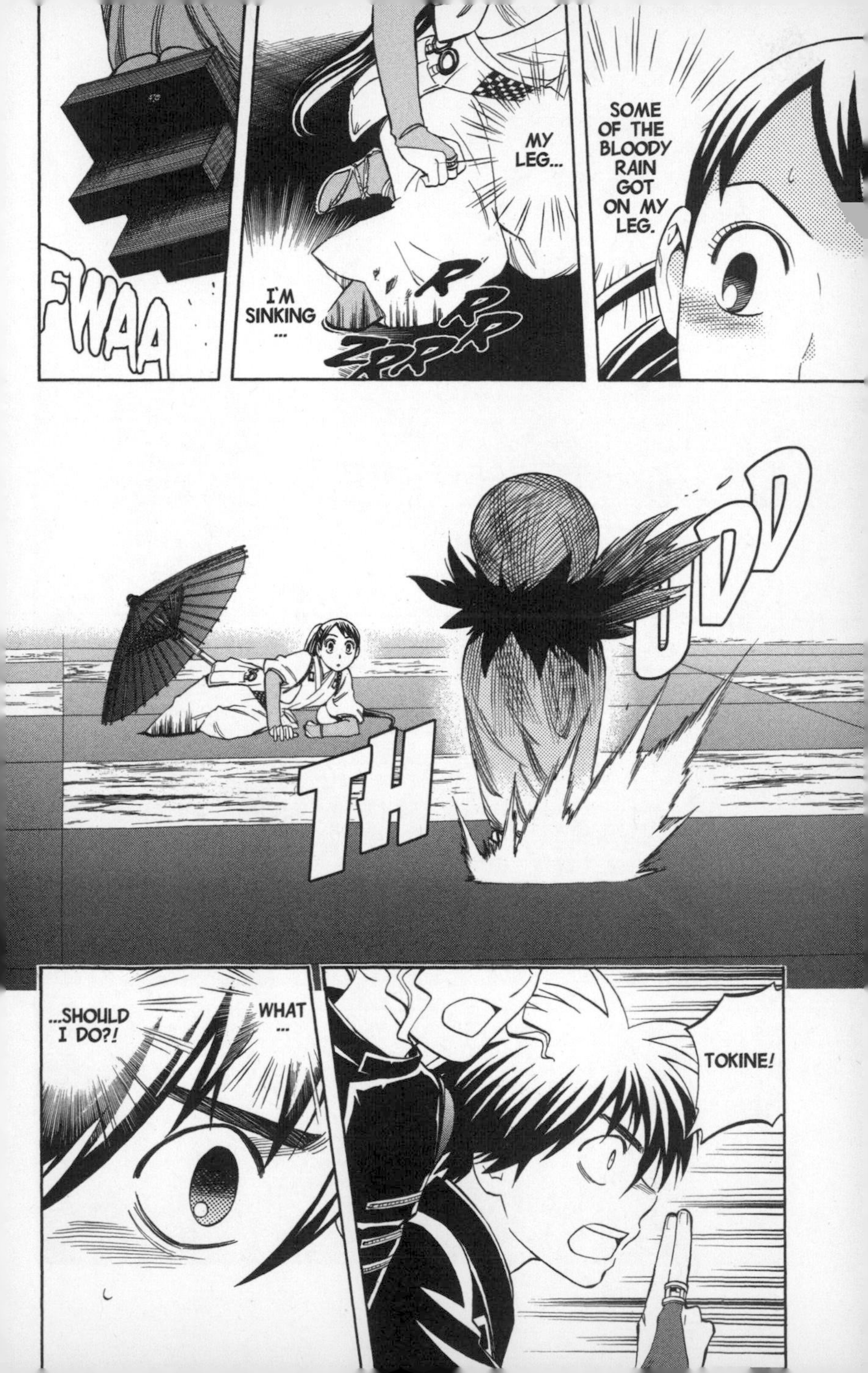
SOME OF THE BLOODY RAIN GOT ON MY LEG.
MY LEG...
I'M SINKING...
FWAA
THUDD
TOKINE!
WHAT...
...SHOULD I DO?!

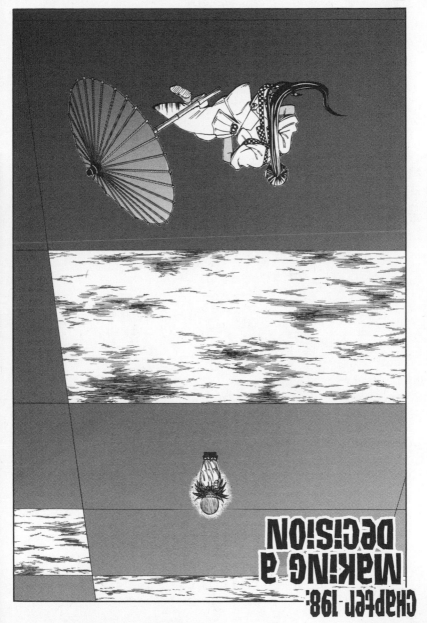

Chapter 198:
MAKING a
DECISION

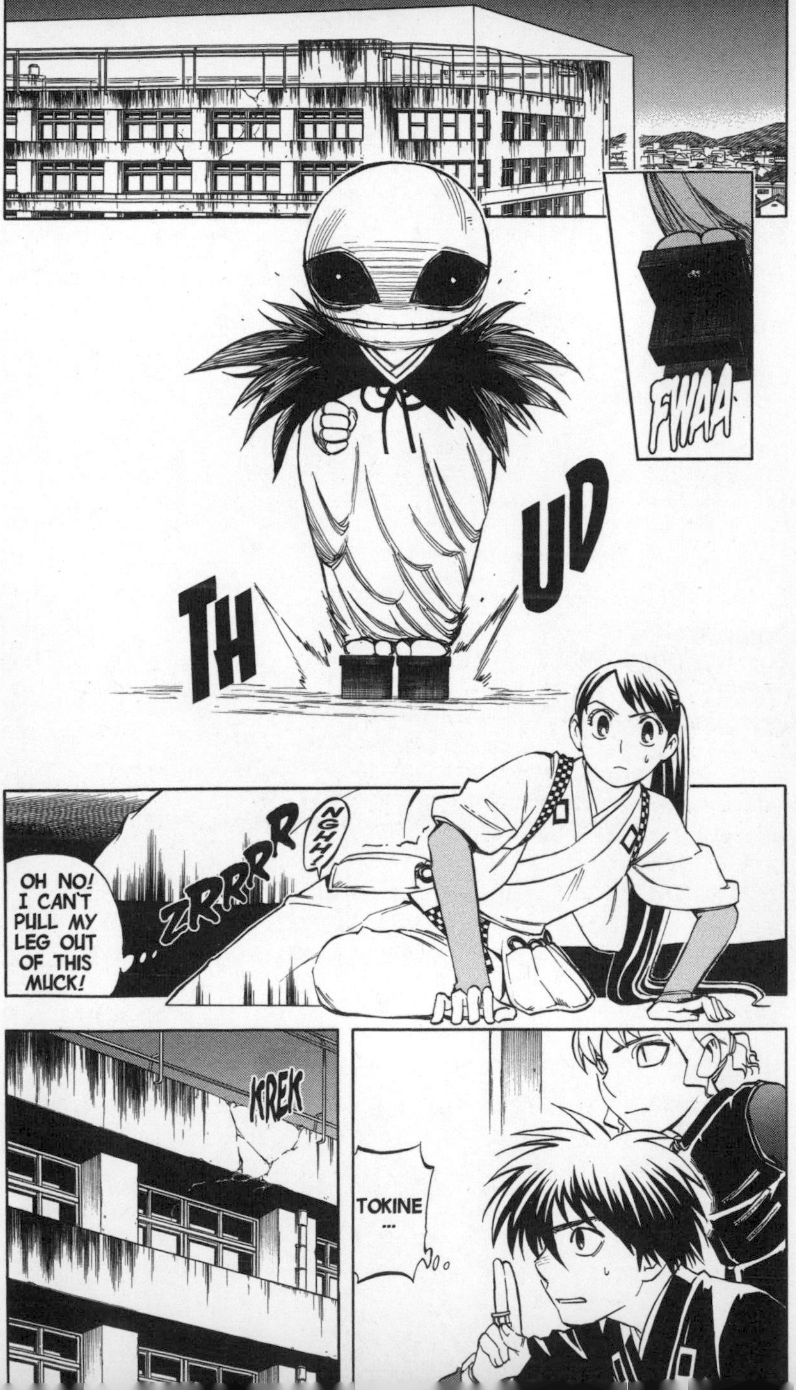
FWAA
THUD
NGHH!
ZRRRR
OH NO! I CAN'T PULL MY LEG OUT OF THIS MUCK!
TOKINE ...
KREK

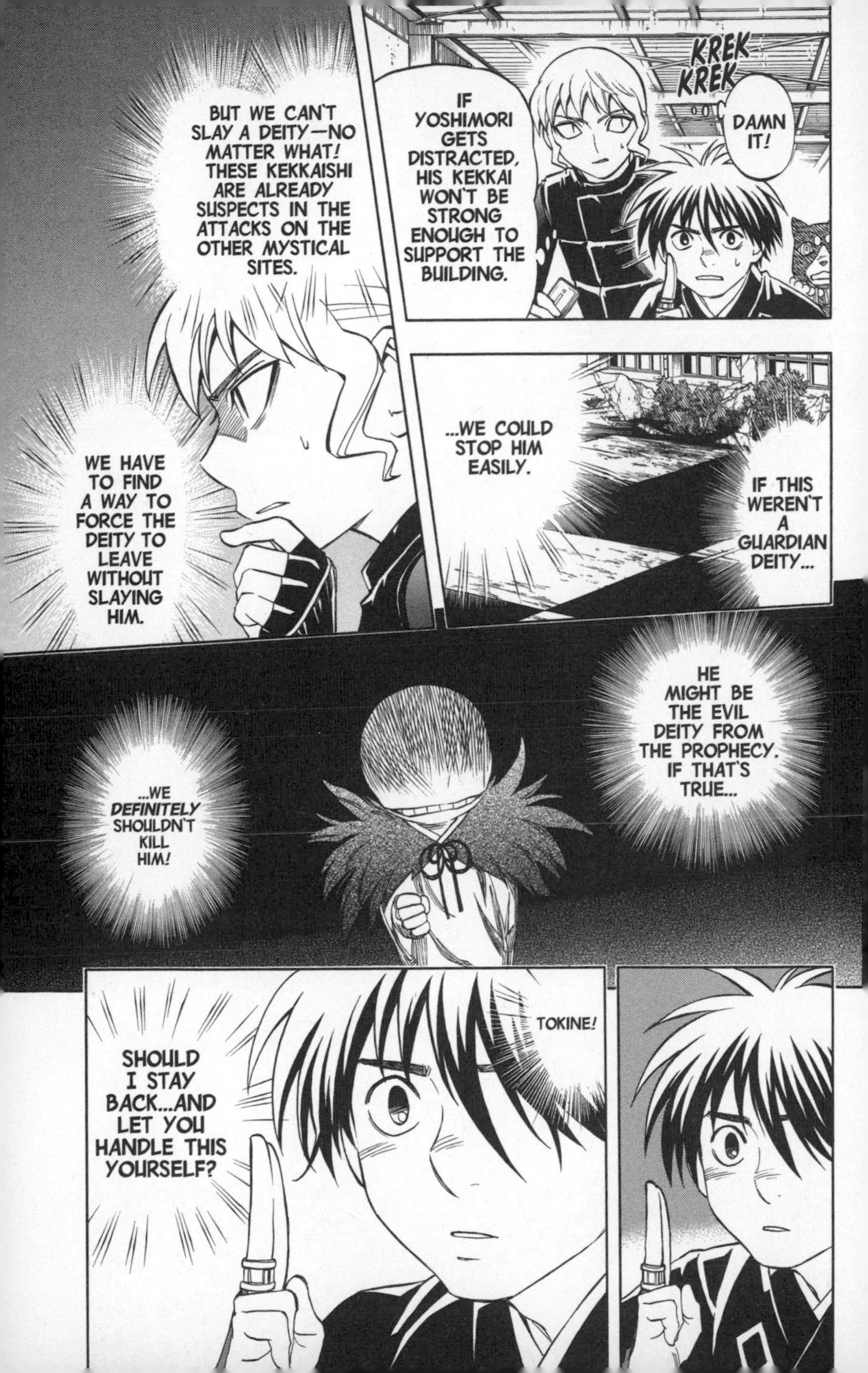
KREK KREK
DAMN IT!
IF YOSHIMORI GETS DISTRACTED, HIS KEKKAI WON'T BE STRONG ENOUGH TO SUPPORT THE BUILDING.
IF THIS WEREN'T A GUARDIAN DEITY...
...WE COULD STOP HIM EASILY.
BUT WE CAN'T SLAY A DEITY—NO MATTER WHAT! THESE KEKKAISHI ARE ALREADY SUSPECTS IN THE ATTACKS ON THE OTHER MYSTICAL SITES.
WE HAVE TO FIND A WAY TO FORCE THE DEITY TO LEAVE WITHOUT SLAYING HIM.
HE MIGHT BE THE EVIL DEITY FROM THE PROPHECY. IF THAT'S TRUE...
...WE *DEFINITELY* SHOULDN'T KILL HIM!
TOKINE!
SHOULD I STAY BACK...AND LET YOU HANDLE THIS YOURSELF?

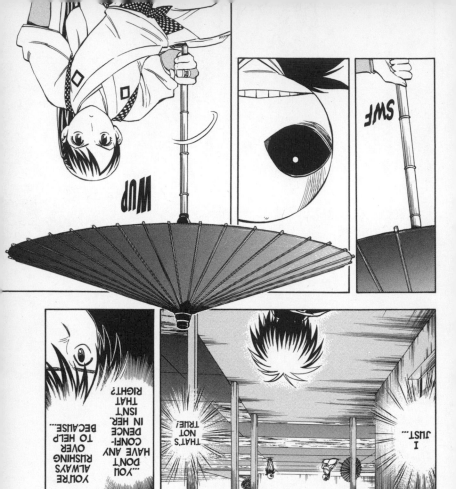

SWF

WUP

...YOU'RE ALWAYS RUSHING OVER TO HELP BECAUSE...

...YOU DON'T HAVE ANY CONFIDENCE IN HER, ISN'T THAT RIGHT?

THAT'S NOT TRUE!

I JUST...

FWAA

THUD

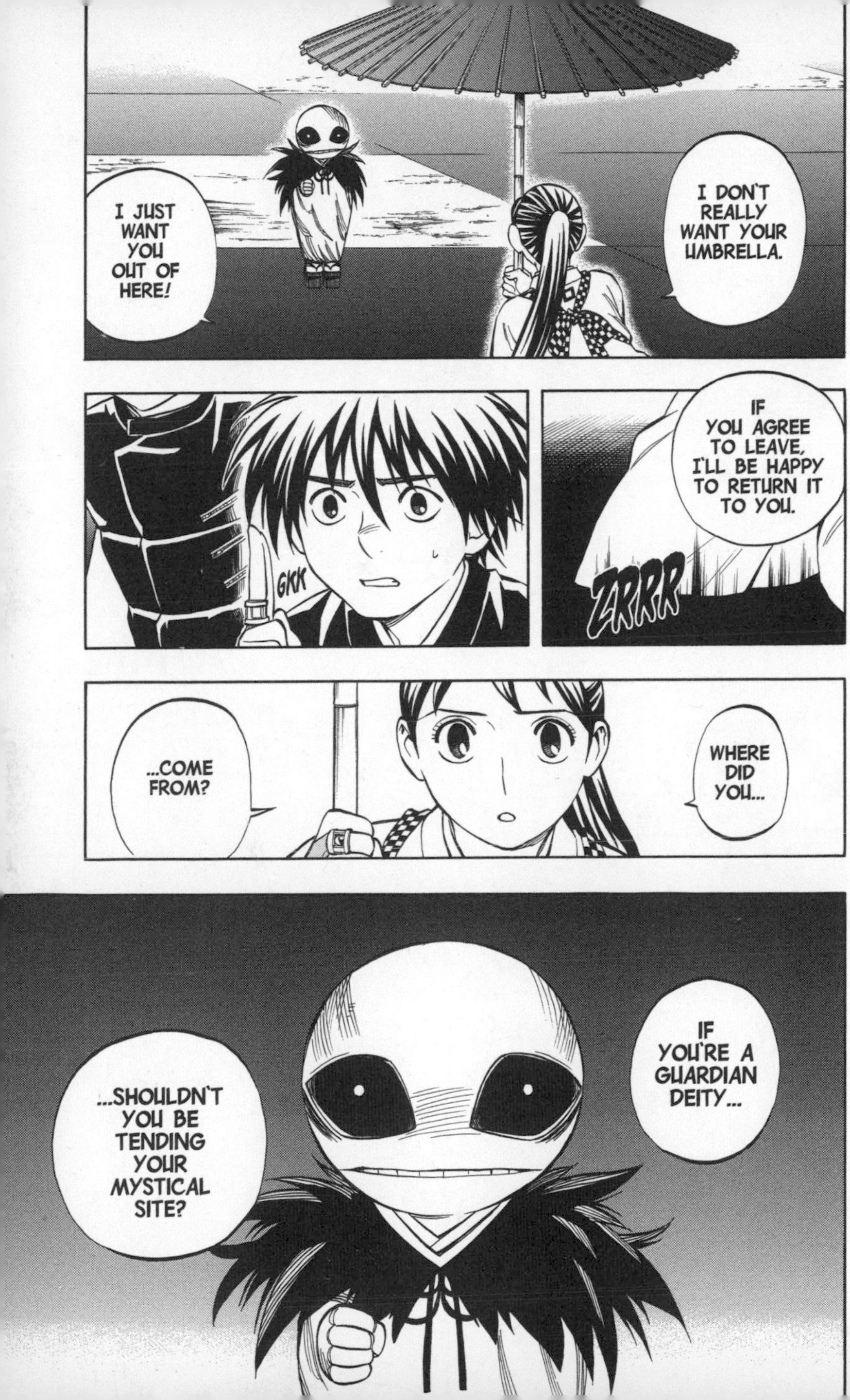
I DON'T REALLY WANT YOUR UMBRELLA.
I JUST WANT YOU OUT OF HERE!
IF YOU AGREE TO LEAVE, I'LL BE HAPPY TO RETURN IT TO YOU.
ZRRR
GKK
WHERE DID YOU...
...COME FROM?
IF YOU'RE A GUARDIAN DEITY...
...SHOULDN'T YOU BE TENDING YOUR MYSTICAL SITE?

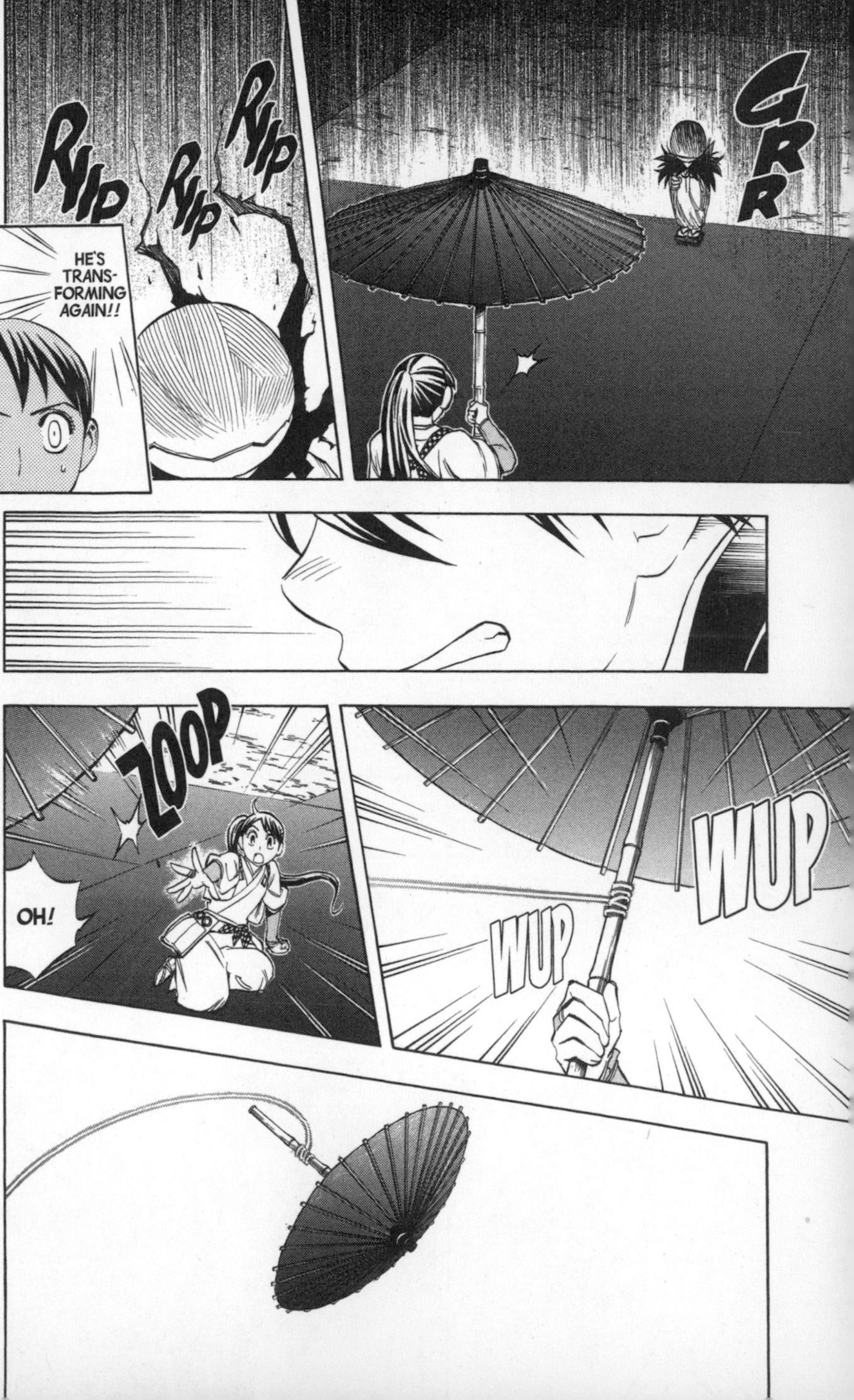
GRR
RIIP RIIP RIIP
HE'S TRANS-FORMING AGAIN!!
WUP
WUP
ZOOP
OH!

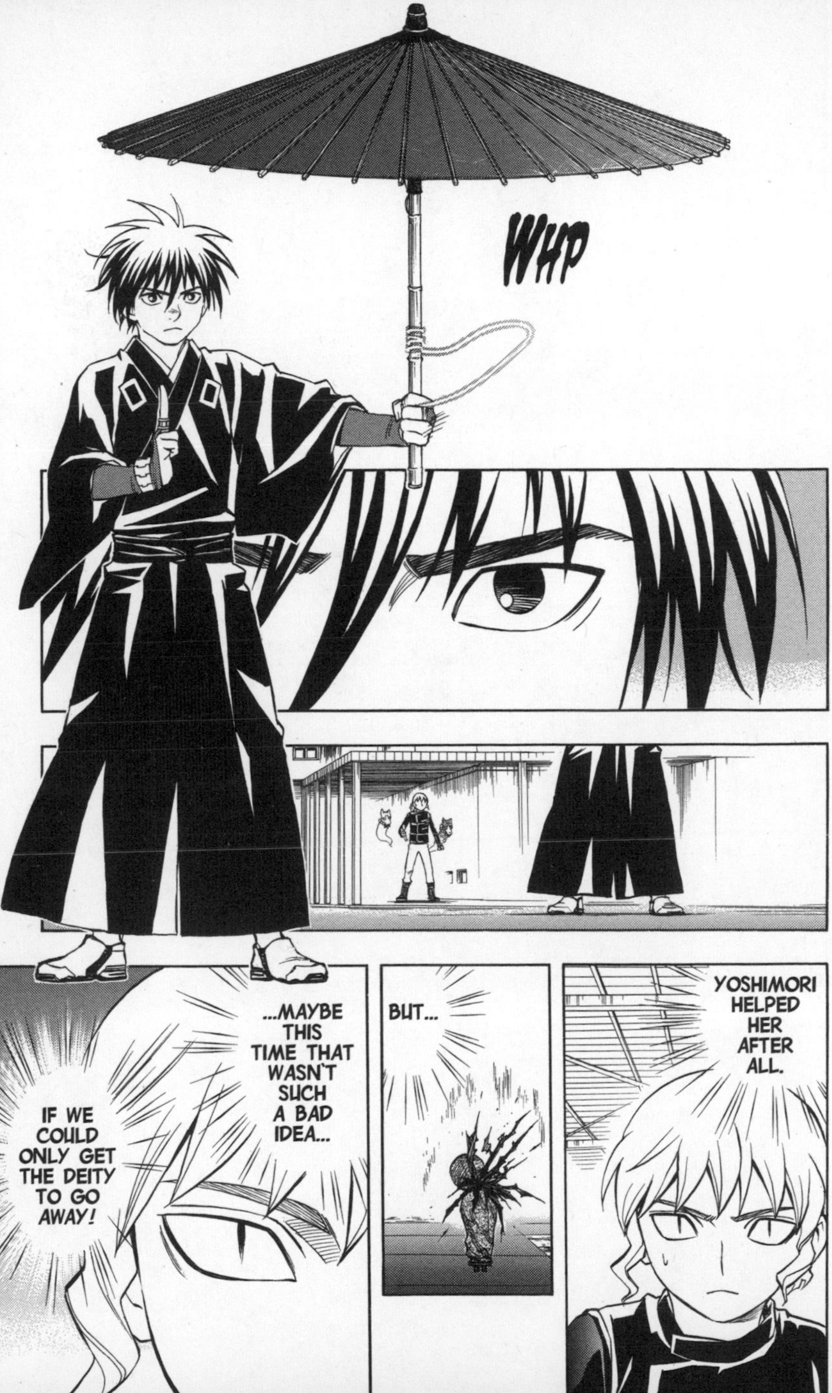
WHP
YOSHIMORI HELPED HER AFTER ALL.
BUT...
...MAYBE THIS TIME THAT WASN'T SUCH A BAD IDEA...
IF WE COULD ONLY GET THE DEITY TO GO AWAY!

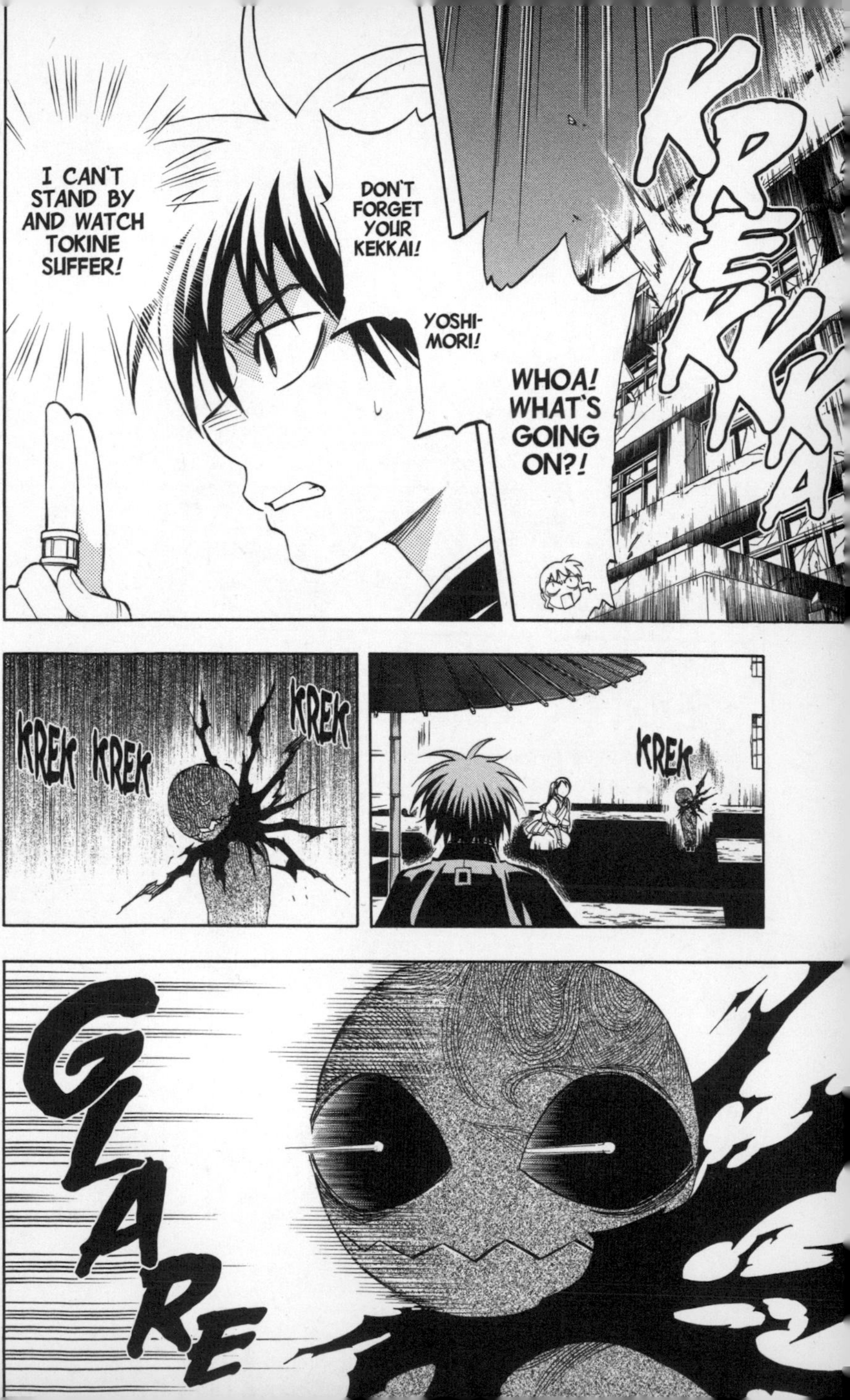
KREKKA
WHOA! WHAT'S GOING ON?!
YOSHI-MORI!
DON'T FORGET YOUR KEKKAI!
I CAN'T STAND BY AND WATCH TOKINE SUFFER!
KREK
KREK
KREK KREK
GLARE

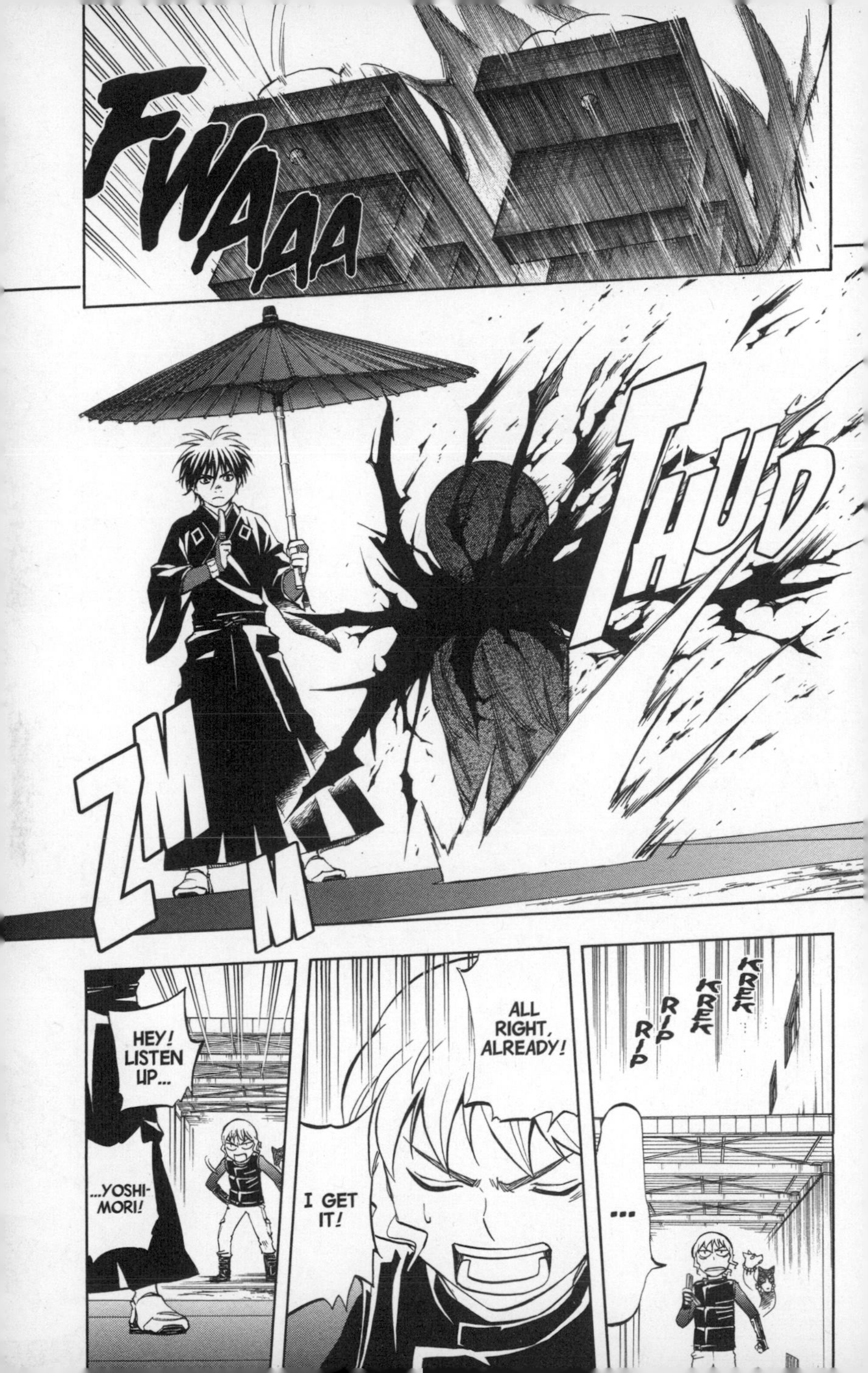
FWAAAA
THUD
ZMMM
KREK KREK
RIP RIP
...
ALL RIGHT, ALREADY!
I GET IT!
HEY! LISTEN UP...
...YOSHI-MORI!

GIVE *ME* THE UMBRELLA.
I'LL TAKE CARE OF IT!
YOU FOCUS ON HOLDING THE BUILDINGS UP!
I'M HALF-AYAKASHI! I CAN MOVE MORE FREELY THAN YOU!
LET *ME* DO IT!
I SAID, "GIVE ME THE UMBREL-LA".
ARE YOU LISTENING ?!
GIVE...
DID THE DEITY JUST SAY SOME-THING?!

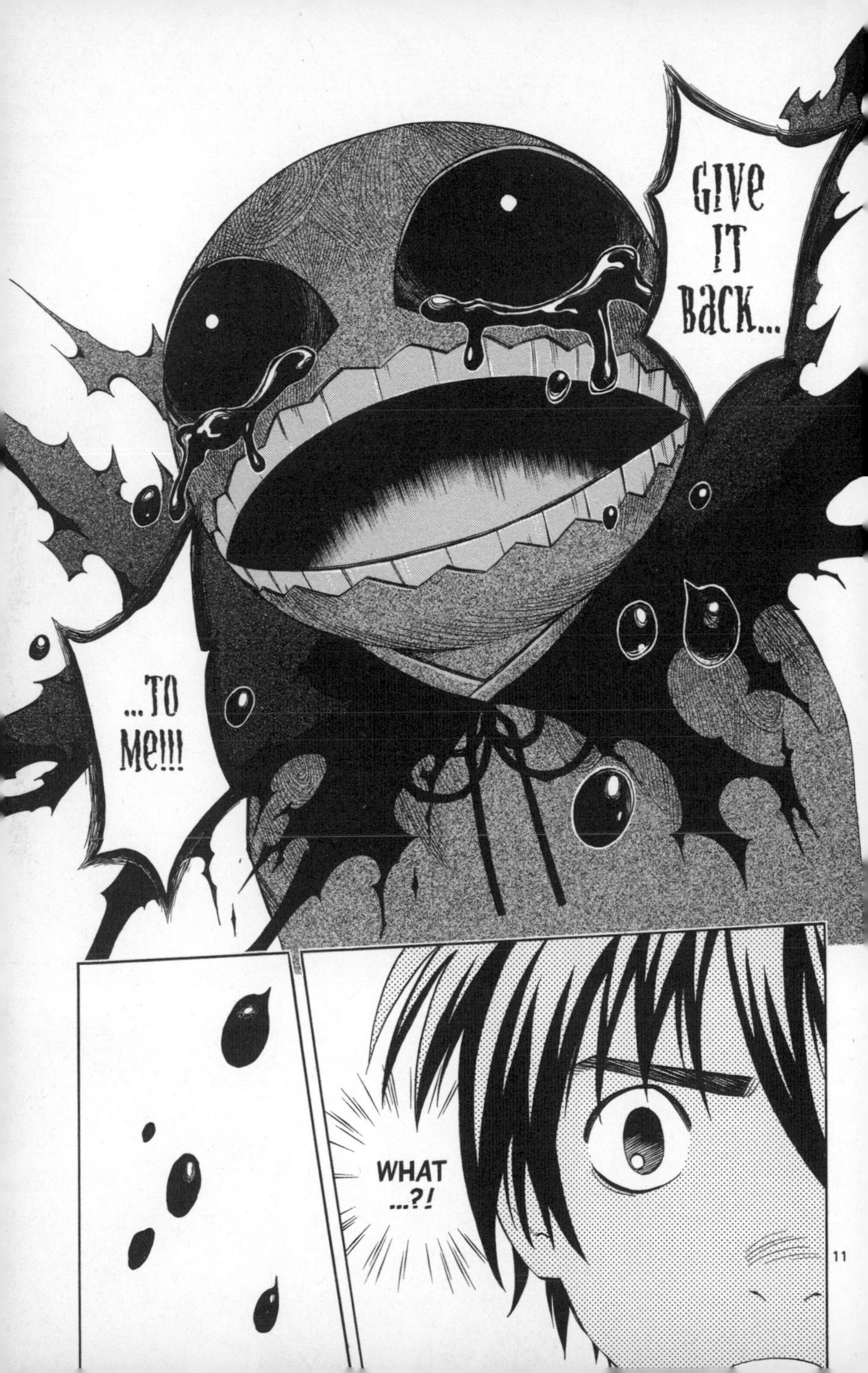
GIVE IT BACK...
...TO ME!!!
WHAT ...?!

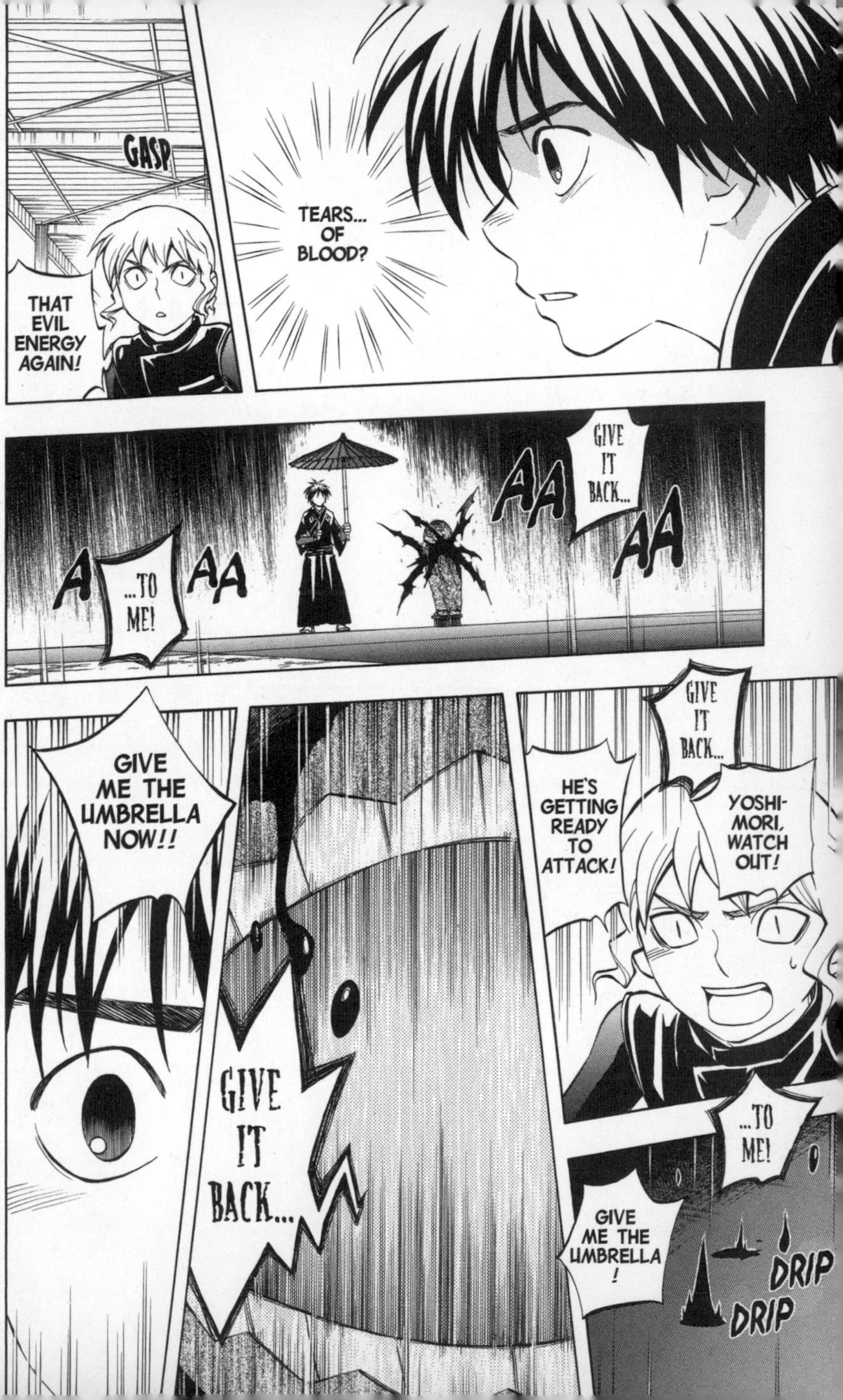
TEARS... OF BLOOD?
GASP
THAT EVIL ENERGY AGAIN!
GIVE IT BACK...
AA
AA
AA
...TO ME!
A
GIVE IT BACK...
HE'S GETTING READY TO ATTACK!
YOSHI-MORI, WATCH OUT!
...TO ME!
GIVE ME THE UMBRELLA!
DRIP
DRIP
GIVE IT BACK...
GIVE ME THE UMBRELLA NOW!!

WHAT THE ...?

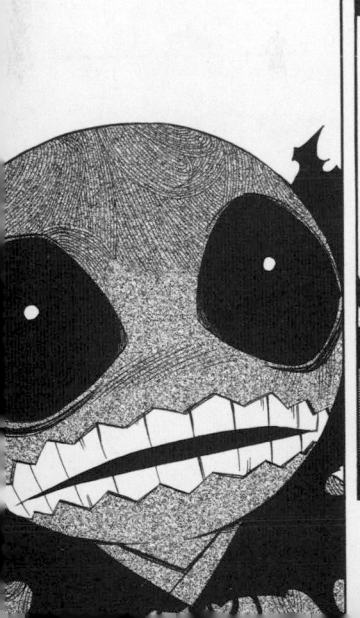

I'M SORRY.

OKAY. IF IT'S THAT IMPORTANT TO YOU. HERE YOU GO.

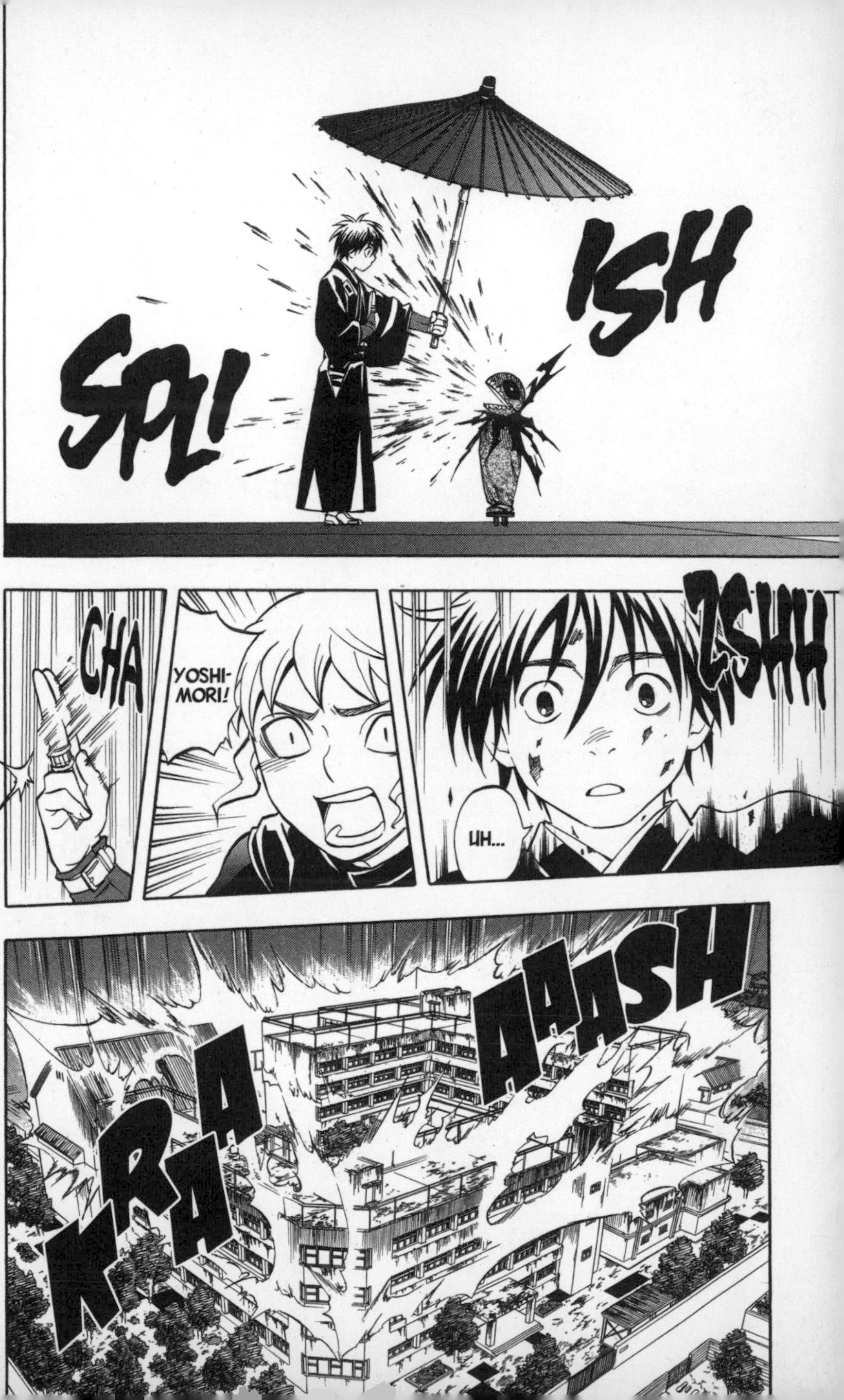
SPL! ISH
ZSHH
UH...
YOSHI-
MORI!
CHA
KRA
AAASH

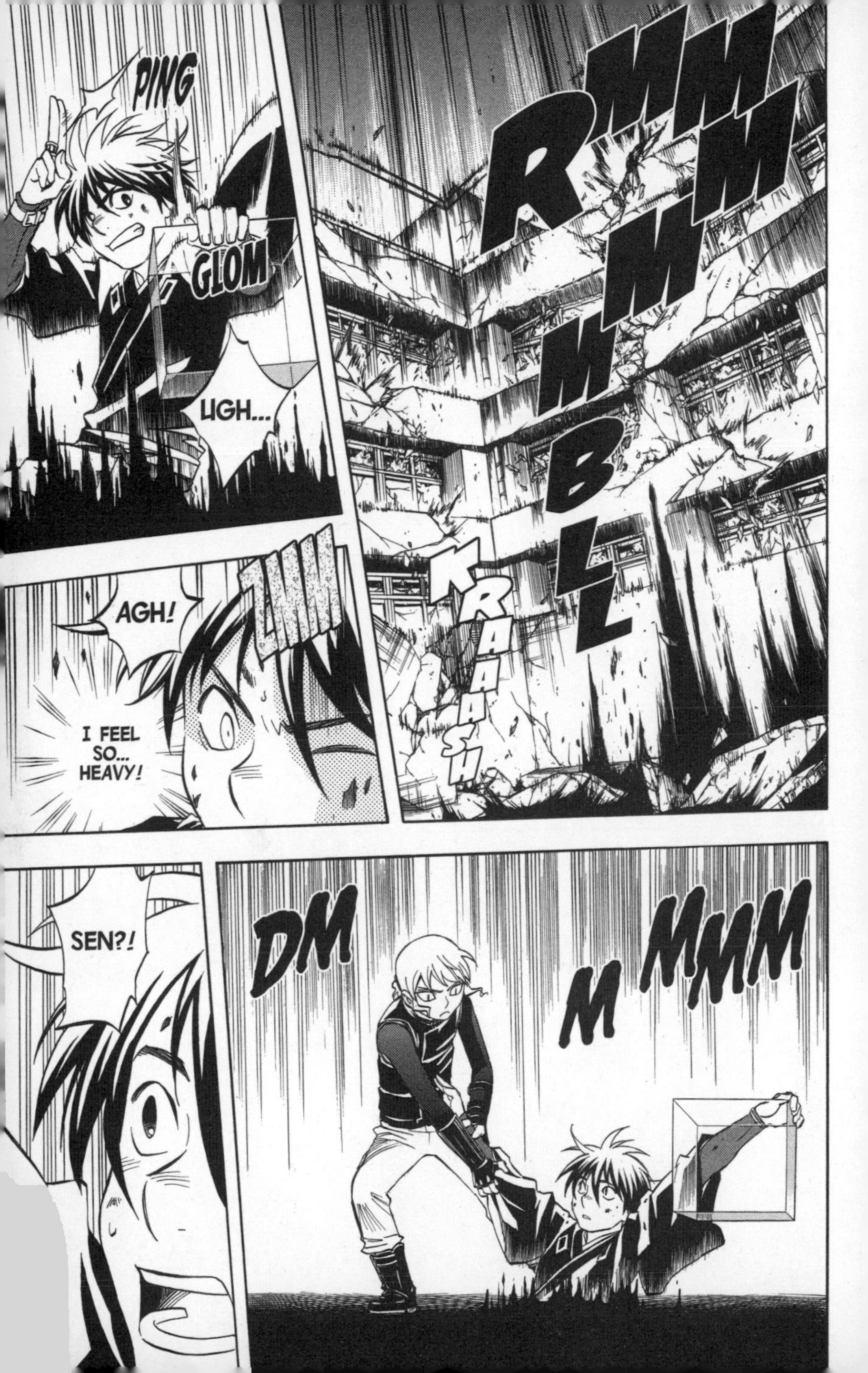
RMMMMMBLL
KRAASH
PING
GLOM
UGH...
AGH!
ZMMM
I FEEL SO... HEAVY!
DM M MMMM
SEN?!

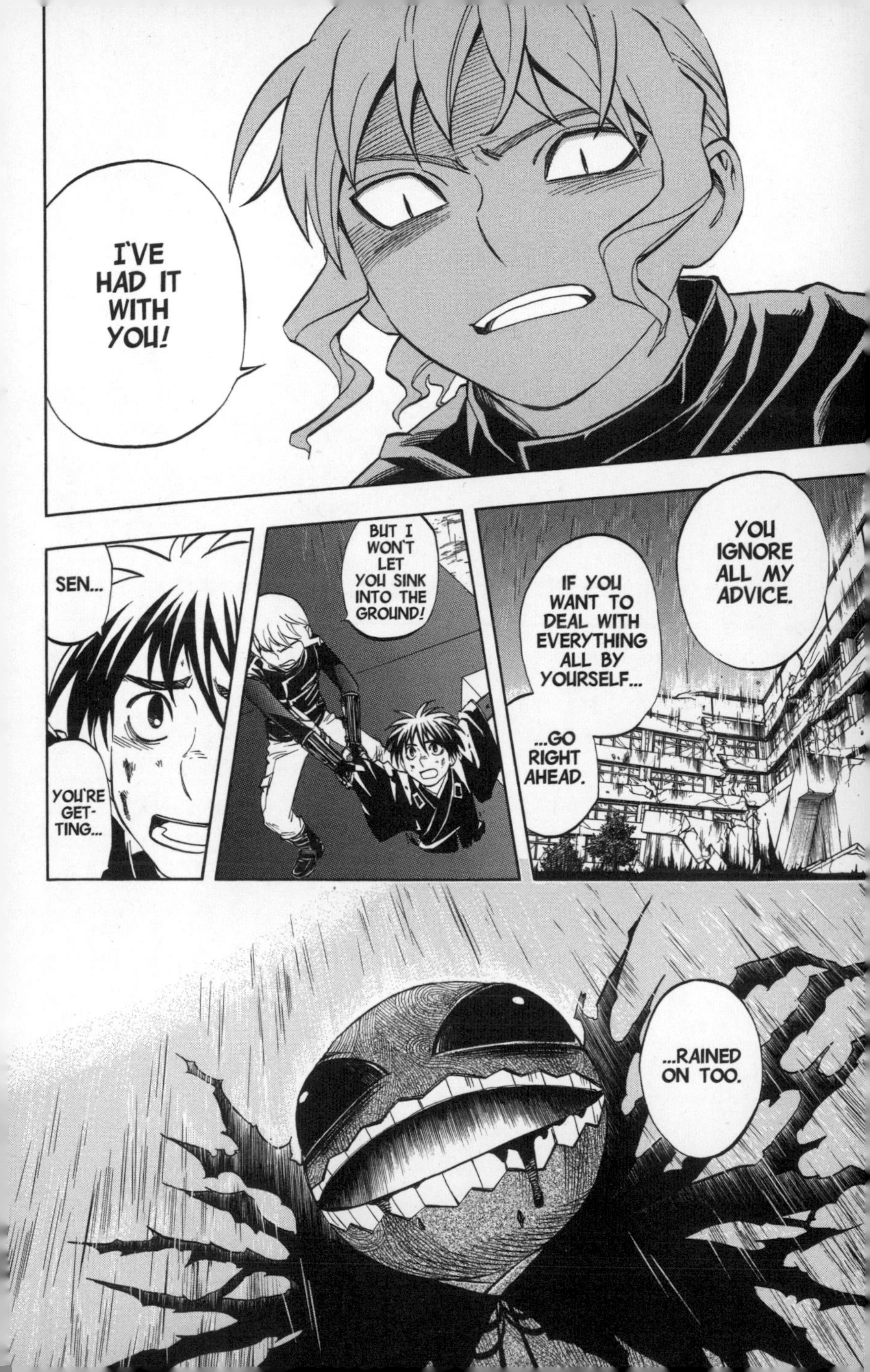
I'VE HAD IT WITH YOU!
YOU IGNORE ALL MY ADVICE.
IF YOU WANT TO DEAL WITH EVERYTHING ALL BY YOURSELF...
...GO RIGHT AHEAD.
BUT I WON'T LET YOU SINK INTO THE GROUND!
SEN...
YOU'RE GET-TING...
...RAINED ON TOO.

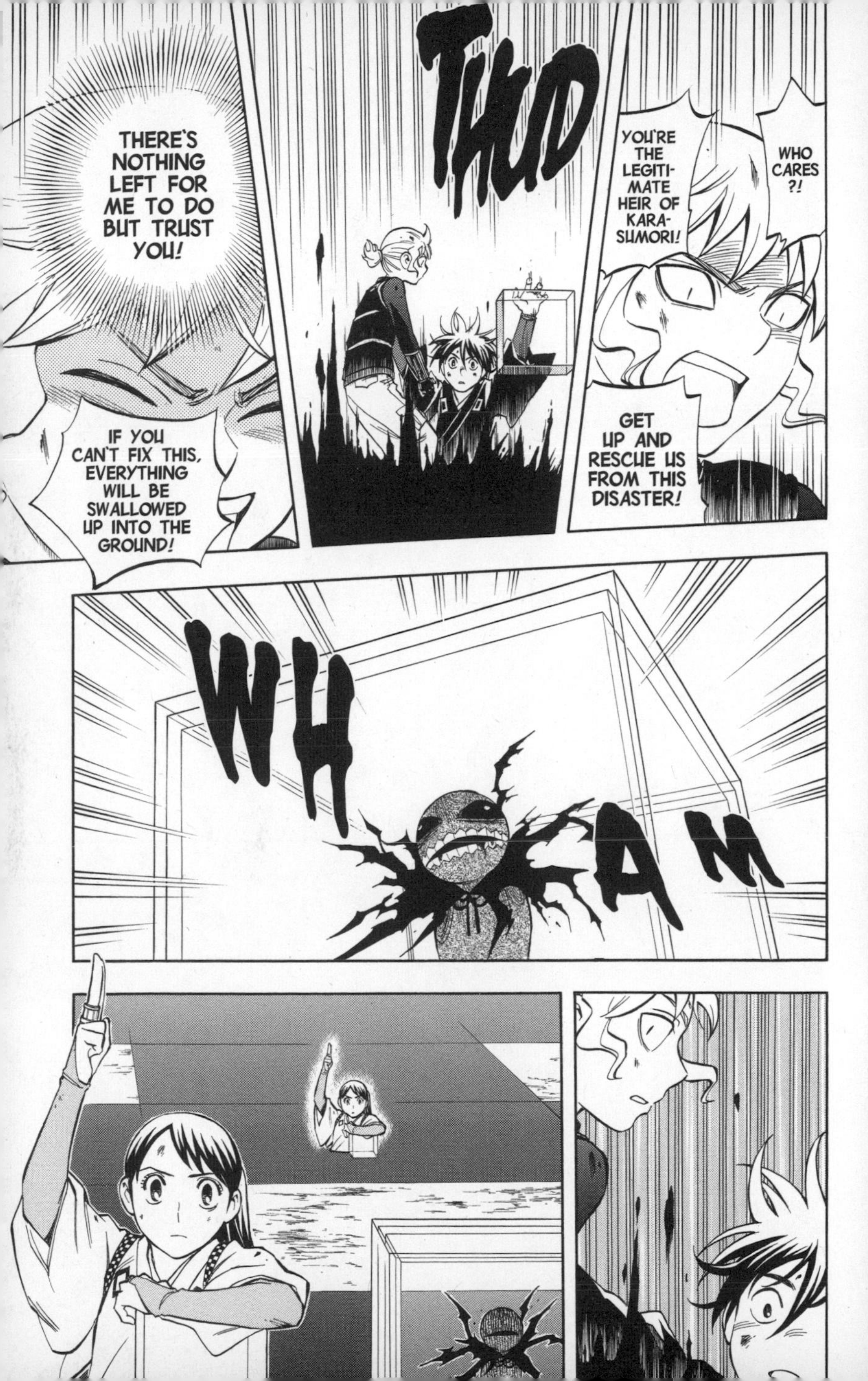
WHO CARES ?!
YOU'RE THE LEGITI- MATE HEIR OF KARA- SUMORI!
GET UP AND RESCUE US FROM THIS DISASTER!
THUD
THERE'S NOTHING LEFT FOR ME TO DO BUT TRUST YOU!
IF YOU CAN'T FIX THIS, EVERYTHING WILL BE SWALLOWED UP INTO THE GROUND!
WHAM

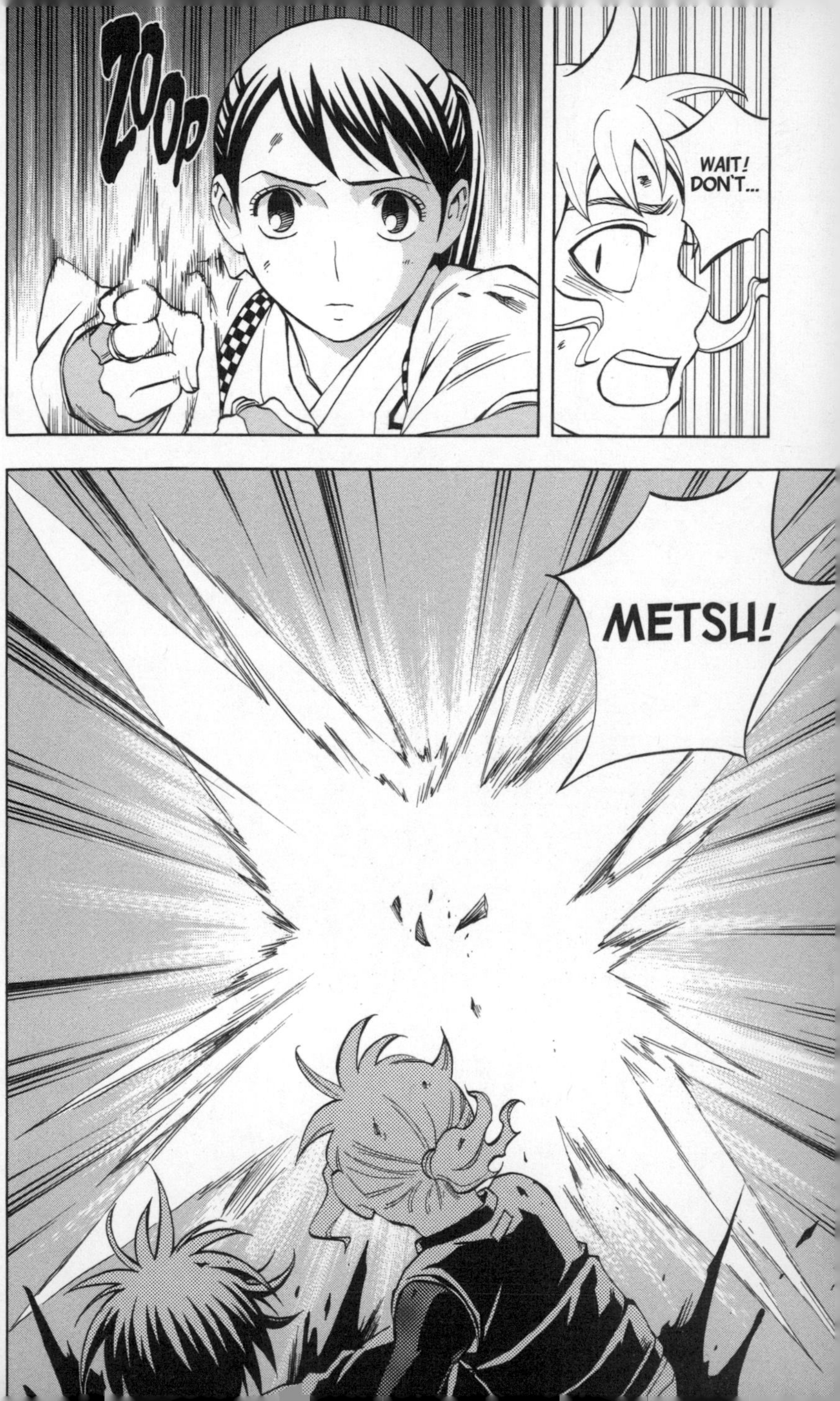
WAIT! DON'T...
ZOOP
METSU!

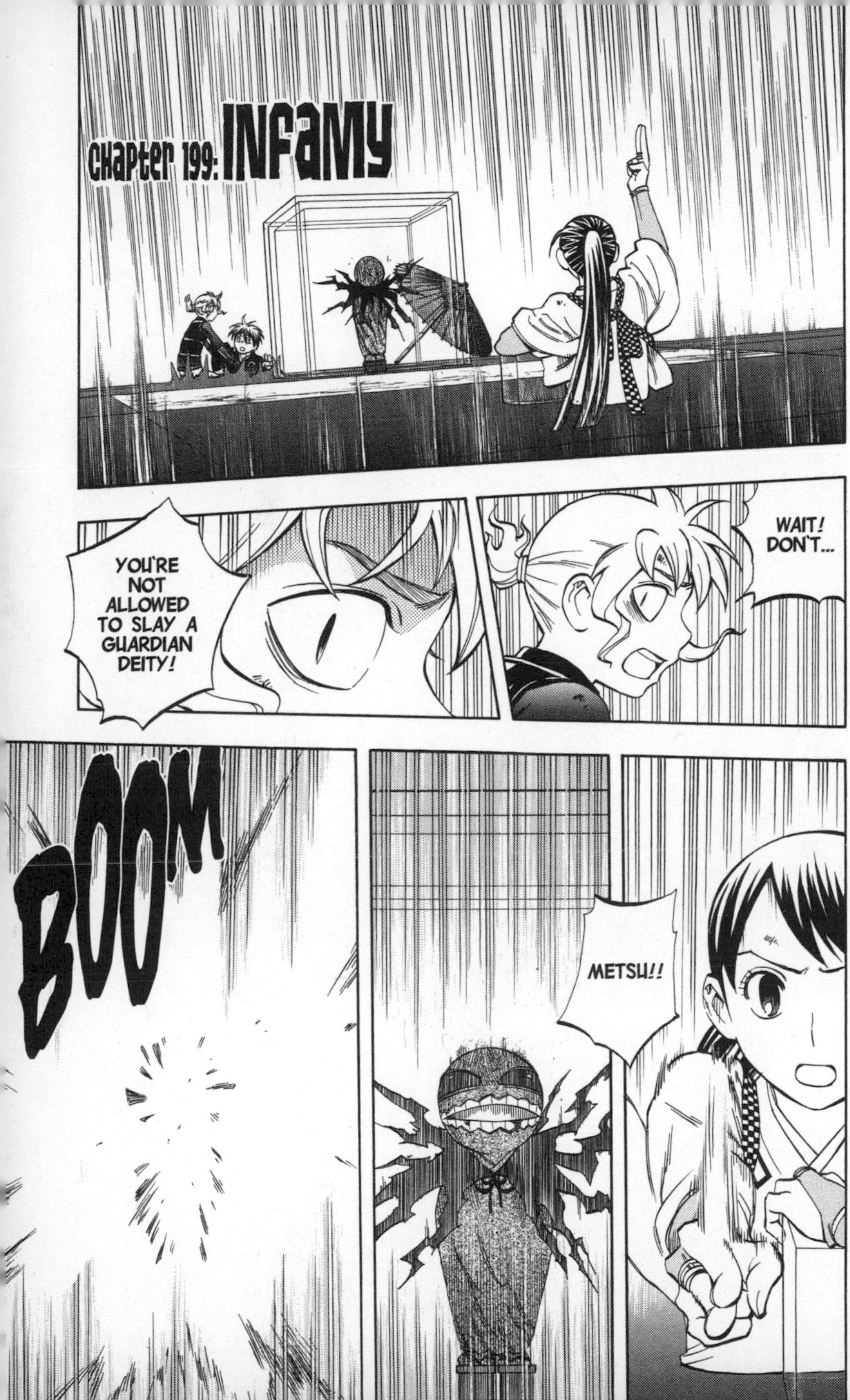
Chapter 199: Infamy
WAIT! DON'T...
YOU'RE NOT ALLOWED TO SLAY A GUARDIAN DEITY!
METSU!!
BOOM

Chapter 199: INFAMY

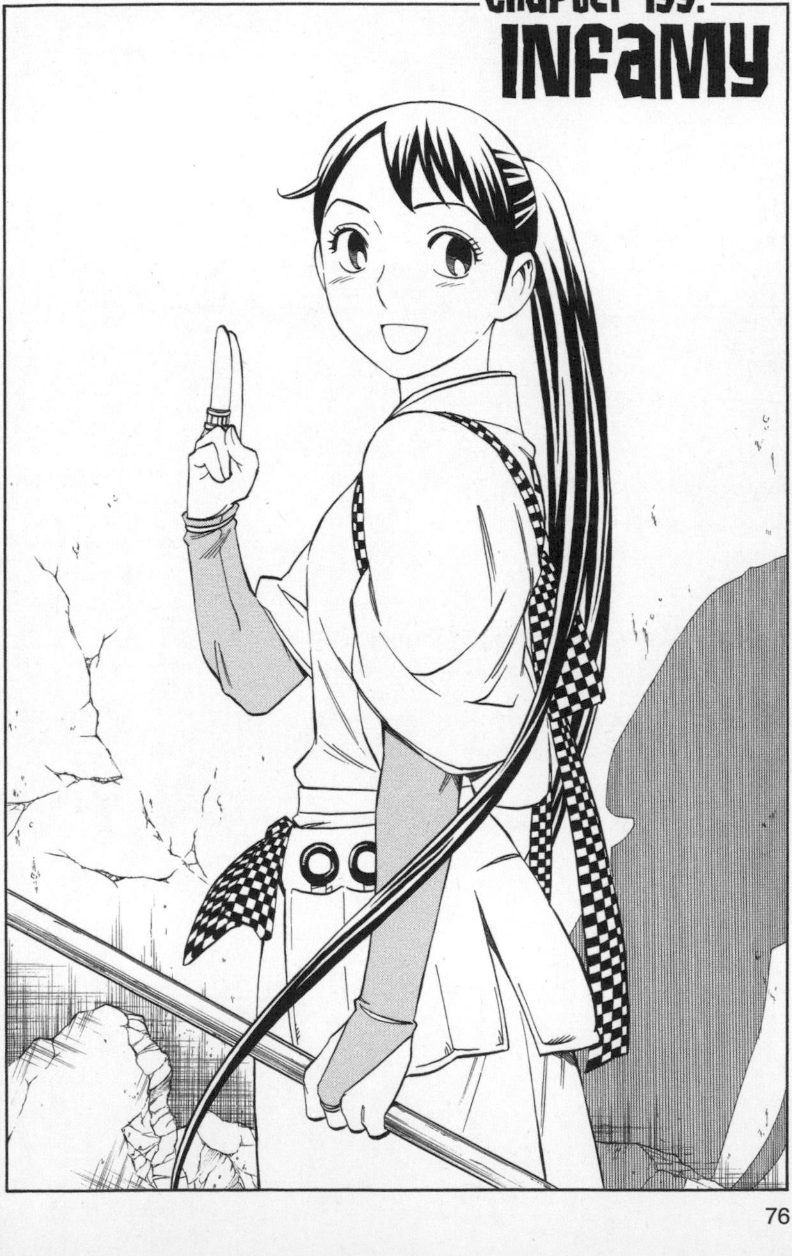

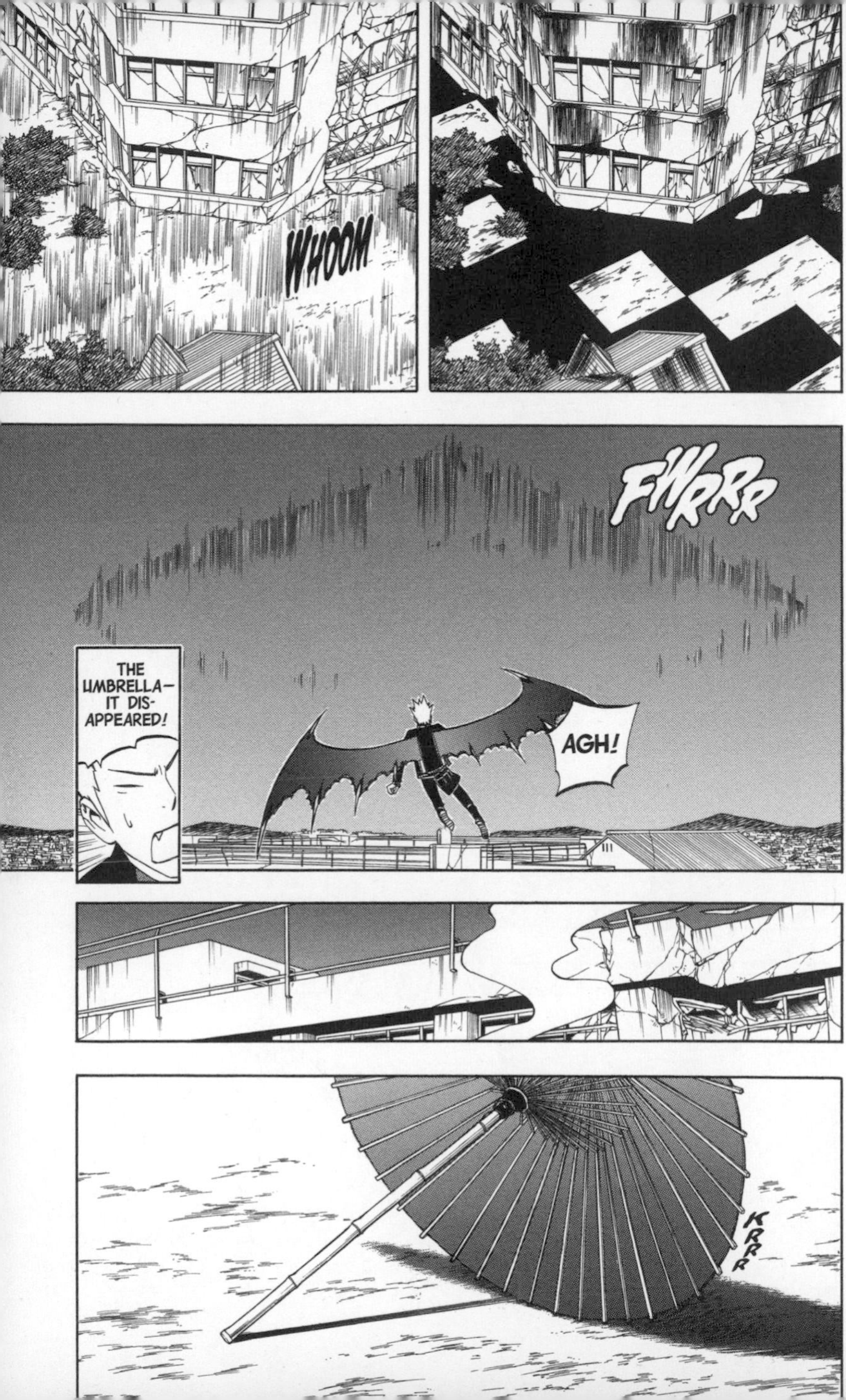
WHOOM
FWRRR
AGH!
THE UMBRELLA—IT DIS-APPEARED!
KRRR

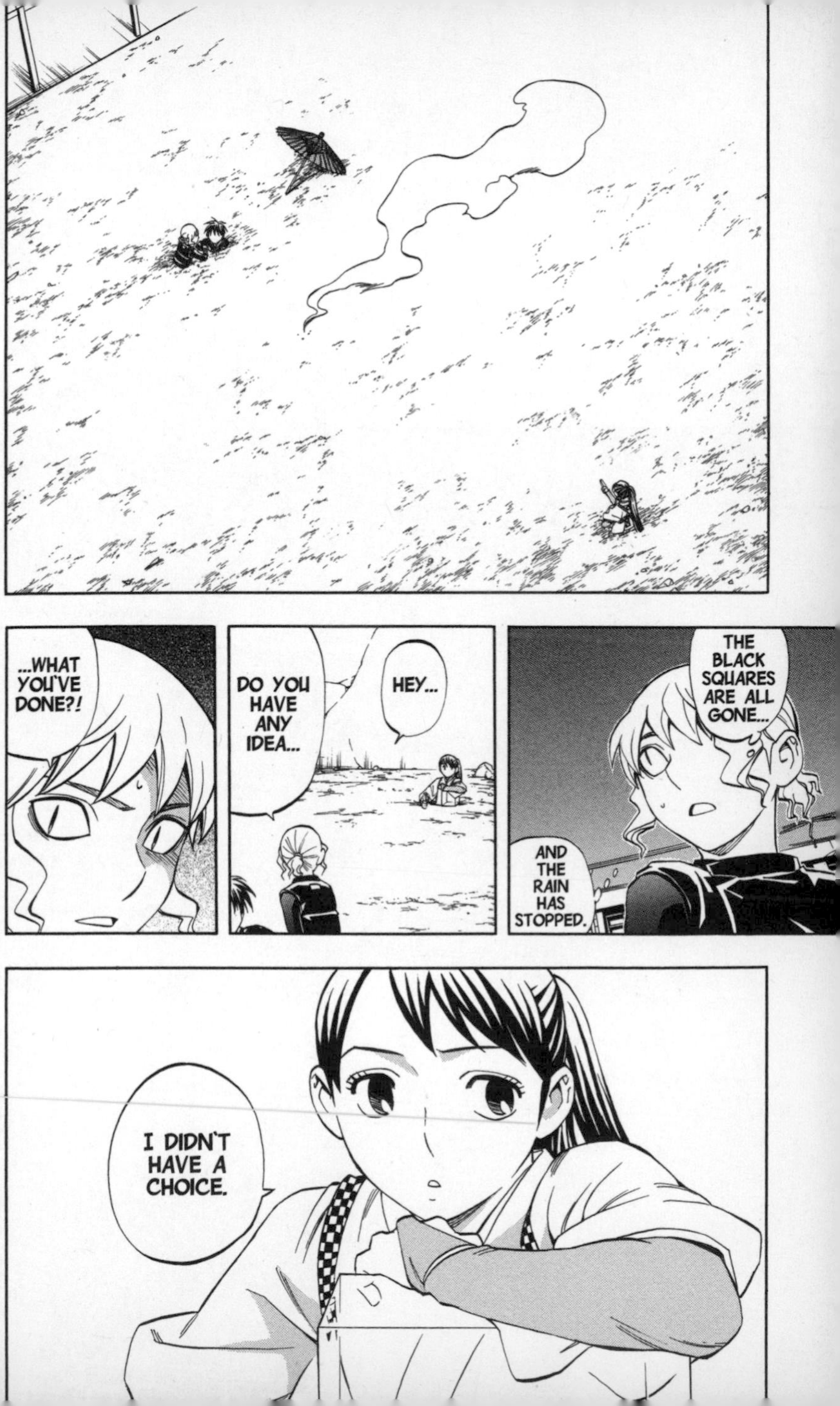
THE BLACK SQUARES ARE ALL GONE...
AND THE RAIN HAS STOPPED.
HEY...
DO YOU HAVE ANY IDEA...
...WHAT YOU'VE DONE?!
I DIDN'T HAVE A CHOICE.

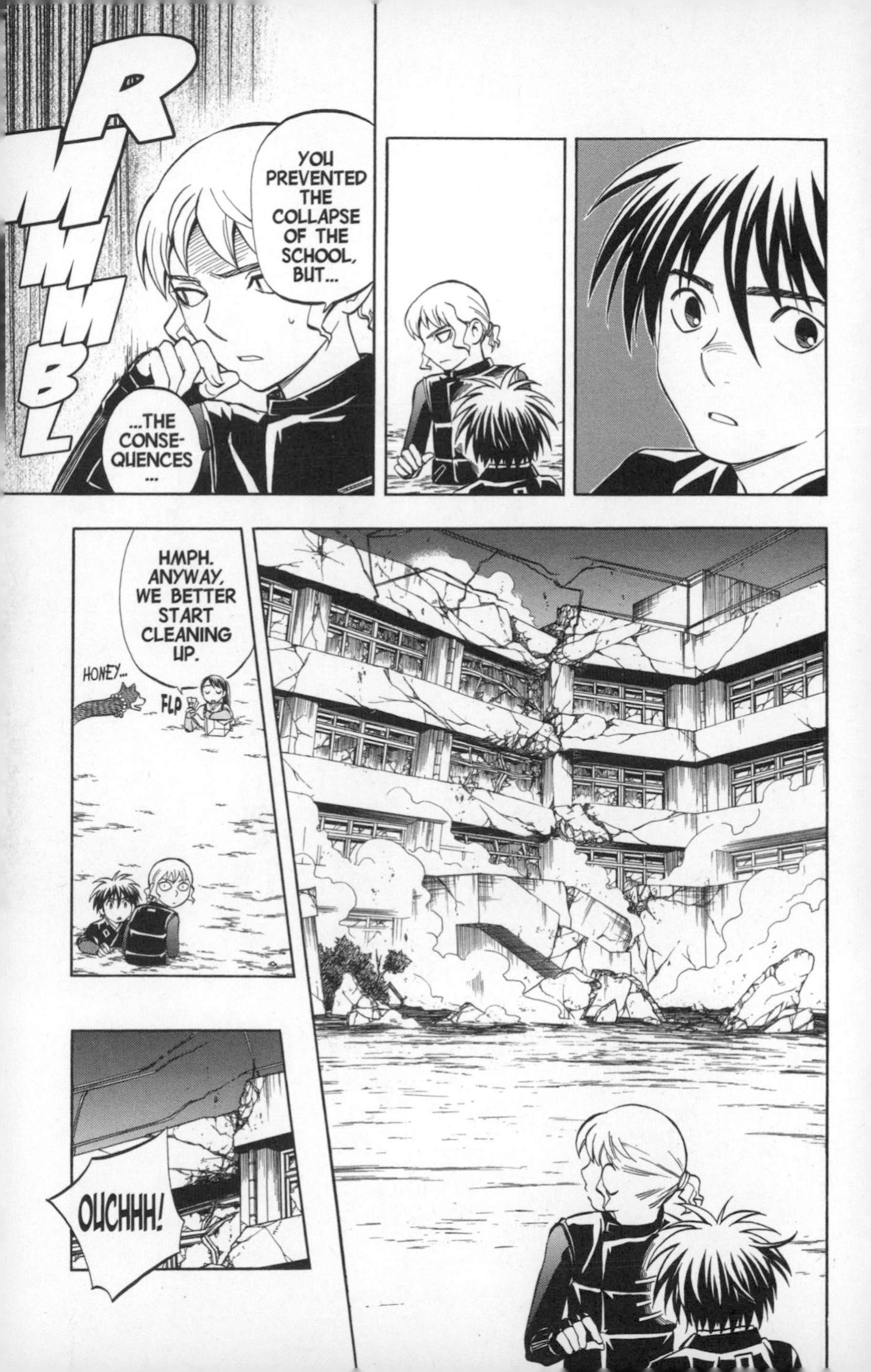
RMMMBL
YOU PREVENTED THE COLLAPSE OF THE SCHOOL, BUT...
...THE CONSE-QUENCES ...
HMPH. ANYWAY, WE BETTER START CLEANING UP.
FLP
HONEY...
OUCHHH!

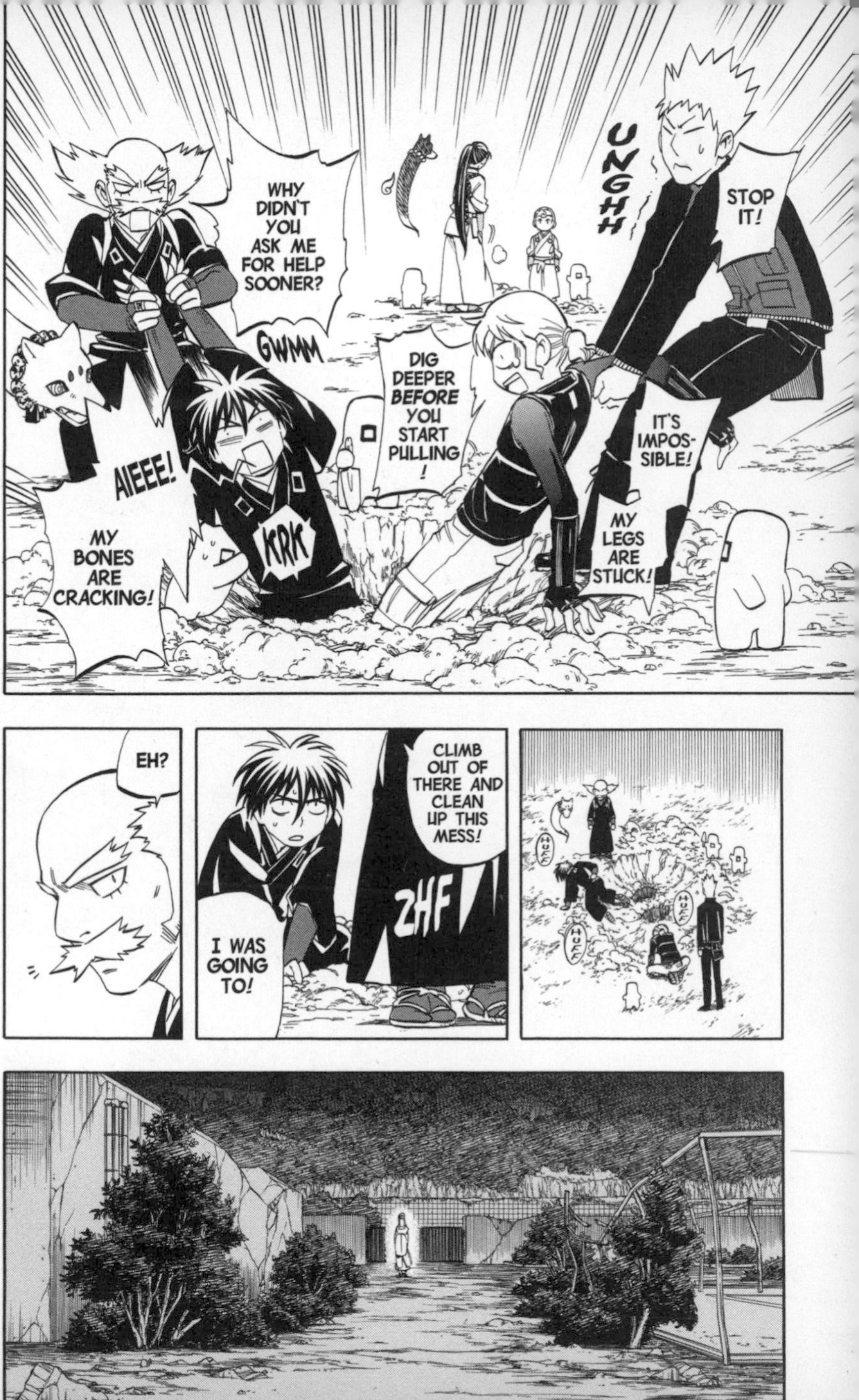
STOP IT!
UNGHH
IT'S IMPOSSIBLE!
MY LEGS ARE STUCK!
DIG DEEPER BEFORE YOU START PULLING!
WHY DIDN'T YOU ASK ME FOR HELP SOONER?
GWMM
AIEEE!
KRK
MY BONES ARE CRACKING!
HUFF
HUFF
HUFF
CLIMB OUT OF THERE AND CLEAN UP THIS MESS!
ZHF
I WAS GOING TO!
EH?

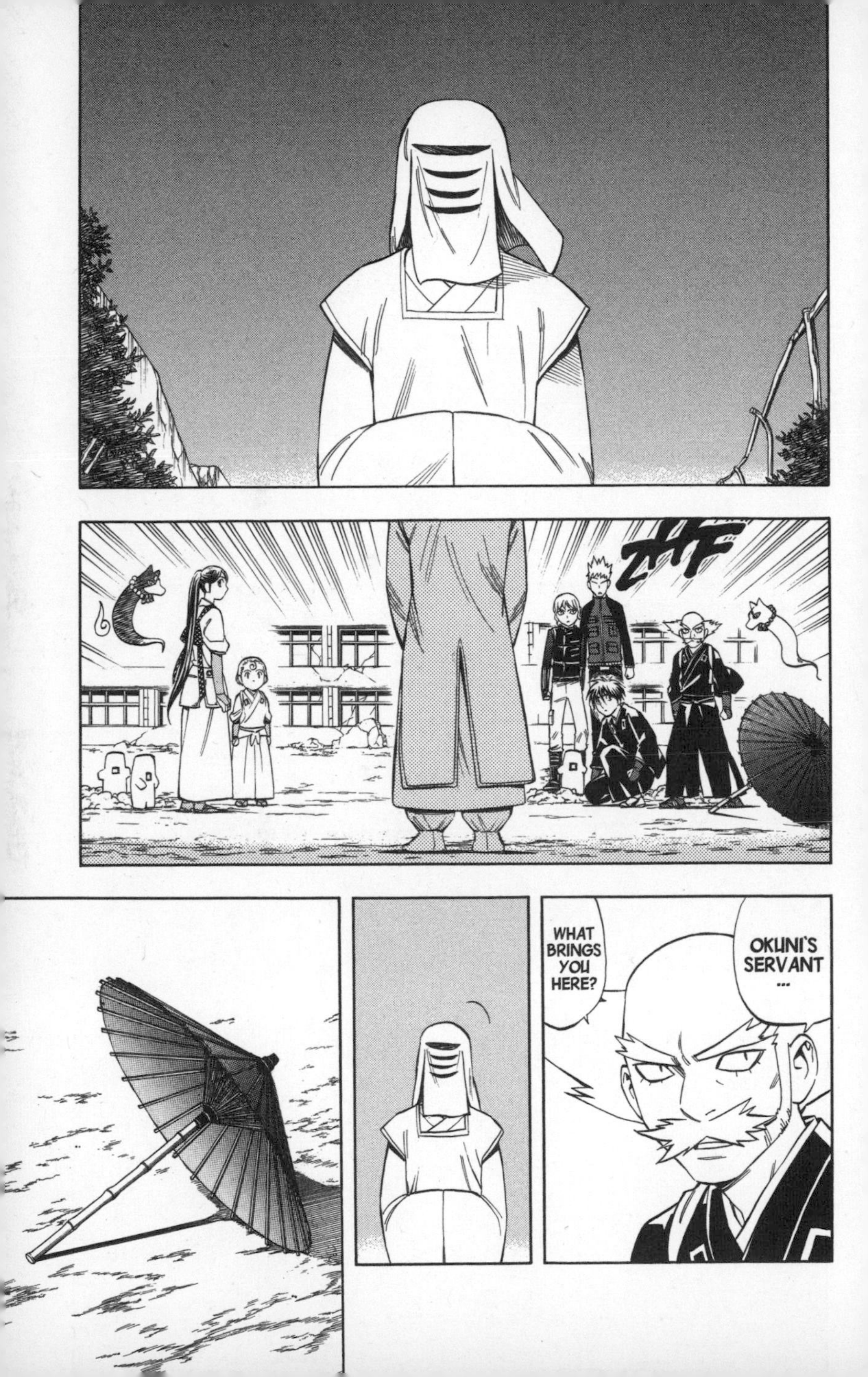
OKUNI'S SERVANT ...
WHAT BRINGS YOU HERE?

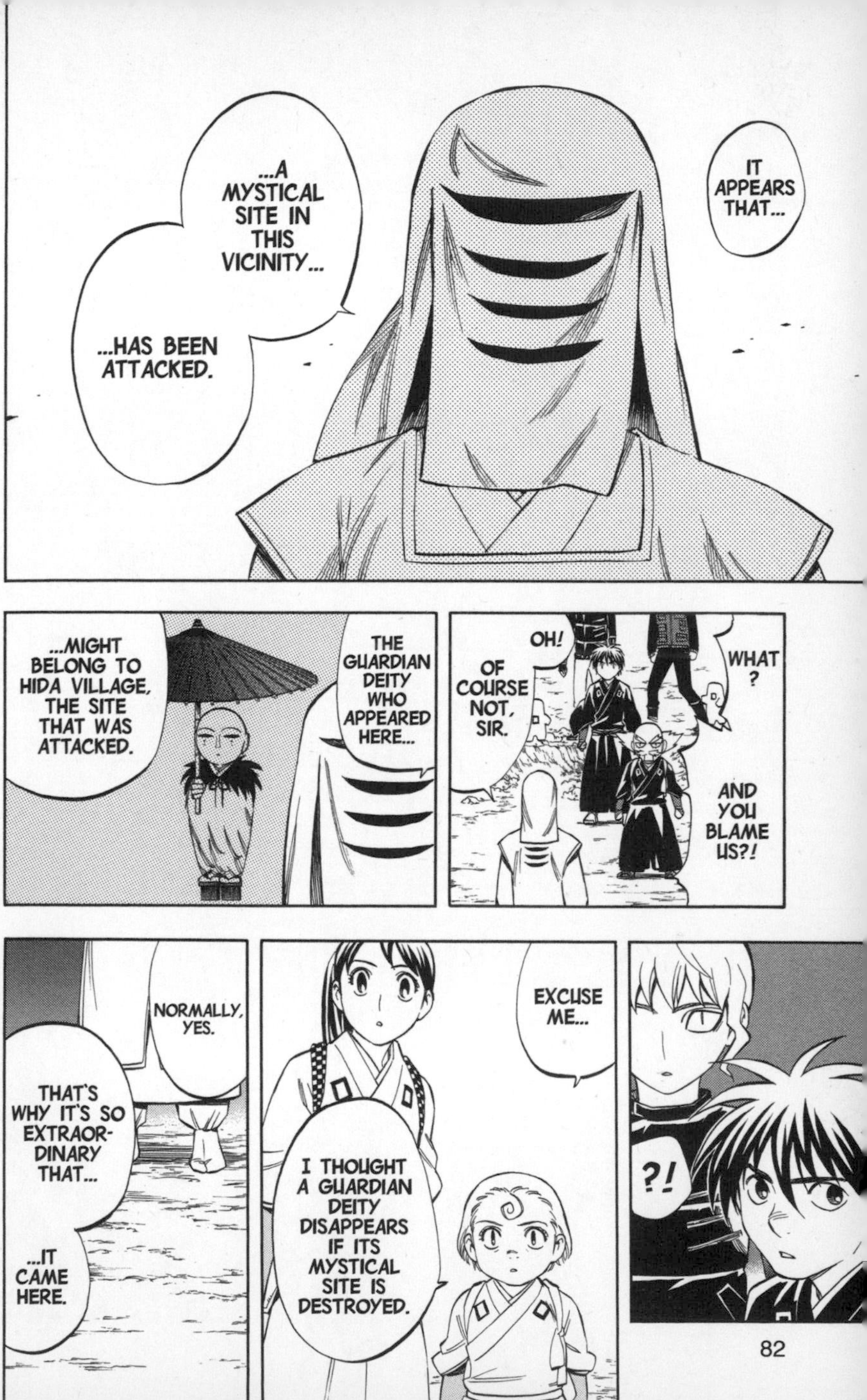
IT APPEARS THAT...
...A MYSTICAL SITE IN THIS VICINITY...
...HAS BEEN ATTACKED.
WHAT ?
OH!
OF COURSE NOT, SIR.
AND YOU BLAME US?!
THE GUARDIAN DEITY WHO APPEARED HERE...
...MIGHT BELONG TO HIDA VILLAGE, THE SITE THAT WAS ATTACKED.
?!
EXCUSE ME...
I THOUGHT A GUARDIAN DEITY DISAPPEARS IF ITS MYSTICAL SITE IS DESTROYED.
NORMALLY, YES.
THAT'S WHY IT'S SO EXTRAOR-DINARY THAT...
...IT CAME HERE.

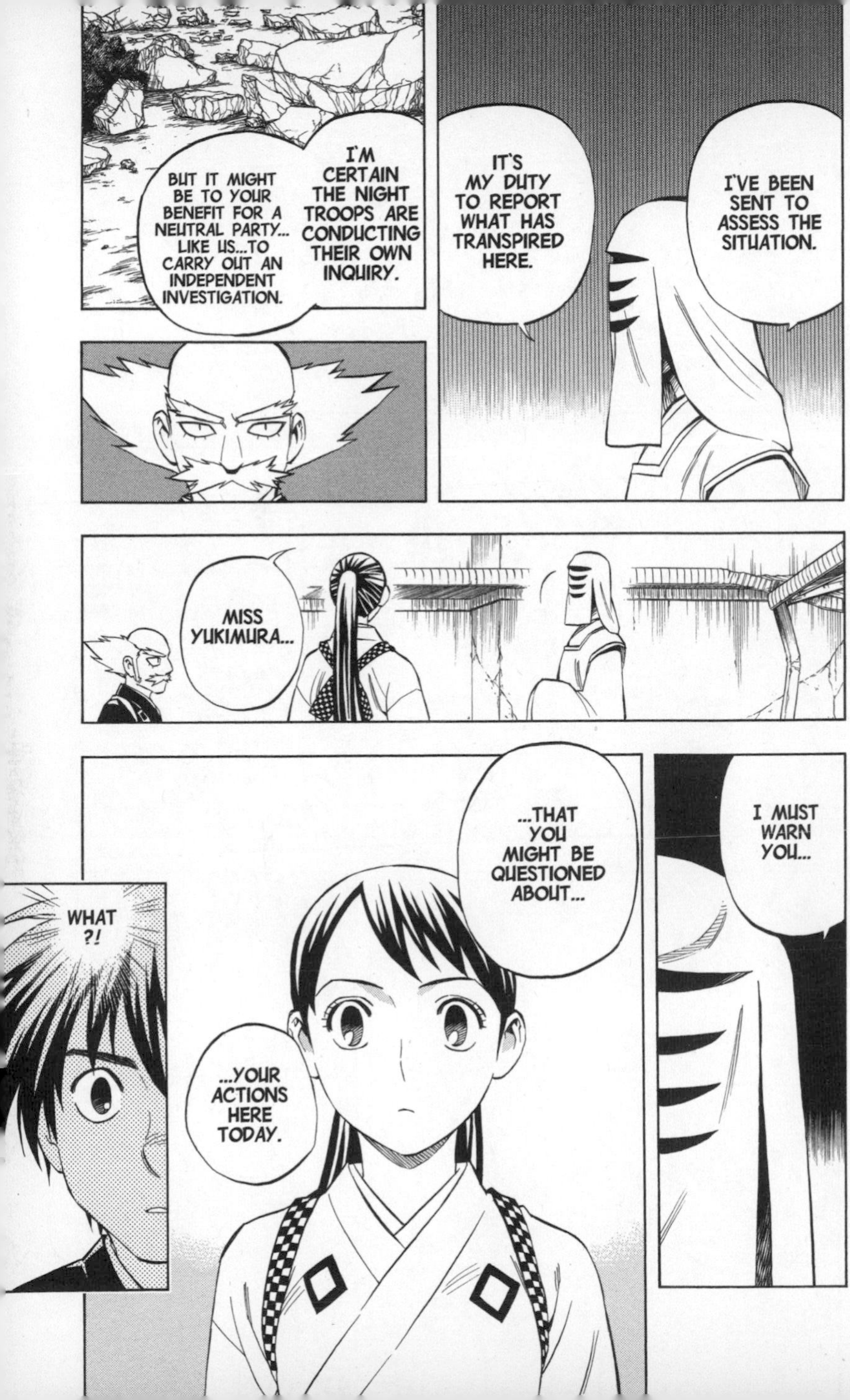
I'VE BEEN SENT TO ASSESS THE SITUATION.
IT'S MY DUTY TO REPORT WHAT HAS TRANSPIRED HERE.
I'M CERTAIN THE NIGHT TROOPS ARE CONDUCTING THEIR OWN INQUIRY.
BUT IT MIGHT BE TO YOUR BENEFIT FOR A NEUTRAL PARTY... LIKE US...TO CARRY OUT AN INDEPENDENT INVESTIGATION.
MISS YUKIMURA...
I MUST WARN YOU...
...THAT YOU MIGHT BE QUESTIONED ABOUT...
...YOUR ACTIONS HERE TODAY.
WHAT ?!

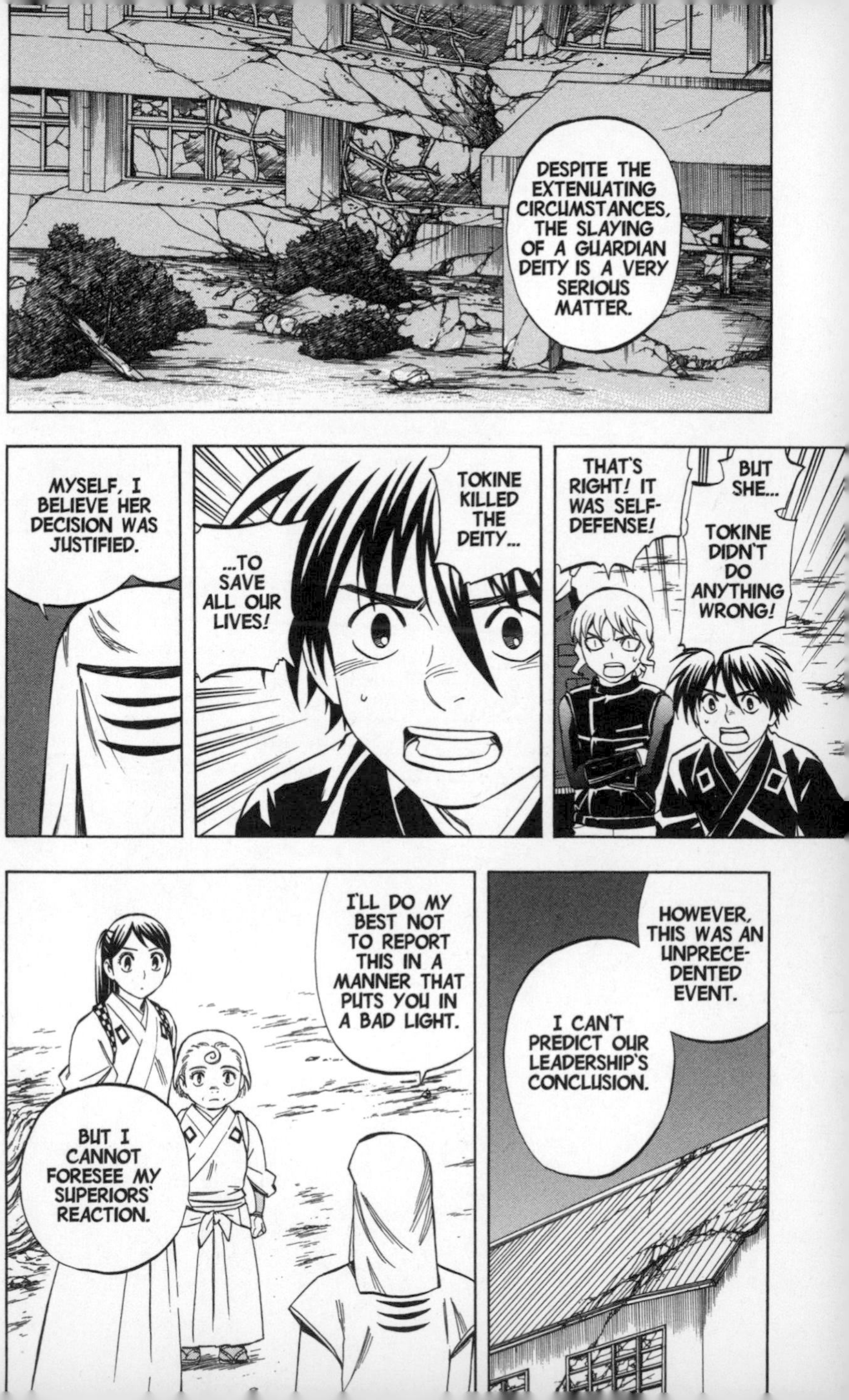
DESPITE THE EXTENUATING CIRCUMSTANCES, THE SLAYING OF A GUARDIAN DEITY IS A VERY SERIOUS MATTER.
BUT SHE...
TOKINE DIDN'T DO ANYTHING WRONG!
THAT'S RIGHT! IT WAS SELF-DEFENSE!
TOKINE KILLED THE DEITY...
...TO SAVE ALL OUR LIVES!
MYSELF, I BELIEVE HER DECISION WAS JUSTIFIED.
HOWEVER, THIS WAS AN UNPRECE-DENTED EVENT.
I CAN'T PREDICT OUR LEADERSHIP'S CONCLUSION.
I'LL DO MY BEST NOT TO REPORT THIS IN A MANNER THAT PUTS YOU IN A BAD LIGHT.
BUT I CANNOT FORESEE MY SUPERIORS' REACTION.

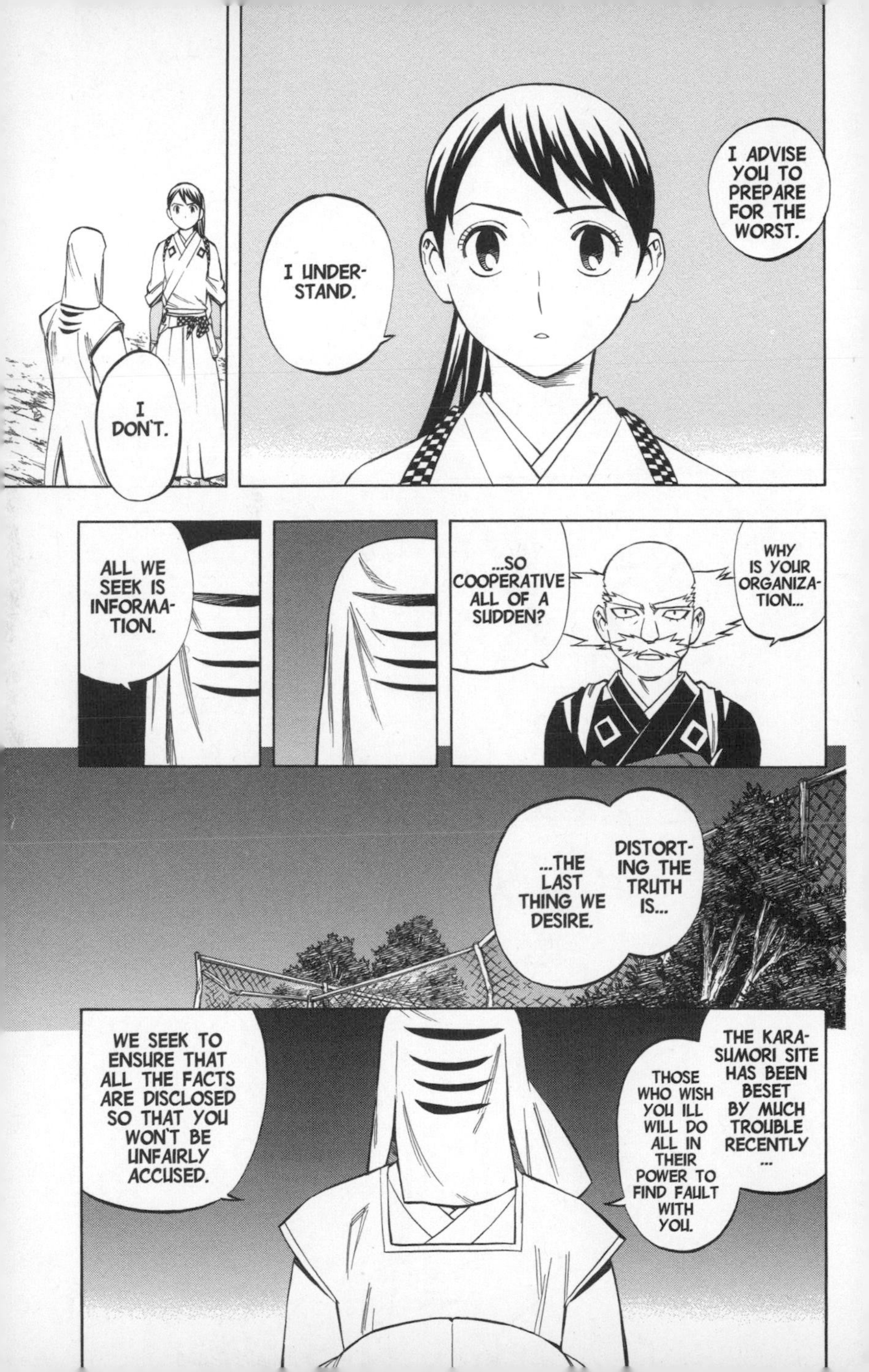
I ADVISE YOU TO PREPARE FOR THE WORST.
I UNDERSTAND.
I DON'T.
WHY IS YOUR ORGANIZATION...
...SO COOPERATIVE ALL OF A SUDDEN?
ALL WE SEEK IS INFORMATION.
DISTORTING THE TRUTH IS...
...THE LAST THING WE DESIRE.
THE KARASUMORI SITE HAS BEEN BESET BY MUCH TROUBLE RECENTLY...
THOSE WHO WISH YOU ILL WILL DO ALL IN THEIR POWER TO FIND FAULT WITH YOU.
WE SEEK TO ENSURE THAT ALL THE FACTS ARE DISCLOSED SO THAT YOU WON'T BE UNFAIRLY ACCUSED.

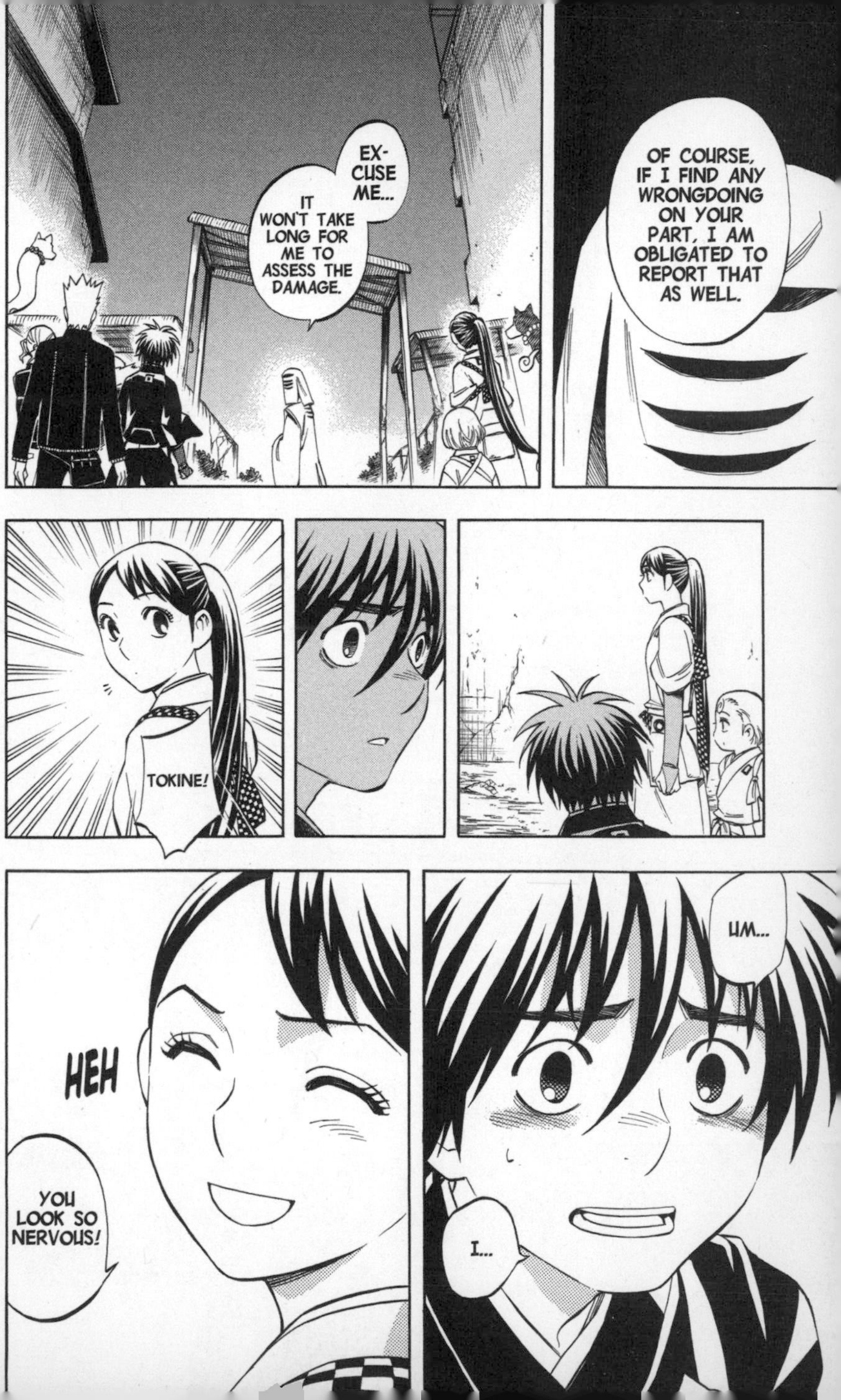
OF COURSE, IF I FIND ANY WRONGDOING ON YOUR PART, I AM OBLIGATED TO REPORT THAT AS WELL.
EX-CUSE ME...
IT WON'T TAKE LONG FOR ME TO ASSESS THE DAMAGE.
TOKINE!
UM...
I...
HEH
YOU LOOK SO NERVOUS!

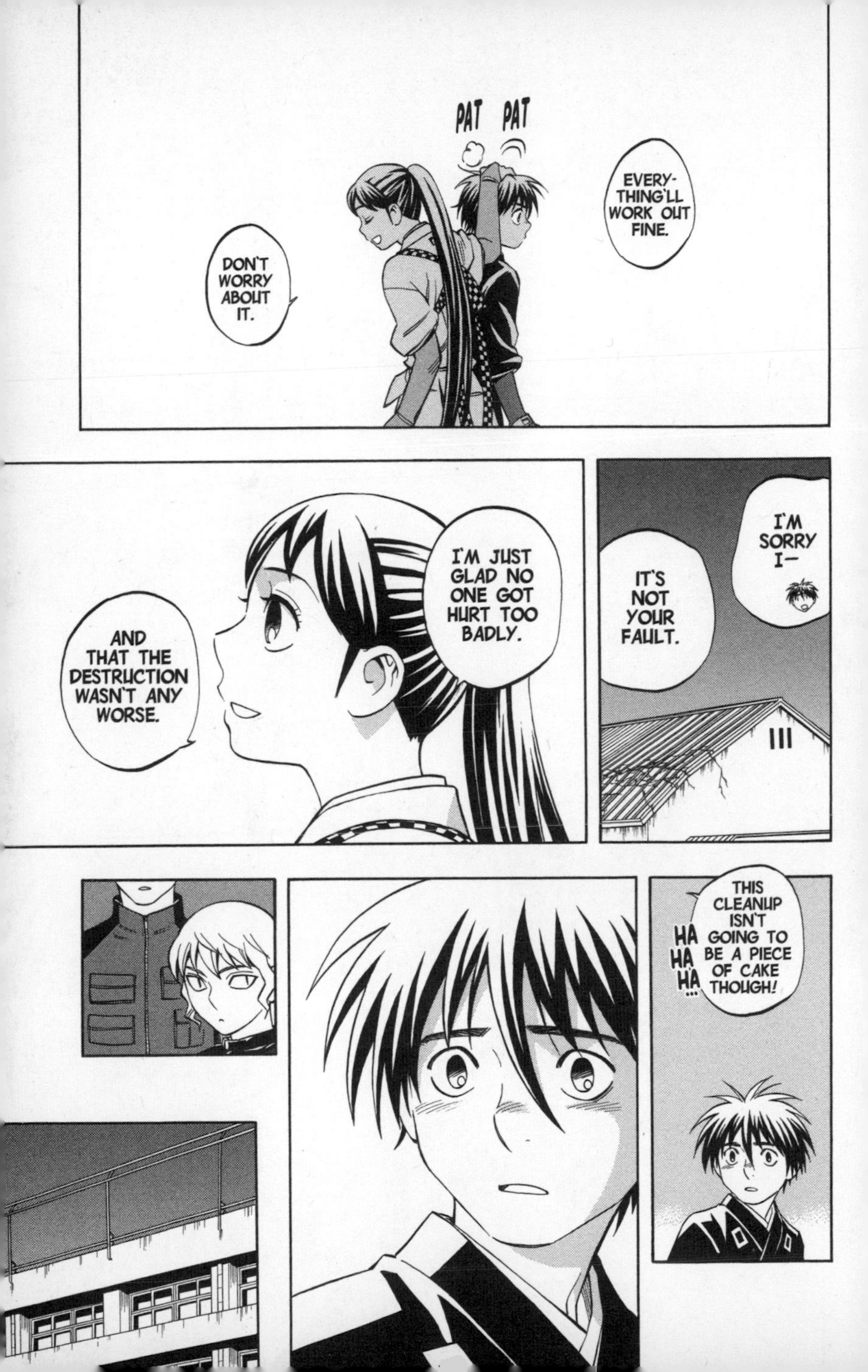
PAT PAT
EVERY-THING'LL WORK OUT FINE.
DON'T WORRY ABOUT IT.
I'M SORRY I—
IT'S NOT YOUR FAULT.
I'M JUST GLAD NO ONE GOT HURT TOO BADLY.
AND THAT THE DESTRUCTION WASN'T ANY WORSE.
THIS CLEANUP ISN'T GOING TO BE A PIECE OF CAKE THOUGH!
HA HA HA...

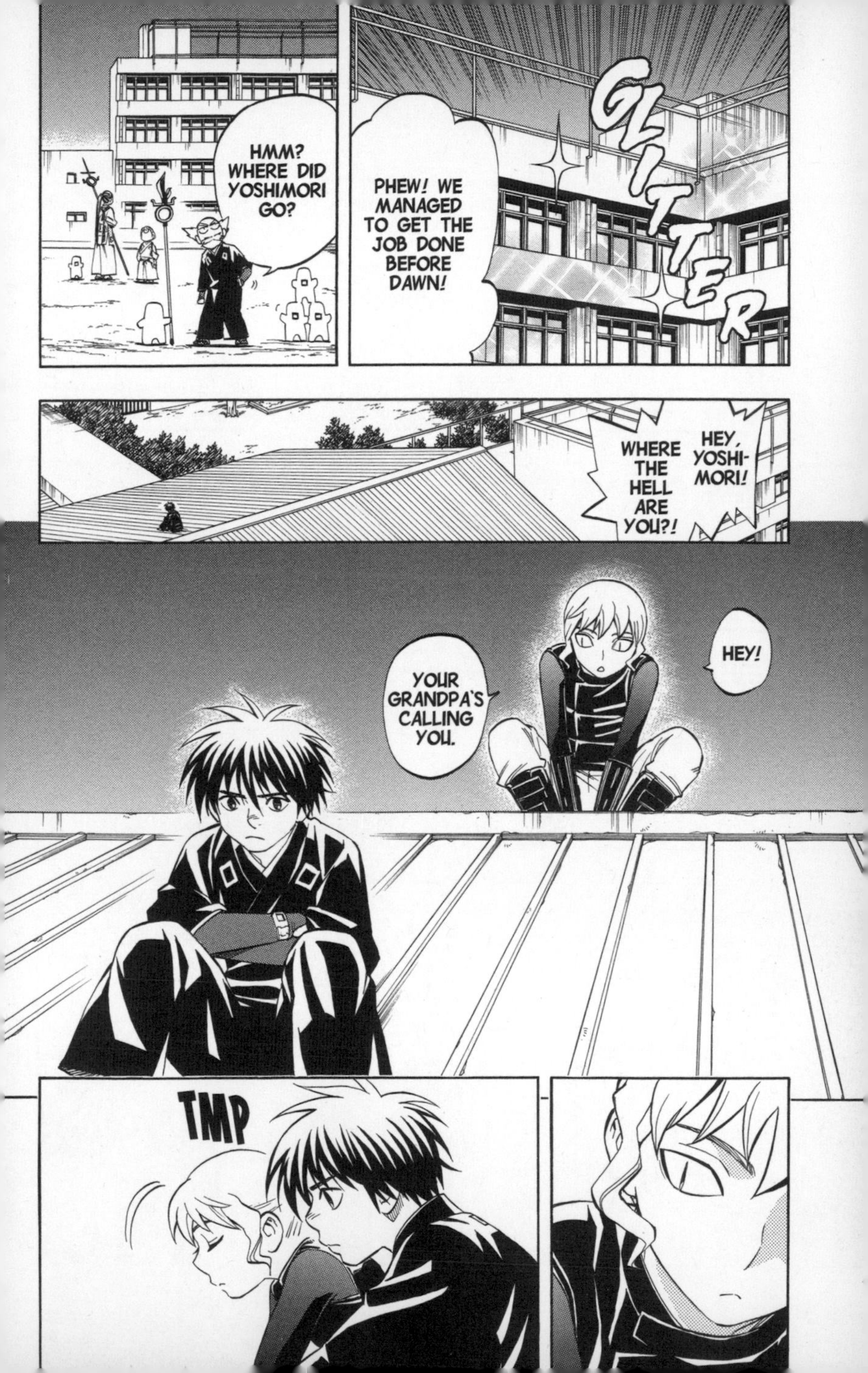
GLITTER
PHEW! WE MANAGED TO GET THE JOB DONE BEFORE DAWN!
HMM? WHERE DID YOSHIMORI GO?
HEY, YOSHIMORI!
WHERE THE HELL ARE YOU?!
HEY!
YOUR GRANDPA'S CALLING YOU.
TMP

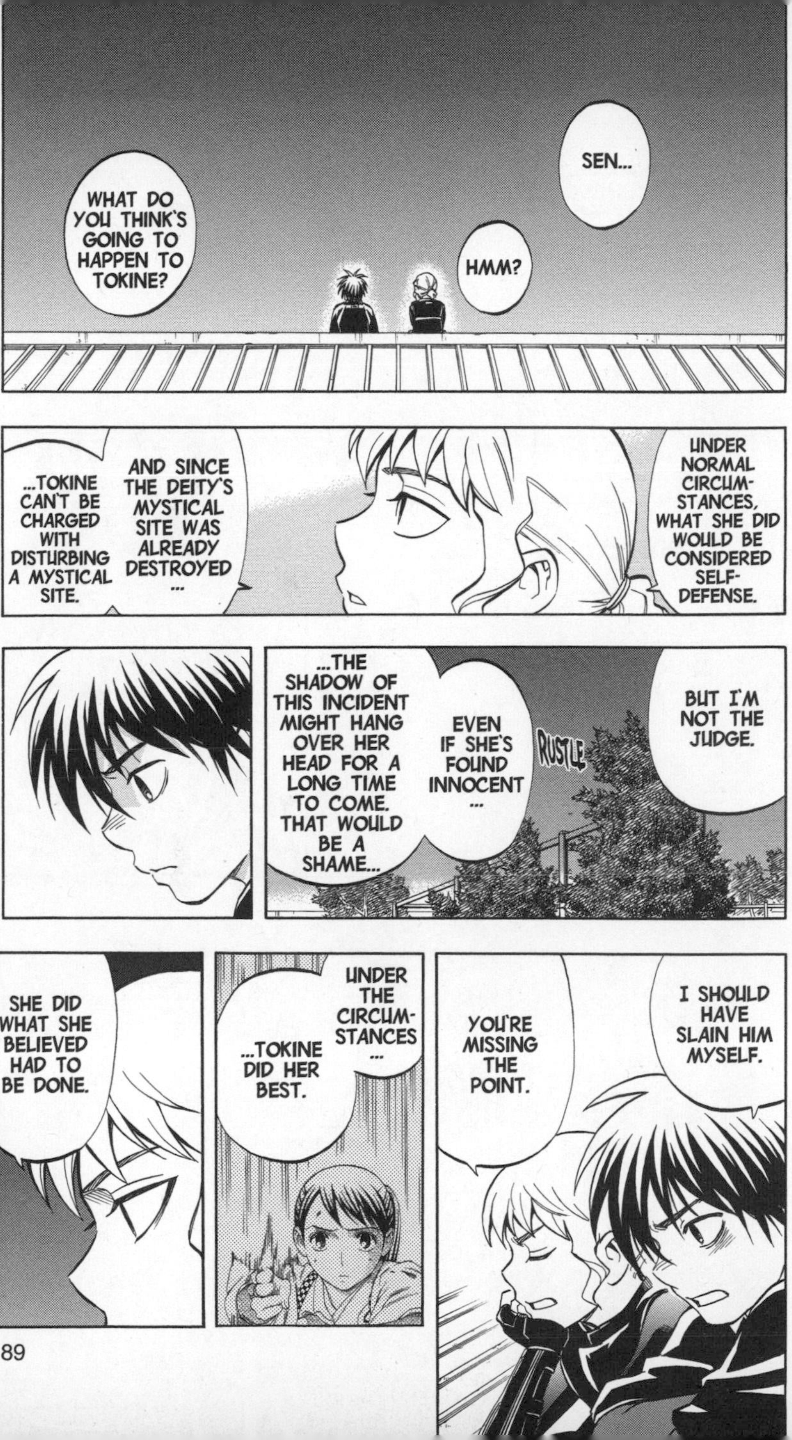
SEN...
HMM?
WHAT DO YOU THINK'S GOING TO HAPPEN TO TOKINE?
UNDER NORMAL CIRCUM-STANCES, WHAT SHE DID WOULD BE CONSIDERED SELF-DEFENSE.
AND SINCE THE DEITY'S MYSTICAL SITE WAS ALREADY DESTROYED ...
...TOKINE CAN'T BE CHARGED WITH DISTURBING A MYSTICAL SITE.
BUT I'M NOT THE JUDGE.
RUSTLE
EVEN IF SHE'S FOUND INNOCENT ...
...THE SHADOW OF THIS INCIDENT MIGHT HANG OVER HER HEAD FOR A LONG TIME TO COME. THAT WOULD BE A SHAME...
I SHOULD HAVE SLAIN HIM MYSELF.
YOU'RE MISSING THE POINT.
UNDER THE CIRCUM-STANCES ...
...TOKINE DID HER BEST.
SHE DID WHAT SHE BELIEVED HAD TO BE DONE.

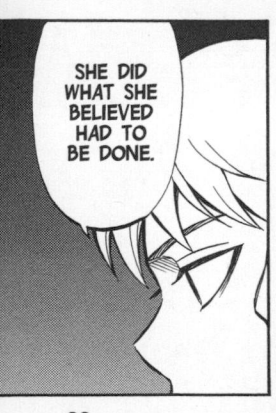

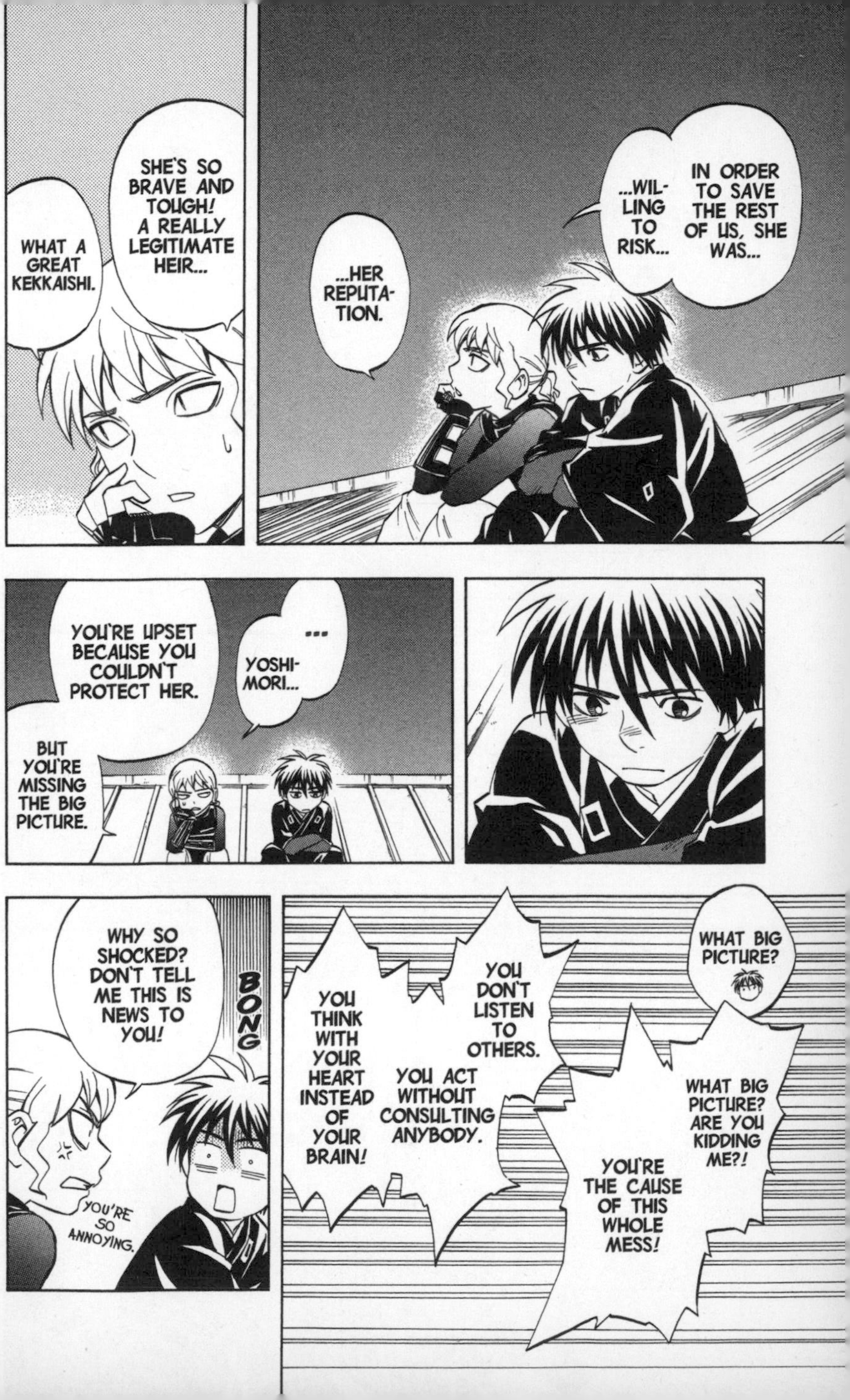
IN ORDER TO SAVE THE REST OF US, SHE WAS...
...WIL-LING TO RISK...
...HER REPUTA-TION.
SHE'S SO BRAVE AND TOUGH! A REALLY LEGITIMATE HEIR...
WHAT A GREAT KEKKAISHI.
...
YOSHI-MORI...
YOU'RE UPSET BECAUSE YOU COULDN'T PROTECT HER.
BUT YOU'RE MISSING THE BIG PICTURE.
WHAT BIG PICTURE?
WHAT BIG PICTURE? ARE YOU KIDDING ME?!
YOU'RE THE CAUSE OF THIS WHOLE MESS!
YOU DON'T LISTEN TO OTHERS.
YOU ACT WITHOUT CONSULTING ANYBODY.
YOU THINK WITH YOUR HEART INSTEAD OF YOUR BRAIN!
BONG
WHY SO SHOCKED? DON'T TELL ME THIS IS NEWS TO YOU!
YOU'RE SO ANNOYING.

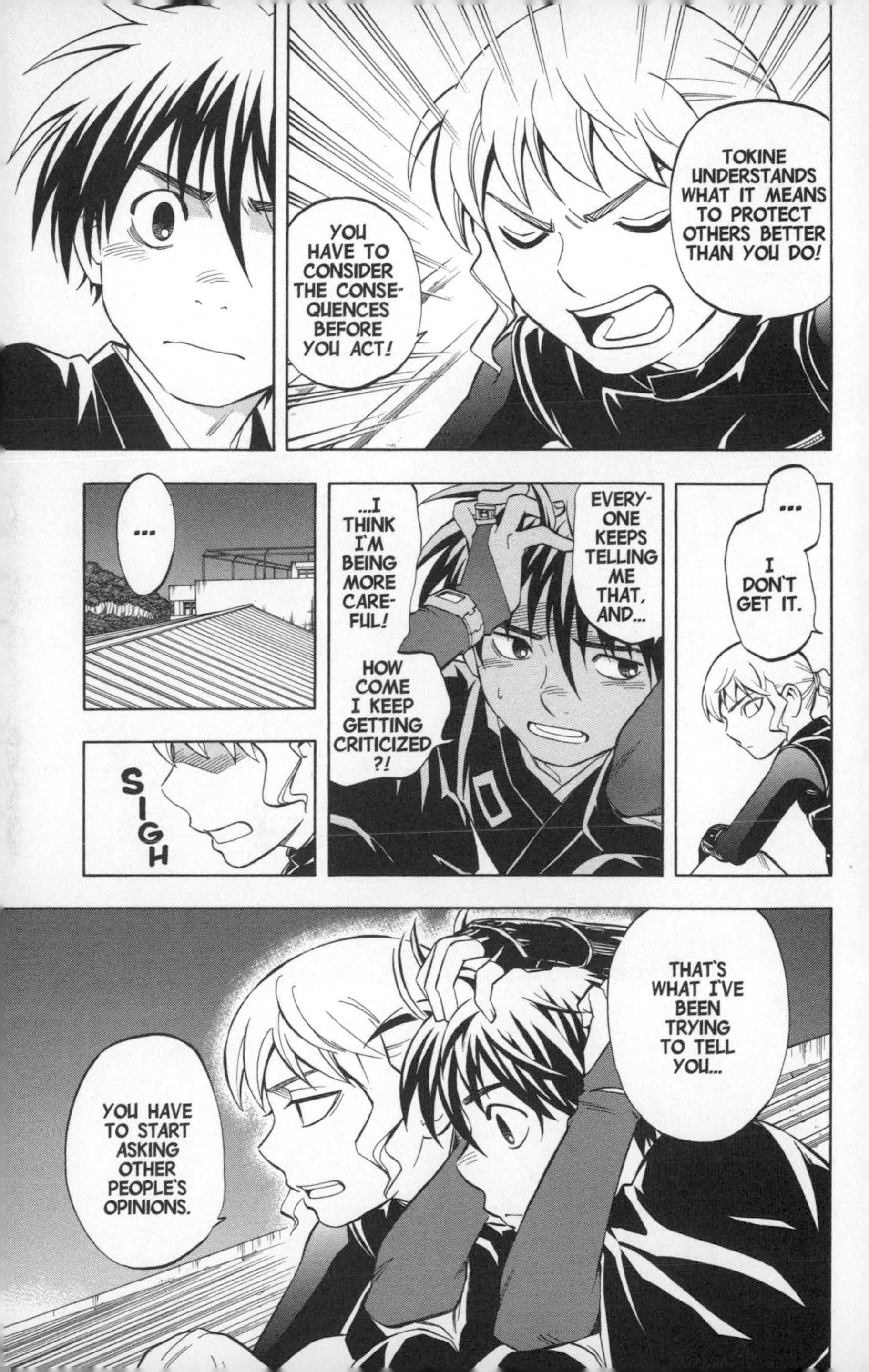
TOKINE UNDERSTANDS WHAT IT MEANS TO PROTECT OTHERS BETTER THAN YOU DO!
YOU HAVE TO CONSIDER THE CONSE-QUENCES BEFORE YOU ACT!
...
I DON'T GET IT.
EVERY-ONE KEEPS TELLING ME THAT, AND...
...I THINK I'M BEING MORE CARE-FUL!
HOW COME I KEEP GETTING CRITICIZED ?!
...
SIGH
THAT'S WHAT I'VE BEEN TRYING TO TELL YOU...
YOU HAVE TO START ASKING OTHER PEOPLE'S OPINIONS.

THANKS, SEN.

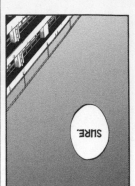

SURE.

I GET IT.

ALL RIGHT.

"...I PROMISE THINGS WILL GET BETTER.

IF YOU DO...."

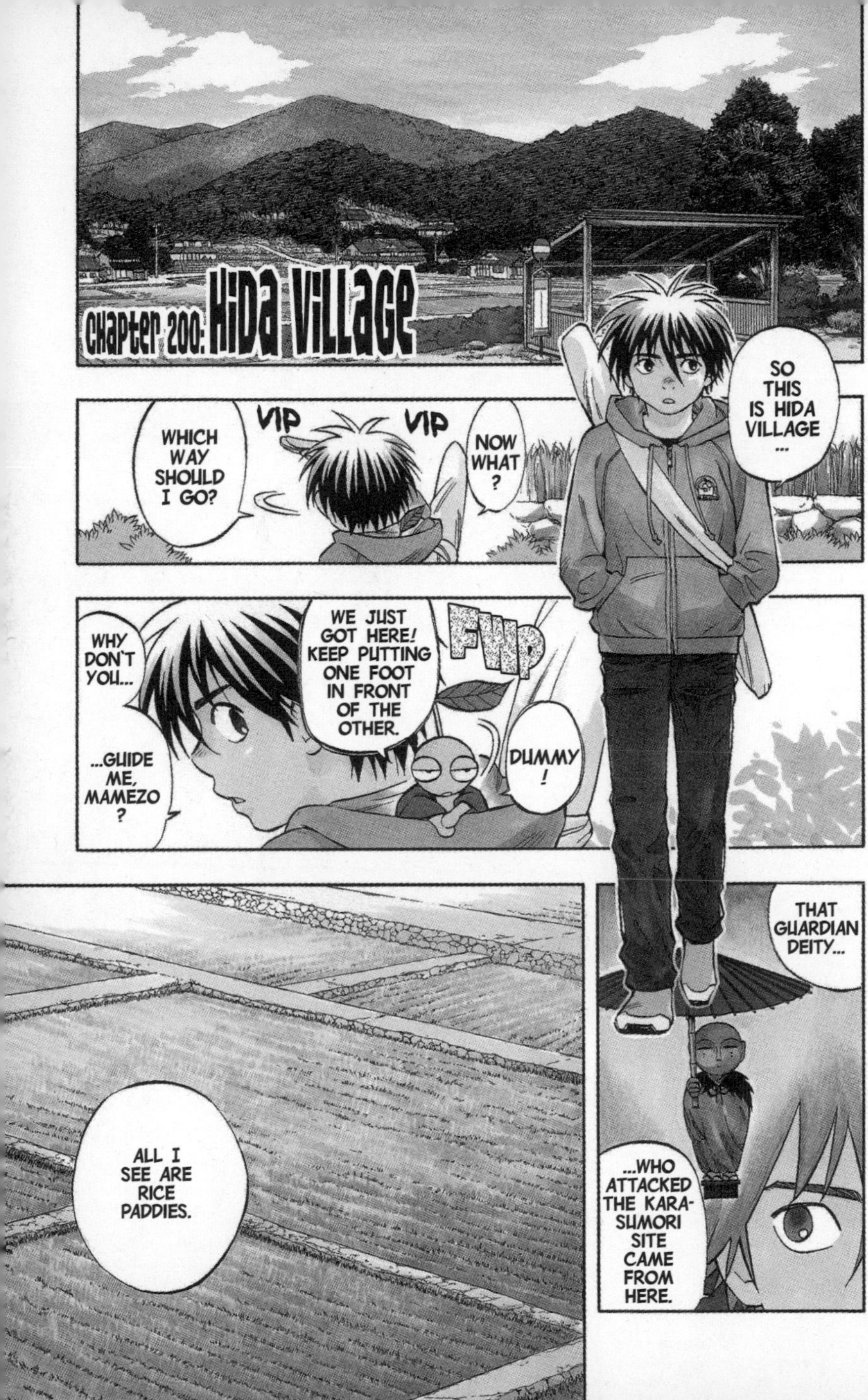
CHAPTER 200: HIDA VILLAGE
SO THIS IS HIDA VILLAGE...
NOW WHAT?
VIP VIP
WHICH WAY SHOULD I GO?
FWP
WE JUST GOT HERE! KEEP PUTTING ONE FOOT IN FRONT OF THE OTHER.
WHY DON'T YOU...
...GUIDE ME, MAMEZO?
DUMMY!
THAT GUARDIAN DEITY...
...WHO ATTACKED THE KARA-SUMORI SITE CAME FROM HERE.
ALL I SEE ARE RICE PADDIES.

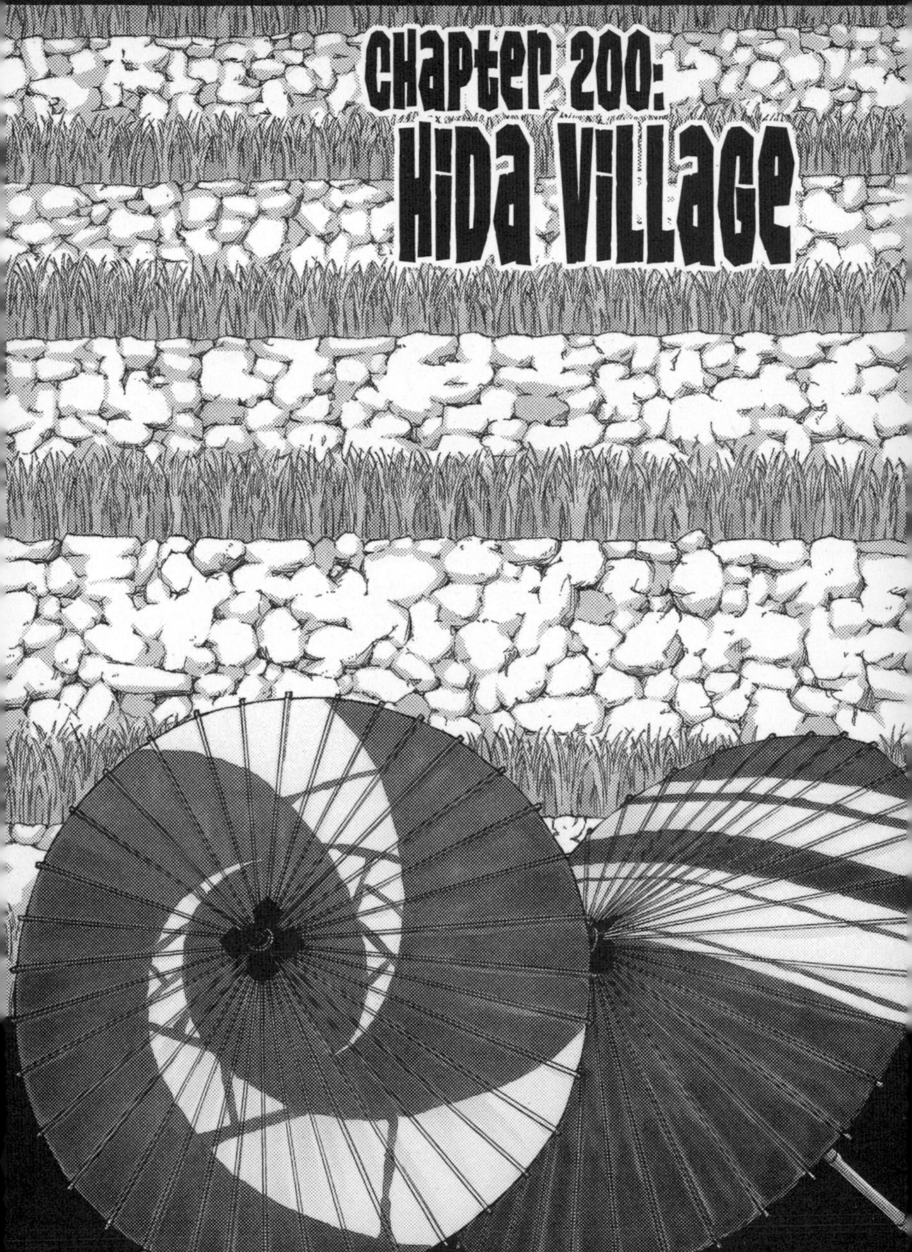
CHAPTER 200:
HIDA VILLAGE

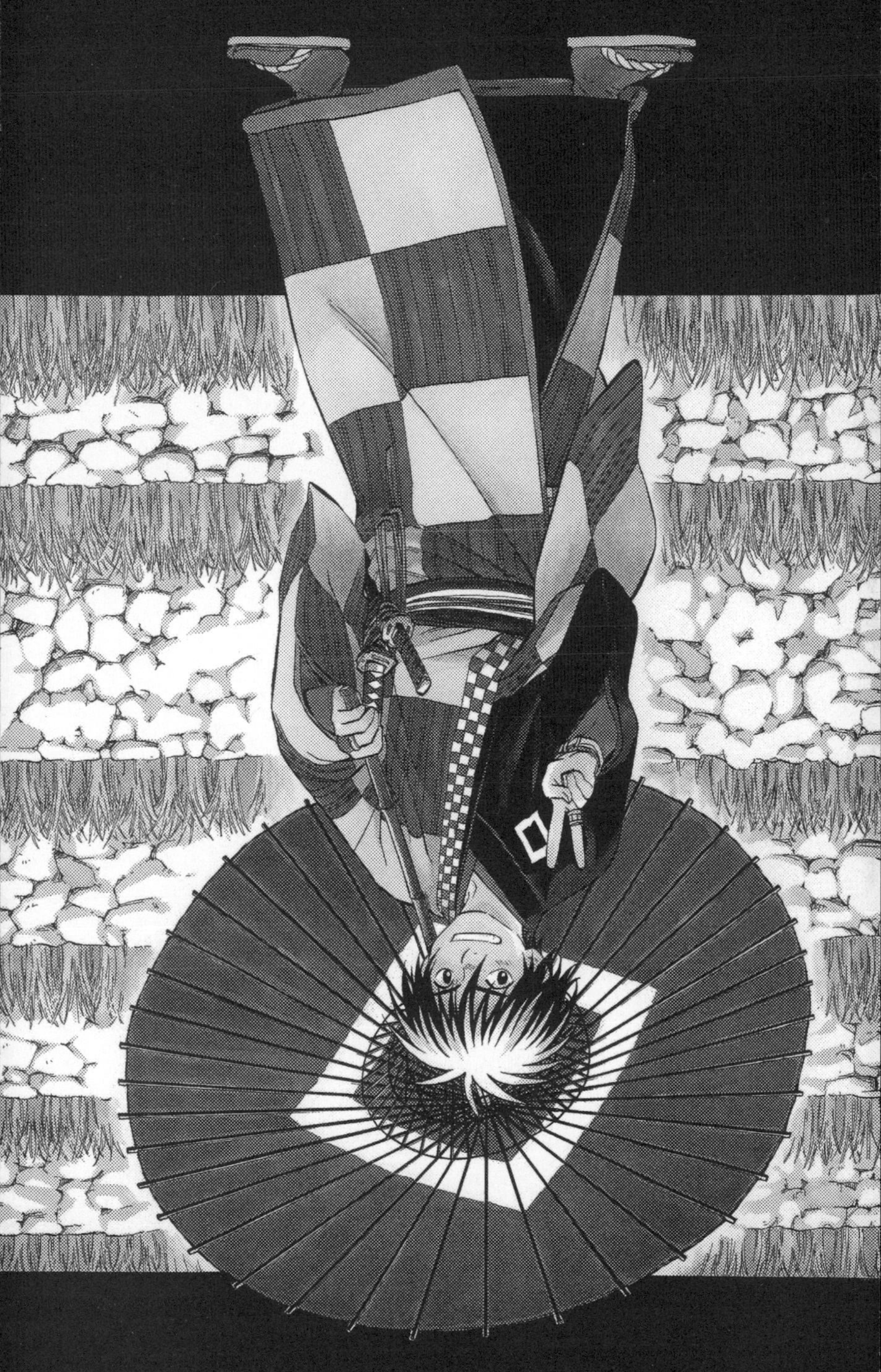

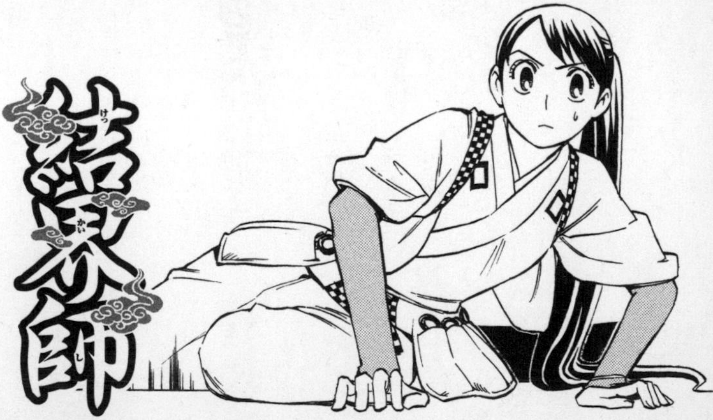
結界師

EARLIER THAT MORNING...
FWWP
KETSU!
NGH!
WBL
OOPS!
WBL

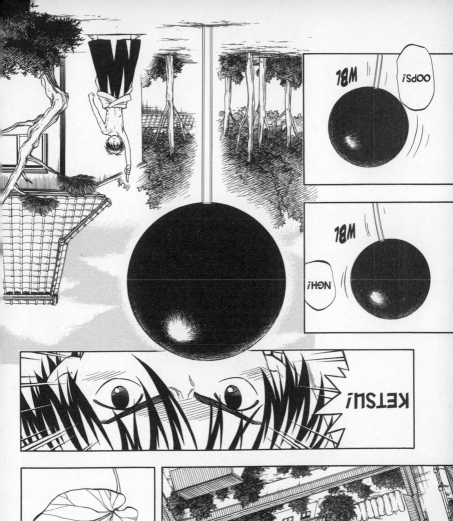

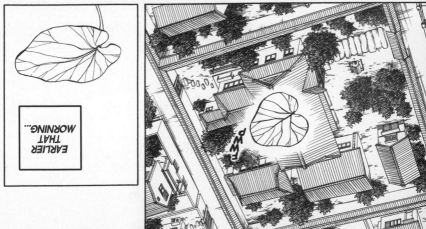

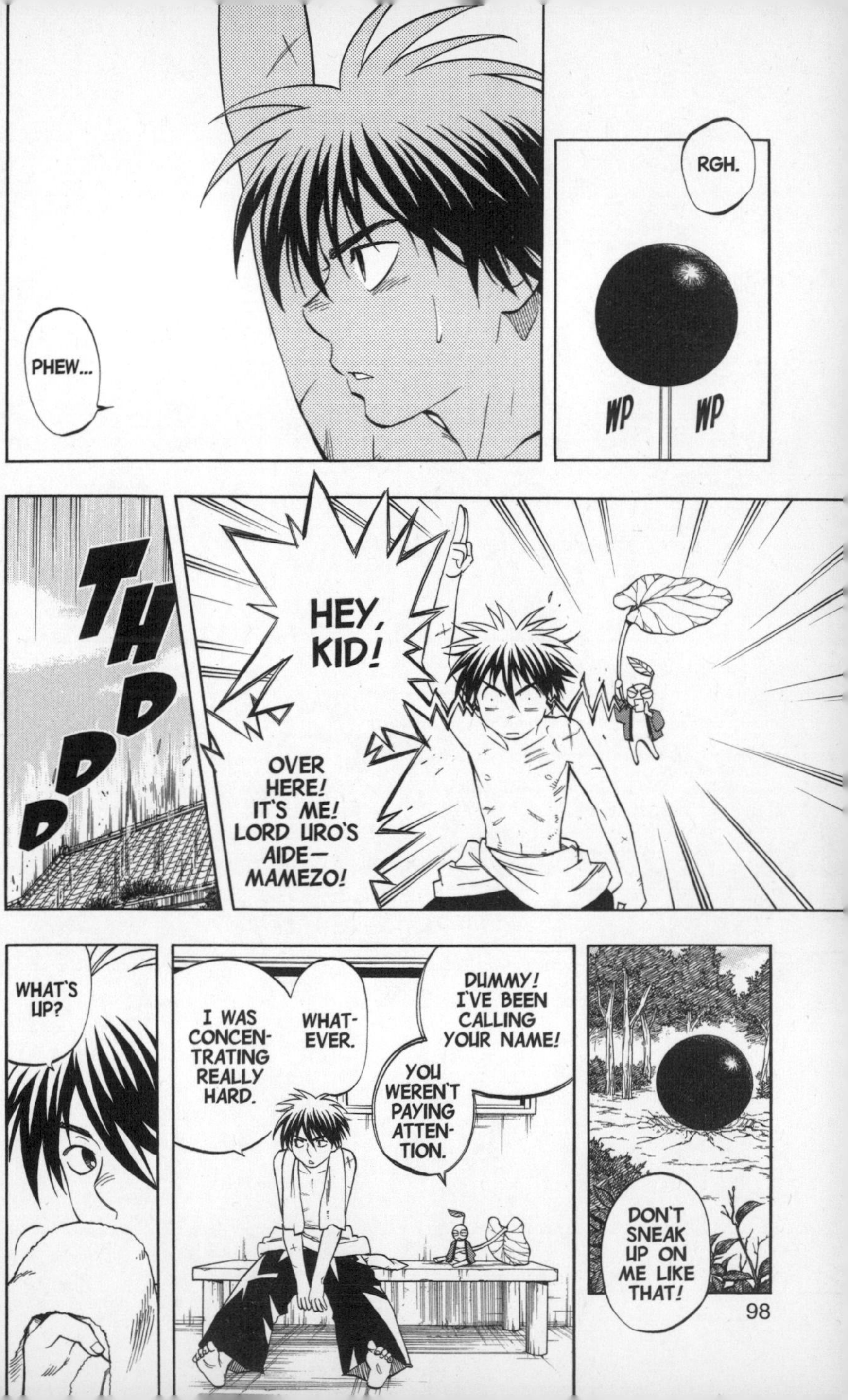
RGH.
WP WP
PHEW...
HEY, KID!
OVER HERE! IT'S ME! LORD URO'S AIDE— MAMEZO!
THDDD
DON'T SNEAK UP ON ME LIKE THAT!
DUMMY! I'VE BEEN CALLING YOUR NAME!
YOU WEREN'T PAYING ATTENTION.
WHAT-EVER.
I WAS CONCEN-TRATING REALLY HARD.
WHAT'S UP?

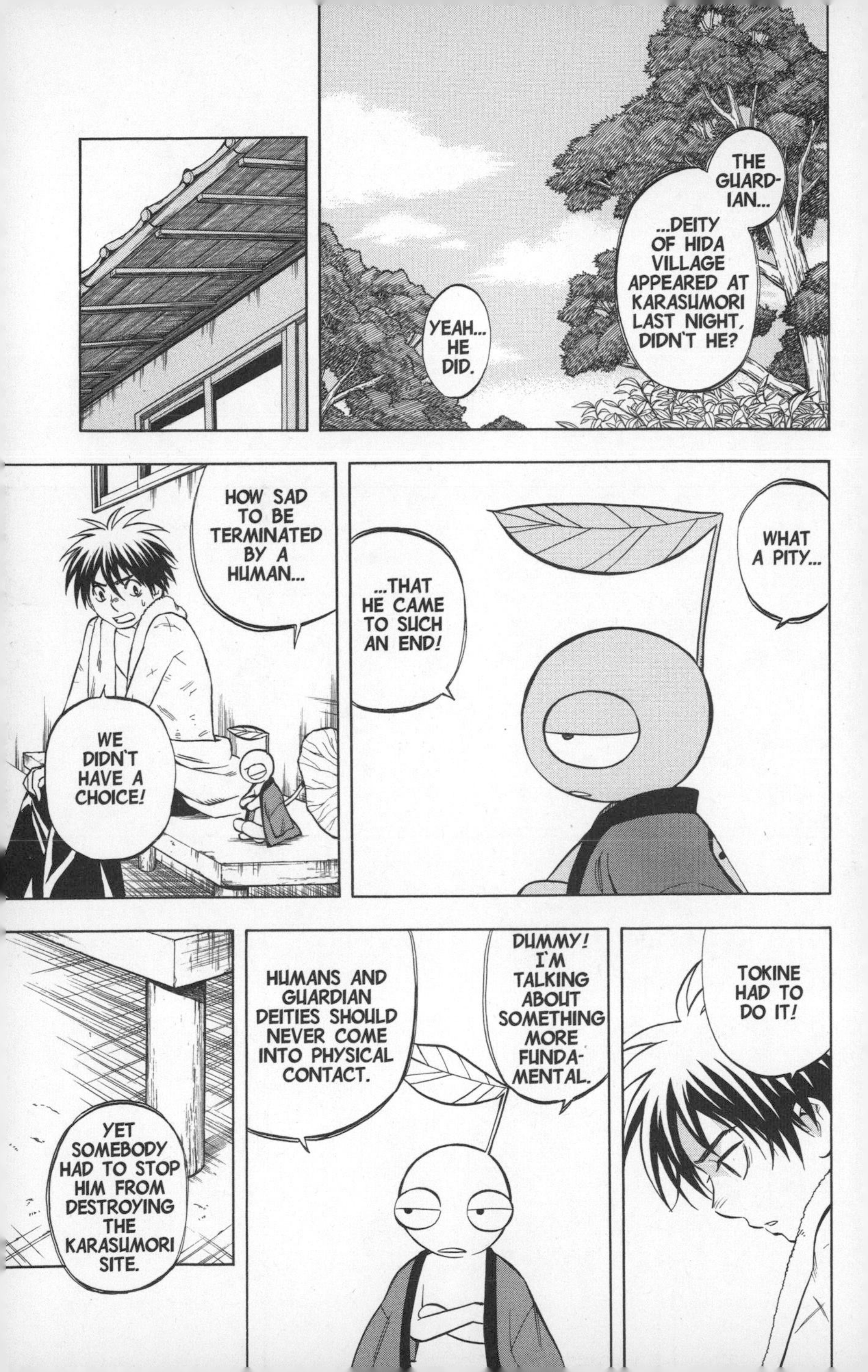
THE GUARDIAN...
...DEITY OF HIDA VILLAGE APPEARED AT KARASUMORI LAST NIGHT, DIDN'T HE?
YEAH... HE DID.
WHAT A PITY...
...THAT HE CAME TO SUCH AN END!
HOW SAD TO BE TERMINATED BY A HUMAN...
WE DIDN'T HAVE A CHOICE!
TOKINE HAD TO DO IT!
DUMMY! I'M TALKING ABOUT SOMETHING MORE FUNDAMENTAL.
HUMANS AND GUARDIAN DEITIES SHOULD NEVER COME INTO PHYSICAL CONTACT.
YET SOMEBODY HAD TO STOP HIM FROM DESTROYING THE KARASUMORI SITE.

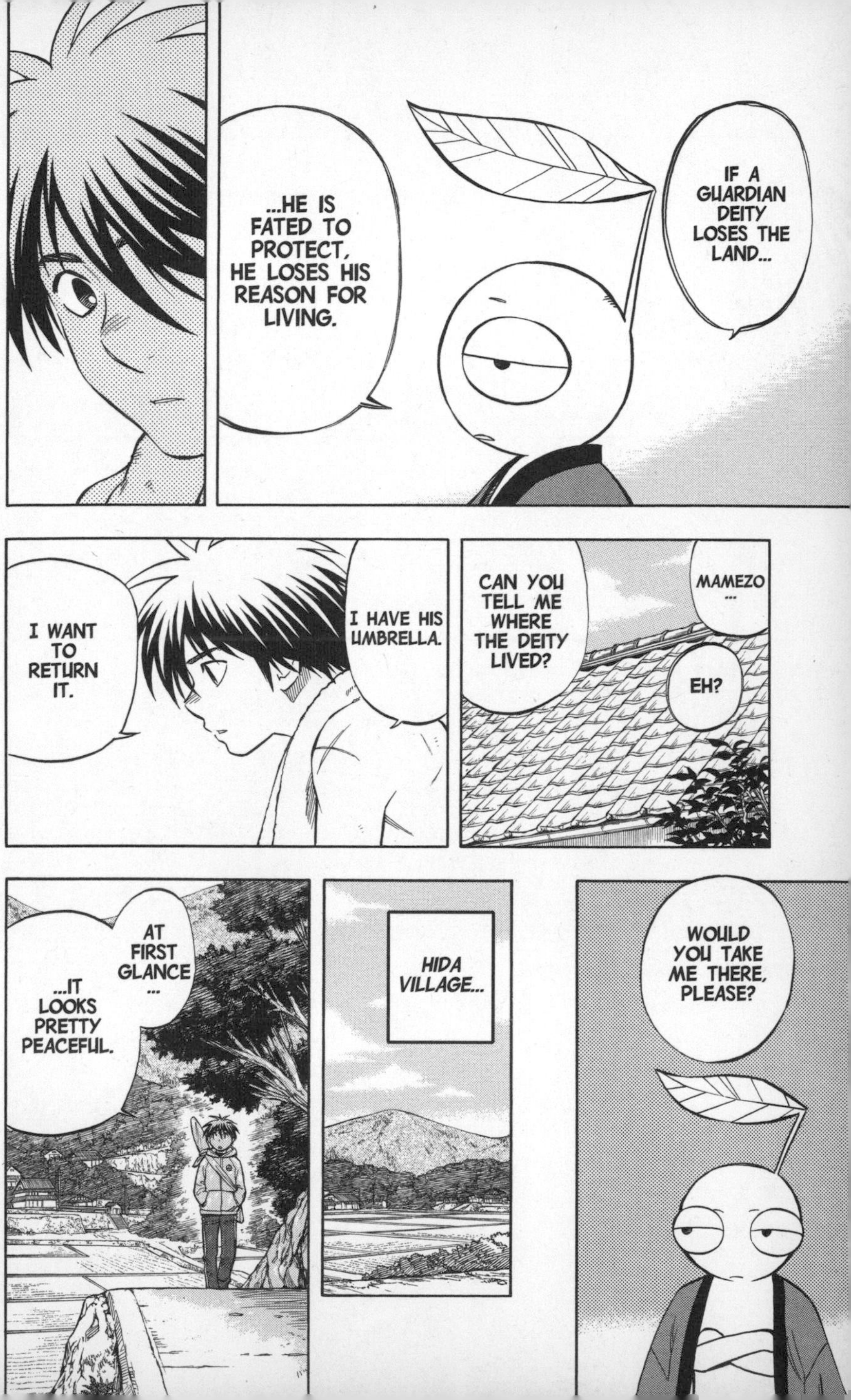
IF A GUARDIAN DEITY LOSES THE LAND...
...HE IS FATED TO PROTECT, HE LOSES HIS REASON FOR LIVING.
MAMEZO ...
EH?
CAN YOU TELL ME WHERE THE DEITY LIVED?
I HAVE HIS UMBRELLA.
I WANT TO RETURN IT.
WOULD YOU TAKE ME THERE, PLEASE?
HIDA VILLAGE...
AT FIRST GLANCE ...
...IT LOOKS PRETTY PEACEFUL.

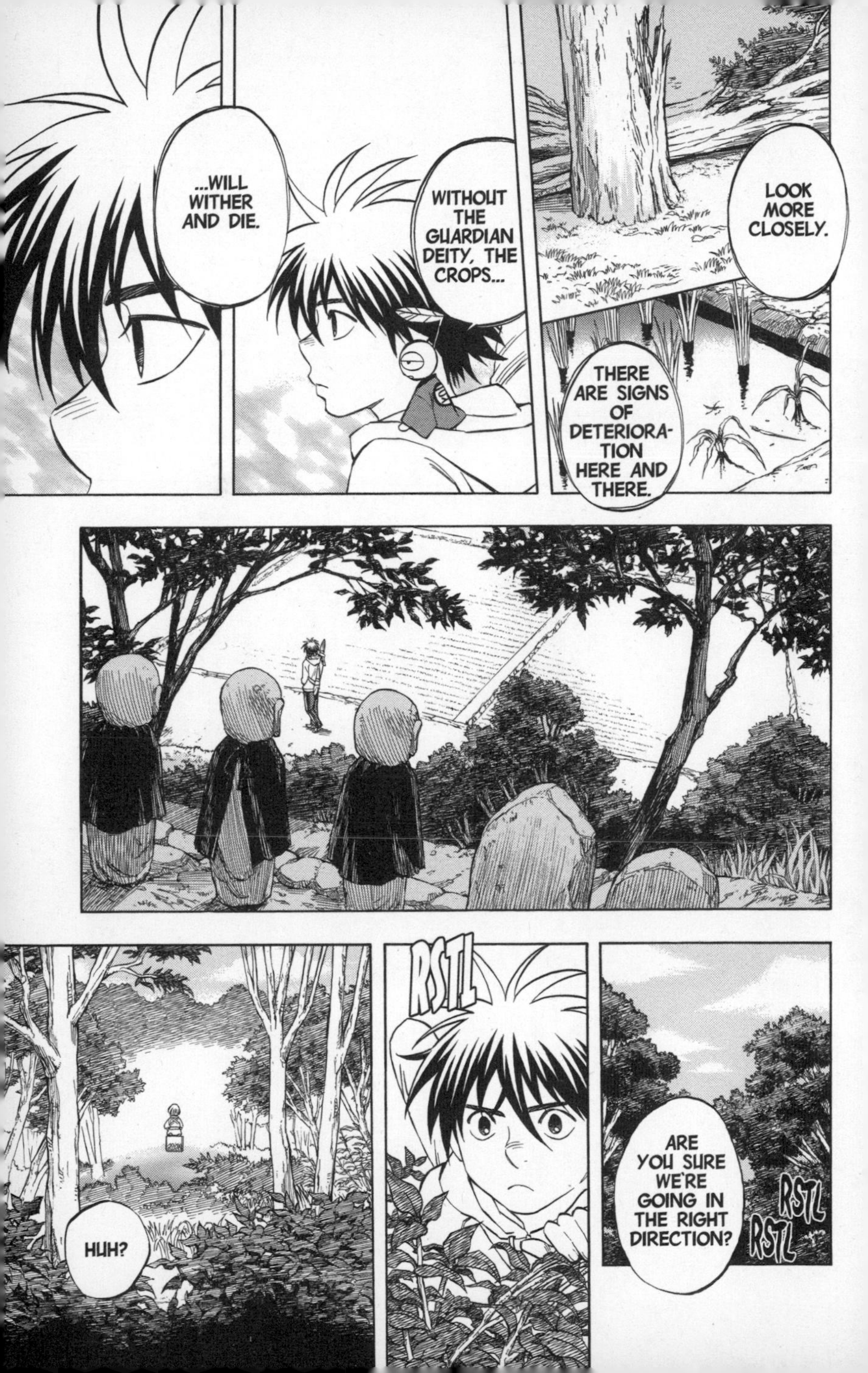
LOOK MORE CLOSELY.
THERE ARE SIGNS OF DETERIORATION HERE AND THERE.
WITHOUT THE GUARDIAN DEITY, THE CROPS...
...WILL WITHER AND DIE.
RSTL RSTL
ARE YOU SURE WE'RE GOING IN THE RIGHT DIRECTION?
RSTL
HUH?

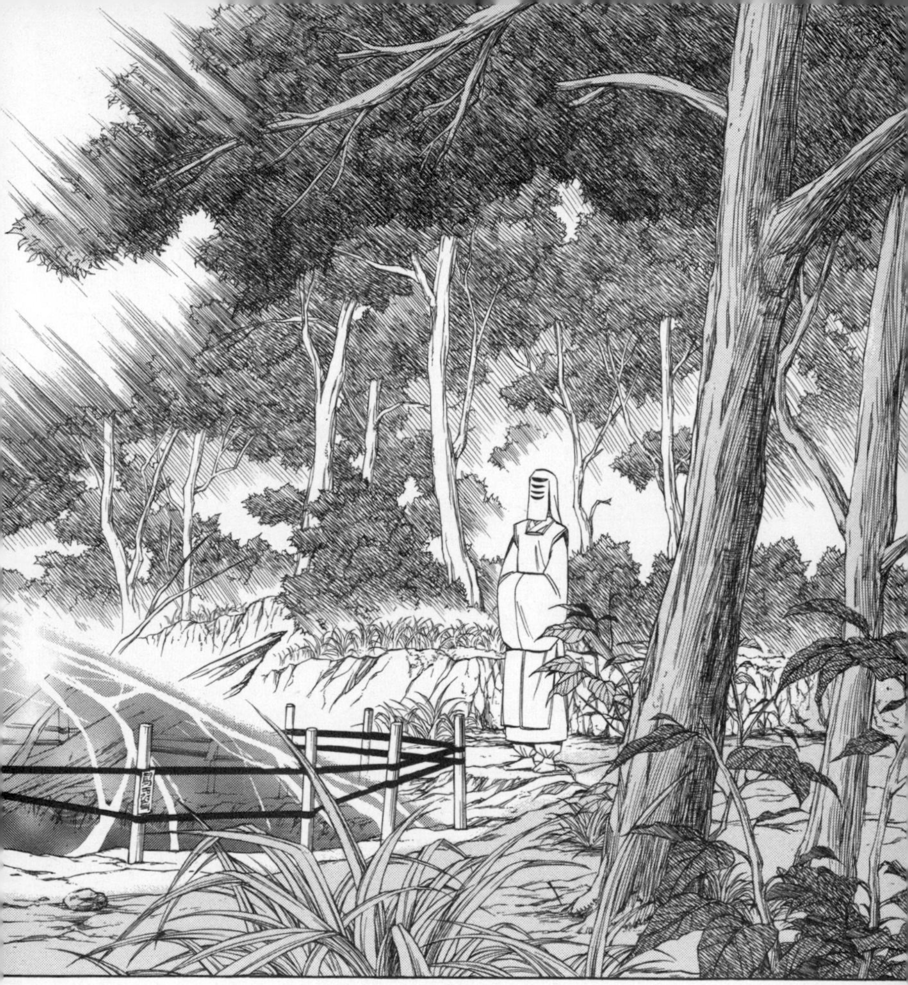
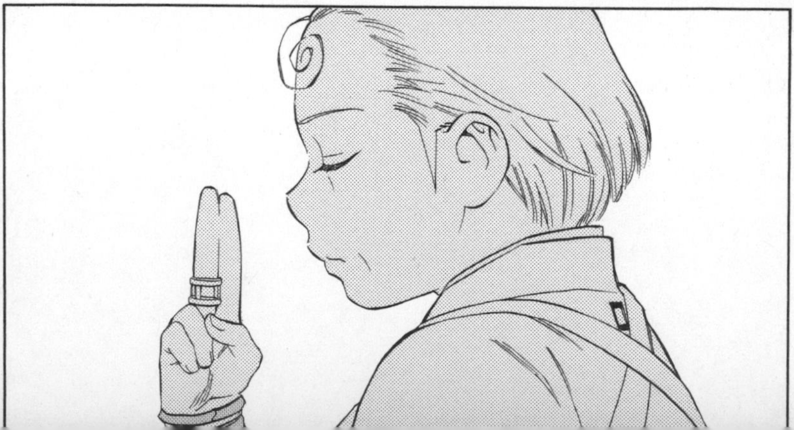

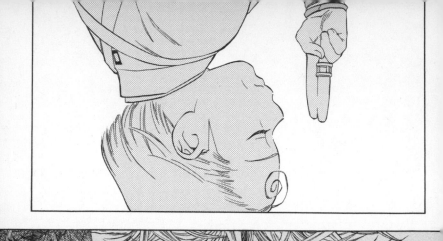

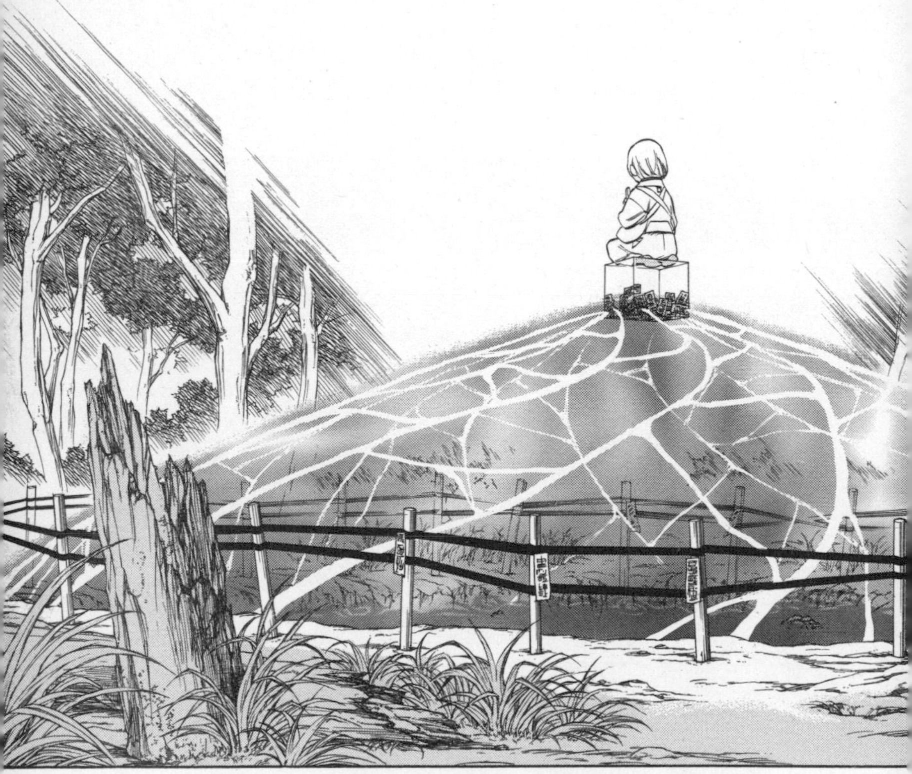
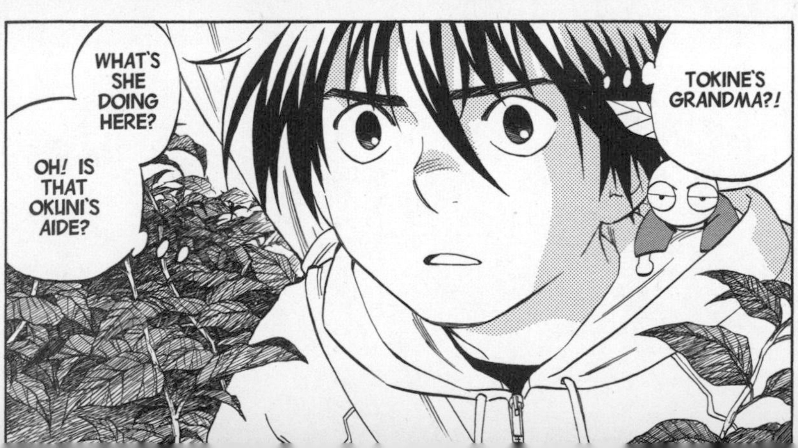
TOKINE'S GRANDMA?!
WHAT'S SHE DOING HERE?
OH! IS THAT OKUNI'S AIDE?

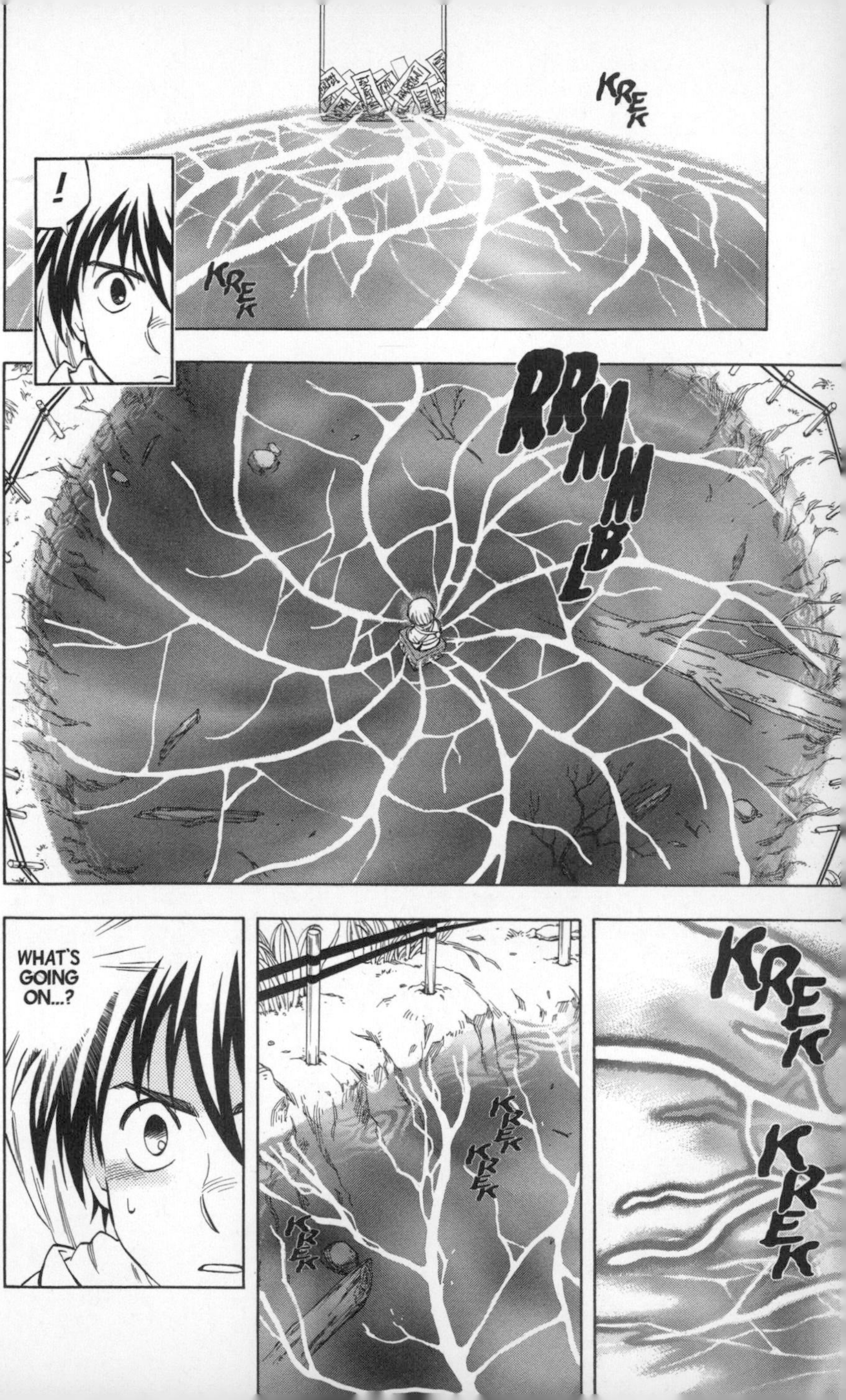
KREK
KREK
!
RRMMMBL
KREK KREK
KREK
KREK
KREK
KREK
WHAT'S GOING ON...?

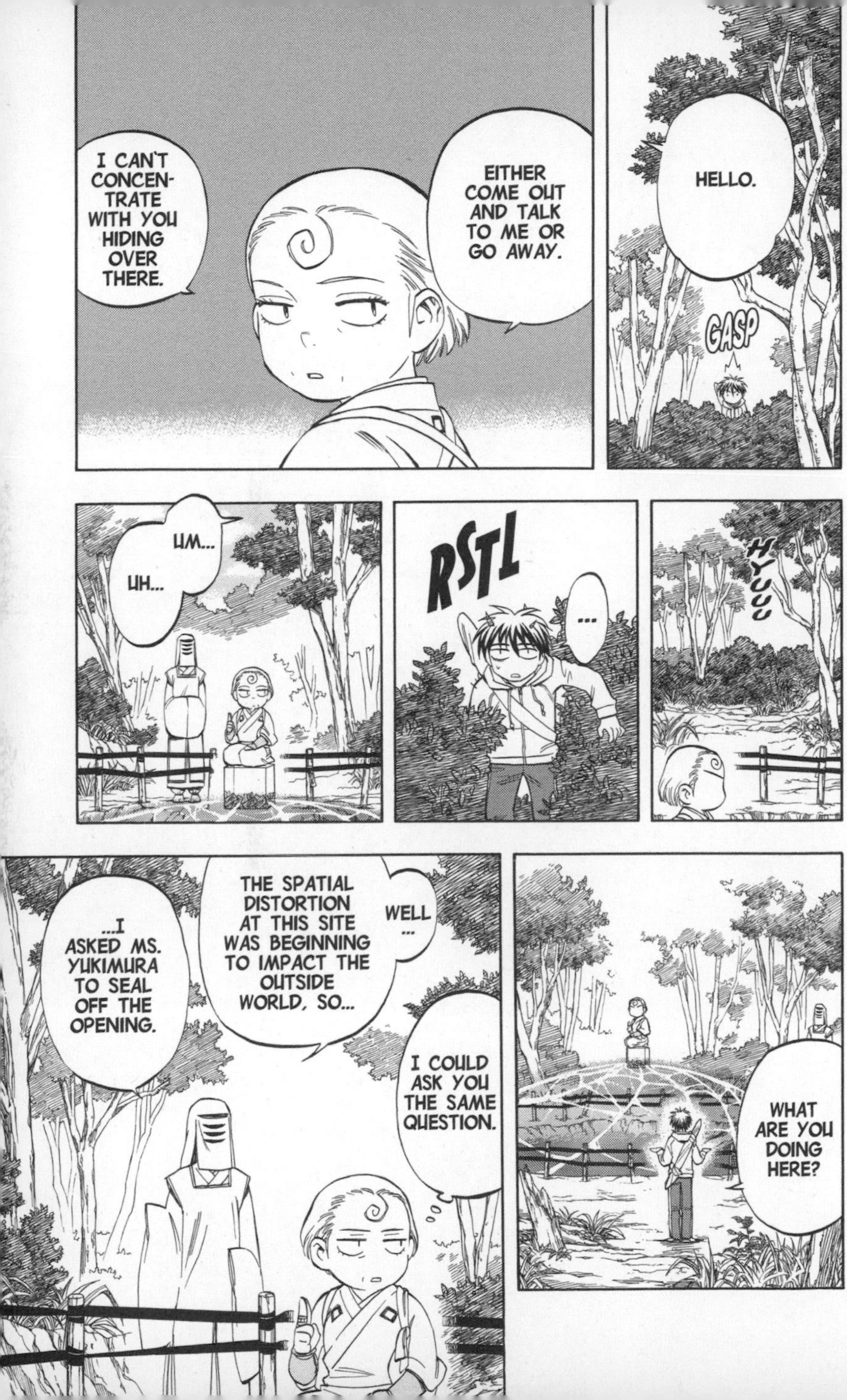
HELLO.
GASP
EITHER COME OUT AND TALK TO ME OR GO AWAY.
I CAN'T CONCEN-TRATE WITH YOU HIDING OVER THERE.
HYUUU
RSTL
...
UM...
UH...
WHAT ARE YOU DOING HERE?
I COULD ASK YOU THE SAME QUESTION.
WELL ...
THE SPATIAL DISTORTION AT THIS SITE WAS BEGINNING TO IMPACT THE OUTSIDE WORLD, SO...
...I ASKED MS. YUKIMURA TO SEAL OFF THE OPENING.

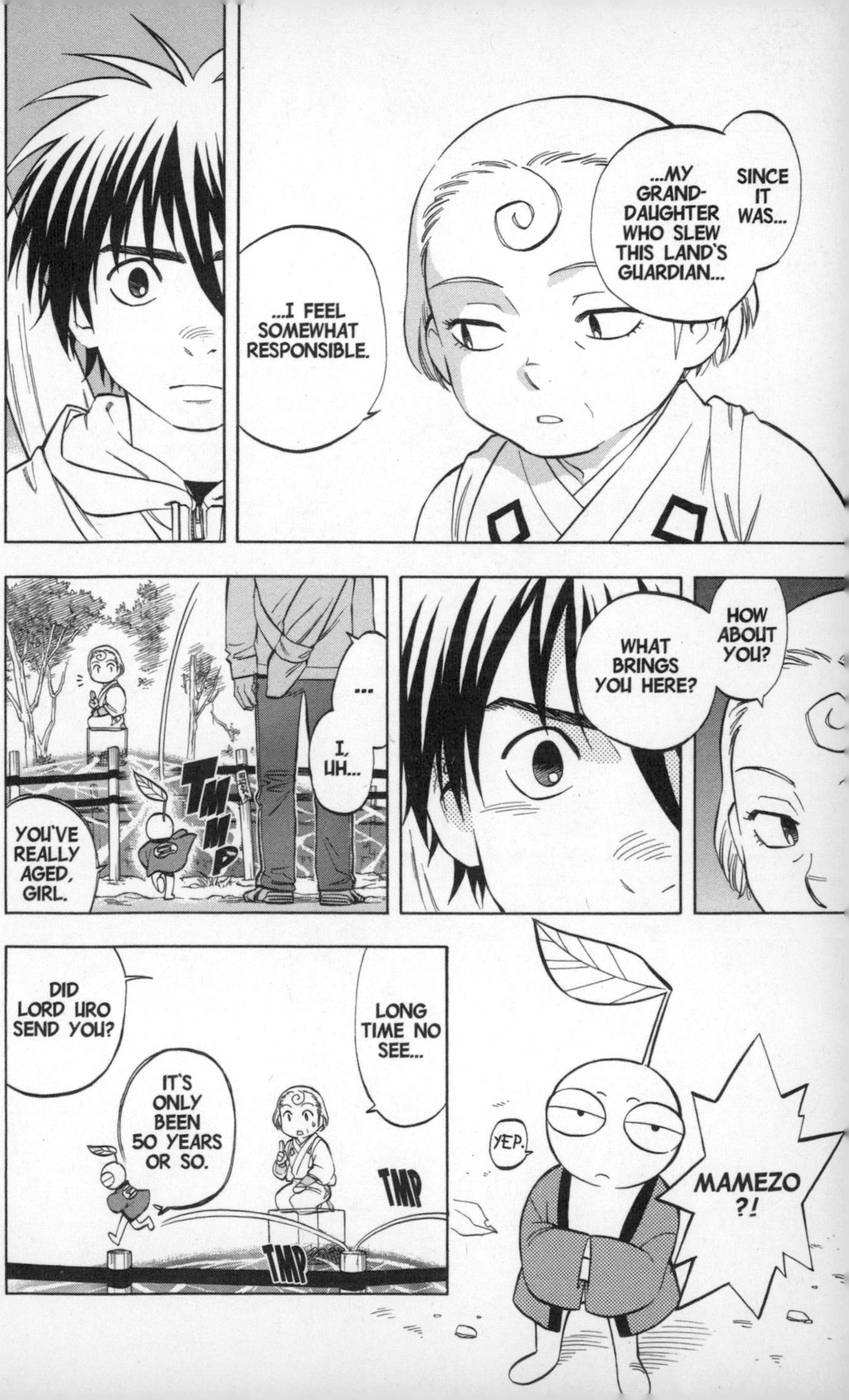
SINCE IT WAS...
...MY GRANDDAUGHTER WHO SLEW THIS LAND'S GUARDIAN...
...I FEEL SOMEWHAT RESPONSIBLE.
HOW ABOUT YOU?
WHAT BRINGS YOU HERE?
...
I, UH...
TMMP
YOU'VE REALLY AGED, GIRL.
MAMEZO ?!
YEP.
LONG TIME NO SEE...
DID LORD URO SEND YOU?
IT'S ONLY BEEN 50 YEARS OR SO.
TMP
TMP

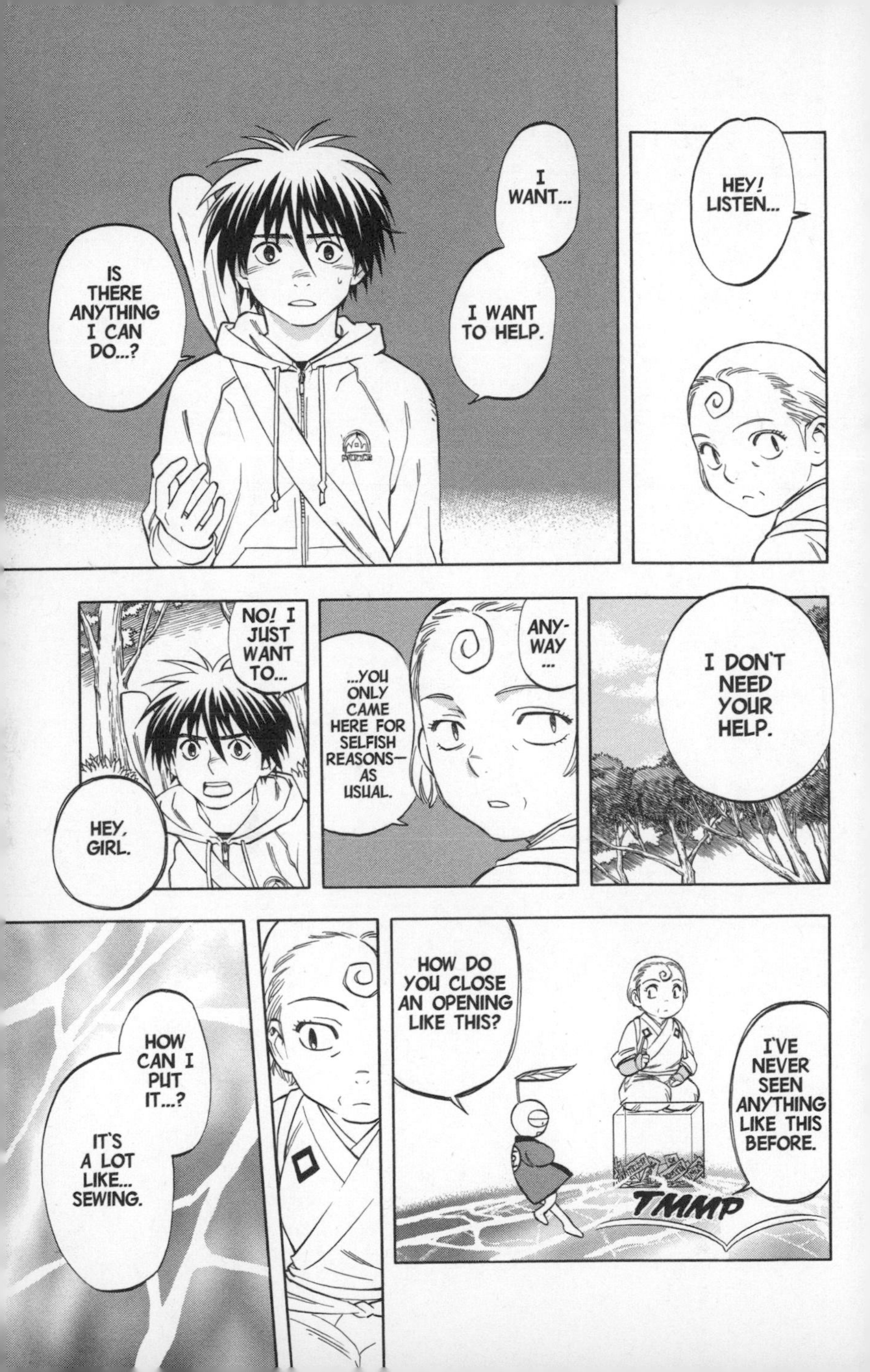
HEY! LISTEN...
I WANT...
I WANT TO HELP.
IS THERE ANYTHING I CAN DO...?
I DON'T NEED YOUR HELP.
ANY-WAY ...
...YOU ONLY CAME HERE FOR SELFISH REASONS—AS USUAL.
NO! I JUST WANT TO...
HEY, GIRL.
I'VE NEVER SEEN ANYTHING LIKE THIS BEFORE.
TMMP
HOW DO YOU CLOSE AN OPENING LIKE THIS?
HOW CAN I PUT IT...?
IT'S A LOT LIKE... SEWING.

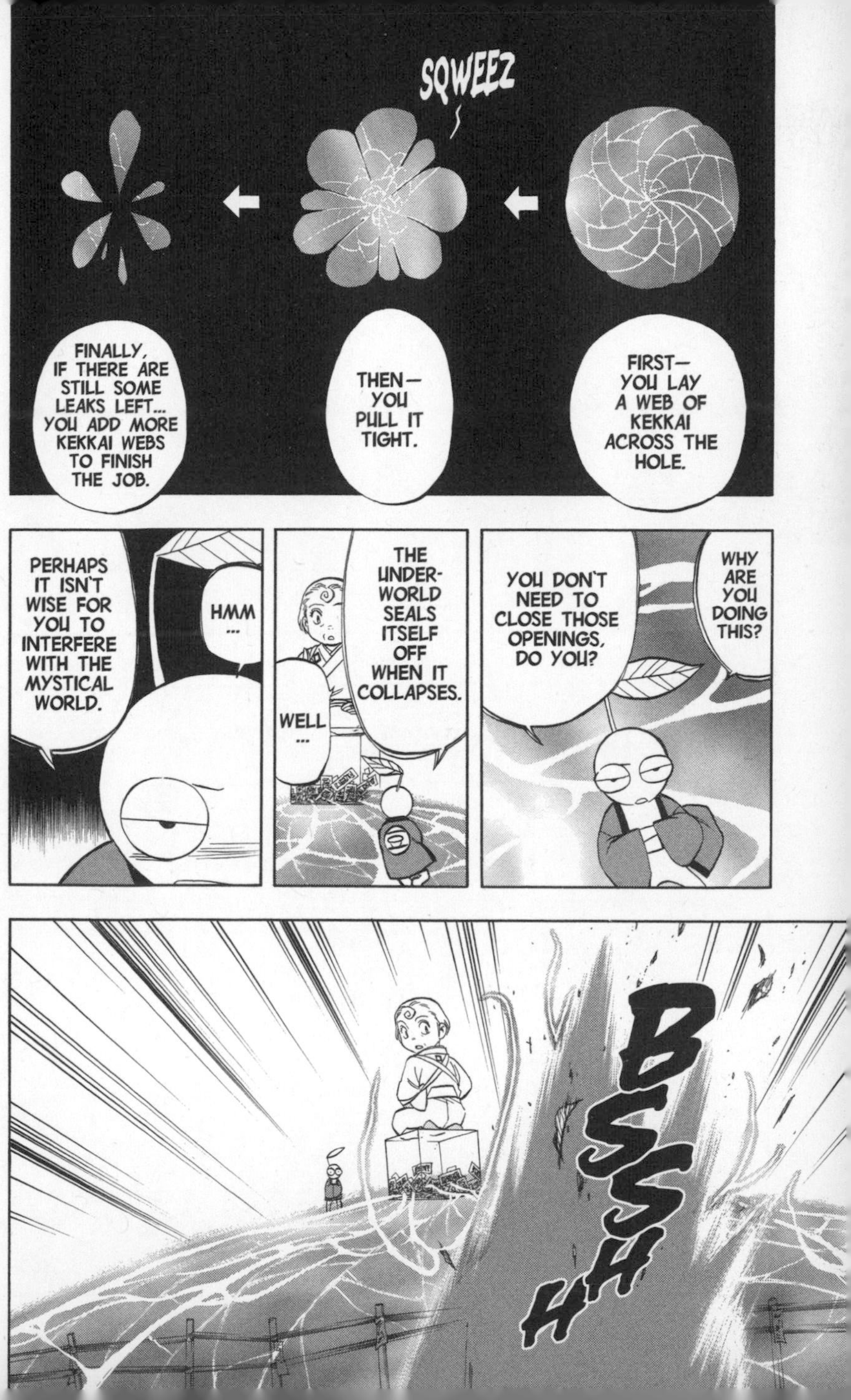
FIRST— YOU LAY A WEB OF KEKKAI ACROSS THE HOLE.
THEN— YOU PULL IT TIGHT.
SQWEEZ
FINALLY, IF THERE ARE STILL SOME LEAKS LEFT... YOU ADD MORE KEKKAI WEBS TO FINISH THE JOB.
WHY ARE YOU DOING THIS?
YOU DON'T NEED TO CLOSE THOSE OPENINGS, DO YOU?
THE UNDER-WORLD SEALS ITSELF OFF WHEN IT COLLAPSES.
WELL ...
HMM ...
PERHAPS IT ISN'T WISE FOR YOU TO INTERFERE WITH THE MYSTICAL WORLD.
BSSHH

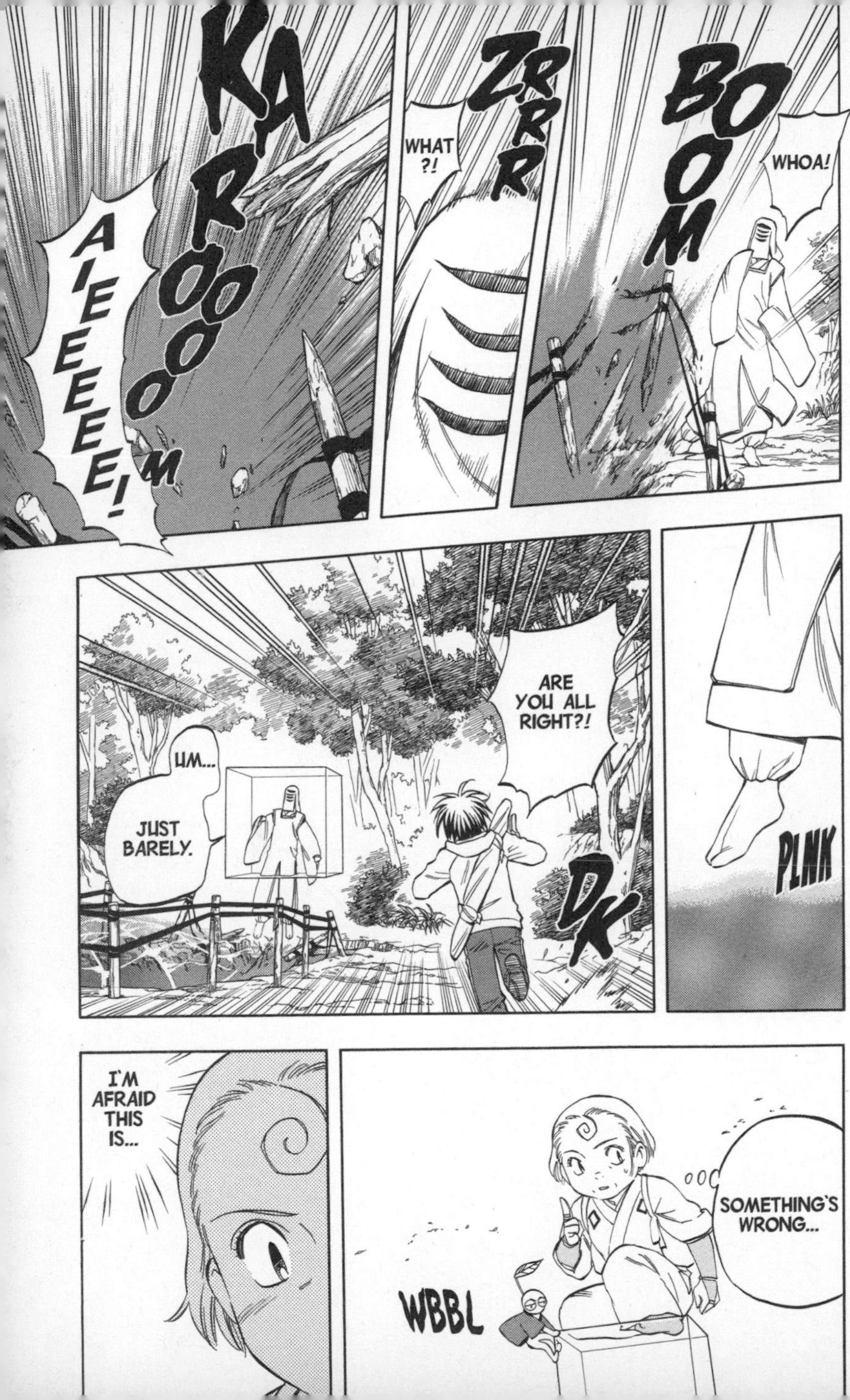
BOOM
WHOA!
ZRRR
WHAT?!
KAROOOOM
AIEEEEEEE!
PLNK
DK
ARE YOU ALL RIGHT?!
UM...
JUST BARELY.
SOMETHING'S WRONG...
WBBL
I'M AFRAID THIS IS...

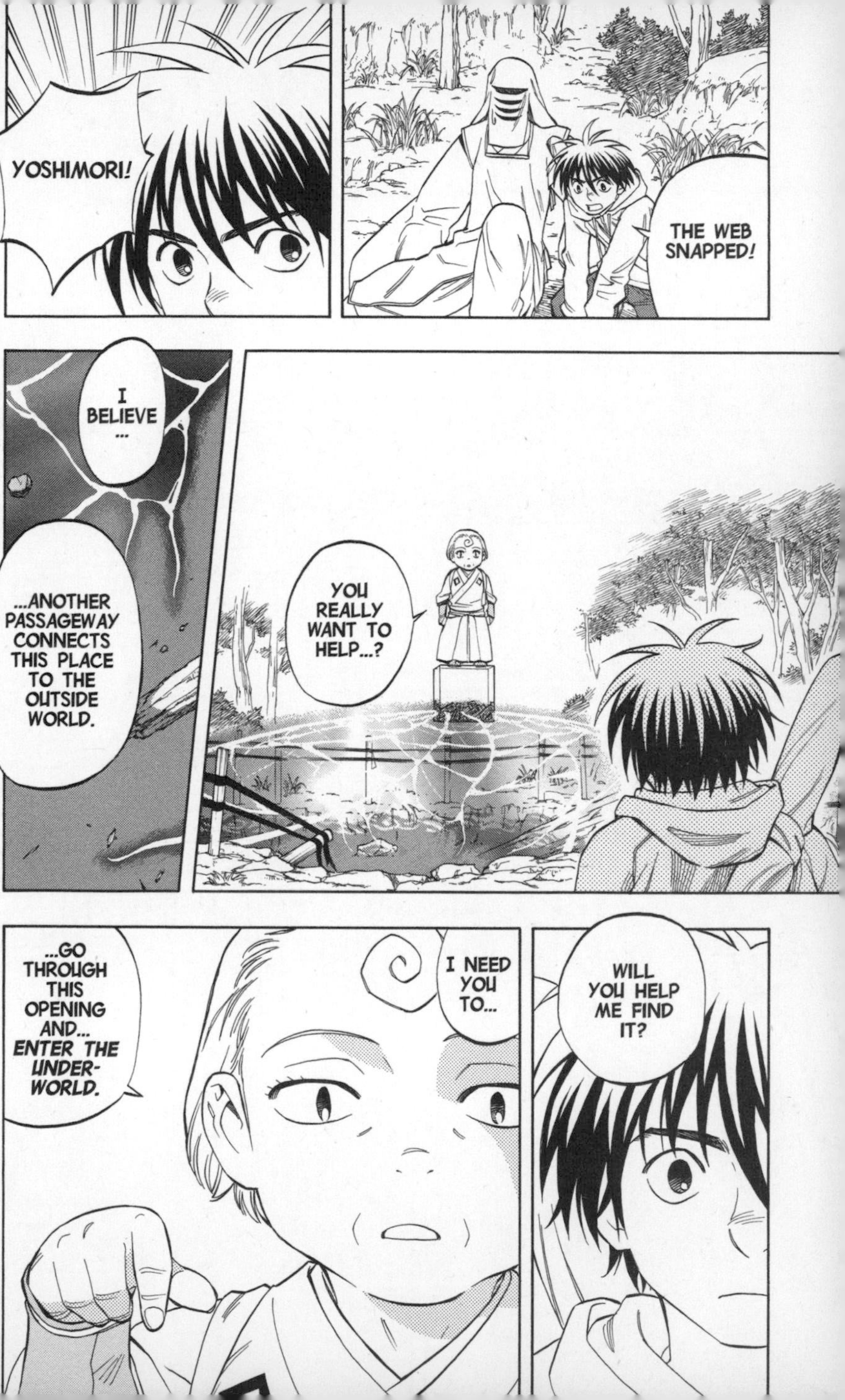
THE WEB SNAPPED!
YOSHIMORI!
YOU REALLY WANT TO HELP...?
I BELIEVE ...
...ANOTHER PASSAGEWAY CONNECTS THIS PLACE TO THE OUTSIDE WORLD.
WILL YOU HELP ME FIND IT?
I NEED YOU TO...
...GO THROUGH THIS OPENING AND... ENTER THE UNDER-WORLD.

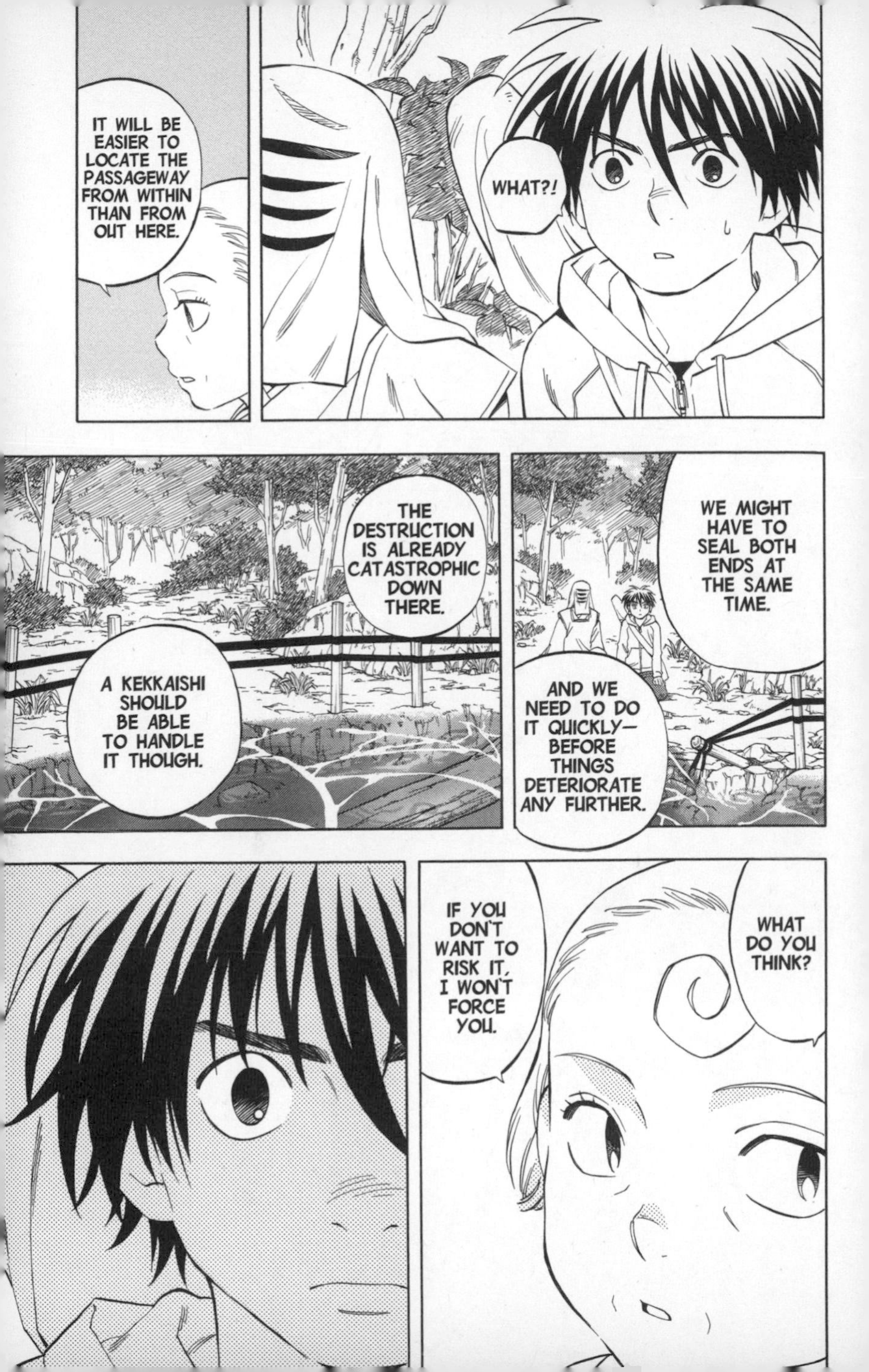
WHAT?!
IT WILL BE EASIER TO LOCATE THE PASSAGEWAY FROM WITHIN THAN FROM OUT HERE.
WE MIGHT HAVE TO SEAL BOTH ENDS AT THE SAME TIME.
AND WE NEED TO DO IT QUICKLY—BEFORE THINGS DETERIORATE ANY FURTHER.
THE DESTRUCTION IS ALREADY CATASTROPHIC DOWN THERE.
A KEKKAISHI SHOULD BE ABLE TO HANDLE IT THOUGH.
WHAT DO YOU THINK?
IF YOU DON'T WANT TO RISK IT, I WON'T FORCE YOU.

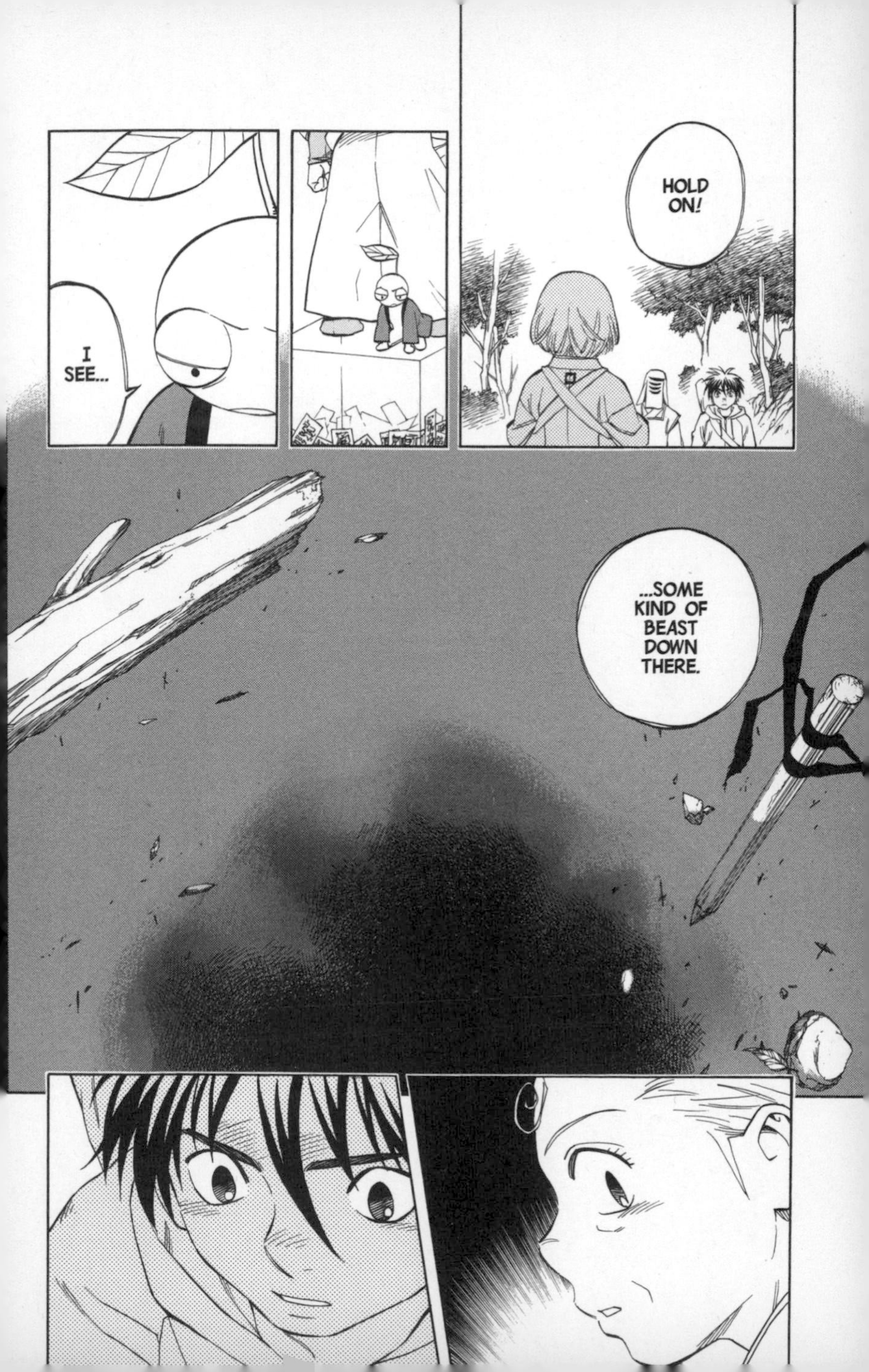
HOLD ON!
I SEE...
...SOME KIND OF BEAST DOWN THERE.

Chapter 201: Requiem

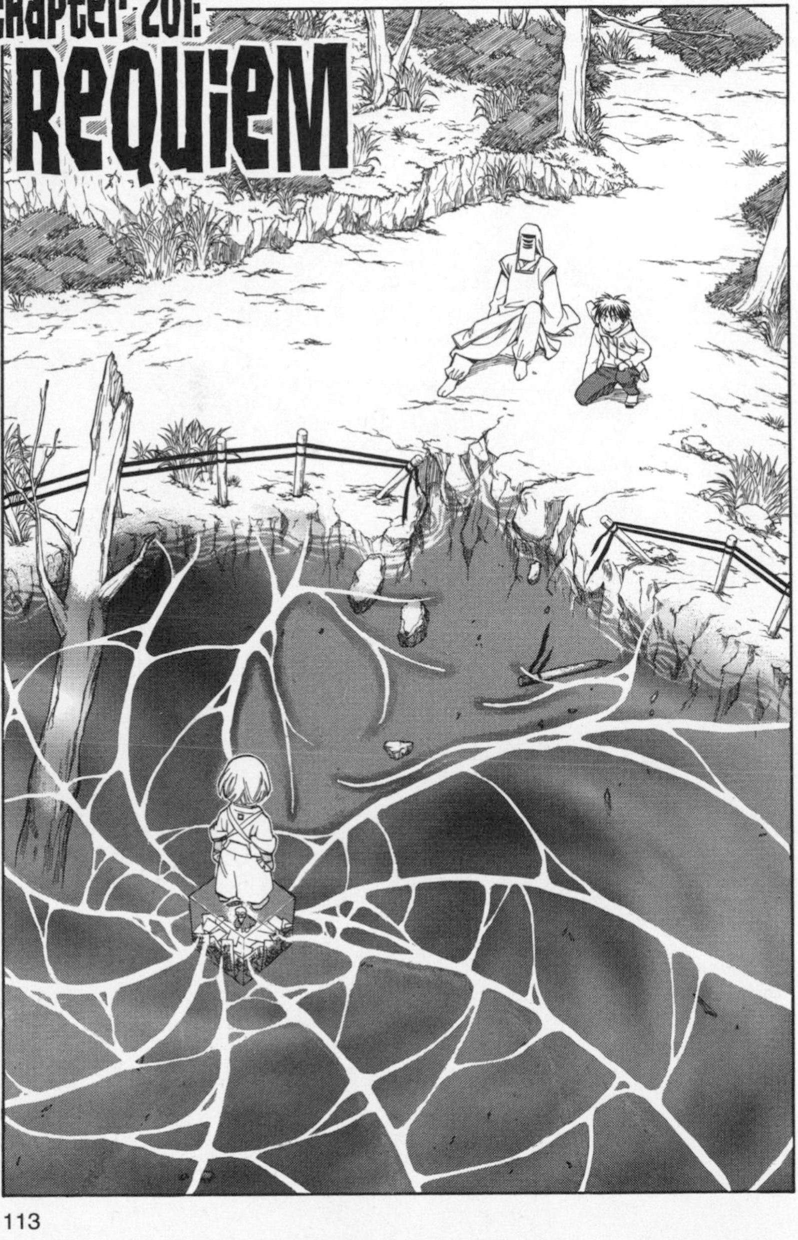

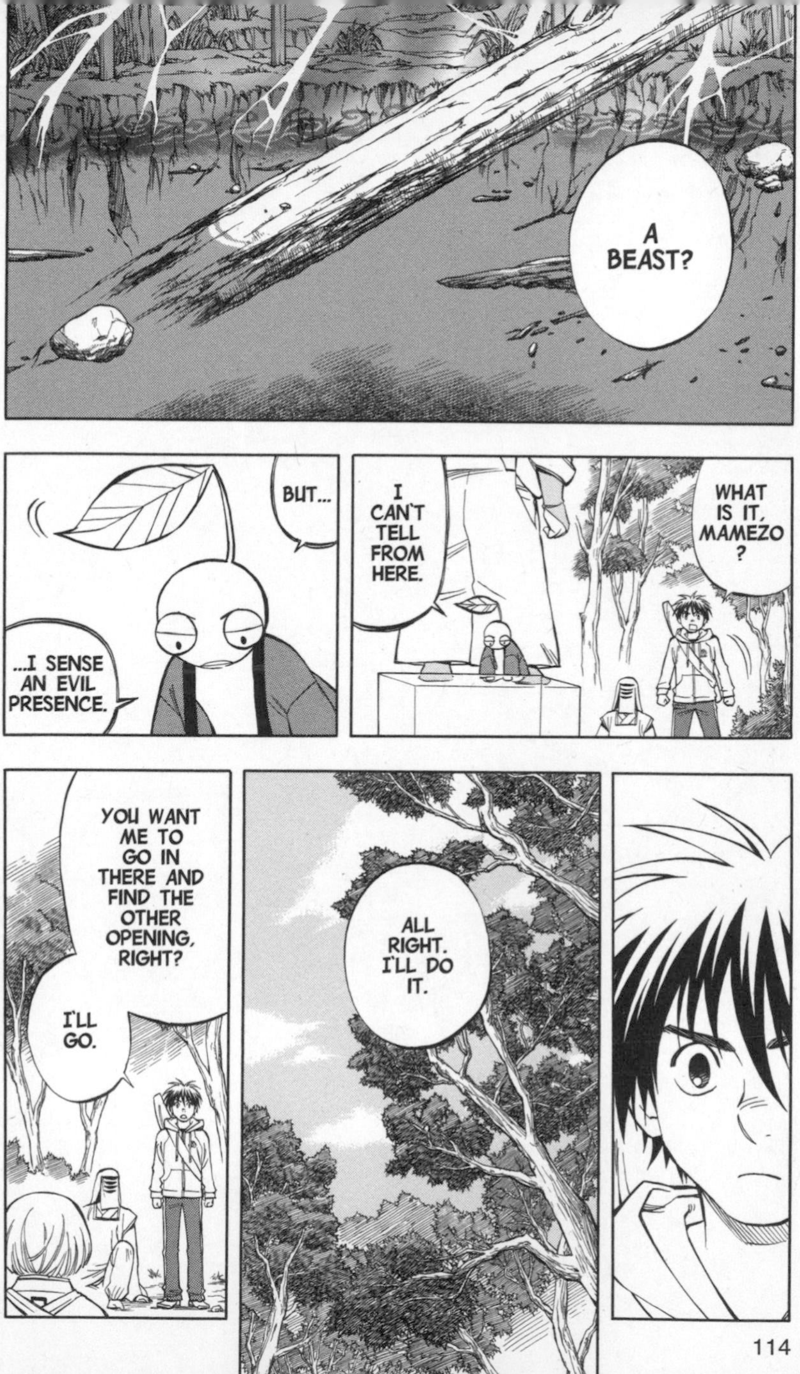
A BEAST?
WHAT IS IT, MAMEZO?
I CAN'T TELL FROM HERE.
BUT...
...I SENSE AN EVIL PRESENCE.
ALL RIGHT. I'LL DO IT.
YOU WANT ME TO GO IN THERE AND FIND THE OTHER OPENING, RIGHT?
I'LL GO.

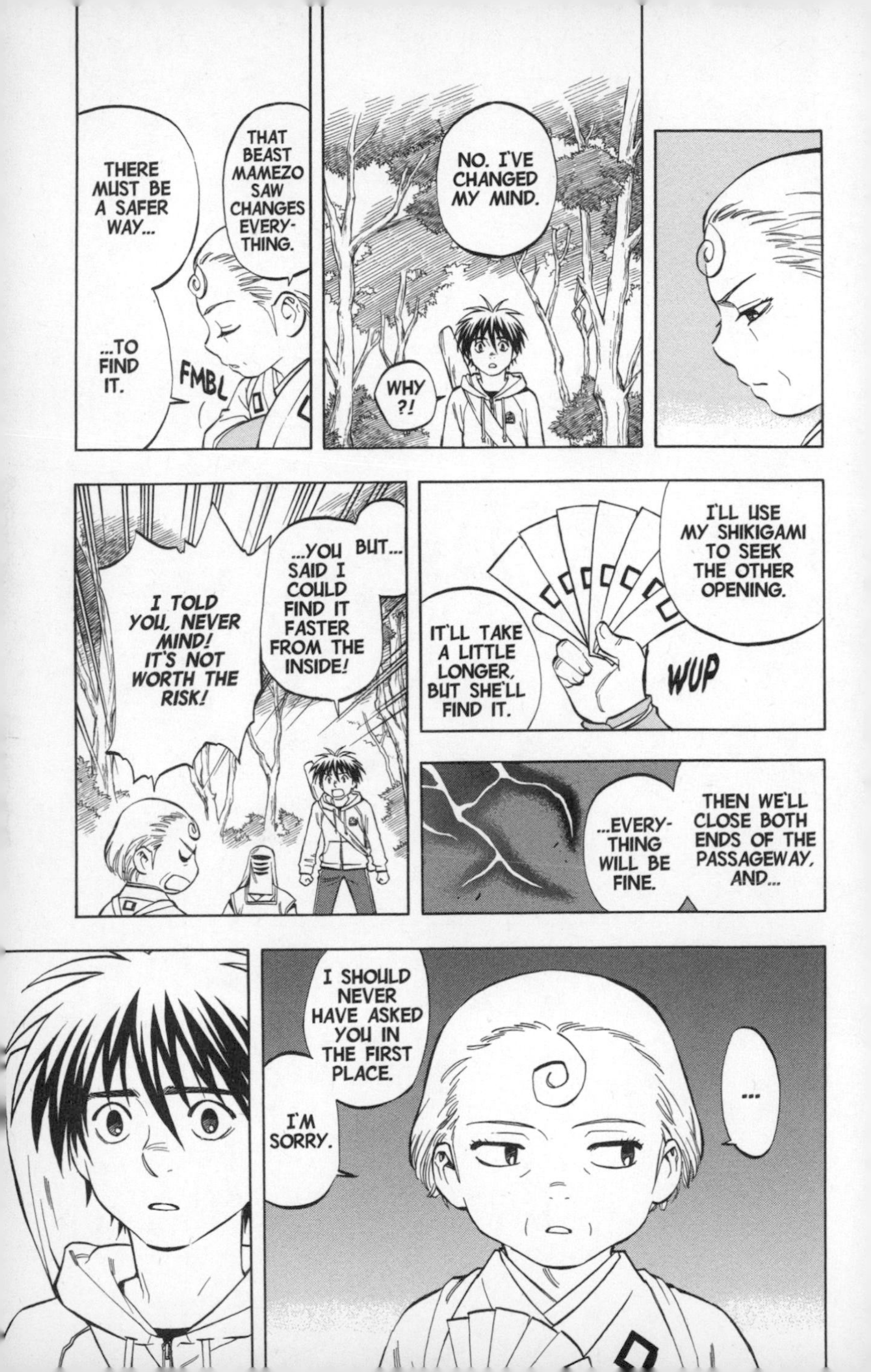
NO. I'VE CHANGED MY MIND.
WHY ?!
THAT BEAST MAMEZO SAW CHANGES EVERY-THING.
THERE MUST BE A SAFER WAY...
...TO FIND IT.
FMBL
I'LL USE MY SHIKIGAMI TO SEEK THE OTHER OPENING.
IT'LL TAKE A LITTLE LONGER, BUT SHE'LL FIND IT.
WUP
THEN WE'LL CLOSE BOTH ENDS OF THE PASSAGEWAY, AND...
...EVERY-THING WILL BE FINE.
BUT...
...YOU SAID I COULD FIND IT FASTER FROM THE INSIDE!
I TOLD YOU, NEVER MIND! IT'S NOT WORTH THE RISK!
...
I SHOULD NEVER HAVE ASKED YOU IN THE FIRST PLACE.
I'M SORRY.

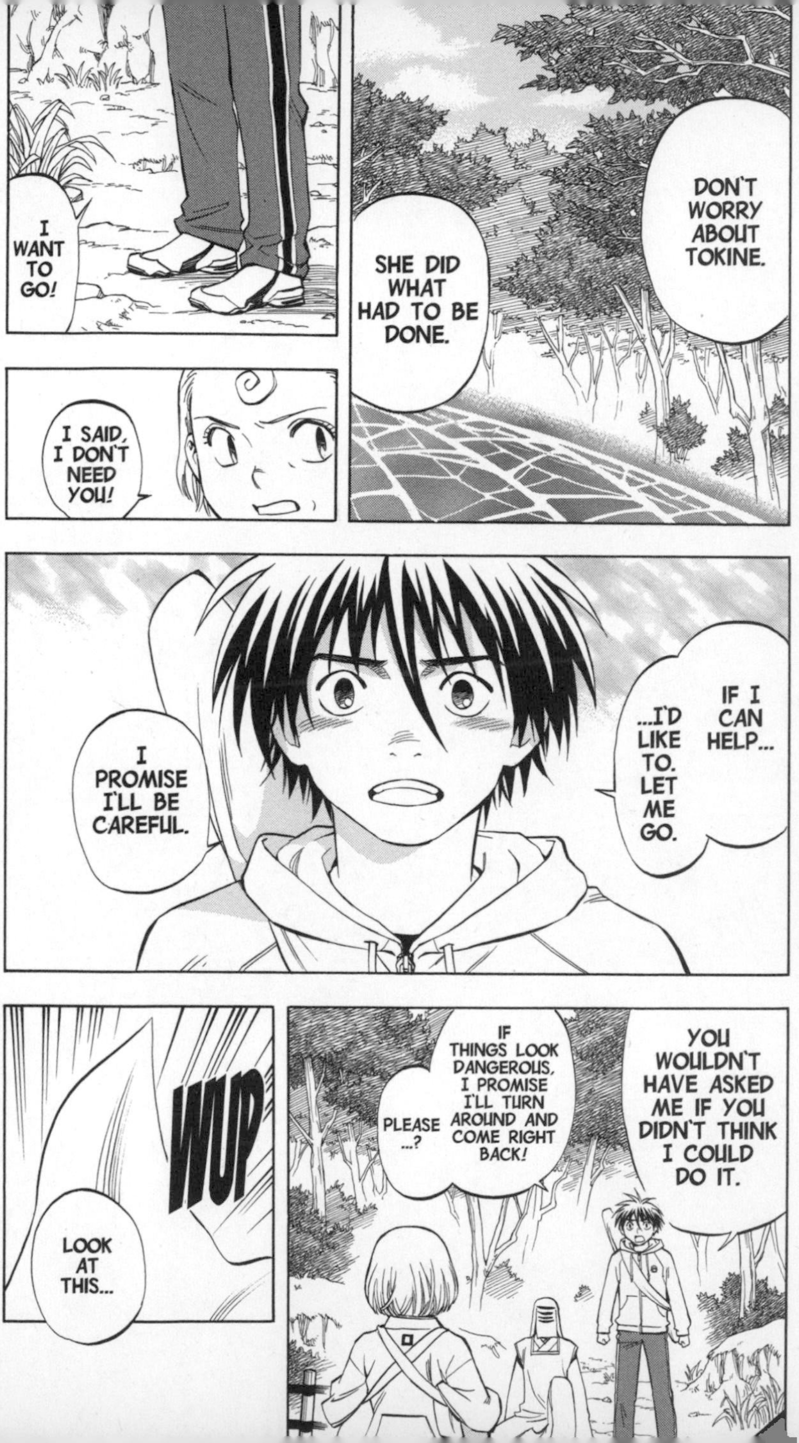
DON'T WORRY ABOUT TOKINE.
SHE DID WHAT HAD TO BE DONE.
I WANT TO GO!
I SAID, I DON'T NEED YOU!
IF I CAN HELP...
...I'D LIKE TO. LET ME GO.
I PROMISE I'LL BE CAREFUL.
YOU WOULDN'T HAVE ASKED ME IF YOU DIDN'T THINK I COULD DO IT.
IF THINGS LOOK DANGEROUS, I PROMISE I'LL TURN AROUND AND COME RIGHT BACK!
PLEASE ...?
WUP
LOOK AT THIS...

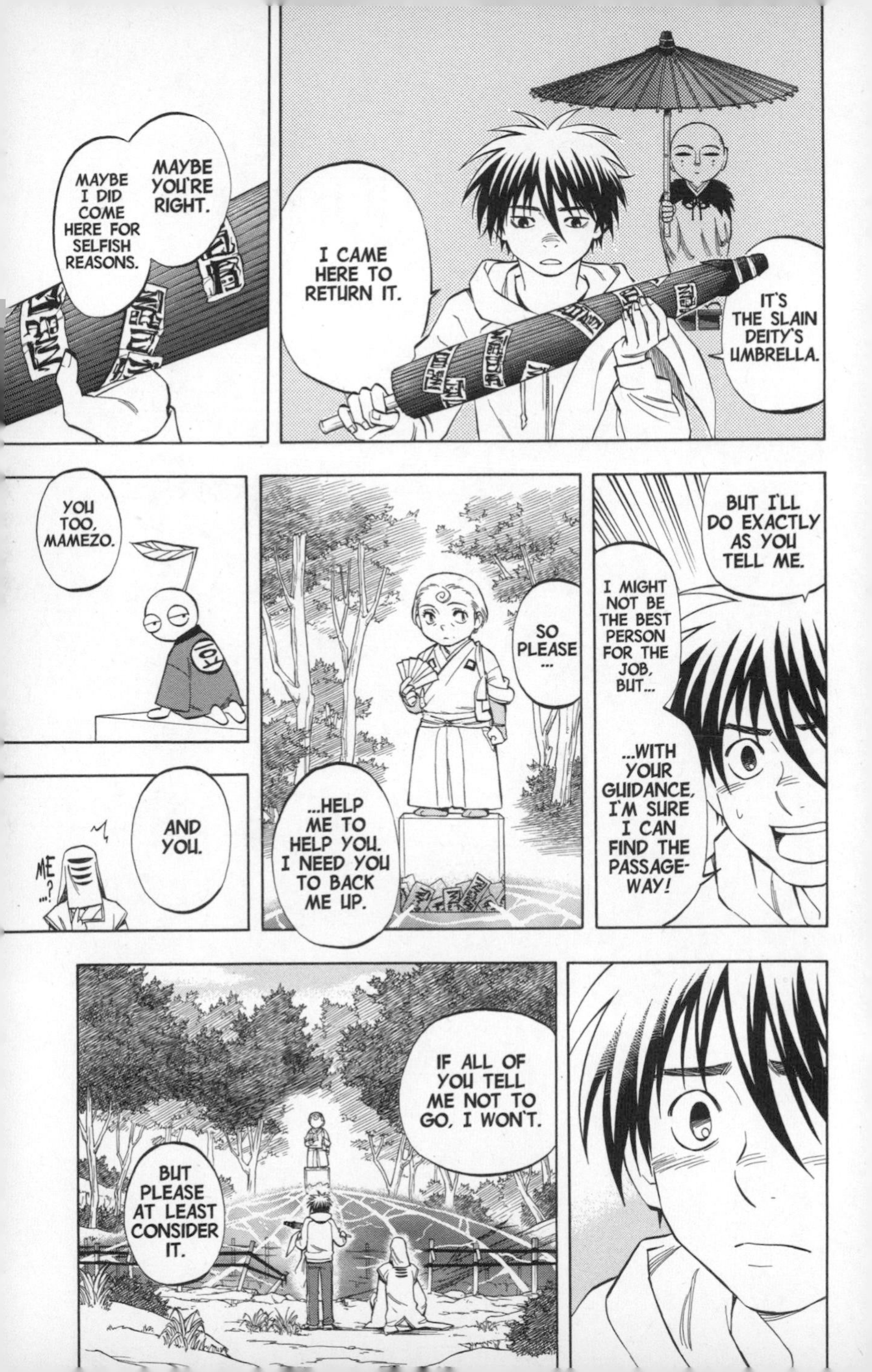
IT'S THE SLAIN DEITY'S UMBRELLA.
I CAME HERE TO RETURN IT.
MAYBE YOU'RE RIGHT.
MAYBE I DID COME HERE FOR SELFISH REASONS.
BUT I'LL DO EXACTLY AS YOU TELL ME.
I MIGHT NOT BE THE BEST PERSON FOR THE JOB, BUT...
...WITH YOUR GUIDANCE, I'M SURE I CAN FIND THE PASSAGE-WAY!
SO PLEASE ...
...HELP ME TO HELP YOU. I NEED YOU TO BACK ME UP.
YOU TOO, MAMEZO.
AND YOU.
ME ...?
IF ALL OF YOU TELL ME NOT TO GO, I WON'T.
BUT PLEASE AT LEAST CONSIDER IT.

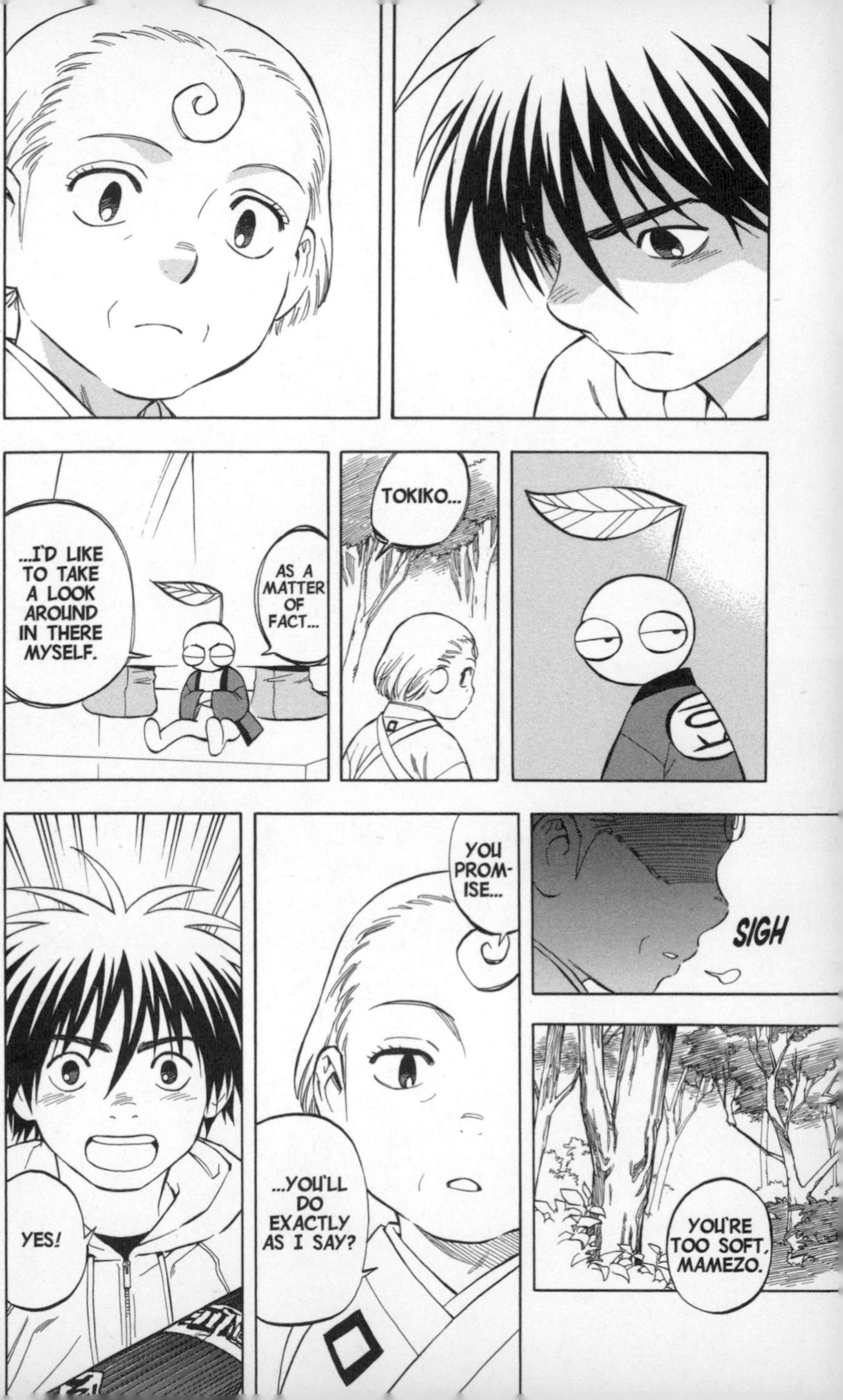
TOKIKO...
AS A MATTER OF FACT...
...I'D LIKE TO TAKE A LOOK AROUND IN THERE MYSELF.
SIGH
YOU'RE TOO SOFT, MAMEZO.
YOU PROMISE...
...YOU'LL DO EXACTLY AS I SAY?
YES!

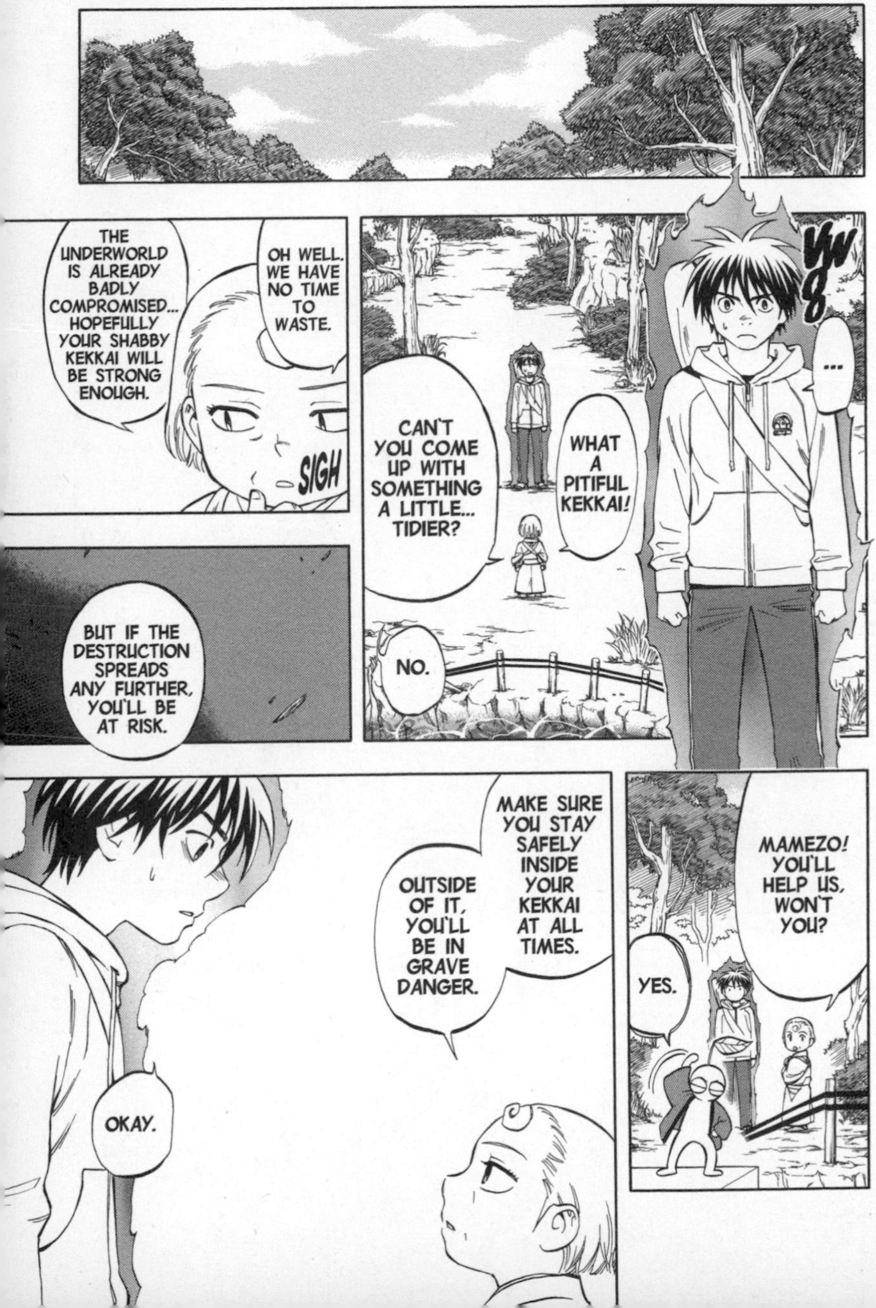
...
WHAT A PITIFUL KEKKAI!
CAN'T YOU COME UP WITH SOMETHING A LITTLE... TIDIER?
NO.
OH WELL. WE HAVE NO TIME TO WASTE.
THE UNDERWORLD IS ALREADY BADLY COMPROMISED... HOPEFULLY YOUR SHABBY KEKKAI WILL BE STRONG ENOUGH.
SIGH
BUT IF THE DESTRUCTION SPREADS ANY FURTHER, YOU'LL BE AT RISK.
MAMEZO! YOU'LL HELP US, WON'T YOU?
YES.
MAKE SURE YOU STAY SAFELY INSIDE YOUR KEKKAI AT ALL TIMES.
OUTSIDE OF IT, YOU'LL BE IN GRAVE DANGER.
OKAY.

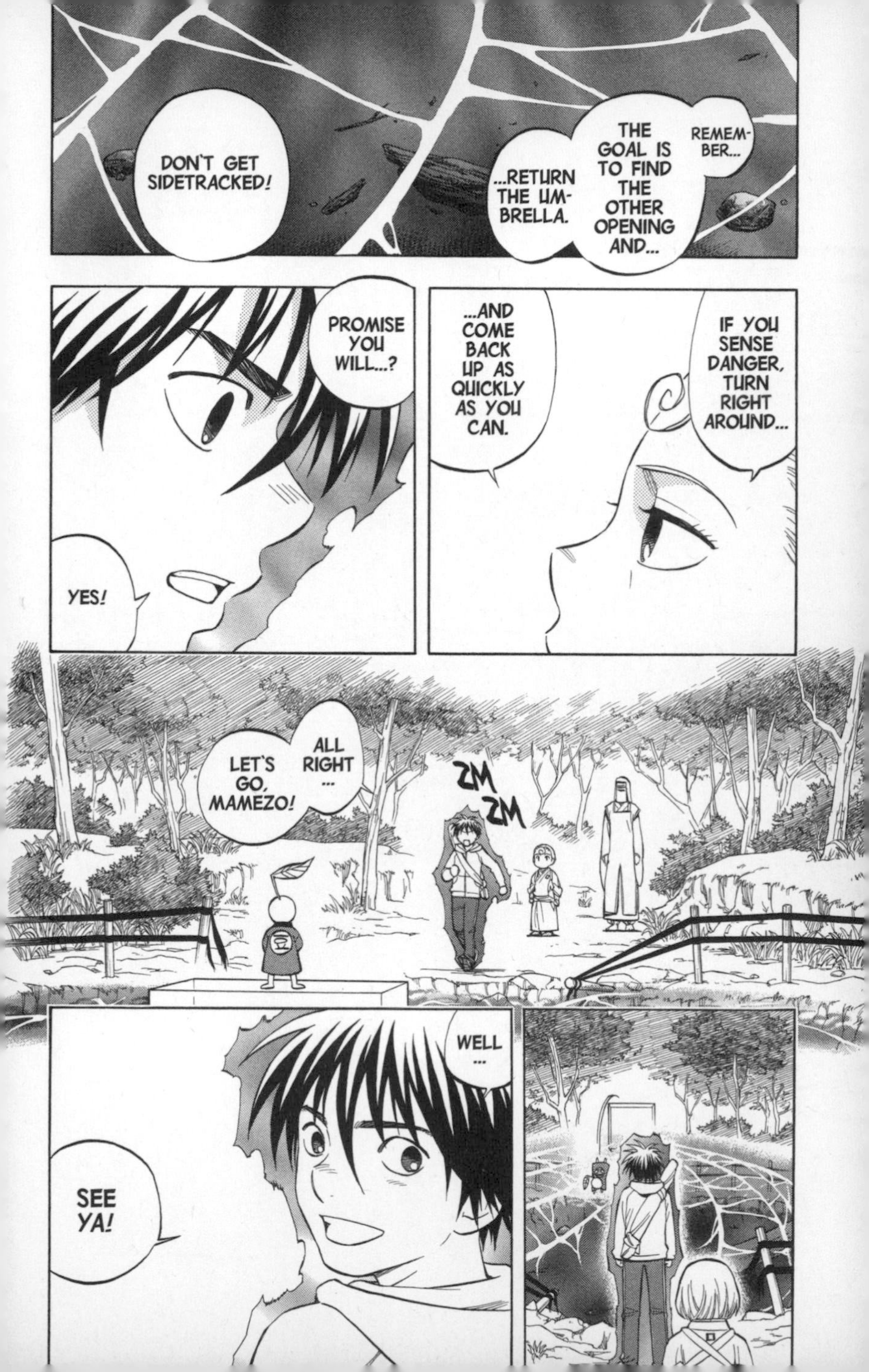
REMEM-
BER...
THE GOAL IS TO FIND THE OTHER OPENING AND...
...RETURN THE UM-
BRELLA.
DON'T GET SIDETRACKED!
IF YOU SENSE DANGER, TURN RIGHT AROUND...
...AND COME BACK UP AS QUICKLY AS YOU CAN.
PROMISE YOU WILL...?
YES!
ZM ZM
ALL RIGHT ... LET'S GO, MAMEZO!
WELL ...
SEE YA!

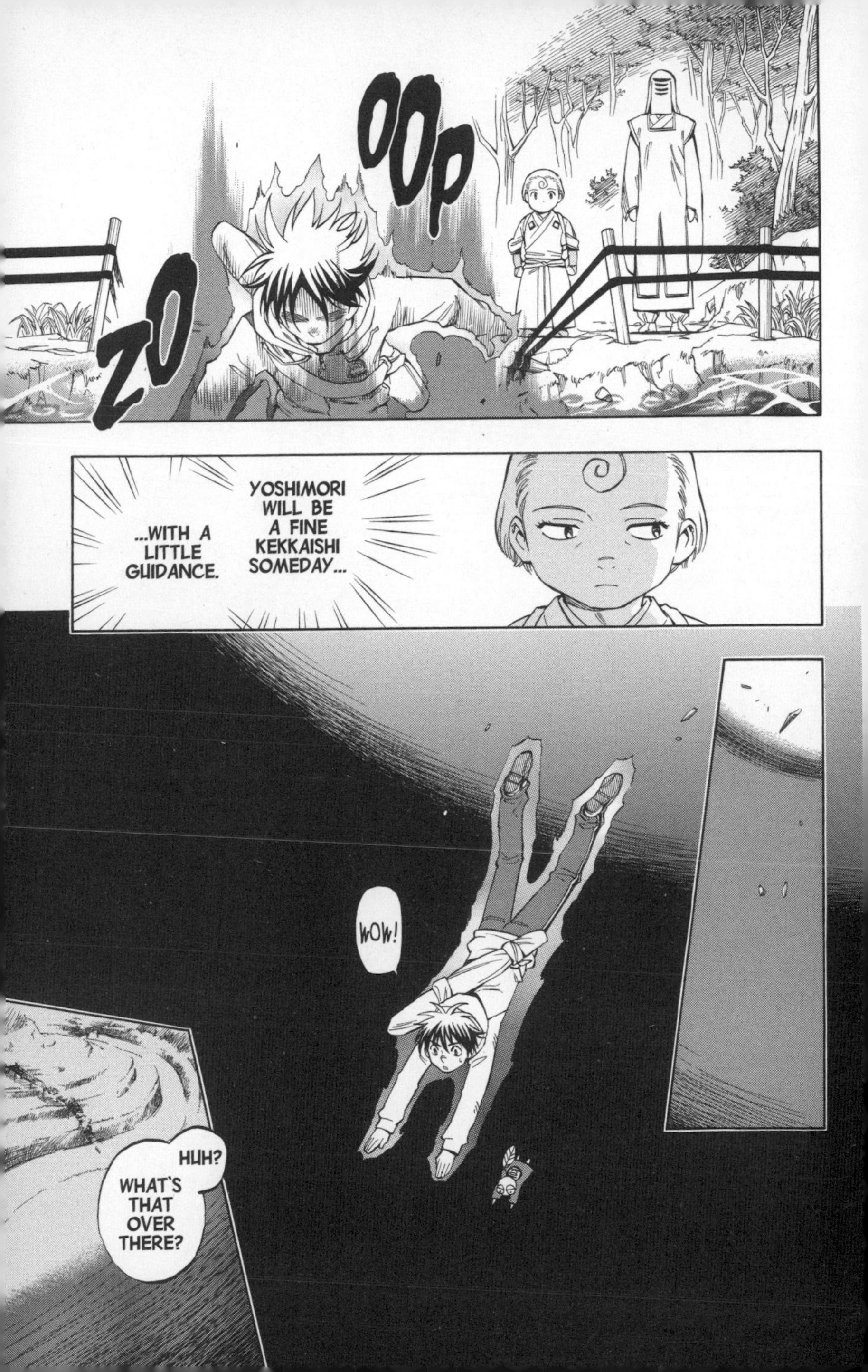
OOP
ZO
YOSHIMORI WILL BE A FINE KEKKAISHI SOMEDAY...
...WITH A LITTLE GUIDANCE.
WOW!
HUH? WHAT'S THAT OVER THERE?

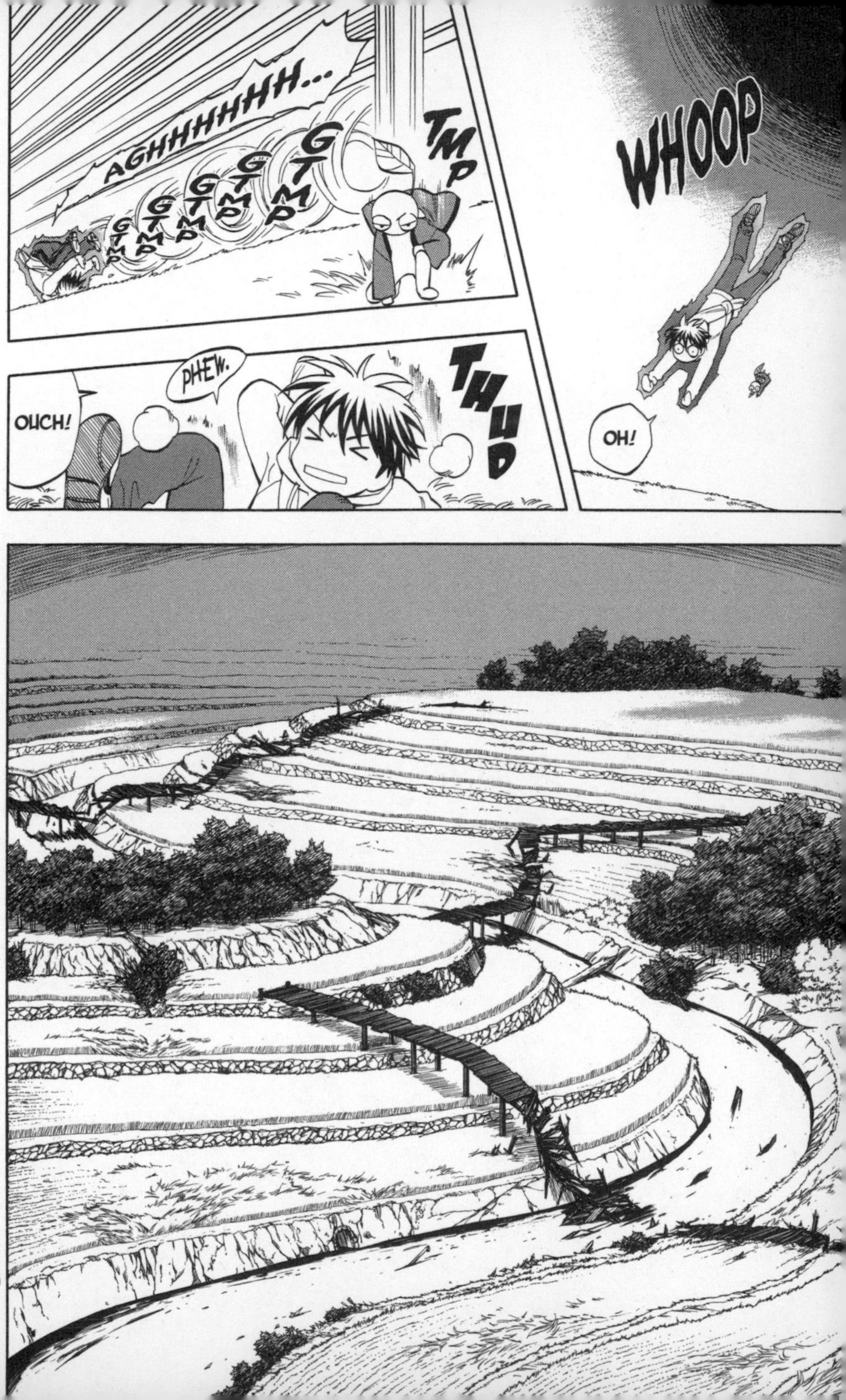
WHOOP
OH!
TMP
GTMP GTMP GTMP GTMP GTMP
AGHHHHHHH...
THUD
PHEW.
OUCH!

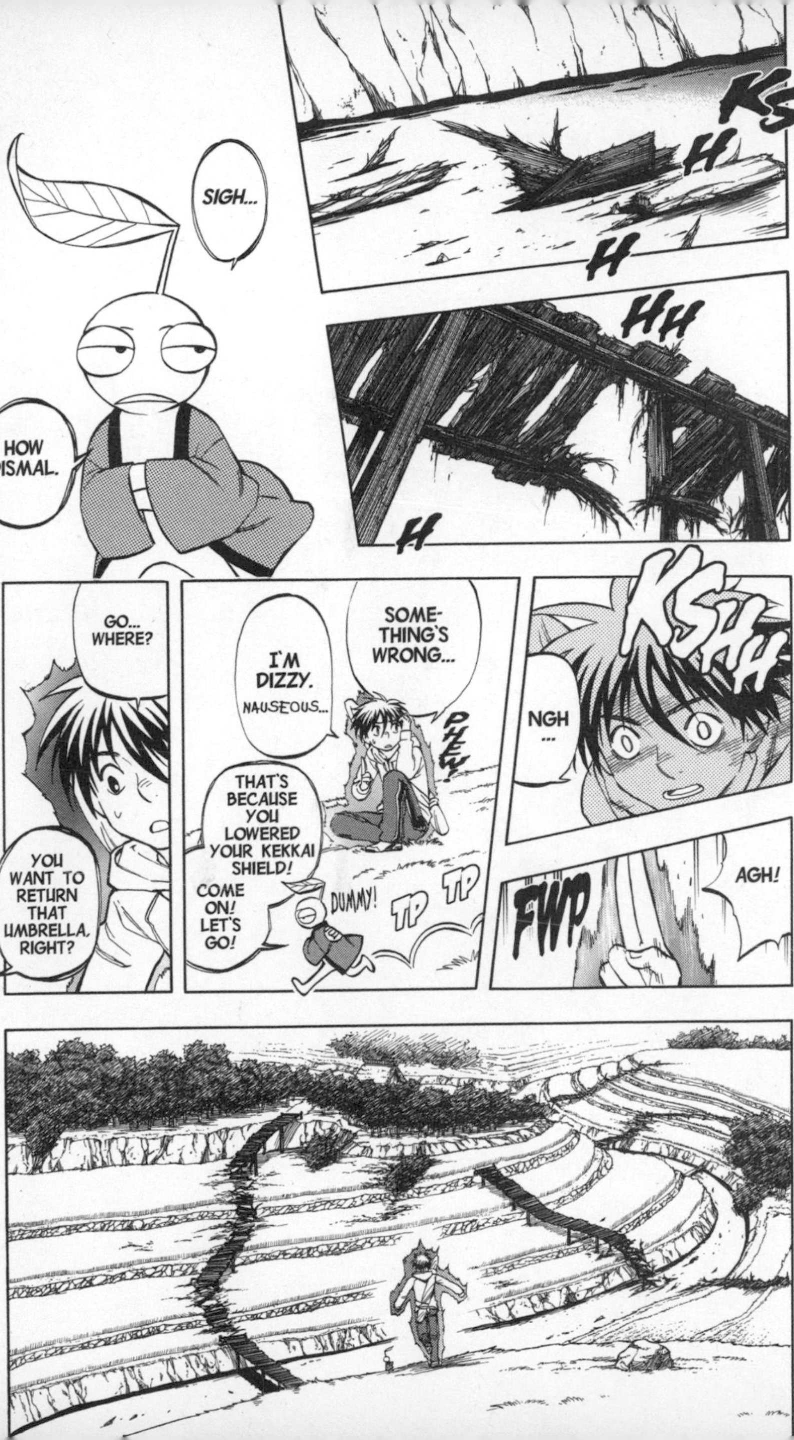
KS
H
H
SIGH...
HH
H
HOW DISMAL.
KSHH
NGH...
AGH!
FWP
SOME-THING'S WRONG...
I'M DIZZY. NAUSEOUS...
PHEW!
THAT'S BECAUSE YOU LOWERED YOUR KEKKAI SHIELD!
DUMMY!
COME ON! LET'S GO!
TP TP
GO... WHERE?
YOU WANT TO RETURN THAT UMBRELLA, RIGHT?

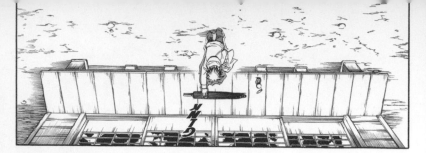

THIS IS WHERE THE GUARDIAN DEITY LIVED.

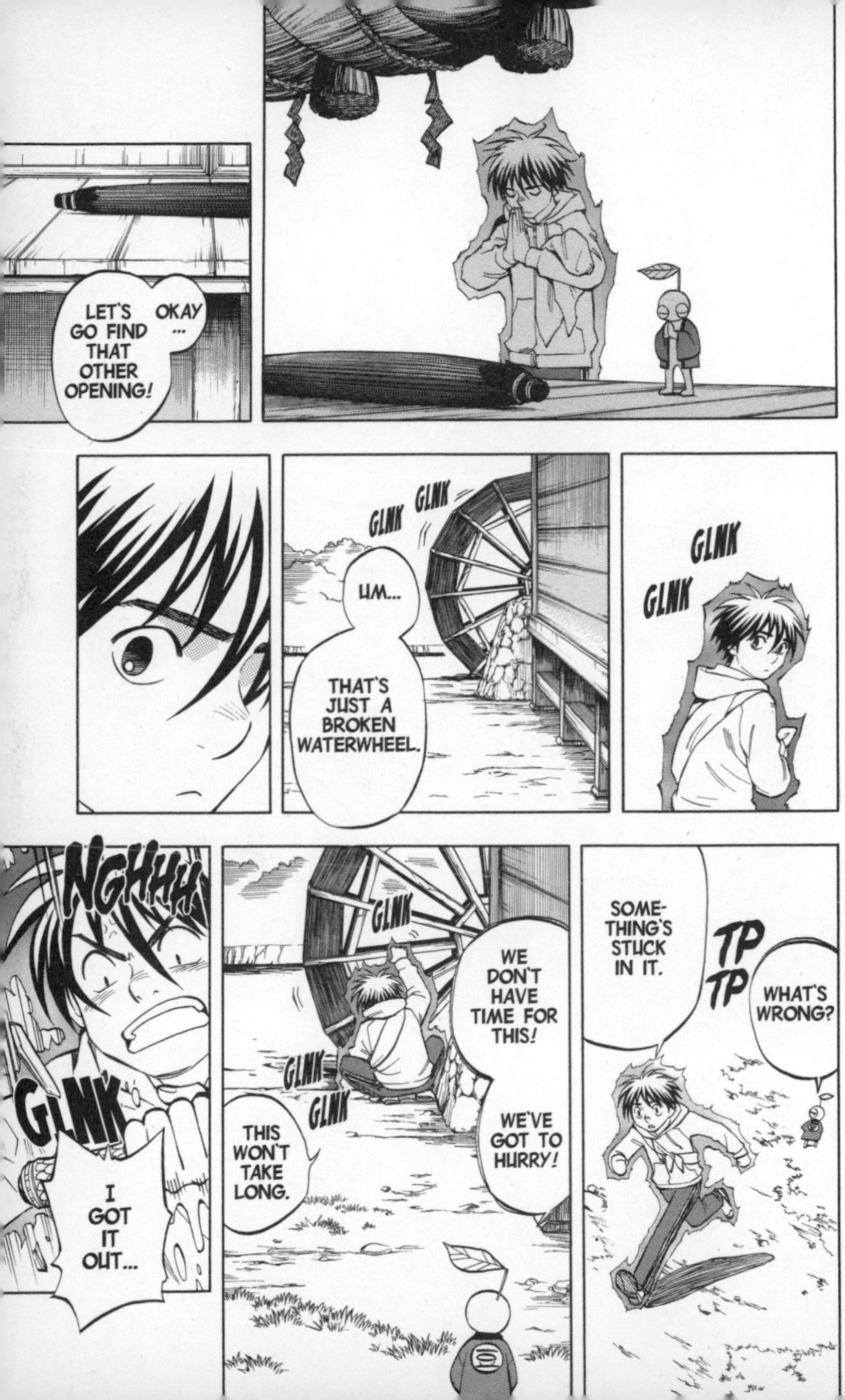
LET'S GO FIND THAT OTHER OPENING!
OKAY ...
GLNK
GLNK
GLNK
GLNK
UM...
THAT'S JUST A BROKEN WATERWHEEL.
TP
TP
WHAT'S WRONG?
SOME-THING'S STUCK IN IT.
WE DON'T HAVE TIME FOR THIS!
WE'VE GOT TO HURRY!
GLNK
GLNK
GLNK
THIS WON'T TAKE LONG.
NGHHH
GLNK
I GOT IT OUT...

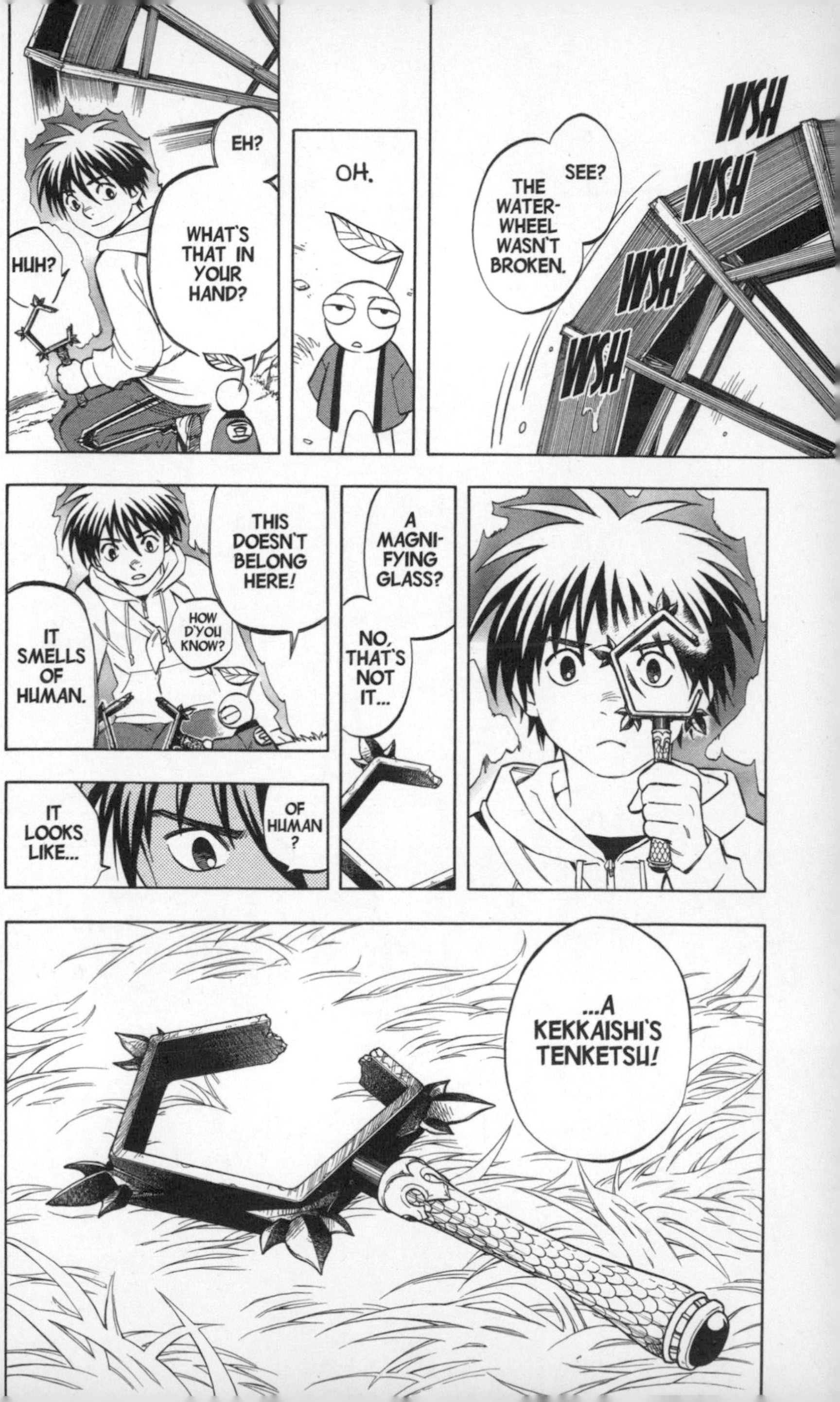
SEE?
THE WATER-WHEEL WASN'T BROKEN.
WSH
WSH
WSH
WSH
OH.
EH?
WHAT'S THAT IN YOUR HAND?
HUH?
A MAGNIFYING GLASS?
NO, THAT'S NOT IT...
THIS DOESN'T BELONG HERE!
HOW D'YOU KNOW?
IT SMELLS OF HUMAN.
OF HUMAN?
IT LOOKS LIKE...
...A KEKKAISHI'S TENKETSU!

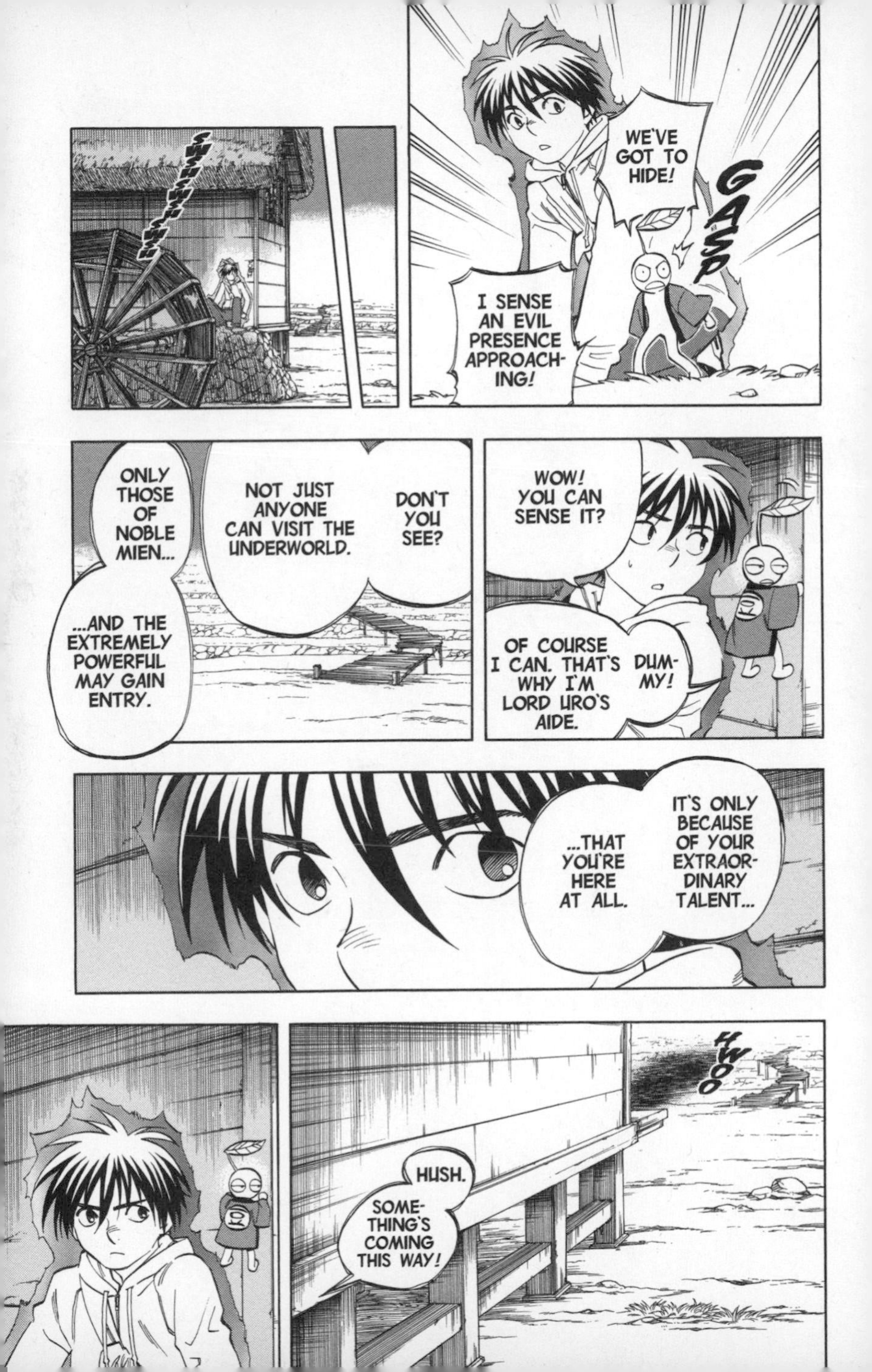
WE'VE GOT TO HIDE!
GASP
I SENSE AN EVIL PRESENCE APPROACH-ING!
WOW! YOU CAN SENSE IT?
OF COURSE I CAN. THAT'S WHY I'M LORD URO'S AIDE.
DUM-MY!
DON'T YOU SEE?
NOT JUST ANYONE CAN VISIT THE UNDERWORLD.
ONLY THOSE OF NOBLE MIEN...
...AND THE EXTREMELY POWERFUL MAY GAIN ENTRY.
IT'S ONLY BECAUSE OF YOUR EXTRAOR-DINARY TALENT...
...THAT YOU'RE HERE AT ALL.
HWOO
HUSH.
SOME-THING'S COMING THIS WAY!

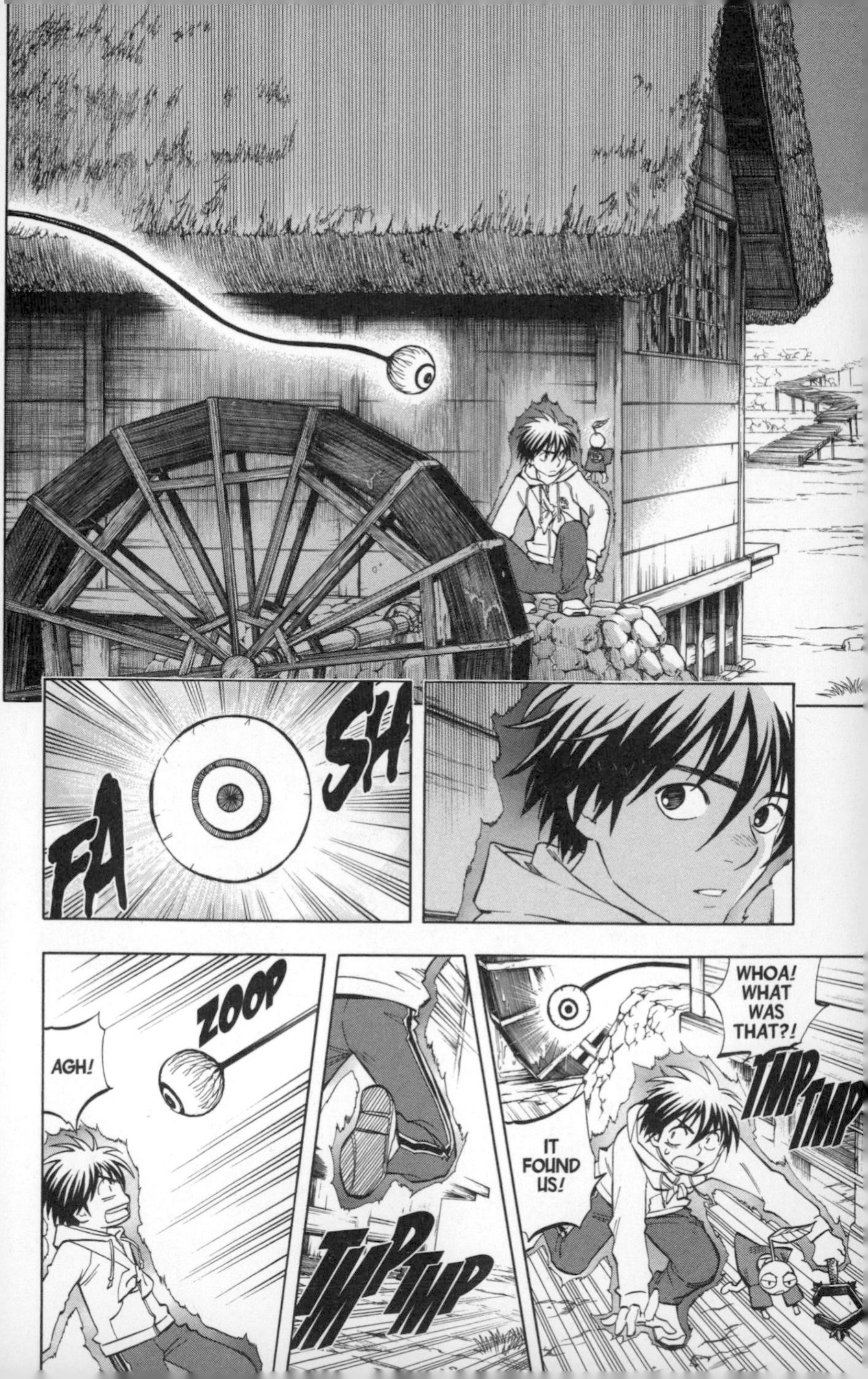
FA
SH
WHOA! WHAT WAS THAT?!
TMP TMP
IT FOUND US!
TMP TMP
ZOOP
AGH!

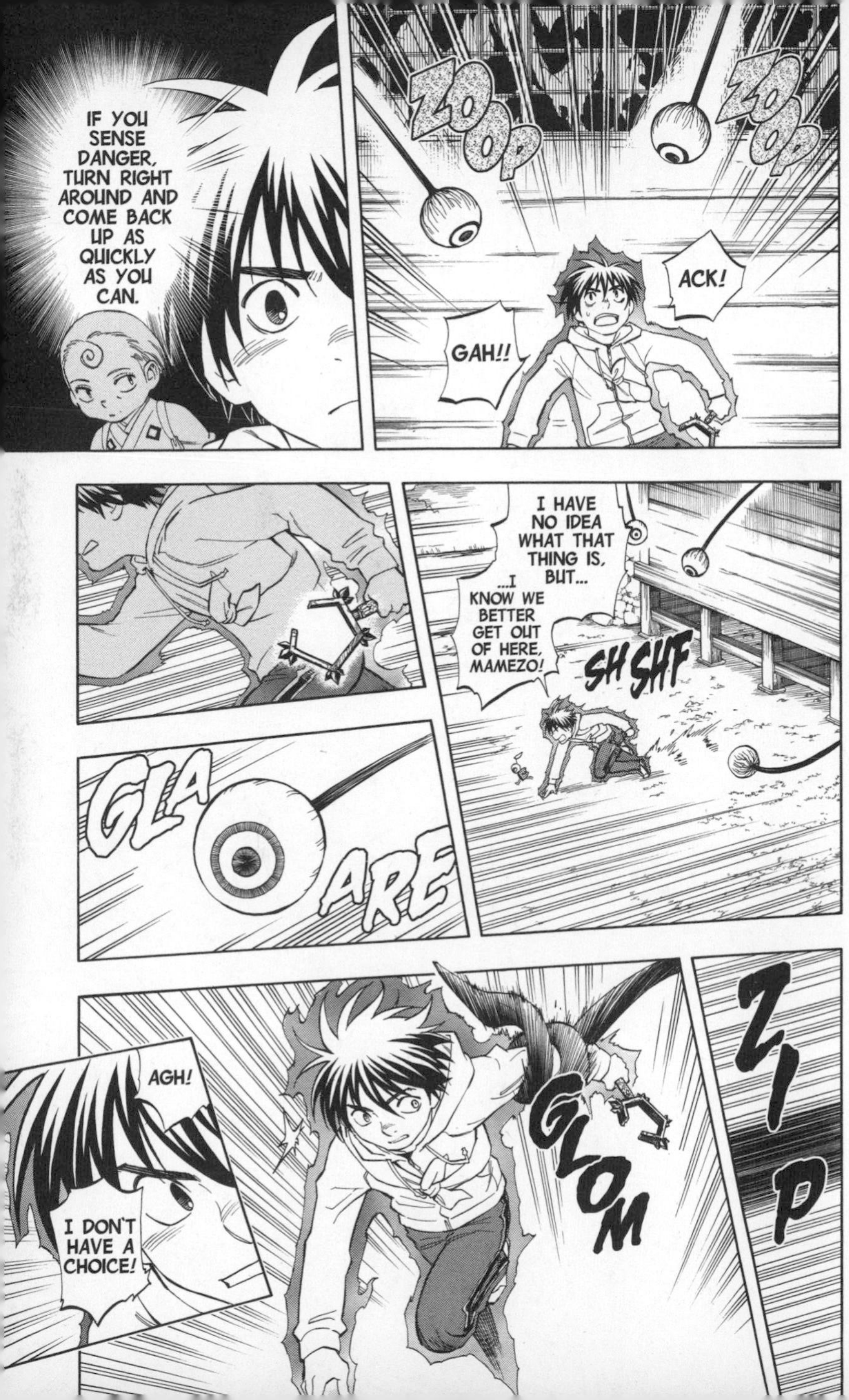
ZOOP
ZOOP
ACK!
GAH!!
IF YOU SENSE DANGER, TURN RIGHT AROUND AND COME BACK UP AS QUICKLY AS YOU CAN.
I HAVE NO IDEA WHAT THAT THING IS, BUT...
...I KNOW WE BETTER GET OUT OF HERE, MAMEZO!
SH SHF
GLA ARE
ZIP
GLOM
AGH!
I DON'T HAVE A CHOICE!

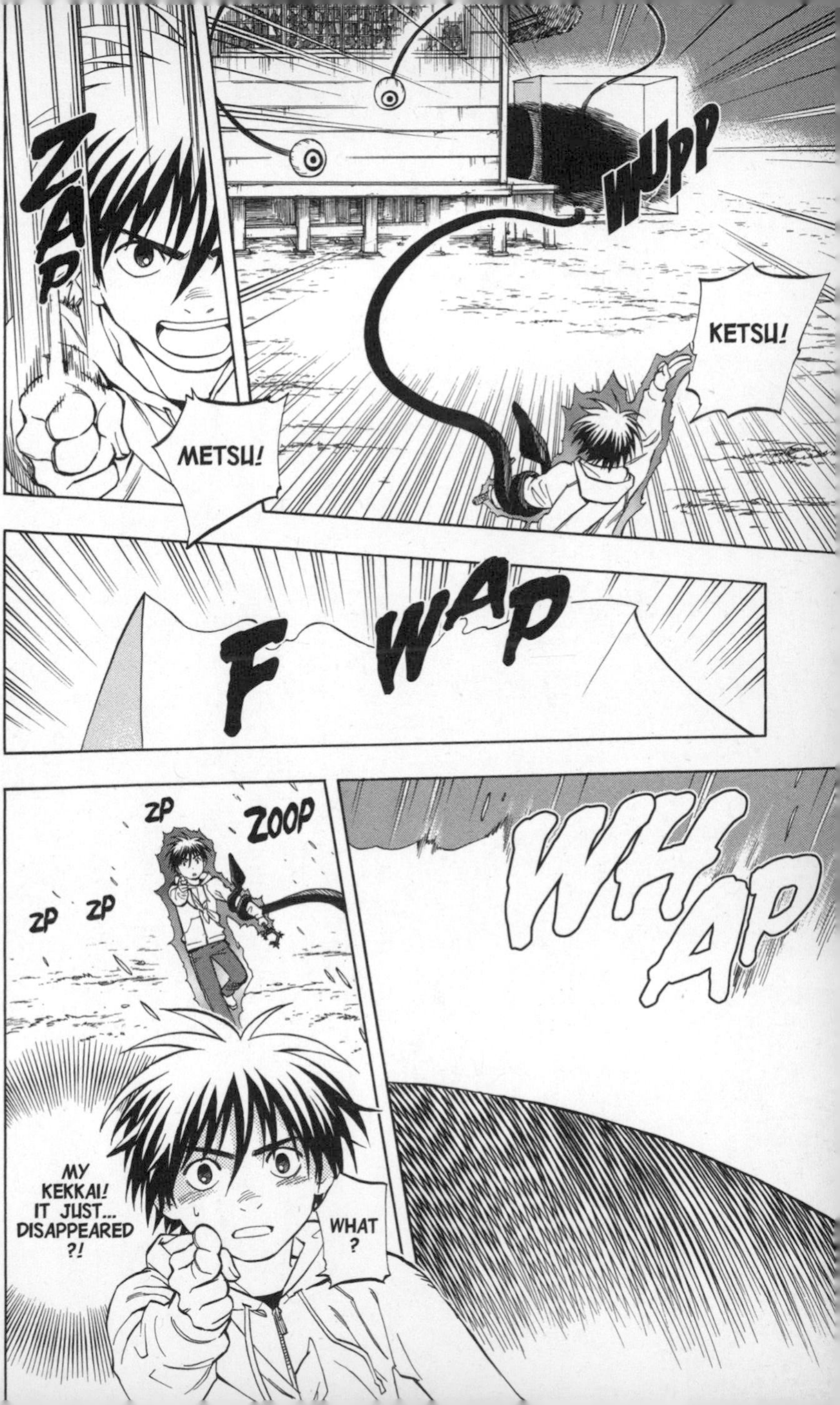
WUPP
KETSU!
ZAP
METSU!
F WAP
WHAP
ZP
ZOOP
ZP ZP
WHAT ?
MY KEKKAI! IT JUST... DISAPPEARED ?!

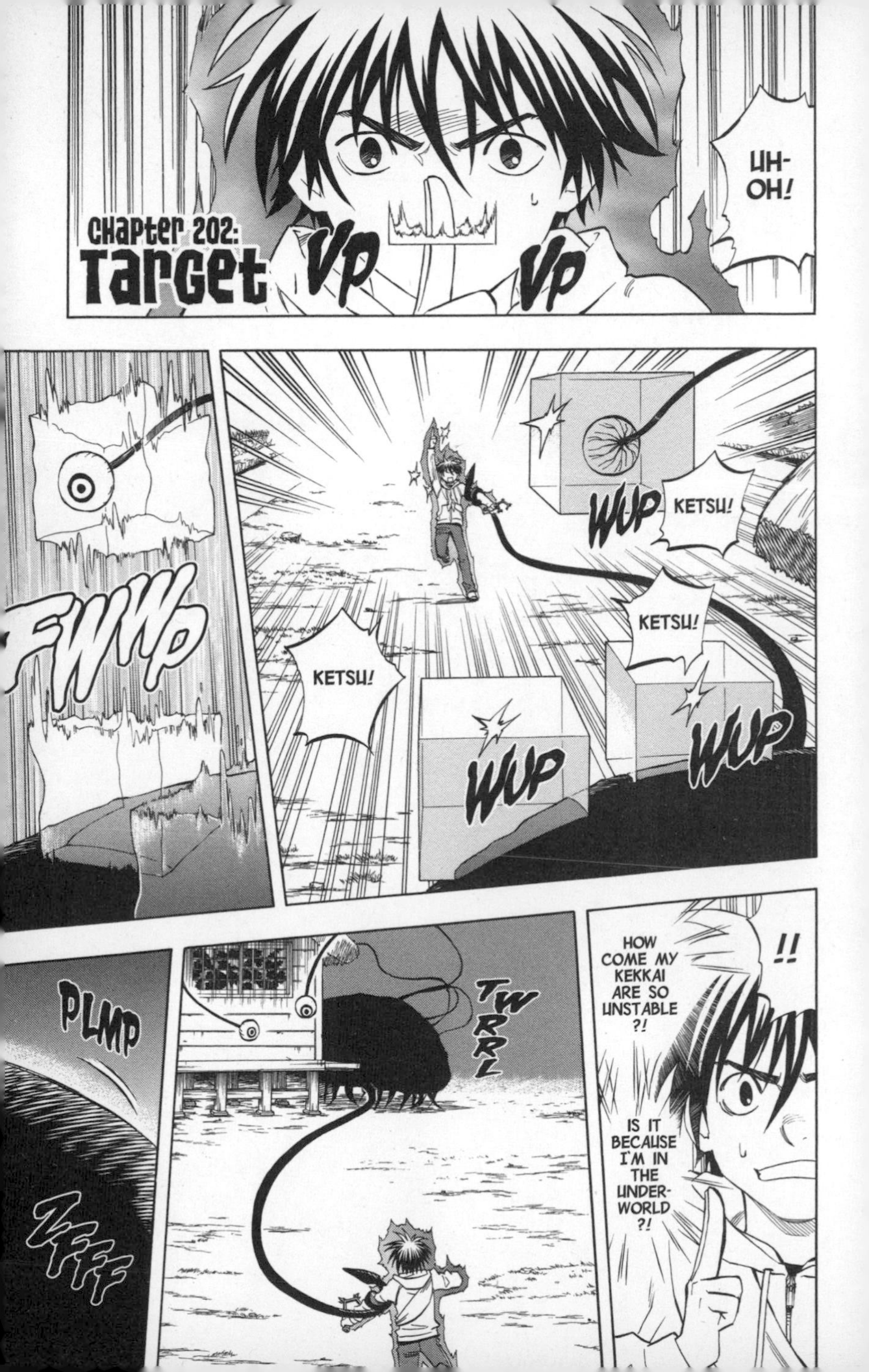
Chapter 202:
Target
UH-OH!
VP
VP
KETSU!
WUP
KETSU!
WUP
KETSU!
WUP
FWMP
!!
HOW COME MY KEKKAI ARE SO UNSTABLE ?!
IS IT BECAUSE I'M IN THE UNDER-WORLD ?!
TWRRL
PLMP
ZFFF

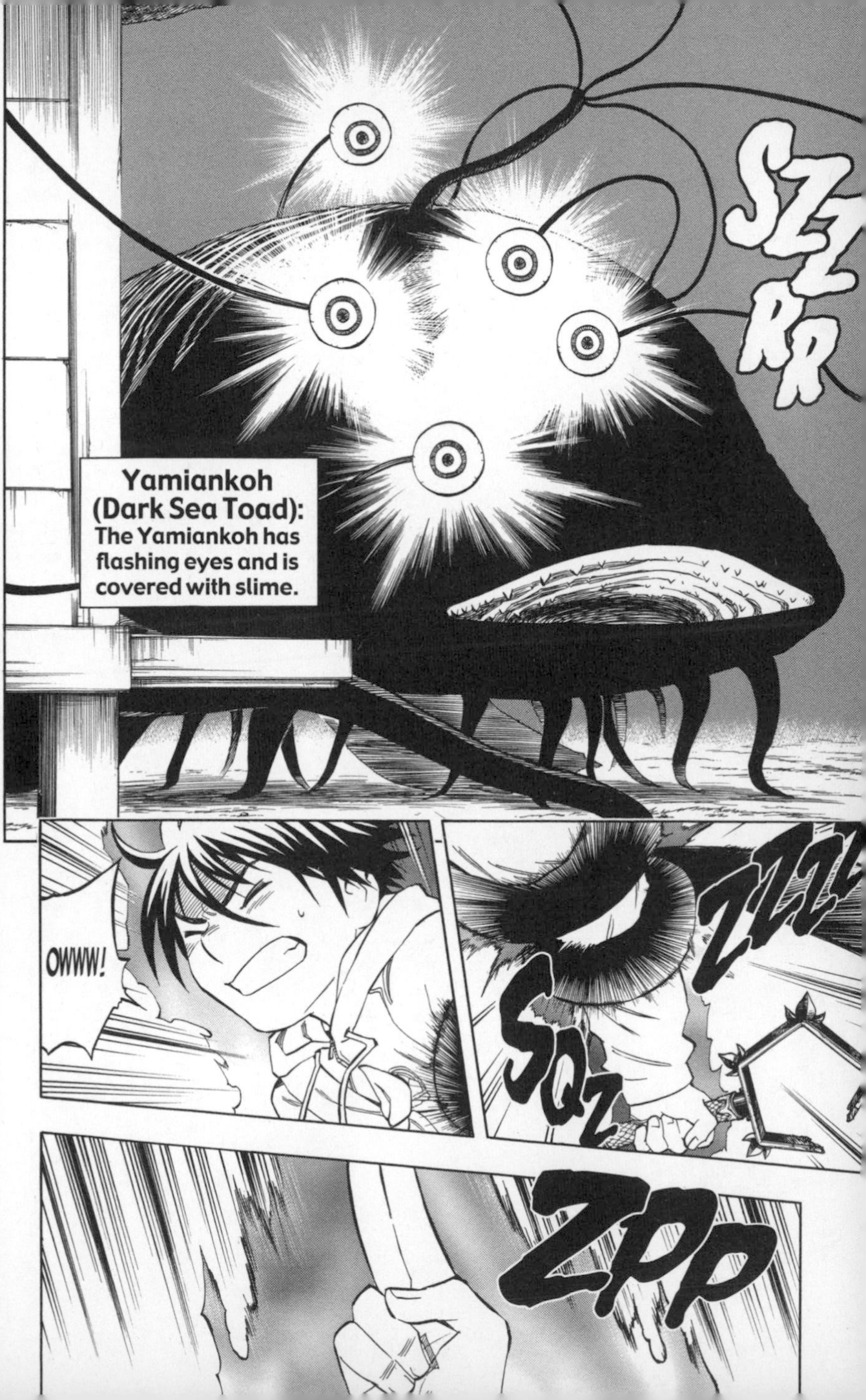
SZZZRR
Yamiankoh
(Dark Sea Toad):
The Yamiankoh has
flashing eyes and is
covered with slime.
ZZZZ
SQZ
OWWW!
ZPP

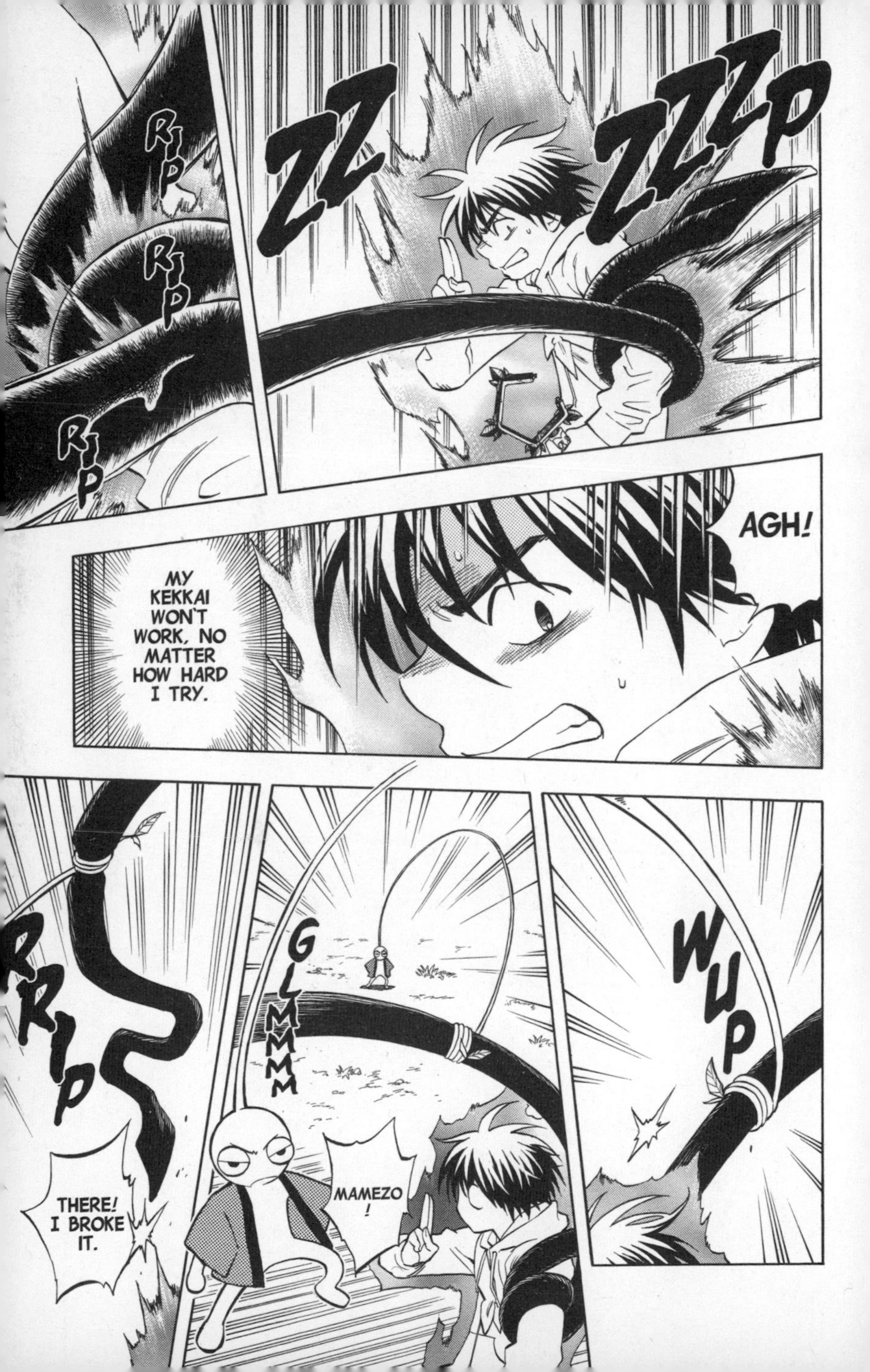
ZZZP
ZZ
RIP
RIP
RIP
AGH!
MY KEKKAI WON'T WORK, NO MATTER HOW HARD I TRY.
WUP
GLMMMM
MAMEZO!
RRIP
THERE! I BROKE IT.

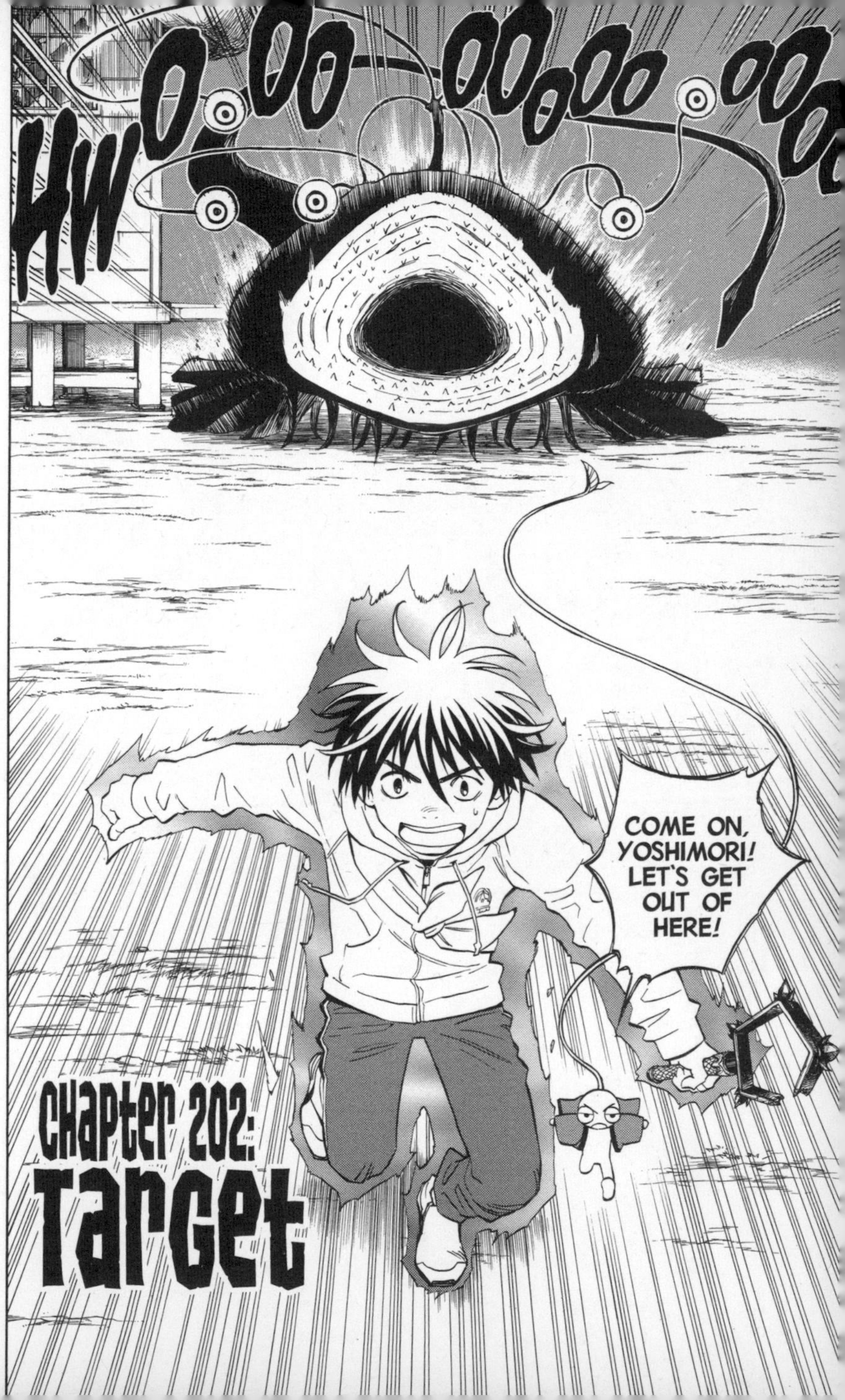
HWO-OO-OOOOO-OOOO
COME ON, YOSHIMORI! LET'S GET OUT OF HERE!
CHAPTER 202: Target

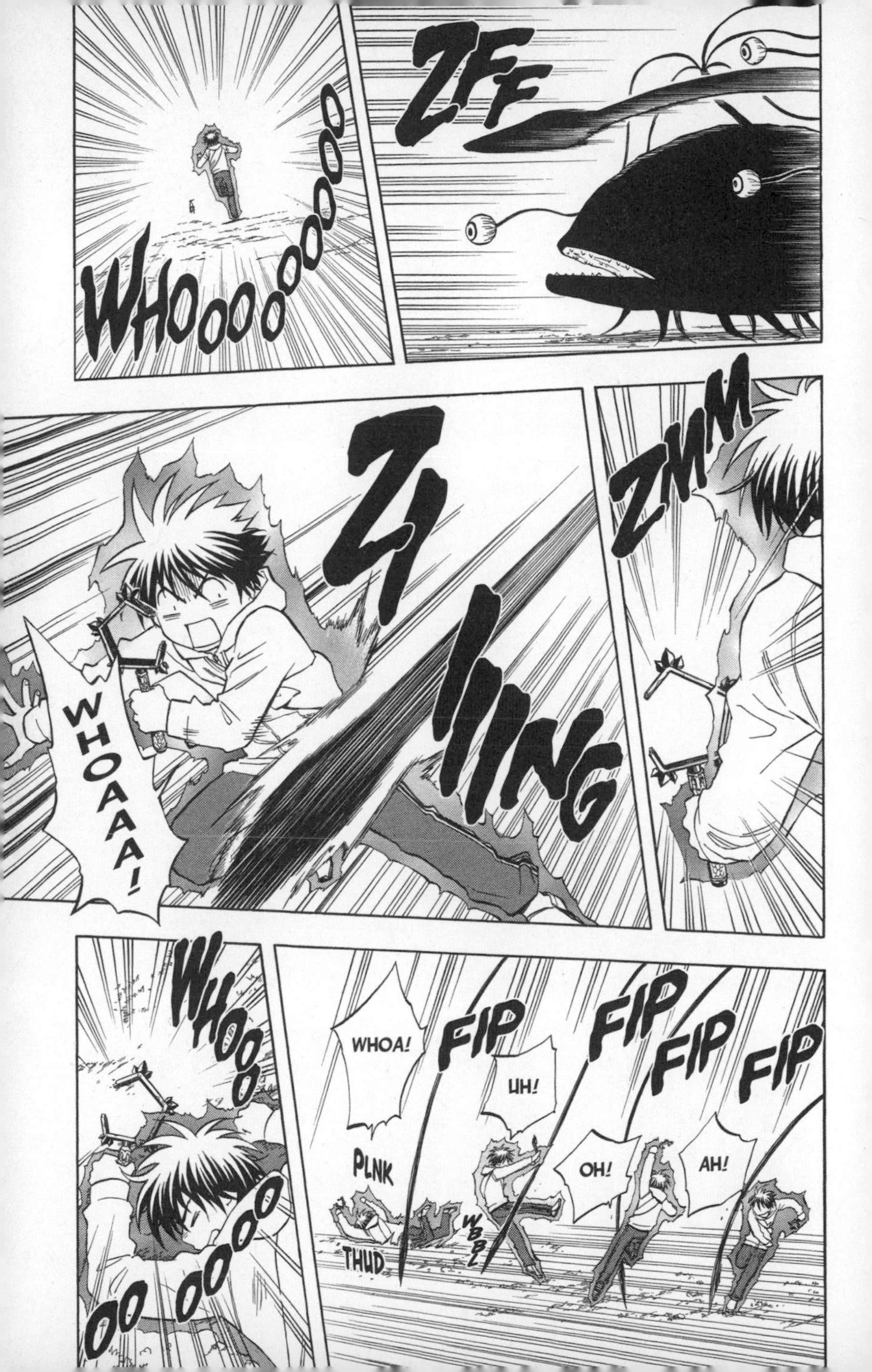
ZFF
WHOOOOOOOOOOOO
ZMM
ZIIING
WHOAAA!
FIP
FIP
FIP
AH!
OH!
FIP
UH!
WBBL
WHOA!
PLNK
THUD
WHOOOOOO OO

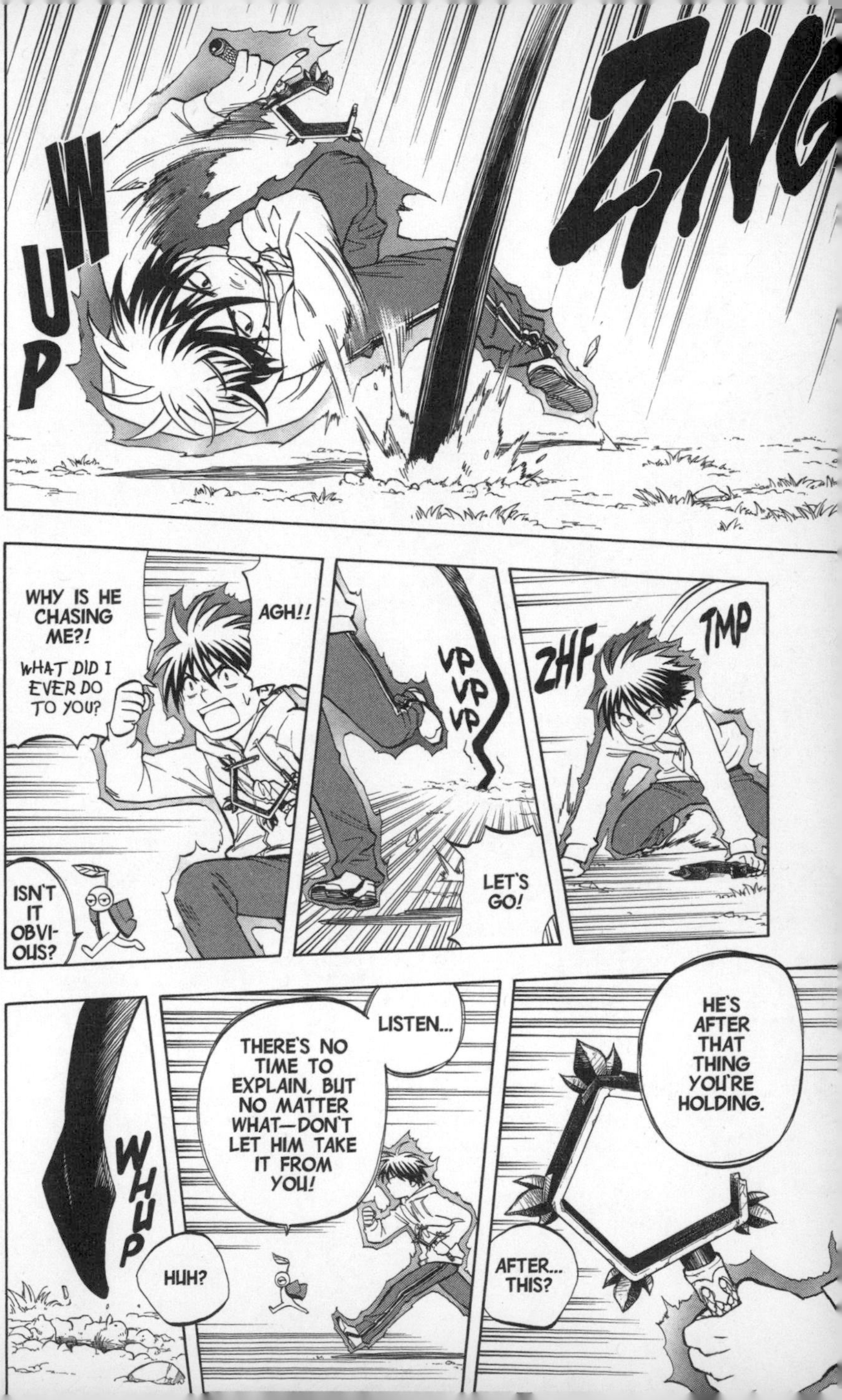
ZING
WUMP
TMP
ZHF
LET'S GO!
VP VP VP
AGH!!
WHY IS HE CHASING ME?!
WHAT DID I EVER DO TO YOU?
ISN'T IT OBVI-OUS?
HE'S AFTER THAT THING YOU'RE HOLDING.
AFTER... THIS?
LISTEN...
THERE'S NO TIME TO EXPLAIN, BUT NO MATTER WHAT—DON'T LET HIM TAKE IT FROM YOU!
HUH?
WHUP

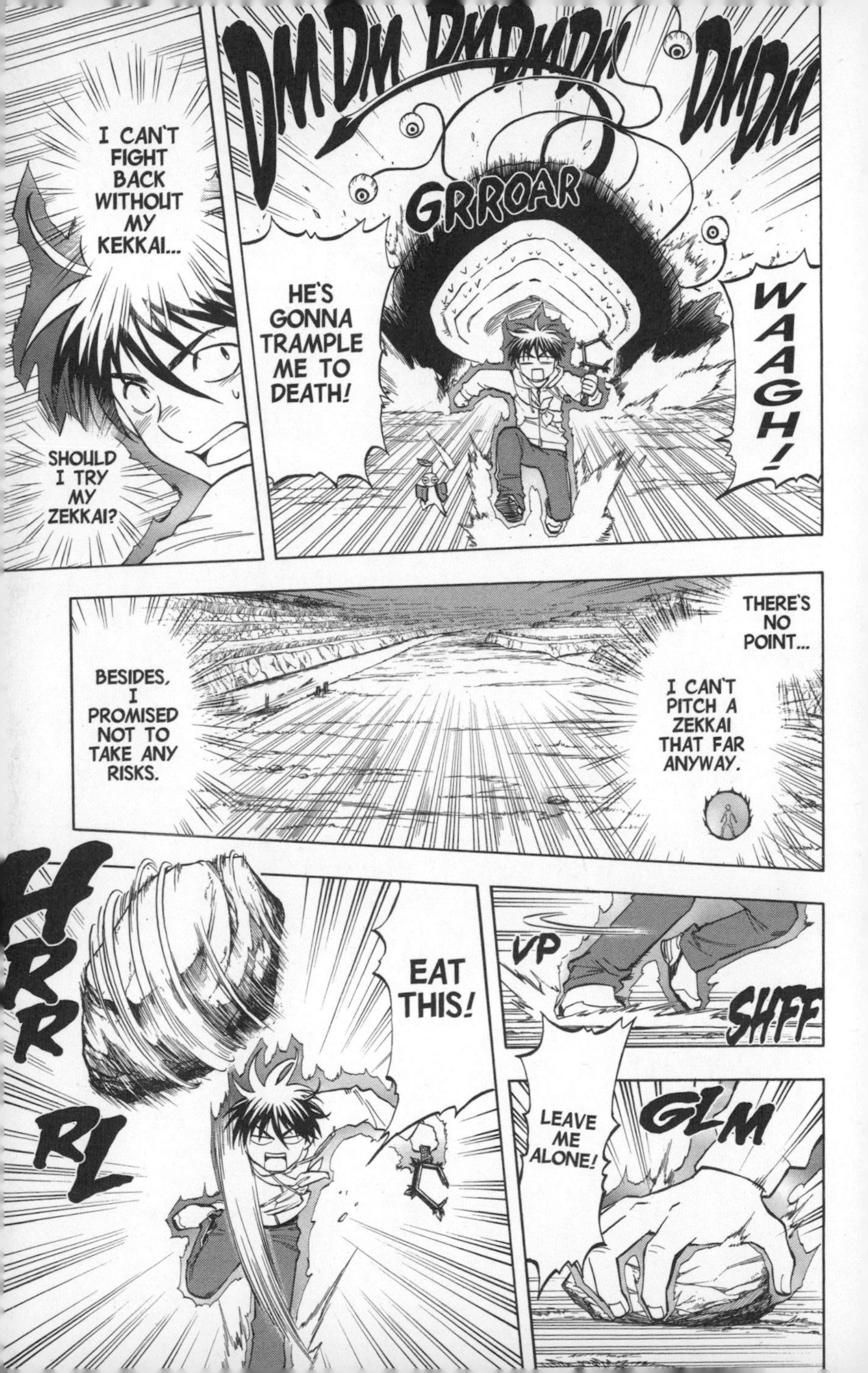
DM DM DMDMDM DMDM
GRROAR
WAAGH!
HE'S GONNA TRAMPLE ME TO DEATH!
I CAN'T FIGHT BACK WITHOUT MY KEKKAI...
SHOULD I TRY MY ZEKKAI?
THERE'S NO POINT...
I CAN'T PITCH A ZEKKAI THAT FAR ANYWAY.
BESIDES, I PROMISED NOT TO TAKE ANY RISKS.
VP
SHFF
GLM
LEAVE ME ALONE!
EAT THIS!
HRRRL

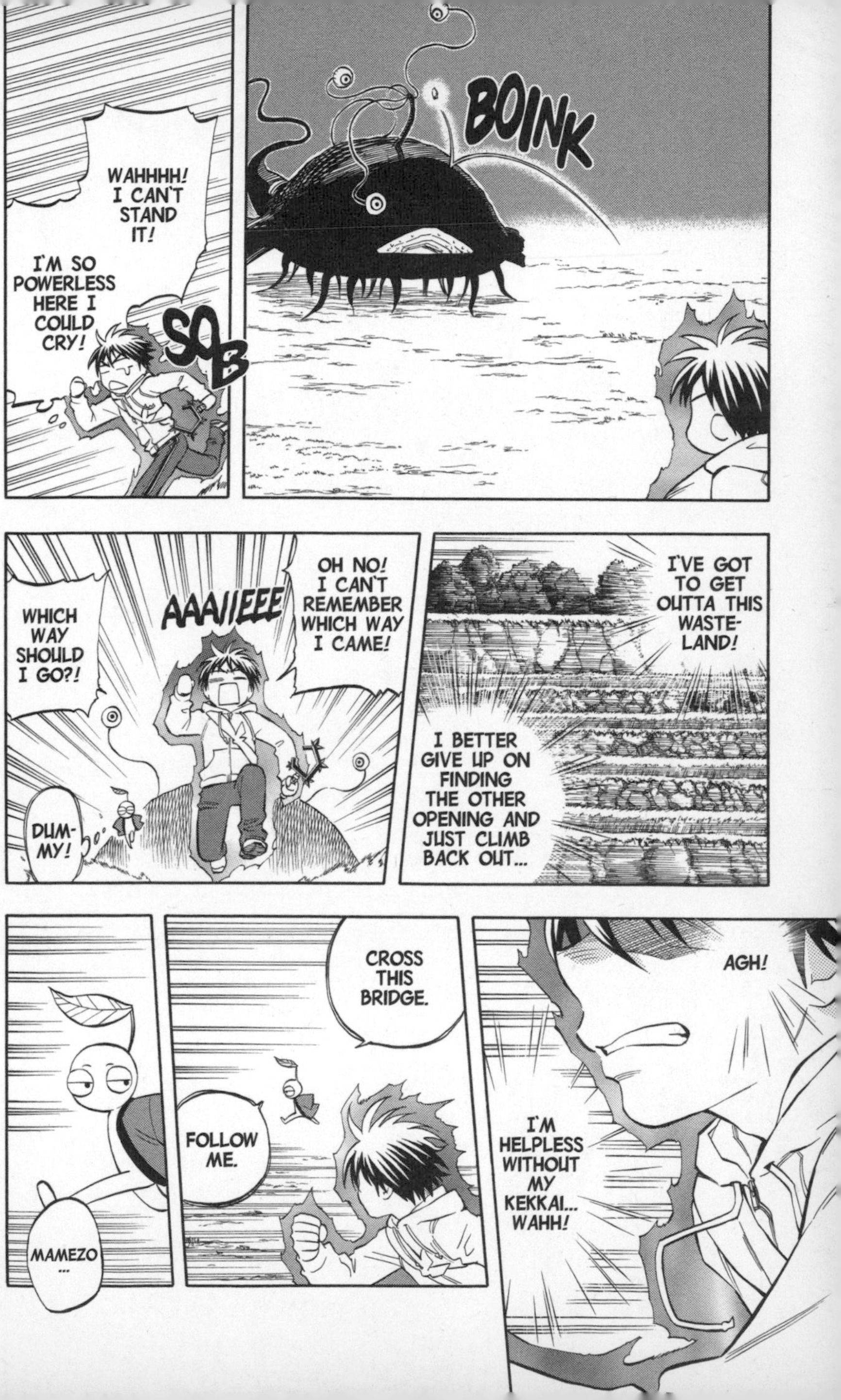
BOINK
WAHHHH! I CAN'T STAND IT!
I'M SO POWERLESS HERE I COULD CRY!
SOB
I'VE GOT TO GET OUTTA THIS WASTE-LAND!
I BETTER GIVE UP ON FINDING THE OTHER OPENING AND JUST CLIMB BACK OUT...
OH NO! I CAN'T REMEMBER WHICH WAY I CAME!
AAAIIEEE
WHICH WAY SHOULD I GO?!
DUM-MY!
AGH!
I'M HELPLESS WITHOUT MY KEKKAI... WAHH!
CROSS THIS BRIDGE.
FOLLOW ME.
MAMEZO ...

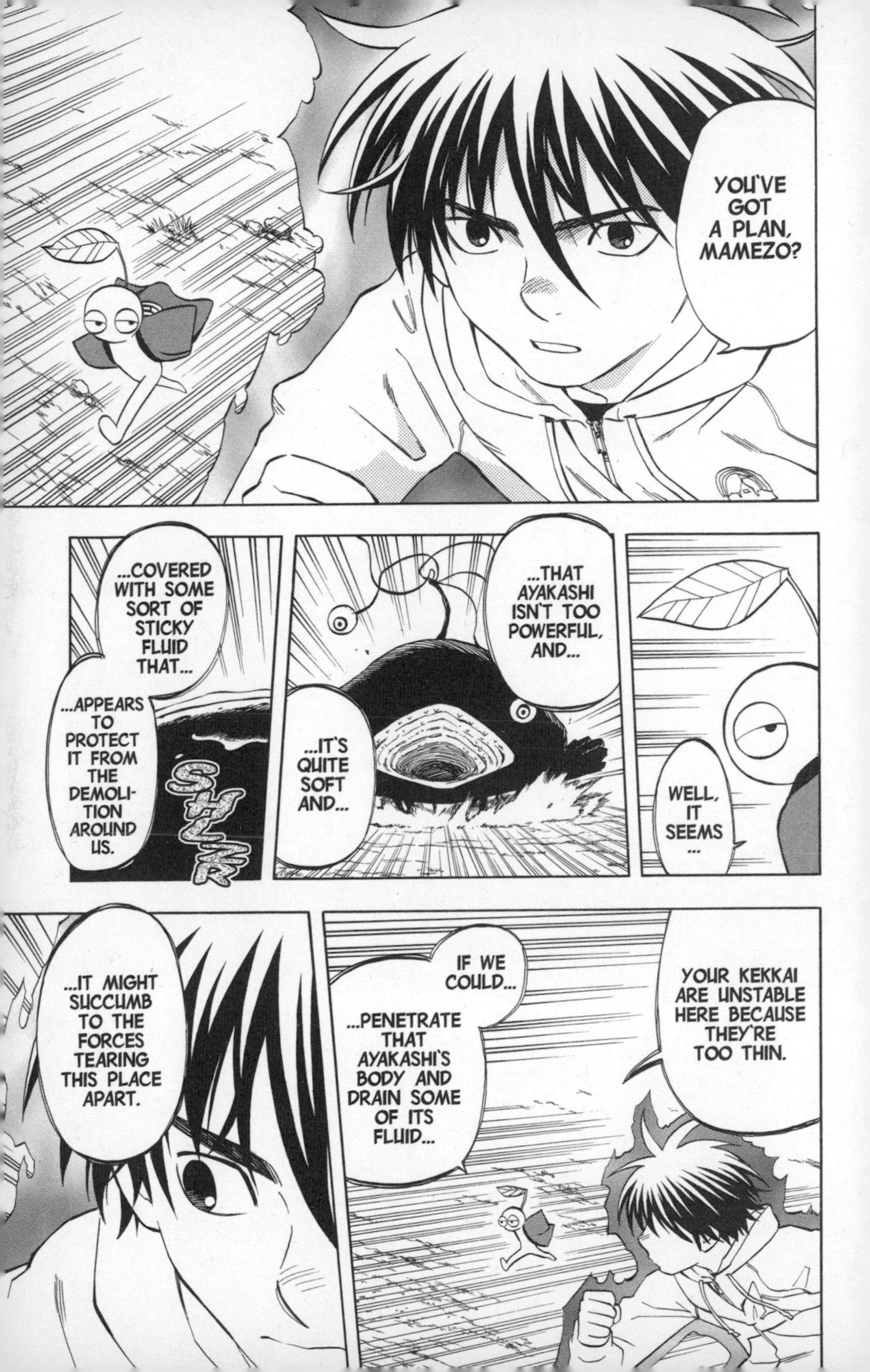
YOU'VE GOT A PLAN, MAMEZO?
WELL, IT SEEMS ...
...THAT AYAKASHI ISN'T TOO POWERFUL, AND...
...IT'S QUITE SOFT AND...
...COVERED WITH SOME SORT OF STICKY FLUID THAT...
...APPEARS TO PROTECT IT FROM THE DEMOLI-TION AROUND US.
SHLR
YOUR KEKKAI ARE UNSTABLE HERE BECAUSE THEY'RE TOO THIN.
IF WE COULD...
...PENETRATE THAT AYAKASHI'S BODY AND DRAIN SOME OF ITS FLUID...
...IT MIGHT SUCCUMB TO THE FORCES TEARING THIS PLACE APART.

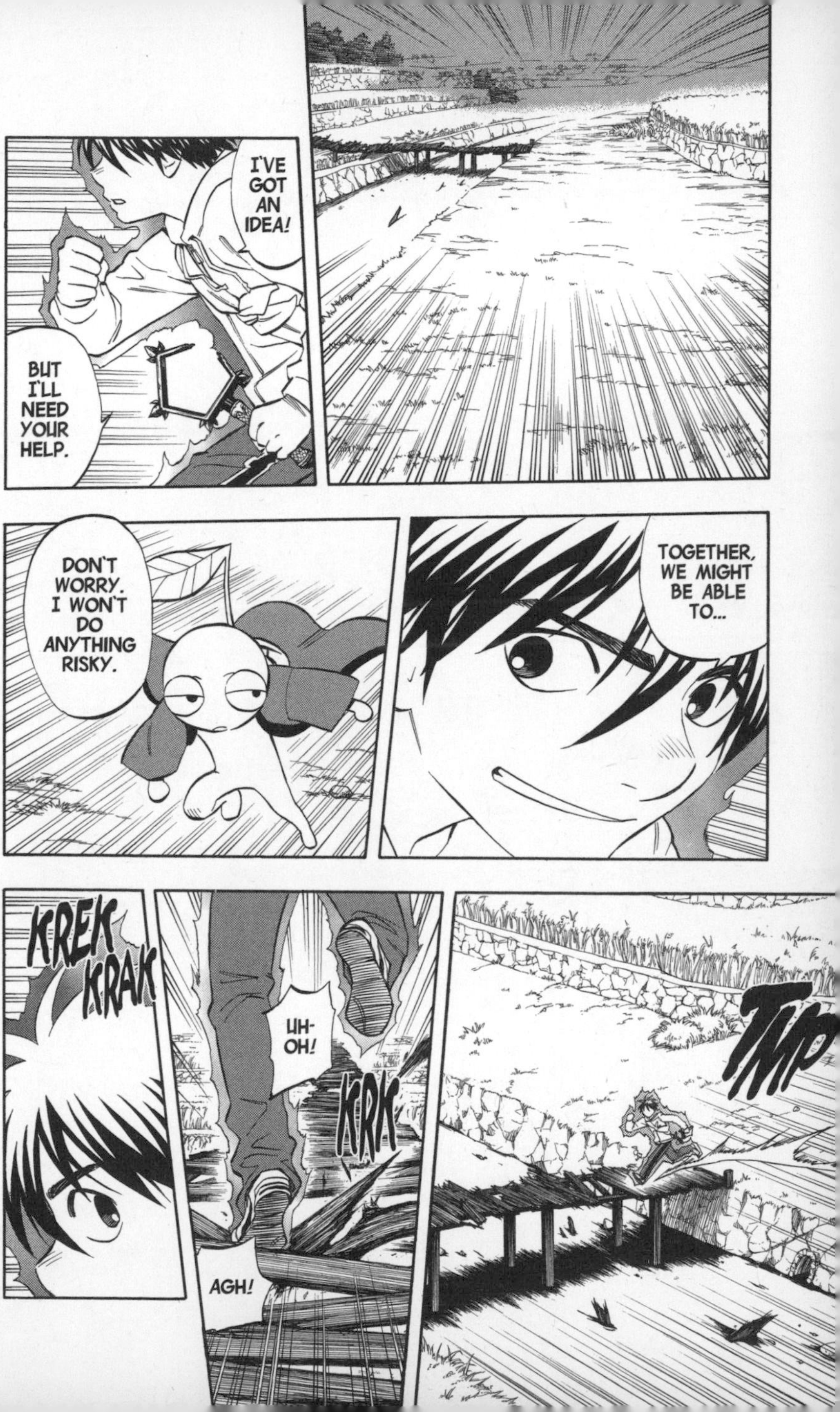
I'VE GOT AN IDEA!
BUT I'LL NEED YOUR HELP.
TOGETHER, WE MIGHT BE ABLE TO...
DON'T WORRY. I WON'T DO ANYTHING RISKY.
TMP
UH-OH!
KRK
AGH!
KREK KRAK

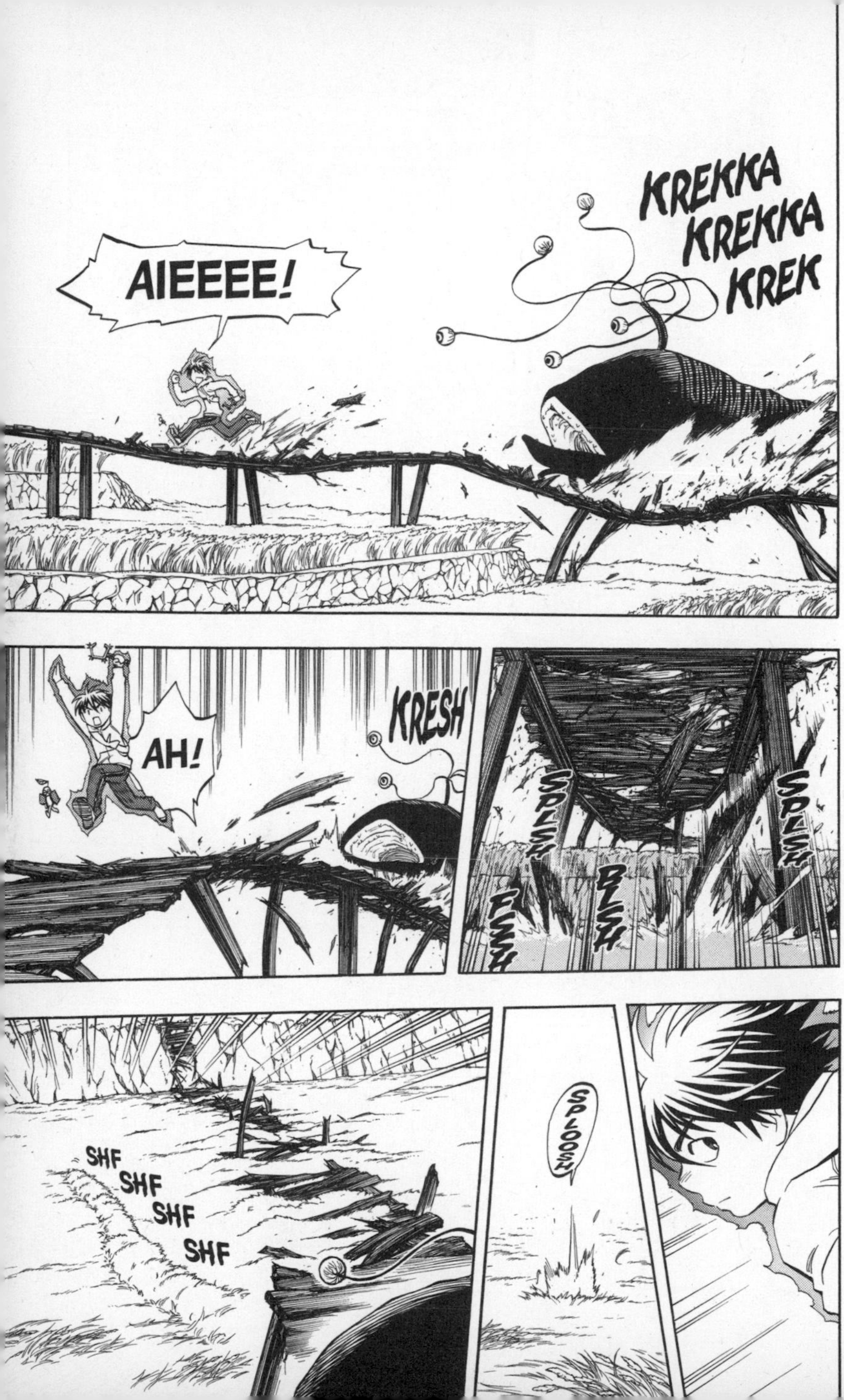
KREKKA KREKKA KREK
AIEEEE!
SPLSH
BLSH
FSSH
SPLSH
KRESH
AH!
SPLOOSH
SHF
SHF
SHF
SHF

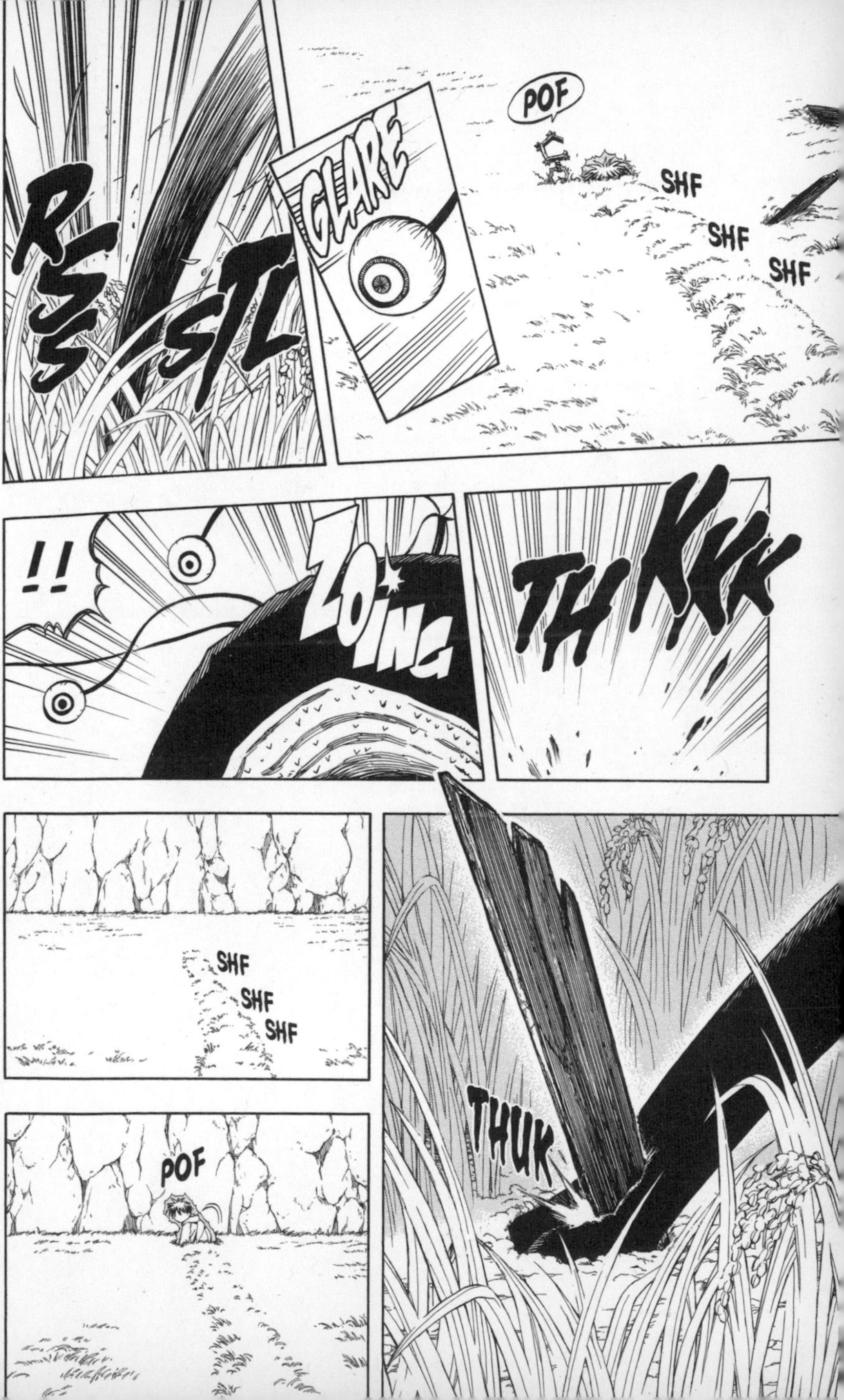
SHF
SHF
SHF
POF
GLARE
R-S-S-STL
THKKK
ZOING
!!
THUK
SHF
SHF
SHF
POF

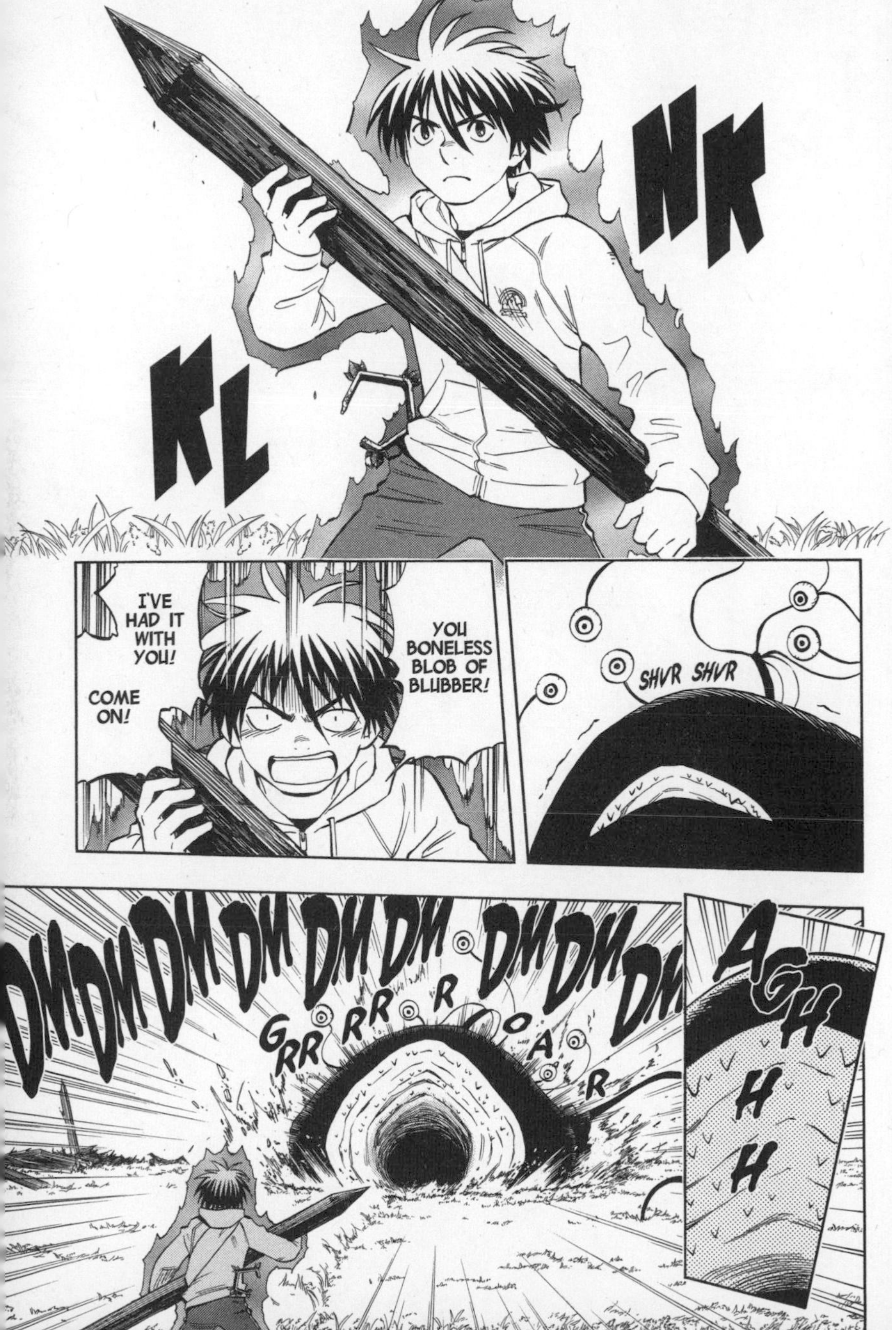
NK
KL
SHVR SHVR
I'VE HAD IT WITH YOU!
YOU BONELESS BLOB OF BLUBBER!
COME ON!
AGHHH
DMDMDMDMDMDMDMDMDMDMDMDM
GRRRRROAR

"...HIS HEAD IS COMPLETELY EXPOSED."

VSH

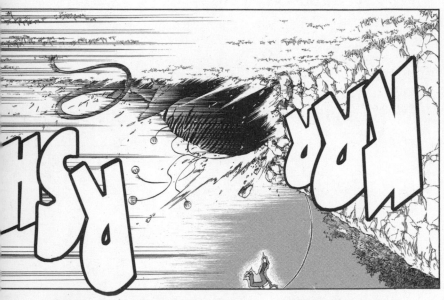

KRR

ASH

PERFECT...

DM DM DM DM DM DM DM DM DM DM DM DM

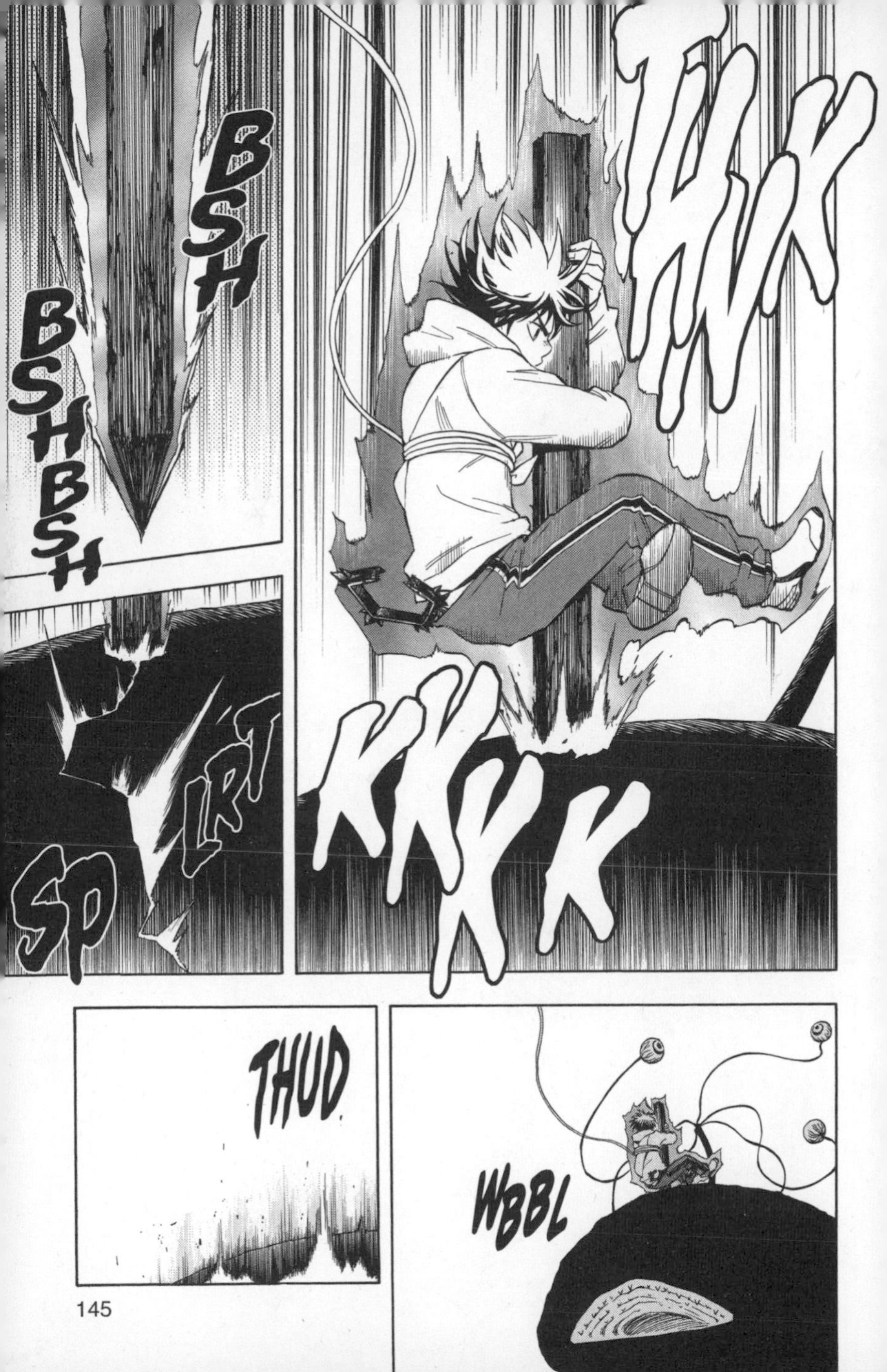
THNK
KKKK
BSH
BSHBSH
SPLIRT
WBBL
THUD

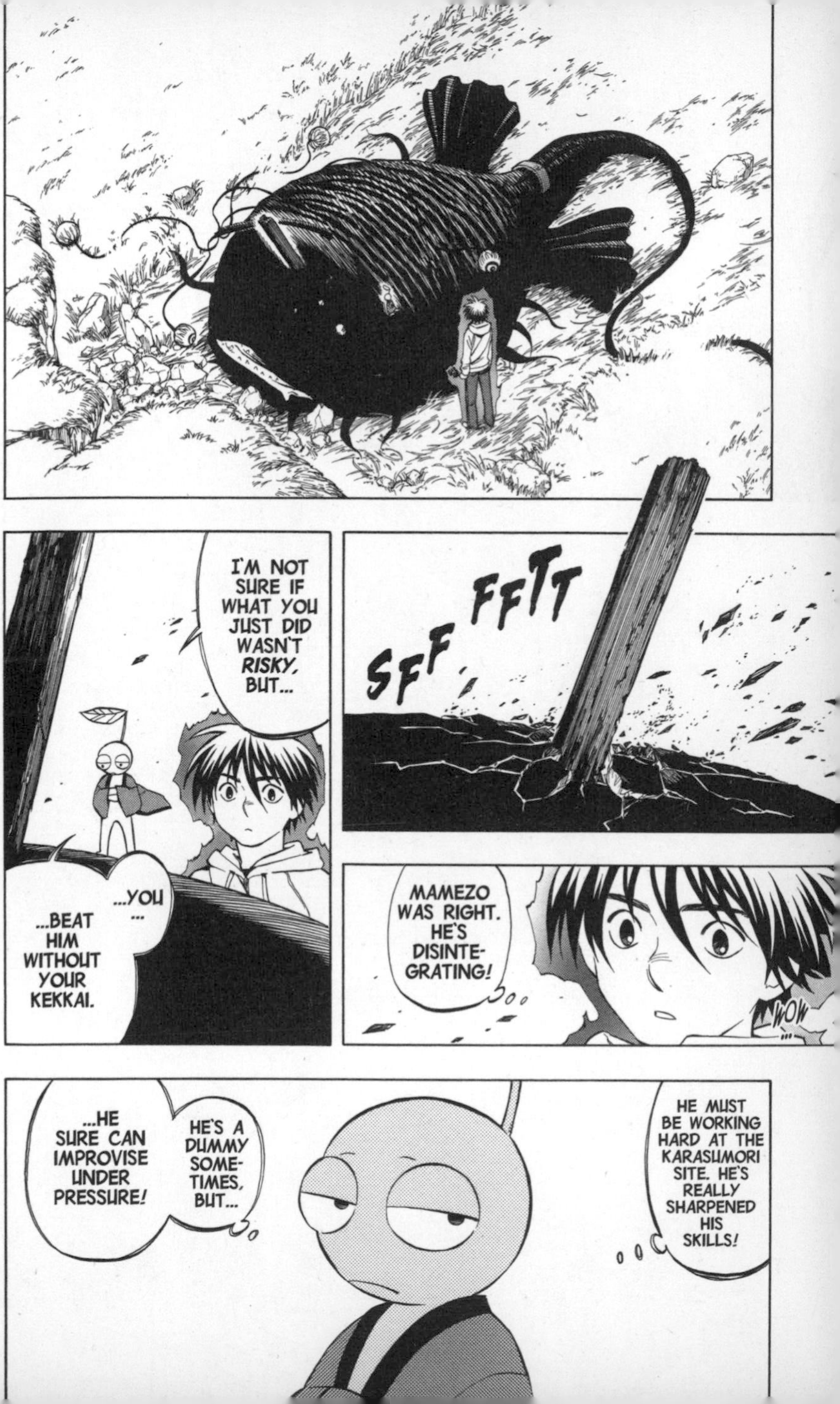
SFF FFTT
WOW...
MAMEZO WAS RIGHT. HE'S DISINTE-GRATING!
I'M NOT SURE IF WHAT YOU JUST DID WASN'T RISKY, BUT...
...YOU...
...BEAT HIM WITHOUT YOUR KEKKAI.
HE MUST BE WORKING HARD AT THE KARASUMORI SITE. HE'S REALLY SHARPENED HIS SKILLS!
HE'S A DUMMY SOME-TIMES, BUT...
...HE SURE CAN IMPROVISE UNDER PRESSURE!

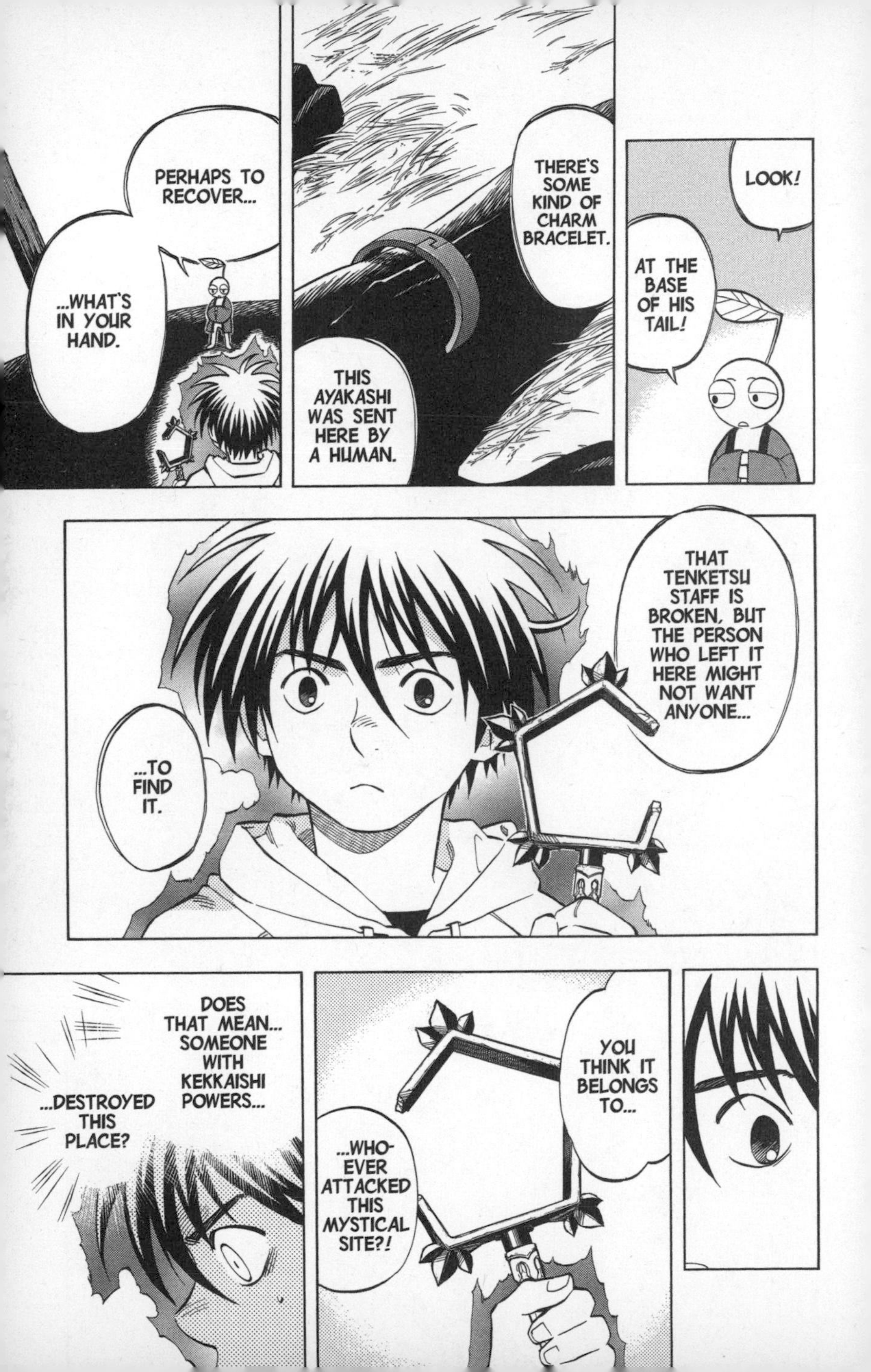
LOOK!
AT THE BASE OF HIS TAIL!
THERE'S SOME KIND OF CHARM BRACELET.
THIS AYAKASHI WAS SENT HERE BY A HUMAN.
PERHAPS TO RECOVER...
...WHAT'S IN YOUR HAND.
THAT TENKETSU STAFF IS BROKEN, BUT THE PERSON WHO LEFT IT HERE MIGHT NOT WANT ANYONE...
...TO FIND IT.
YOU THINK IT BELONGS TO...
...WHO-EVER ATTACKED THIS MYSTICAL SITE?!
DOES THAT MEAN... SOMEONE WITH KEKKAISHI POWERS...
...DESTROYED THIS PLACE?

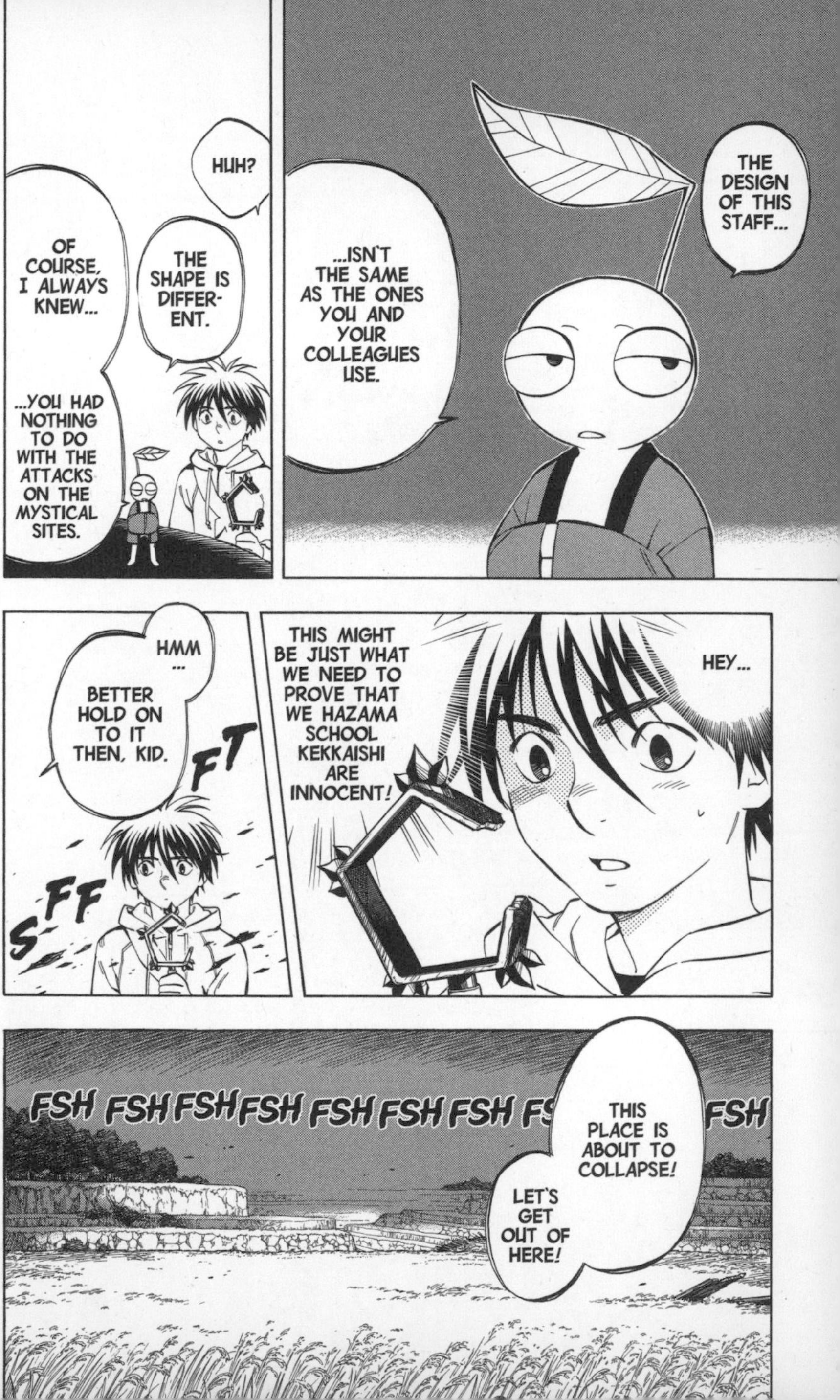
THE DESIGN OF THIS STAFF...
...ISN'T THE SAME AS THE ONES YOU AND YOUR COLLEAGUES USE.
HUH?
THE SHAPE IS DIFFER-ENT.
OF COURSE, I ALWAYS KNEW...
...YOU HAD NOTHING TO DO WITH THE ATTACKS ON THE MYSTICAL SITES.
HEY...
THIS MIGHT BE JUST WHAT WE NEED TO PROVE THAT WE HAZAMA SCHOOL KEKKAISHI ARE INNOCENT!
HMM...
BETTER HOLD ON TO IT THEN, KID.
FT
SFF
FSH FSH FSH FSH FSH FSH FSH FS FSH
THIS PLACE IS ABOUT TO COLLAPSE!
LET'S GET OUT OF HERE!

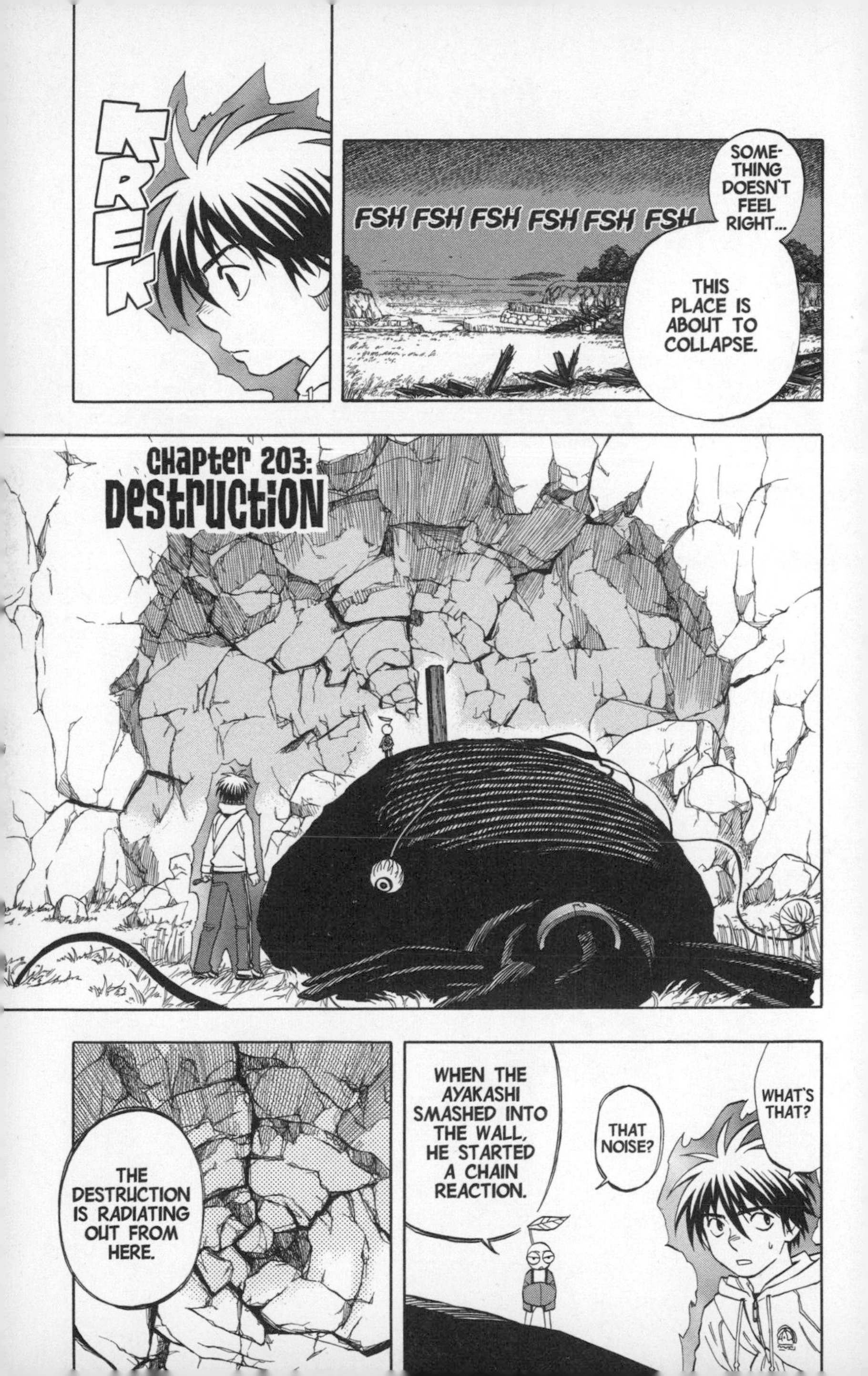
SOME-THING DOESN'T FEEL RIGHT...
FSH FSH FSH FSH FSH FSH
THIS PLACE IS ABOUT TO COLLAPSE.
KREK
Chapter 203: Destruction
WHAT'S THAT?
THAT NOISE?
WHEN THE AYAKASHI SMASHED INTO THE WALL, HE STARTED A CHAIN REACTION.
THE DESTRUCTION IS RADIATING OUT FROM HERE.

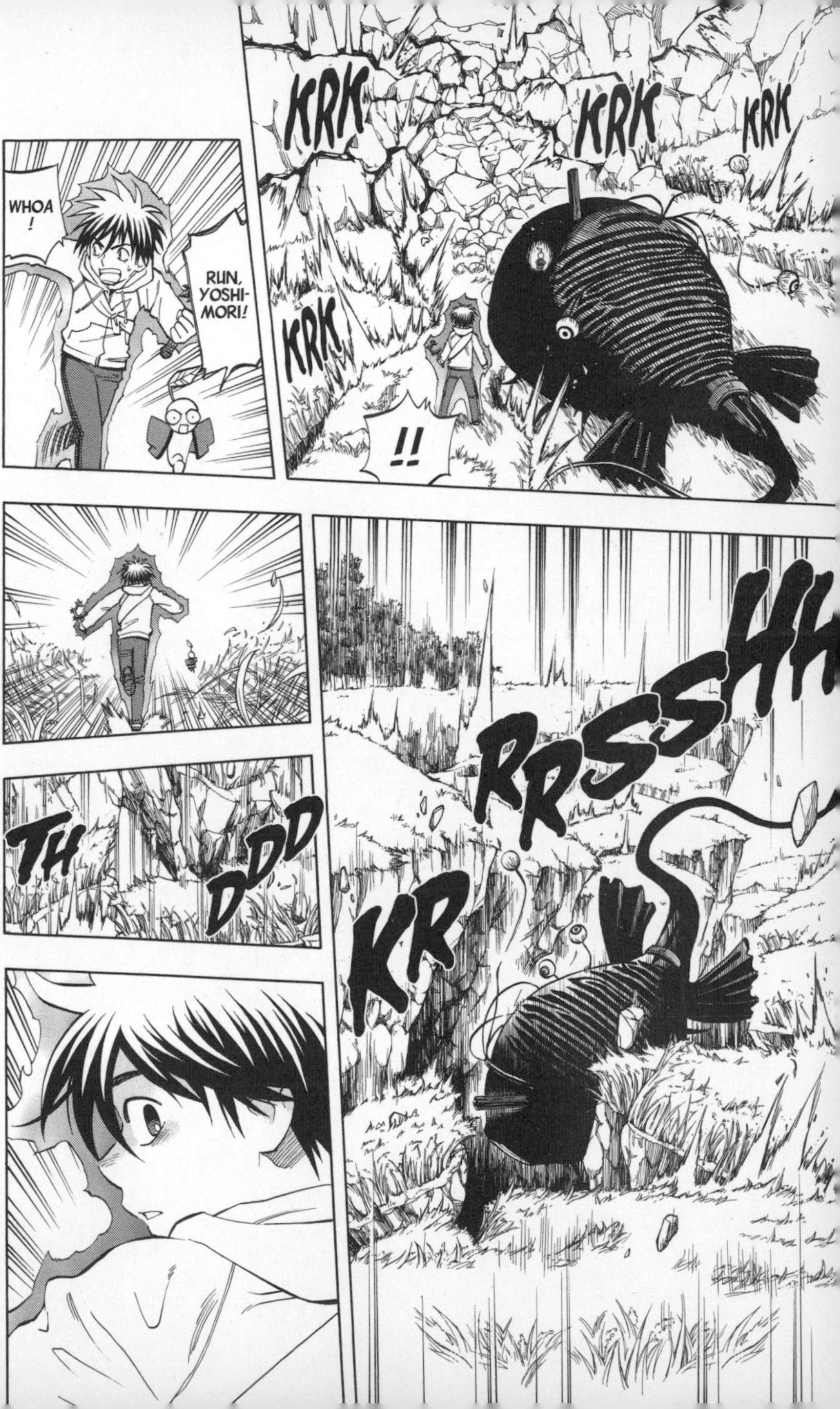
KRK
KRK
KRK
KRK
!!
WHOA!
RUN, YOSHIMORI!
KRRSSHH
TH DDD

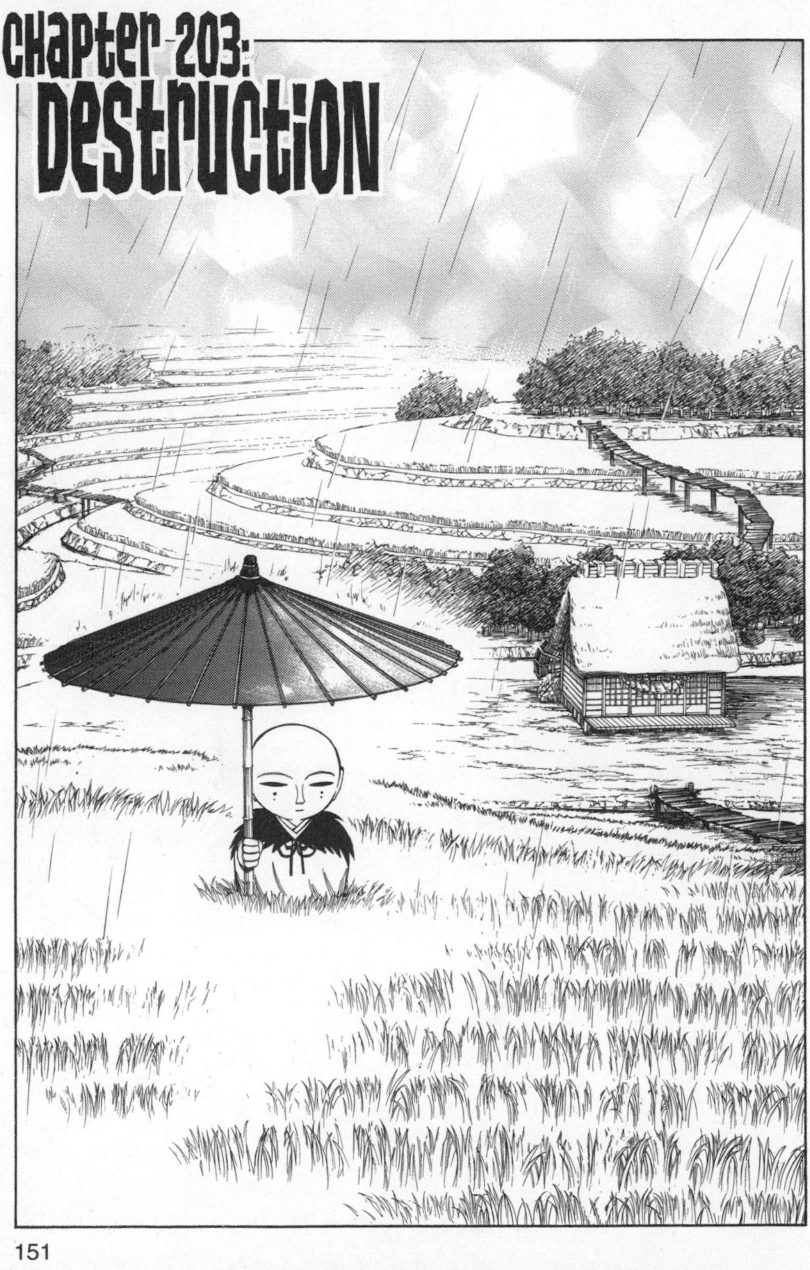
Chapter 203:
Destruction

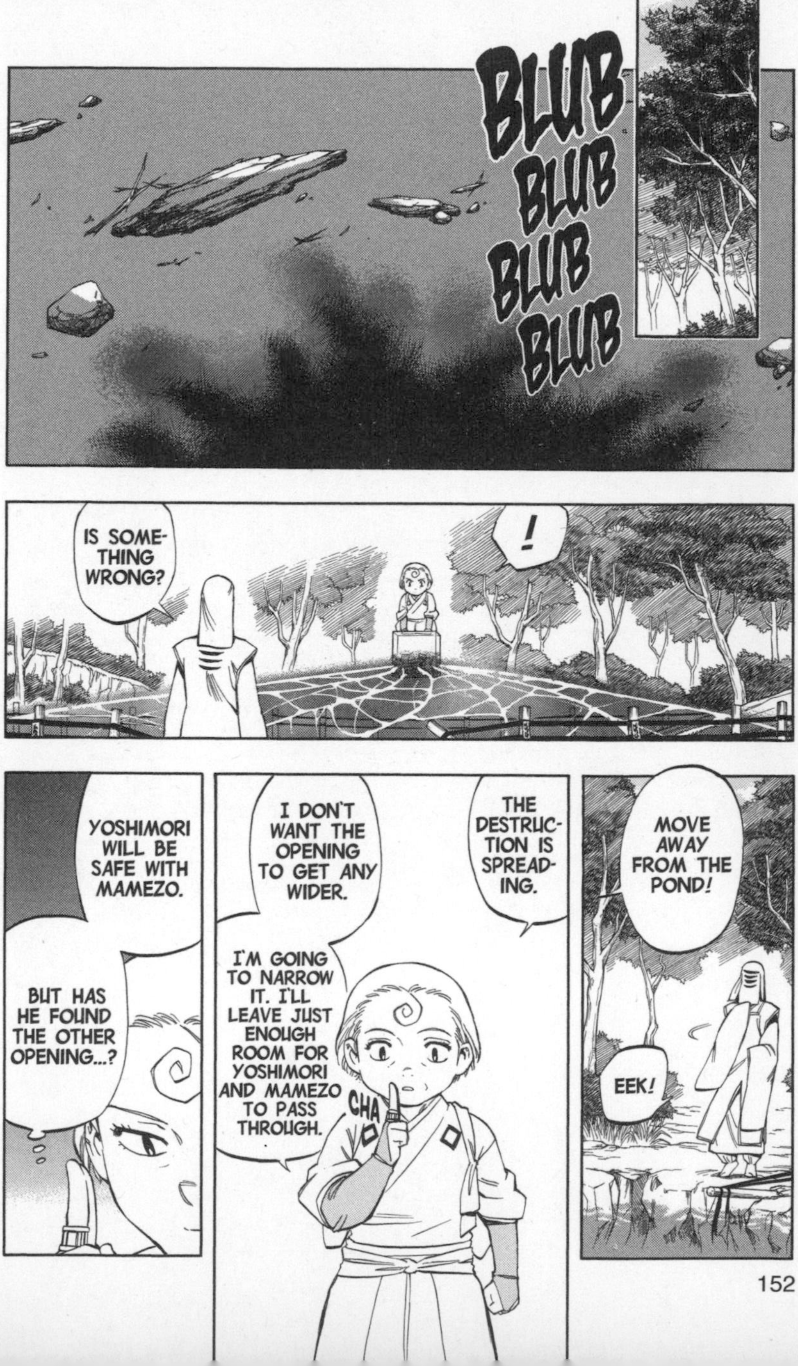
BLUB BLUB BLUB BLUB
!
IS SOME-THING WRONG?
MOVE AWAY FROM THE POND!
EEK!
THE DESTRUC-TION IS SPREAD-ING.
I DON'T WANT THE OPENING TO GET ANY WIDER.
I'M GOING TO NARROW IT. I'LL LEAVE JUST ENOUGH ROOM FOR YOSHIMORI AND MAMEZO TO PASS THROUGH.
CHA
YOSHIMORI WILL BE SAFE WITH MAMEZO.
BUT HAS HE FOUND THE OTHER OPENING...?

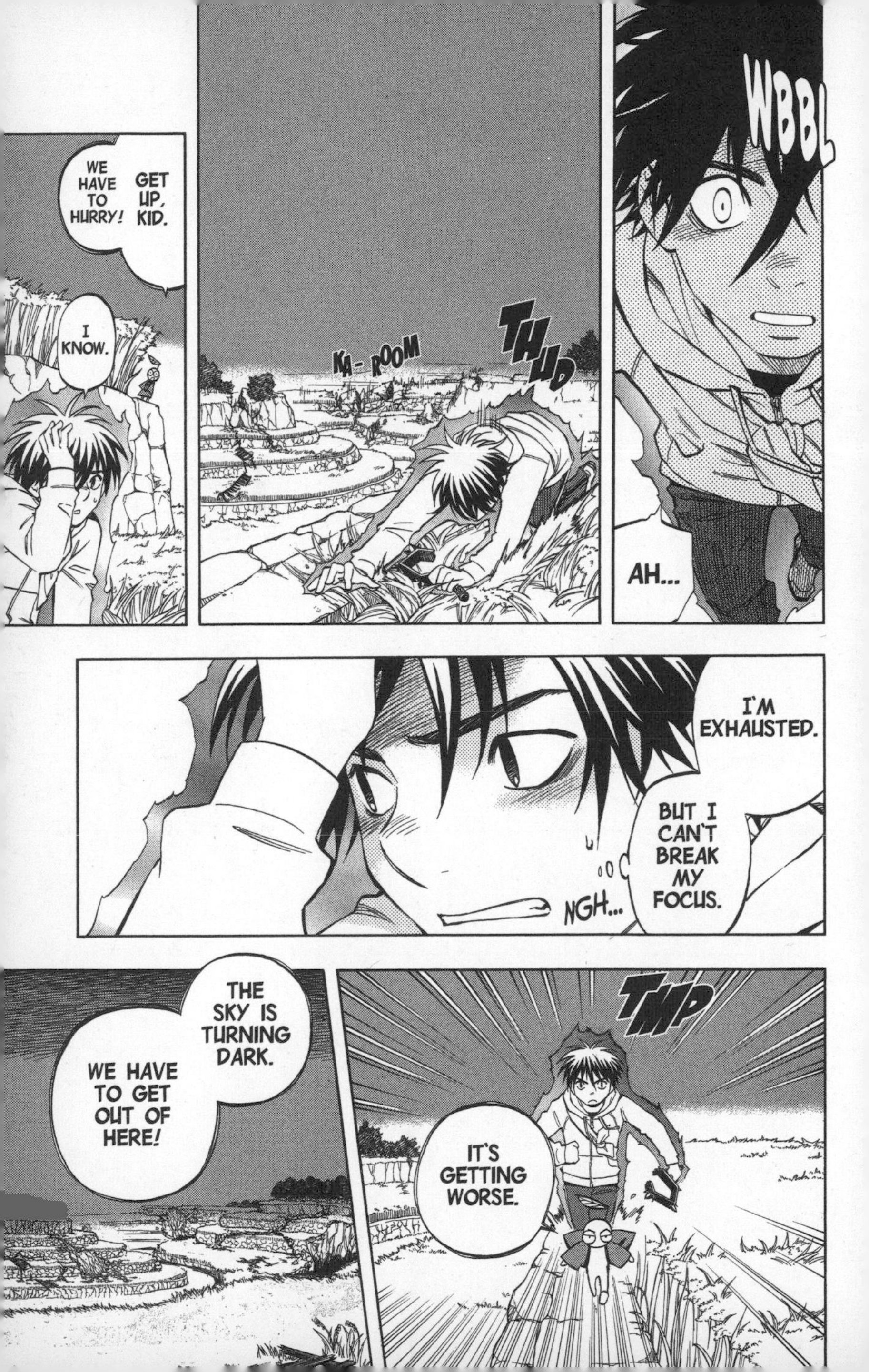
WBBL
AH...
THUD
KA-ROOM
GET UP, KID.
WE HAVE TO HURRY!
I KNOW.
I'M EXHAUSTED.
BUT I CAN'T BREAK MY FOCUS.
NGH...
TMP
IT'S GETTING WORSE.
THE SKY IS TURNING DARK.
WE HAVE TO GET OUT OF HERE!

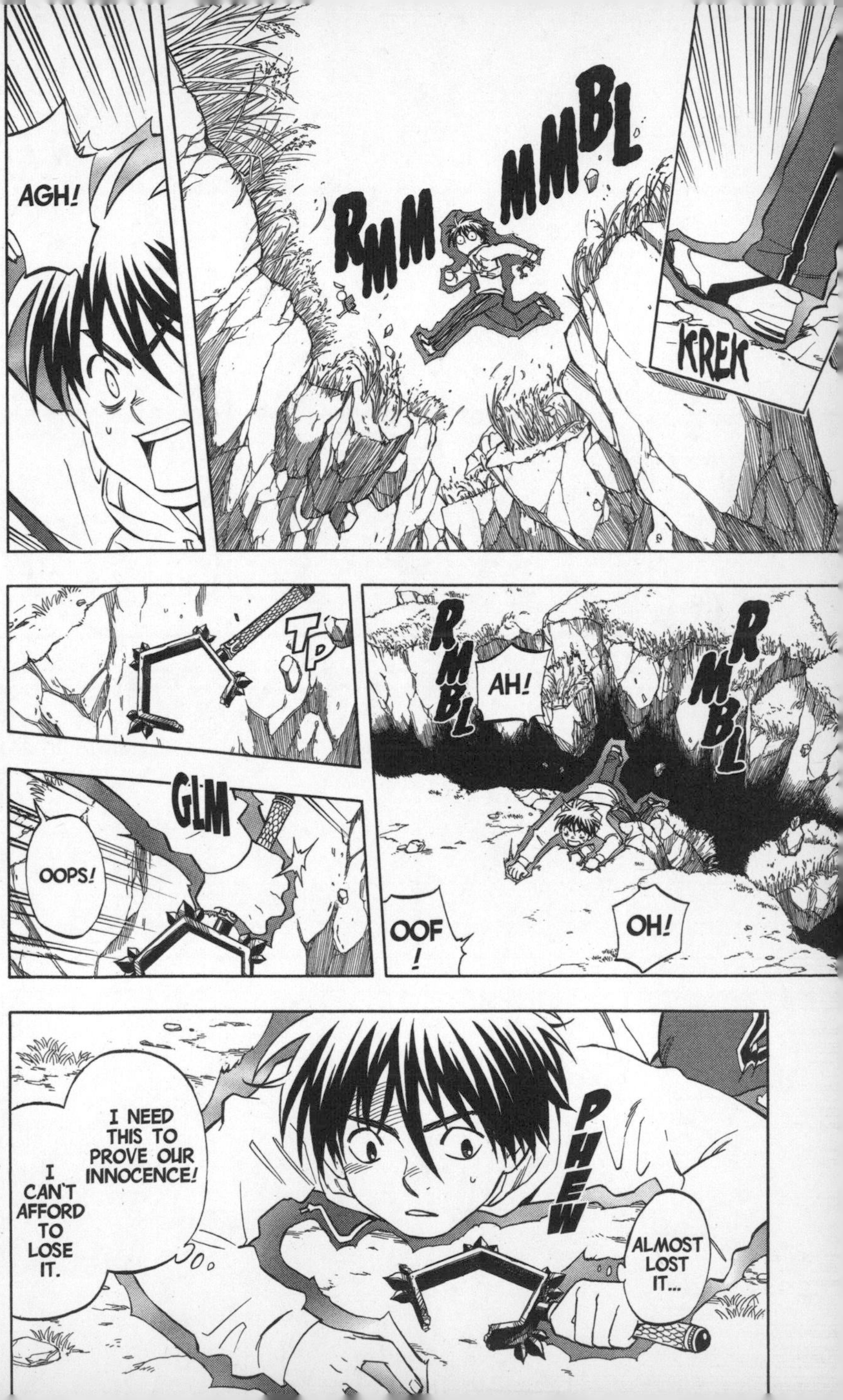
KREK
RMM MMBL
AGH!
RMBL
AH!
RMBL
OH!
OOF!
TP
GLM
OOPS!
PHEW
ALMOST LOST IT...
I NEED THIS TO PROVE OUR INNOCENCE!
I CAN'T AFFORD TO LOSE IT.

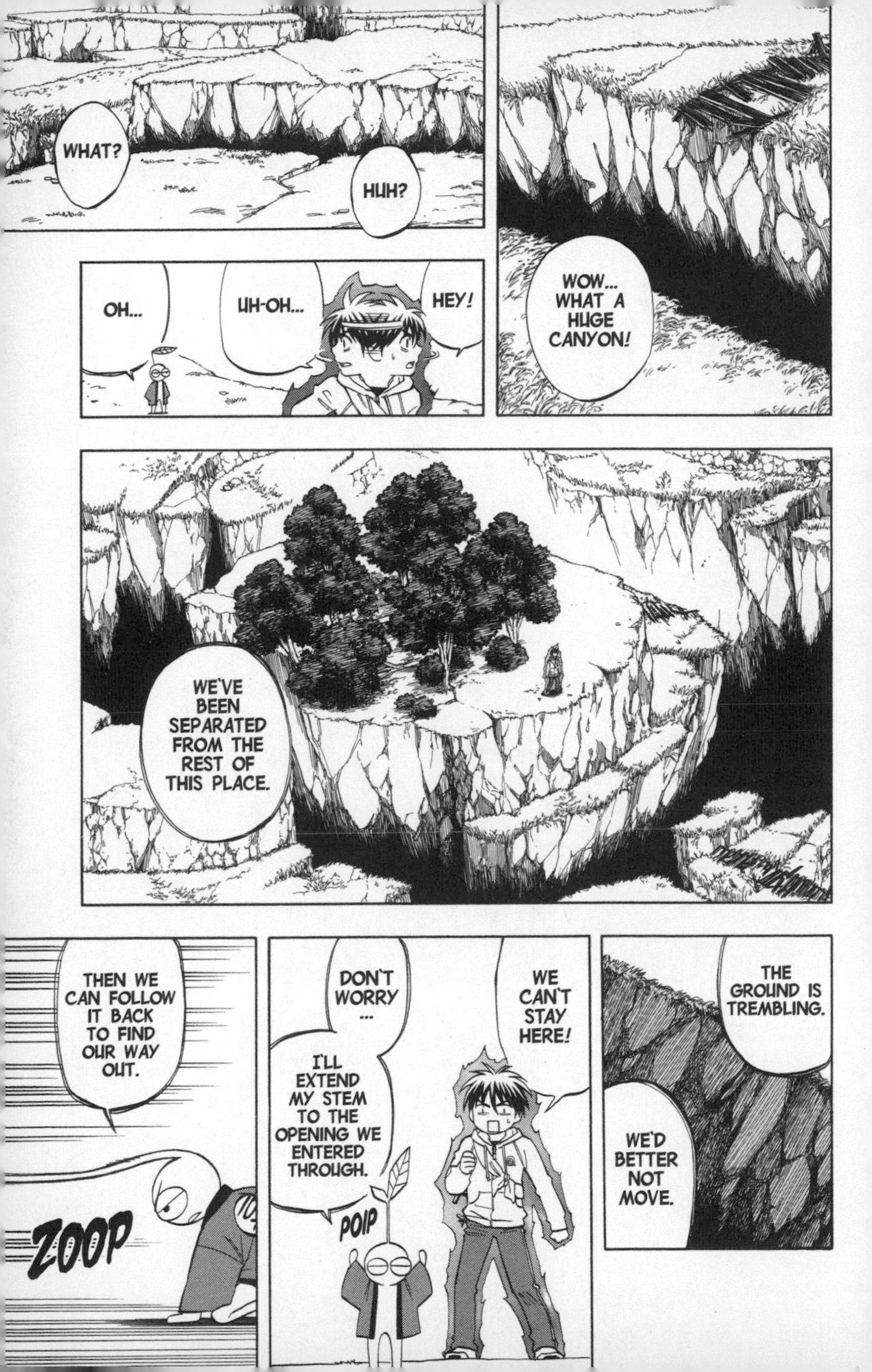
WOW... WHAT A HUGE CANYON!
WHAT?
HUH?
HEY!
UH-OH...
OH...
WE'VE BEEN SEPARATED FROM THE REST OF THIS PLACE.
THE GROUND IS TREMBLING.
WE'D BETTER NOT MOVE.
WE CAN'T STAY HERE!
DON'T WORRY ...
I'LL EXTEND MY STEM TO THE OPENING WE ENTERED THROUGH.
POIP
THEN WE CAN FOLLOW IT BACK TO FIND OUR WAY OUT.
ZOOP

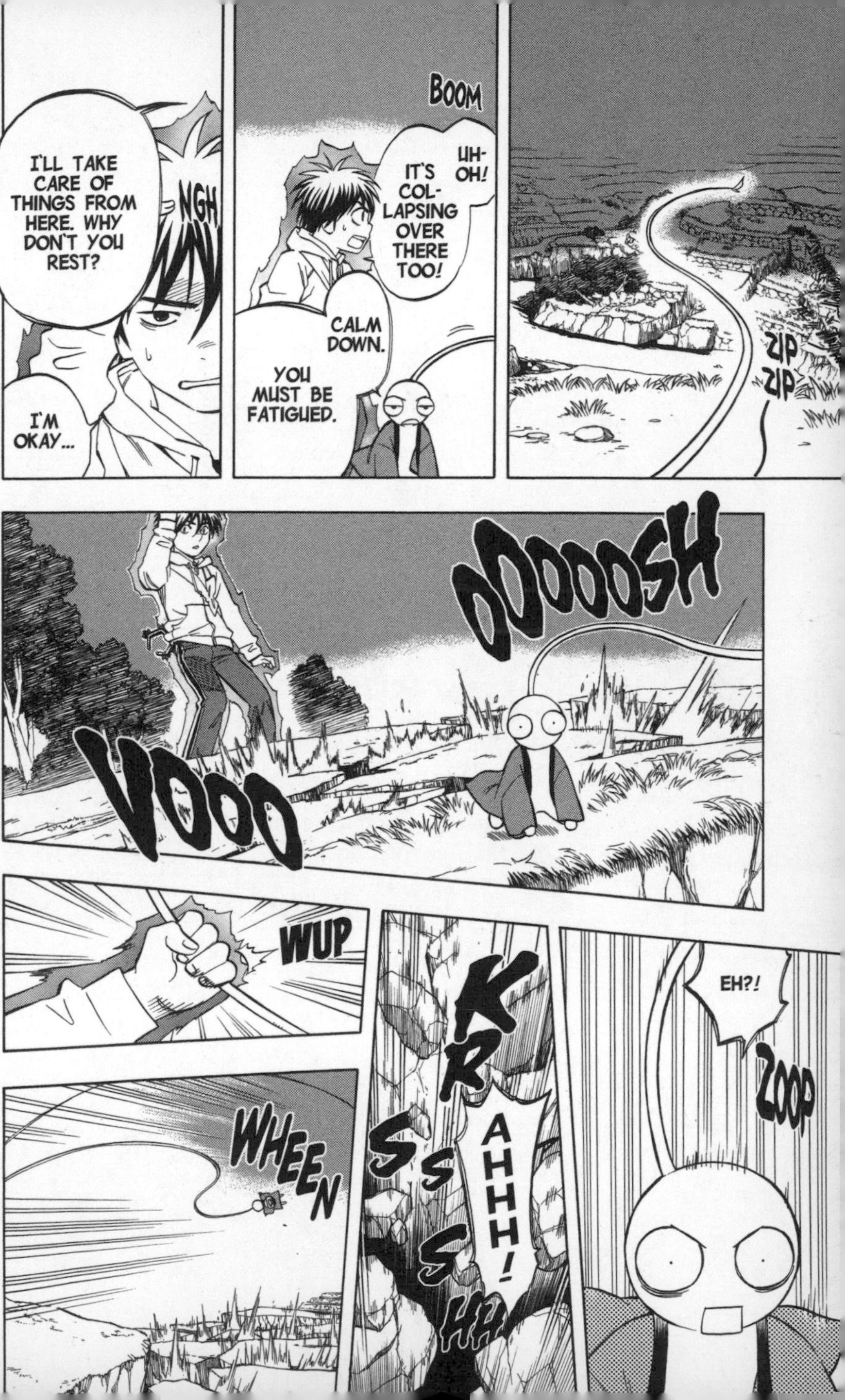
ZIP ZIP
BOOM
UH-OH! IT'S COL-LAPSING OVER THERE TOO!
CALM DOWN.
YOU MUST BE FATIGUED.
I'LL TAKE CARE OF THINGS FROM HERE. WHY DON'T YOU REST?
NGH
I'M OKAY...
OOOOOSH
VOOO
EH?!
ZOOP
KR
SSSHH
AHHH!
WUP
WHEEN

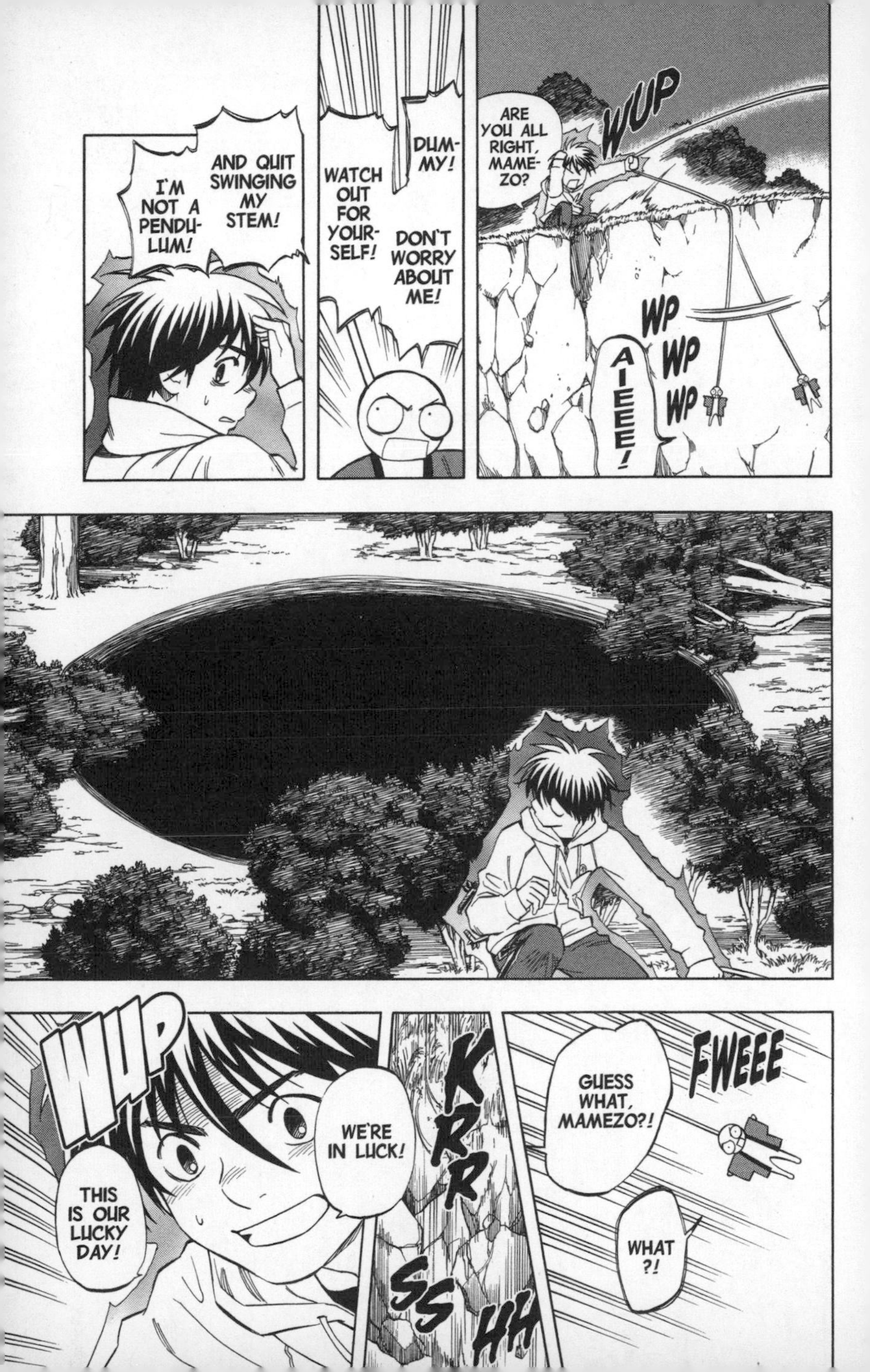
WUP
ARE YOU ALL RIGHT, MAME-ZO?
WP WP WP
AIEEE!
DUM-MY!
WATCH OUT FOR YOUR-SELF!
DON'T WORRY ABOUT ME!
AND QUIT SWINGING MY STEM!
I'M NOT A PENDU-LUM!
FWEEE
GUESS WHAT, MAMEZO?!
WHAT ?!
KRR
SSHH
WE'RE IN LUCK!
WUP
THIS IS OUR LUCKY DAY!

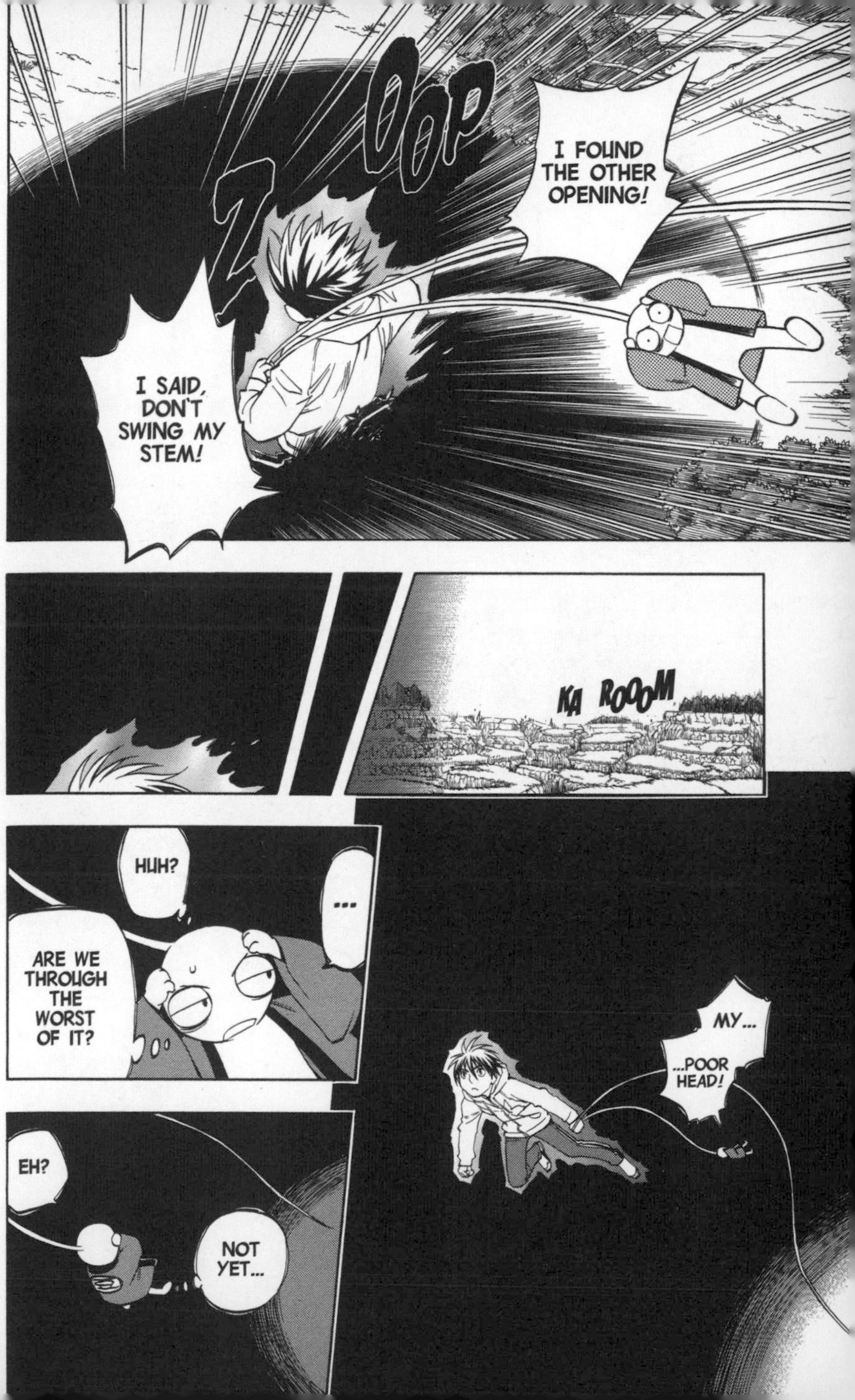
I FOUND THE OTHER OPENING!
ZOOP
I SAID, DON'T SWING MY STEM!
KA ROOOM
MY...
...POOR HEAD!
...
HUH?
ARE WE THROUGH THE WORST OF IT?
EH?
NOT YET...

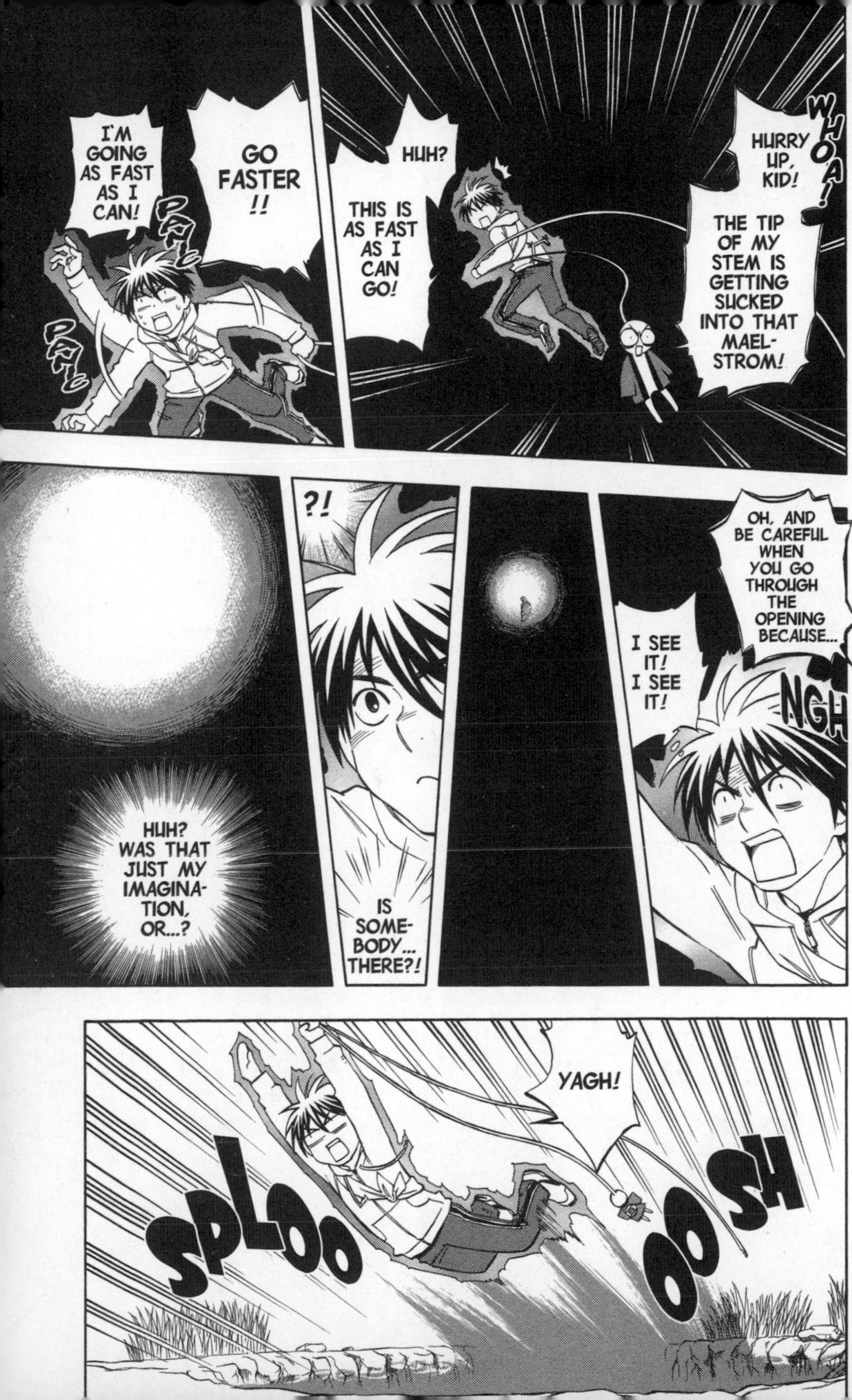
HURRY UP, KID!
WHOA!
THE TIP OF MY STEM IS GETTING SUCKED INTO THAT MAEL-STROM!
HUH?
THIS IS AS FAST AS I CAN GO!
GO FASTER !!
I'M GOING AS FAST AS I CAN!
PANT
PANT
OH, AND BE CAREFUL WHEN YOU GO THROUGH THE OPENING BECAUSE...
NGH
I SEE IT! I SEE IT!
?!
IS SOME-BODY... THERE?!
HUH? WAS THAT JUST MY IMAGINA-TION, OR...?
YAGH!
SPLOO
OOSH

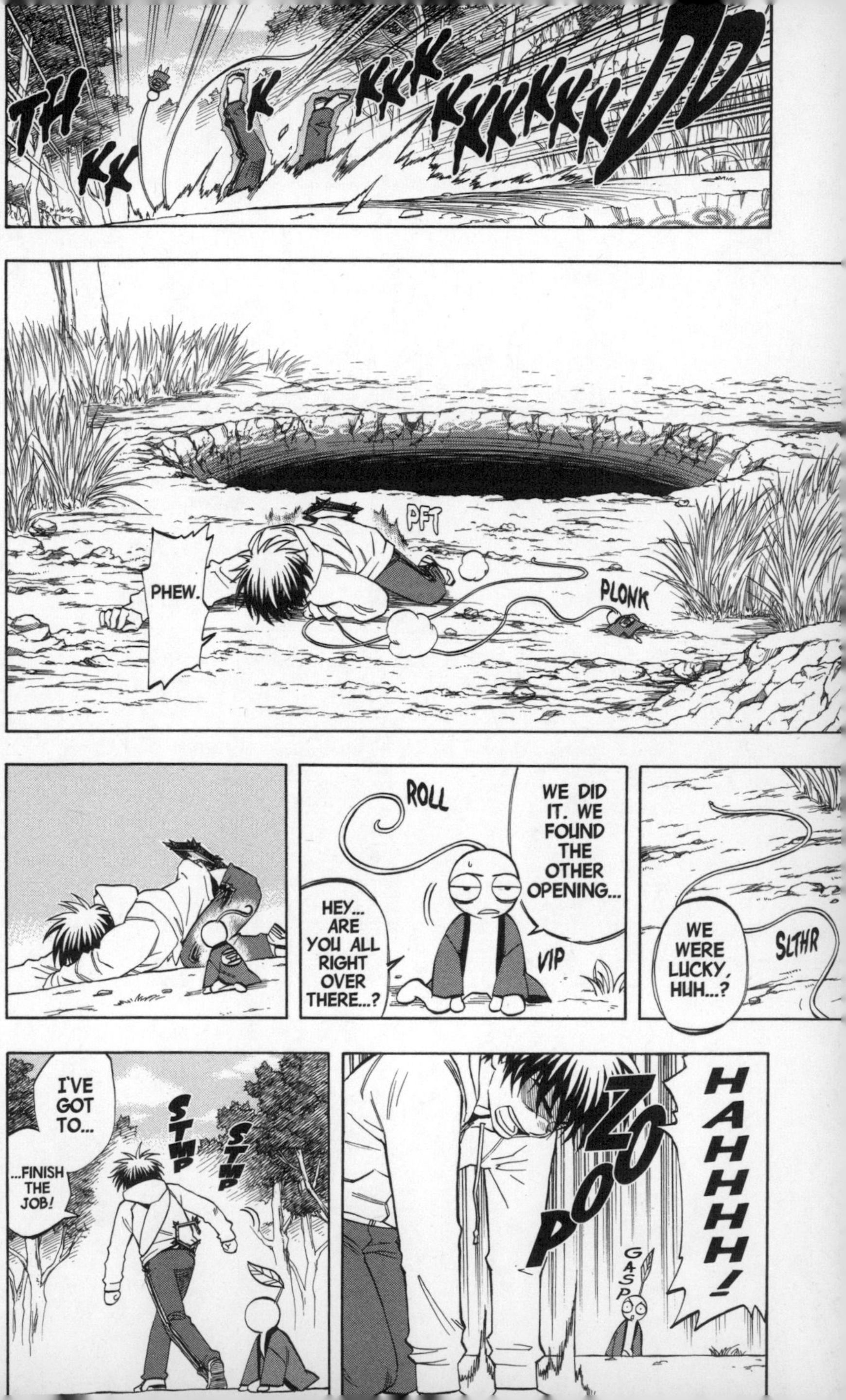
THKKKKKKKKKKKKDD
PFT
PHEW.
PLONK
SLTHR
WE WERE LUCKY, HUH...?
WE DID IT. WE FOUND THE OTHER OPENING...
ROLL
HEY... ARE YOU ALL RIGHT OVER THERE...?
VIP
ZOOP
HAHHHHH!
GASP
I'VE GOT TO...
...FINISH THE JOB!
STMP
STMP

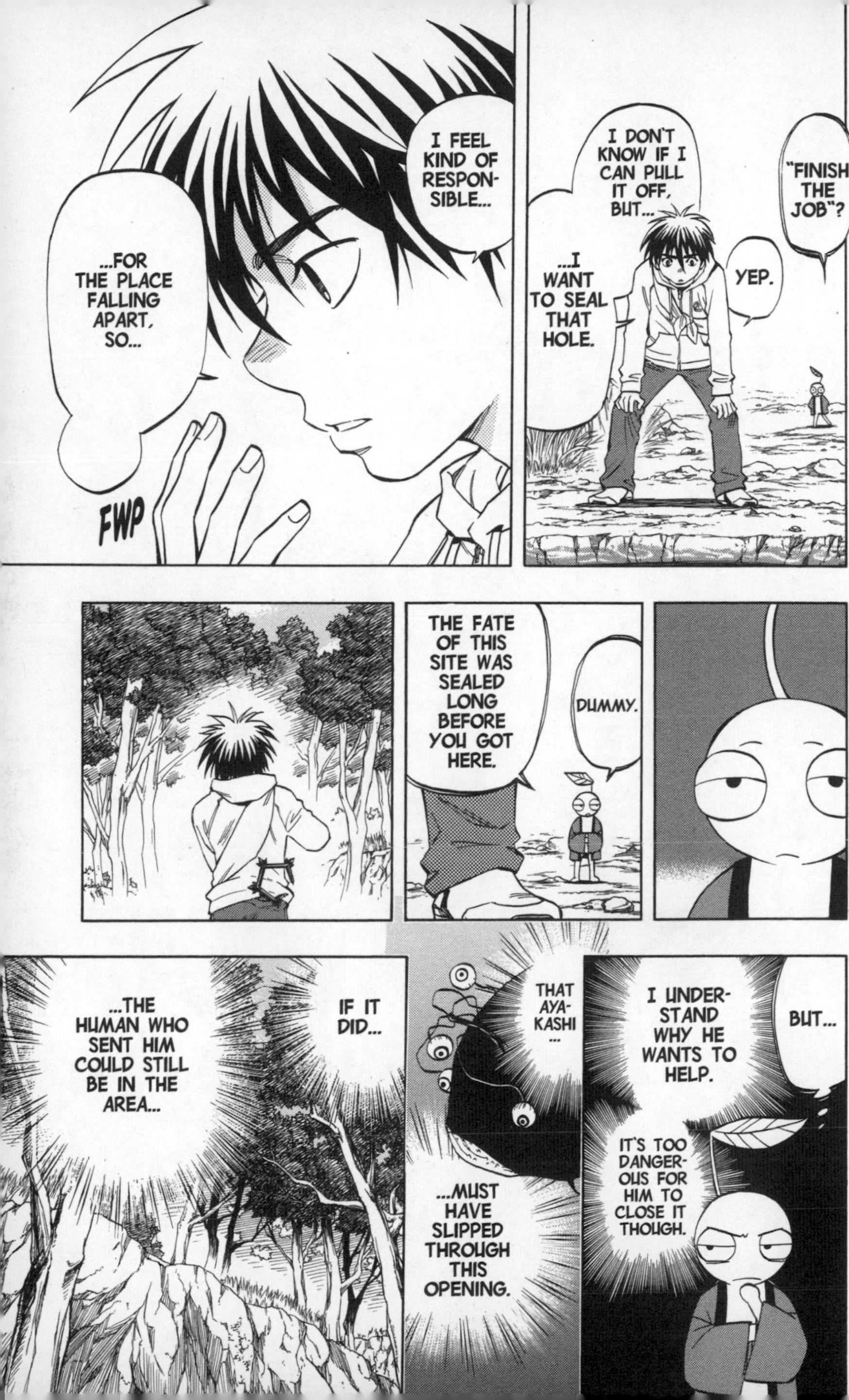
"FINISH THE JOB"?
YEP.
I DON'T KNOW IF I CAN PULL IT OFF, BUT...
...I WANT TO SEAL THAT HOLE.
I FEEL KIND OF RESPONSIBLE...
...FOR THE PLACE FALLING APART, SO...
FWP
DUMMY.
THE FATE OF THIS SITE WAS SEALED LONG BEFORE YOU GOT HERE.
BUT...
I UNDERSTAND WHY HE WANTS TO HELP.
IT'S TOO DANGEROUS FOR HIM TO CLOSE IT THOUGH.
THAT AYAKASHI...
...MUST HAVE SLIPPED THROUGH THIS OPENING.
IF IT DID...
...THE HUMAN WHO SENT HIM COULD STILL BE IN THE AREA...

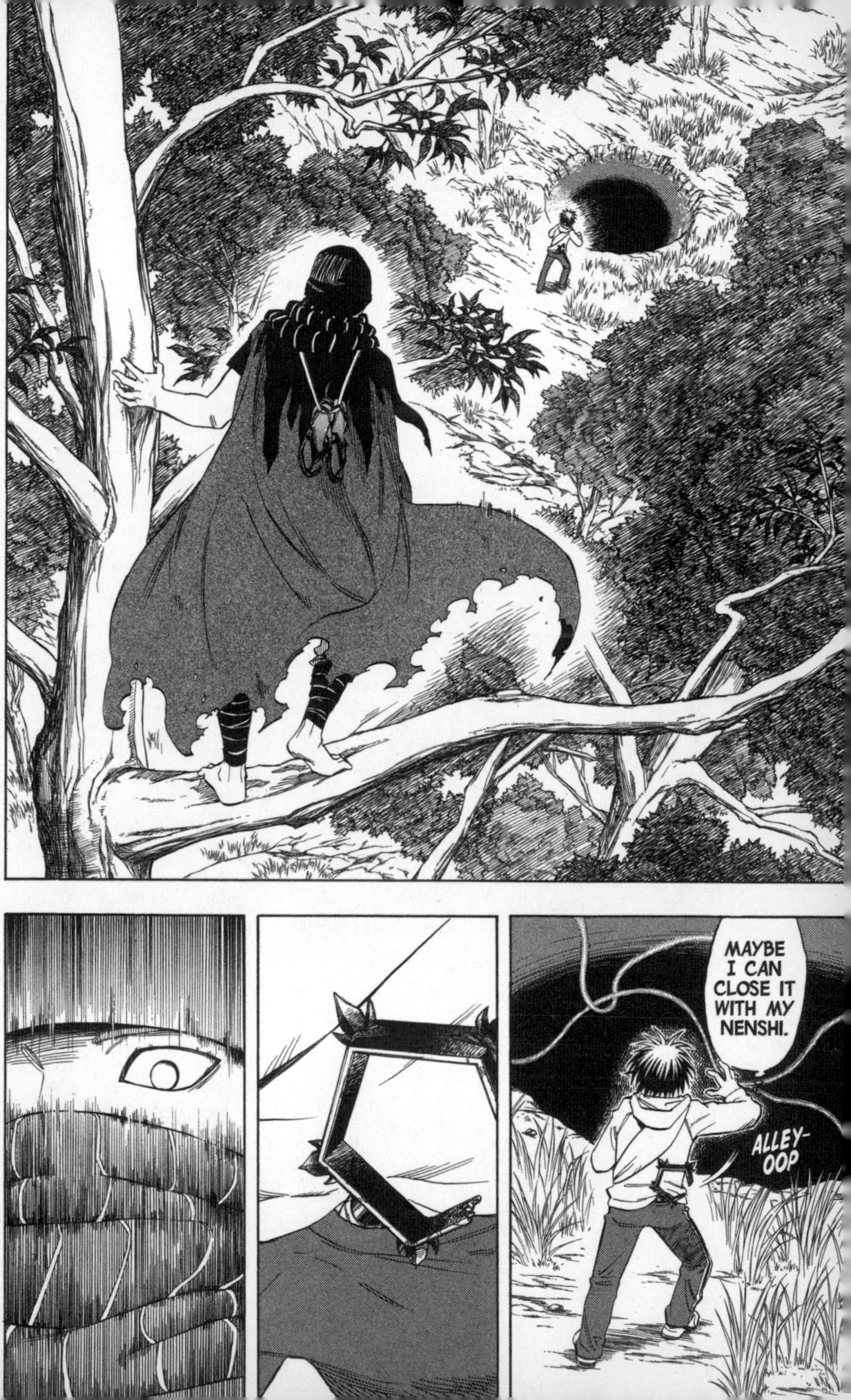
MAYBE I CAN CLOSE IT WITH MY NENSHI.
ALLEY-OOP

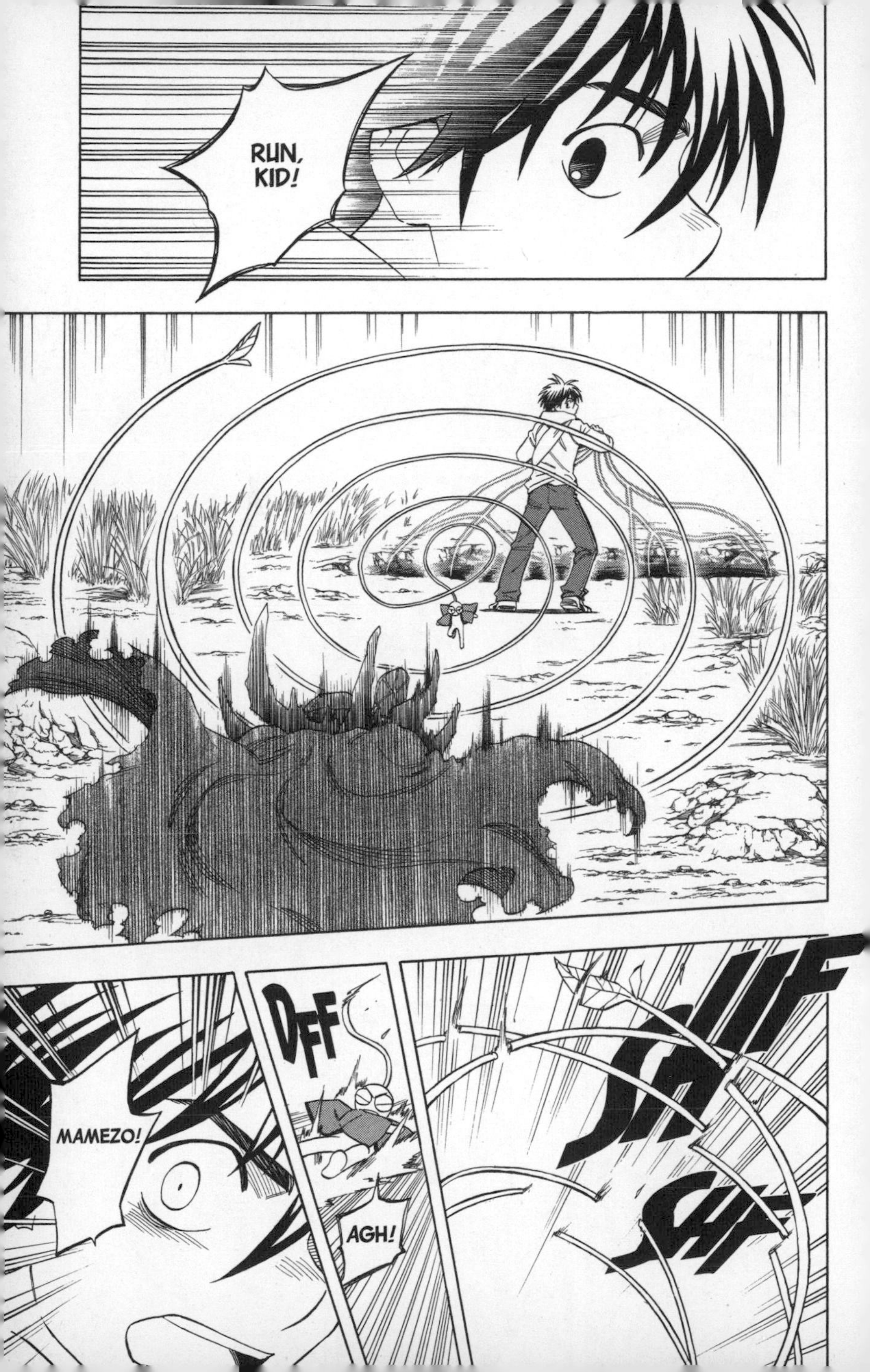
RUN, KID!
SHFF
SHFF
DFF
AGH!
MAMEZO!

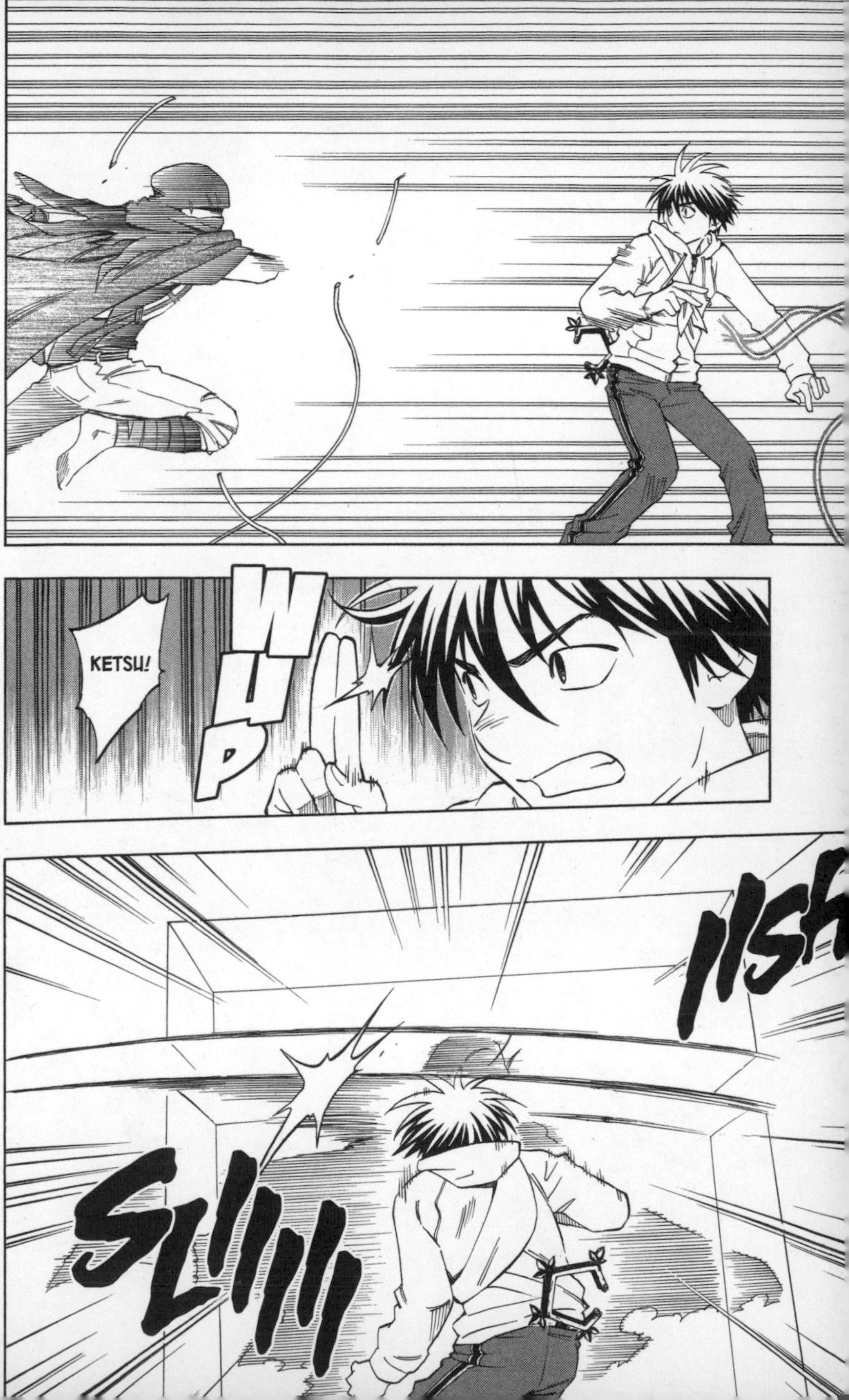
KETSU!
PUW
SLIIIII
IISH

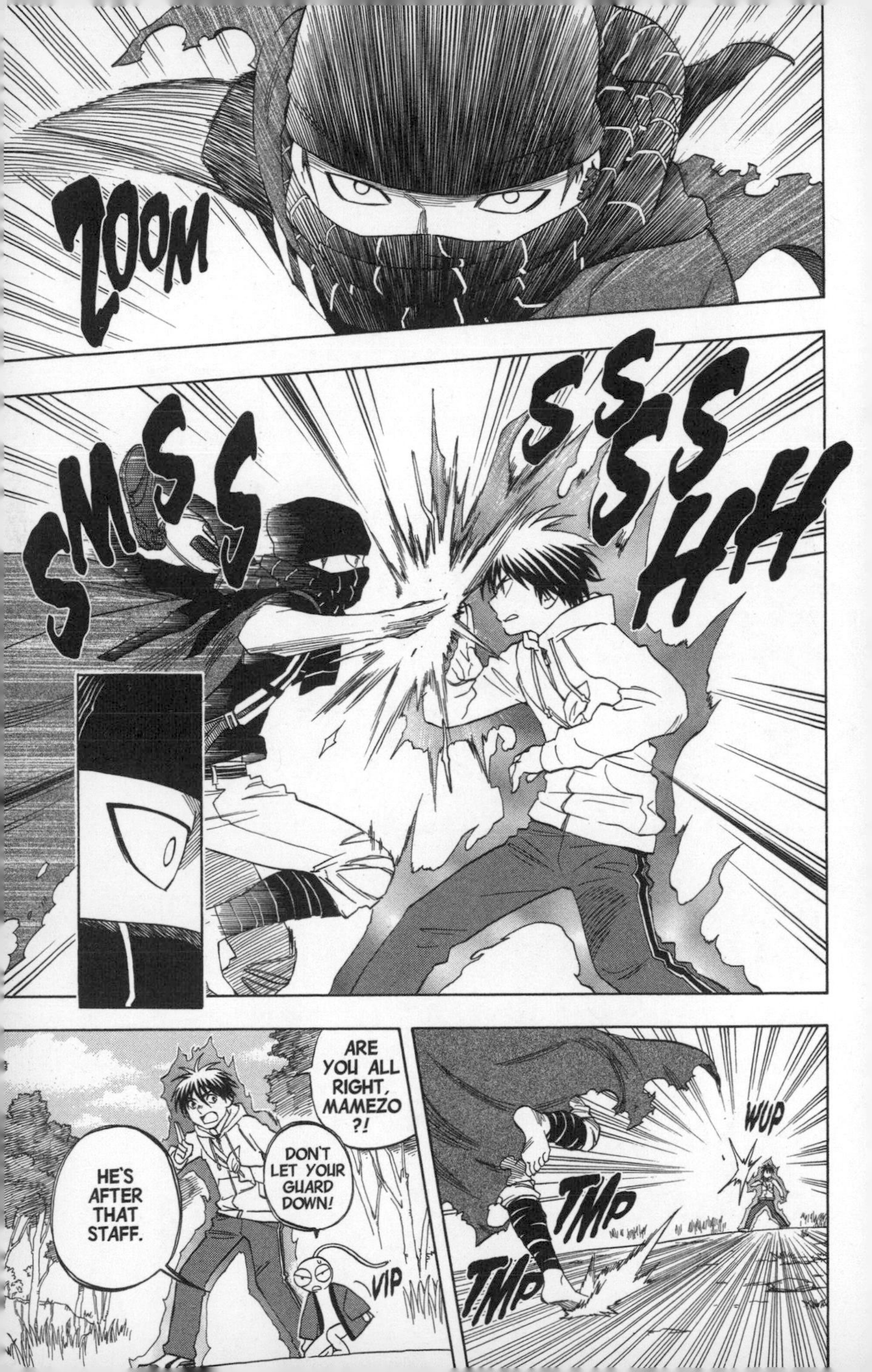
ZOOM
SSSSHH
SMSS
WUP
TMP
TMP
ARE YOU ALL RIGHT, MAMEZO?!
DON'T LET YOUR GUARD DOWN!
HE'S AFTER THAT STAFF.
VIP

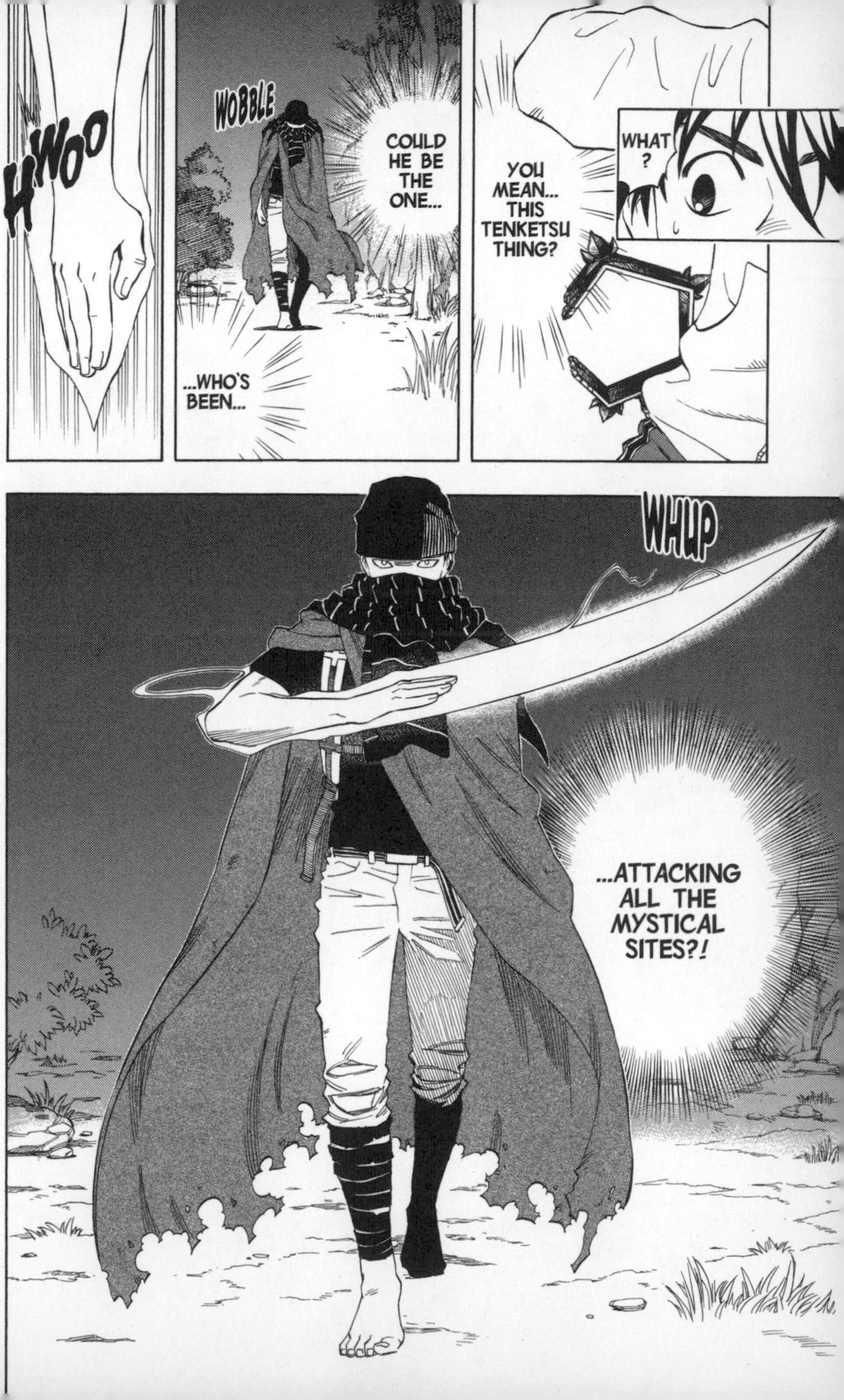
WHAT
?
YOU MEAN... THIS TENKETSU THING?
COULD HE BE THE ONE...
WOBBLE
...WHO'S BEEN...
HWOO
WHUP
...ATTACKING ALL THE MYSTICAL SITES?!

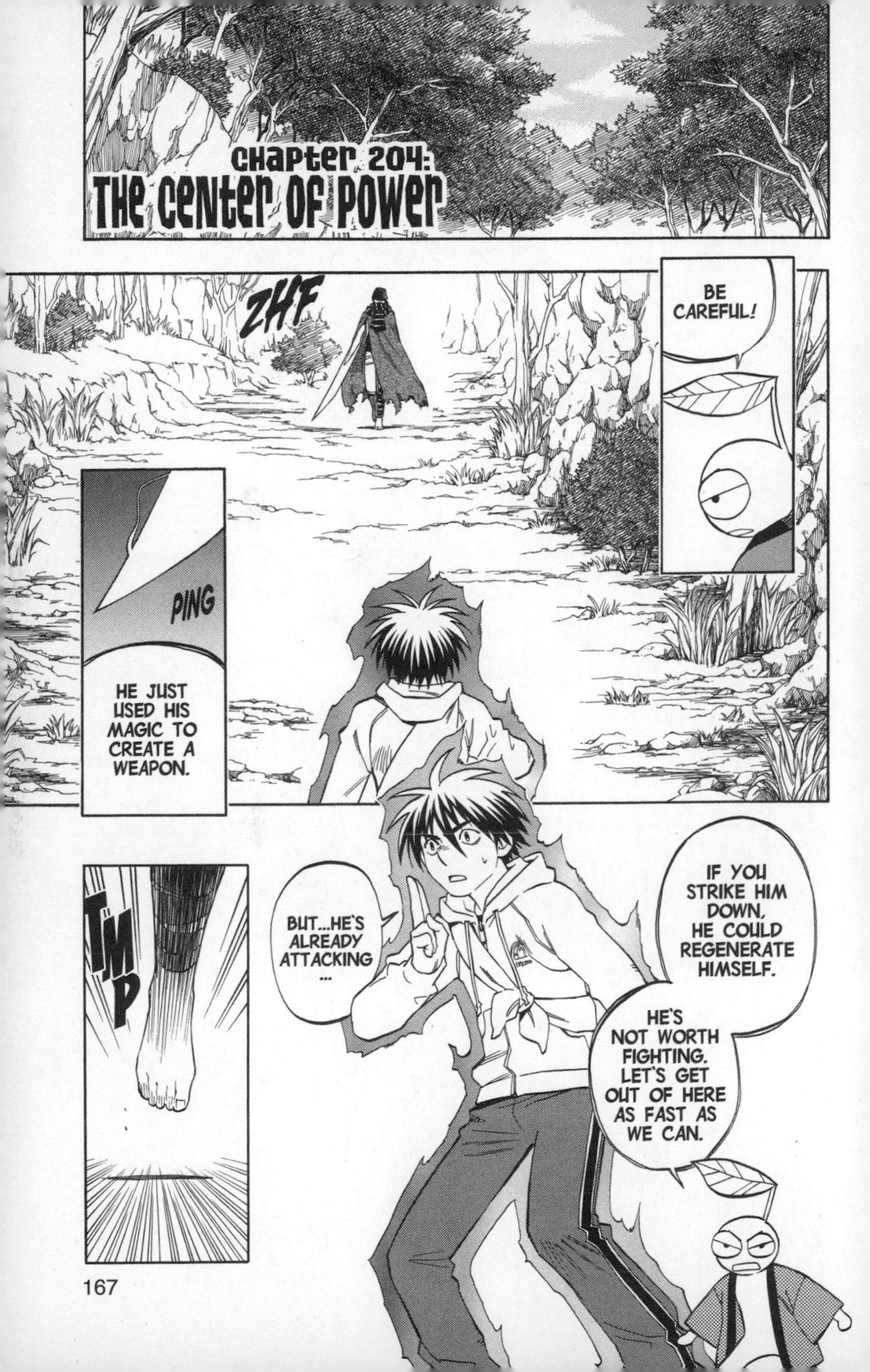
Chapter 204:
The Center of Power
BE CAREFUL!
ZHF
PING
HE JUST USED HIS MAGIC TO CREATE A WEAPON.
IF YOU STRIKE HIM DOWN, HE COULD REGENERATE HIMSELF.
HE'S NOT WORTH FIGHTING. LET'S GET OUT OF HERE AS FAST AS WE CAN.
BUT...HE'S ALREADY ATTACKING...
TMP

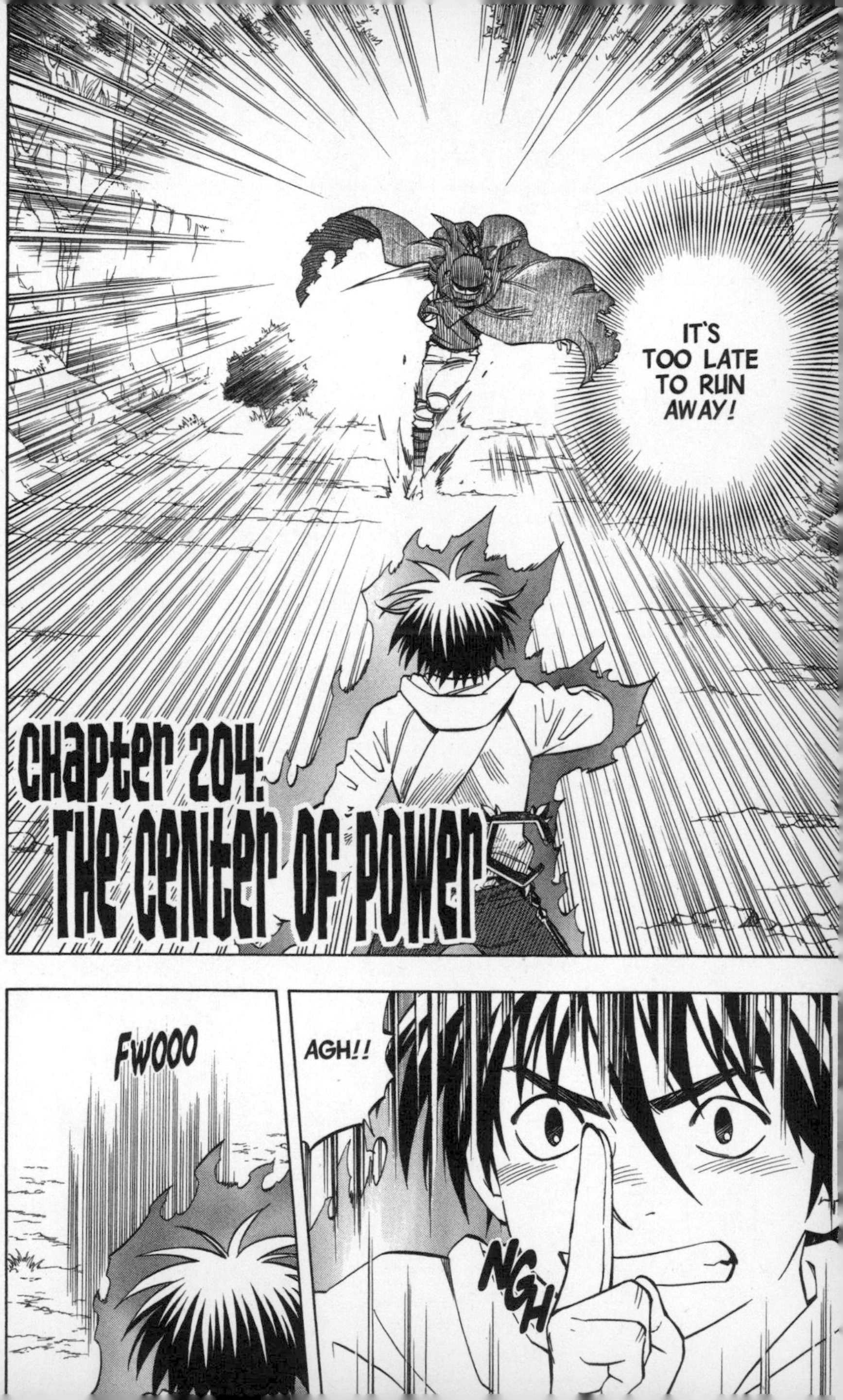
IT'S TOO LATE TO RUN AWAY!
CHAPTER 204: THE CENTER OF POWER
AGH!!
NGH
FWOOO

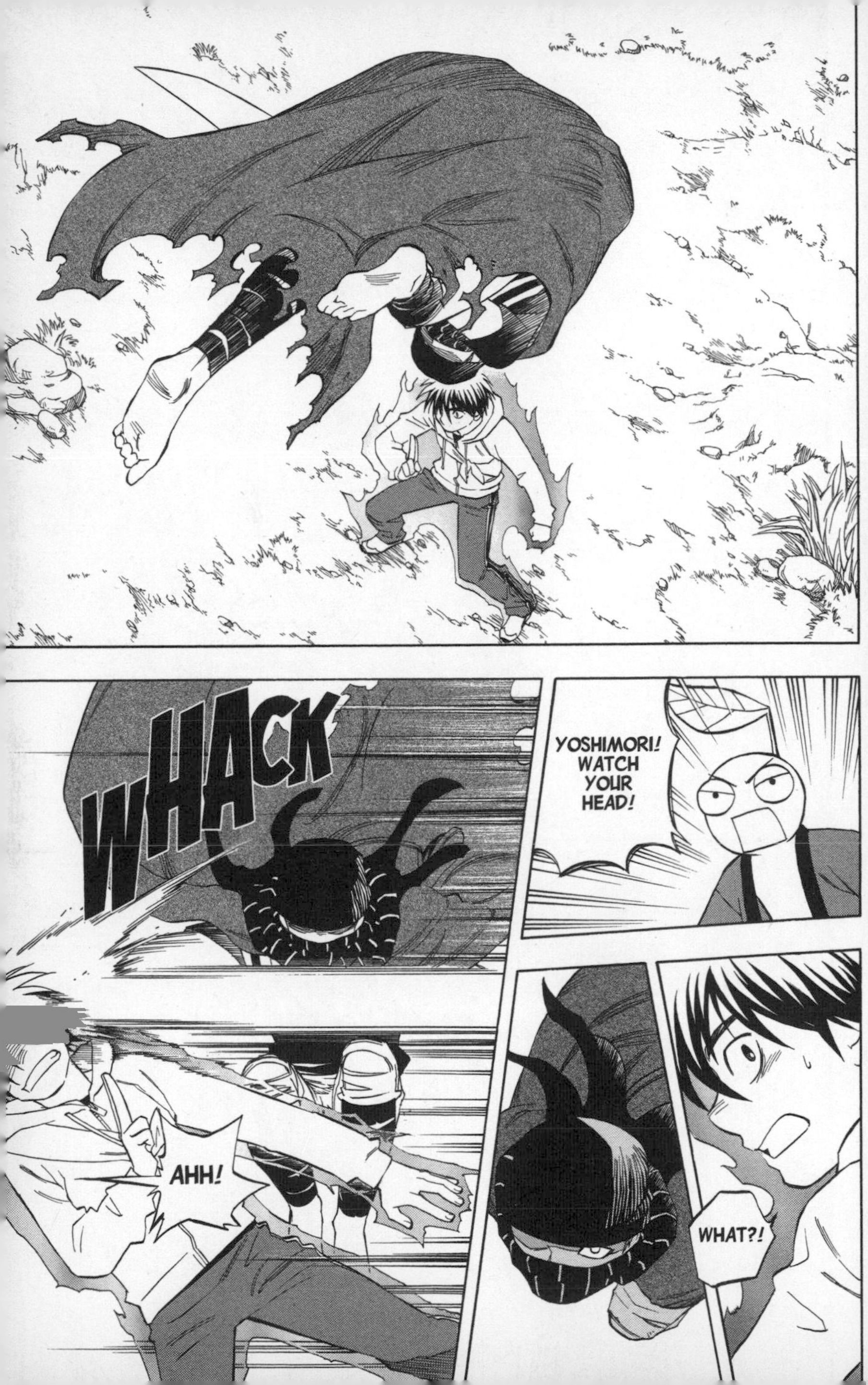
YOSHIMORI! WATCH YOUR HEAD!
WHAT?!
WHACK
AHH!

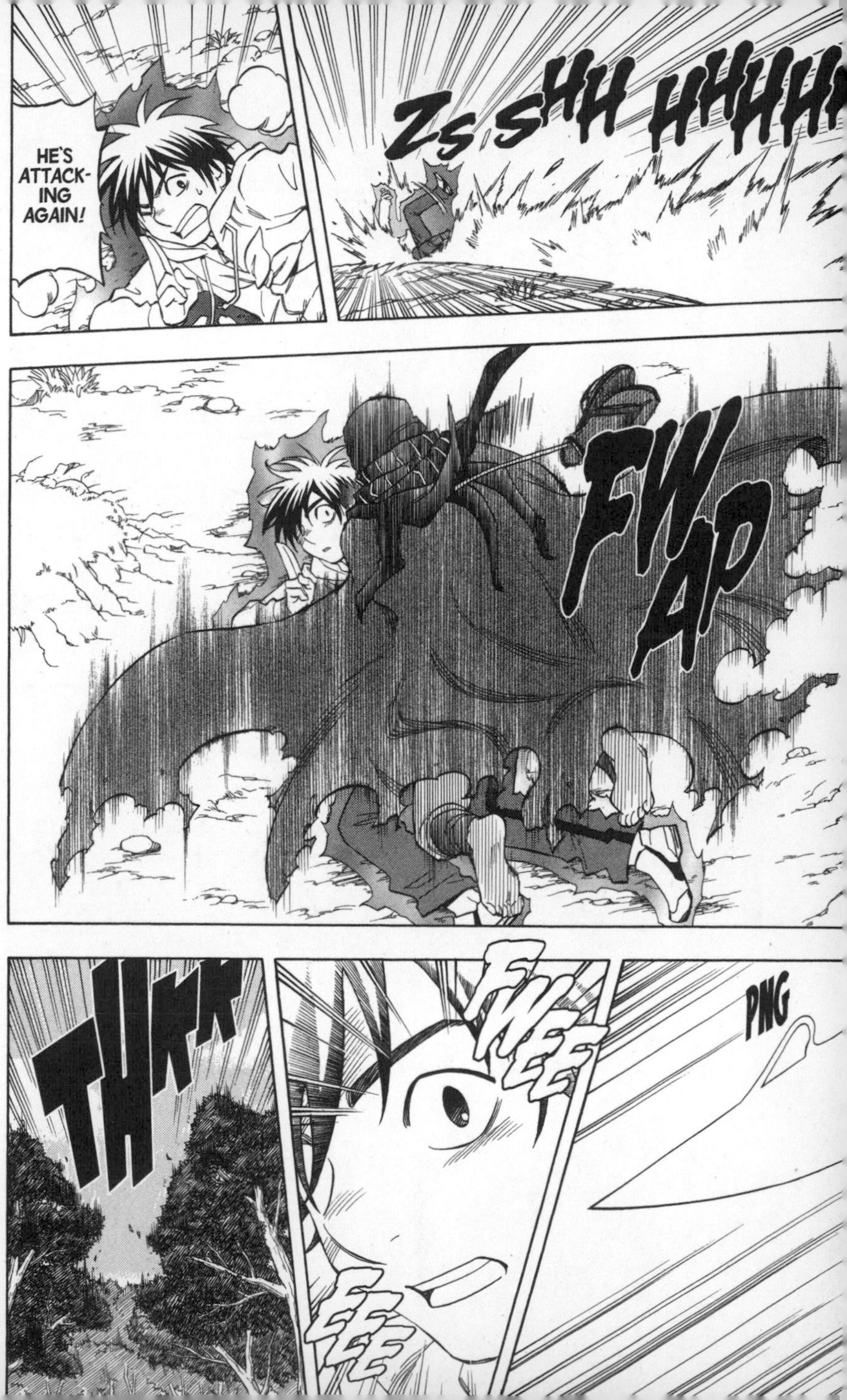

ZSSHH HHHH
HE'S ATTACK-ING AGAIN!
FWAP
PNG
FWEE
EEEE
THKK

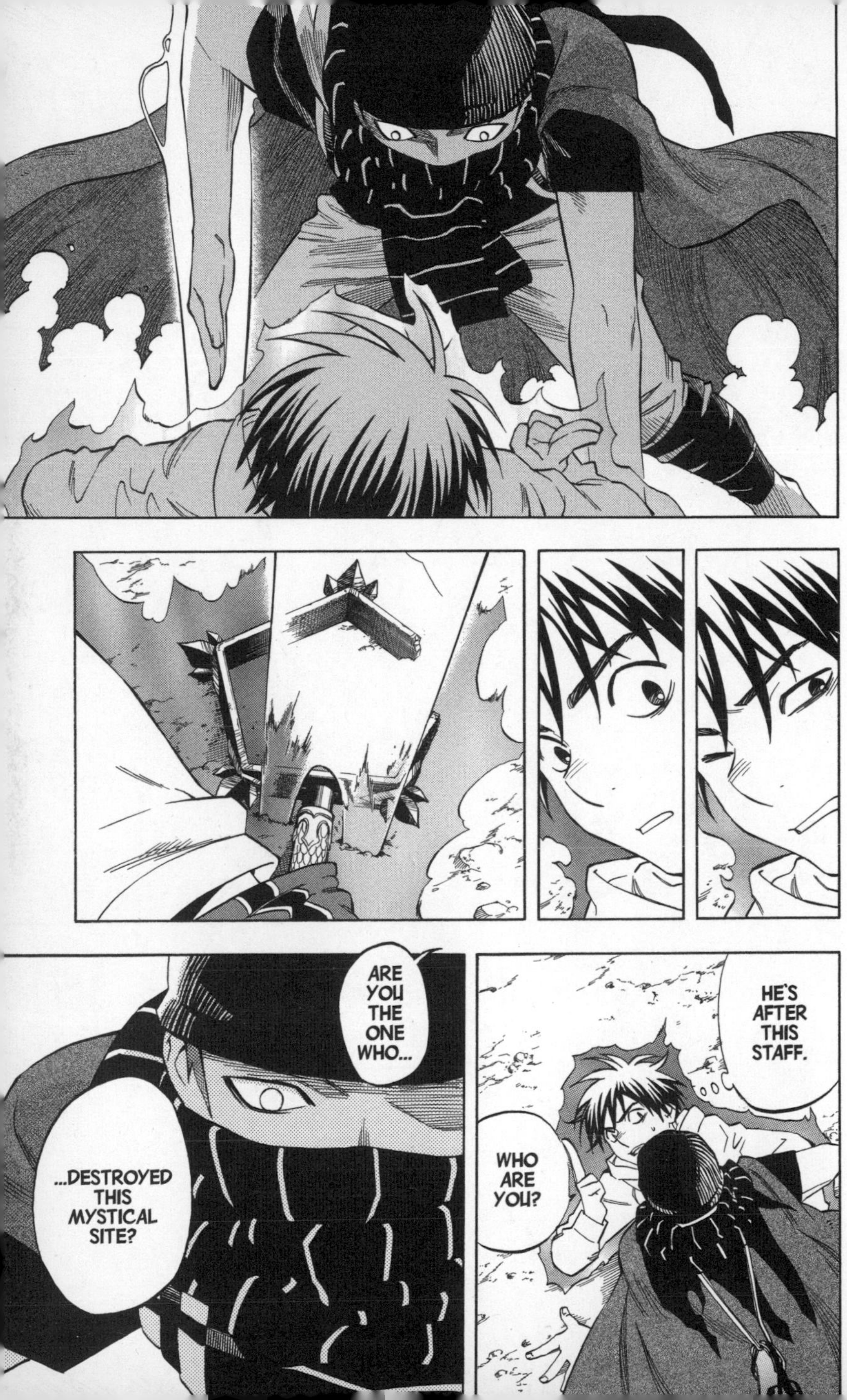
HE'S AFTER THIS STAFF.
WHO ARE YOU?
ARE YOU THE ONE WHO...
...DESTROYED THIS MYSTICAL SITE?

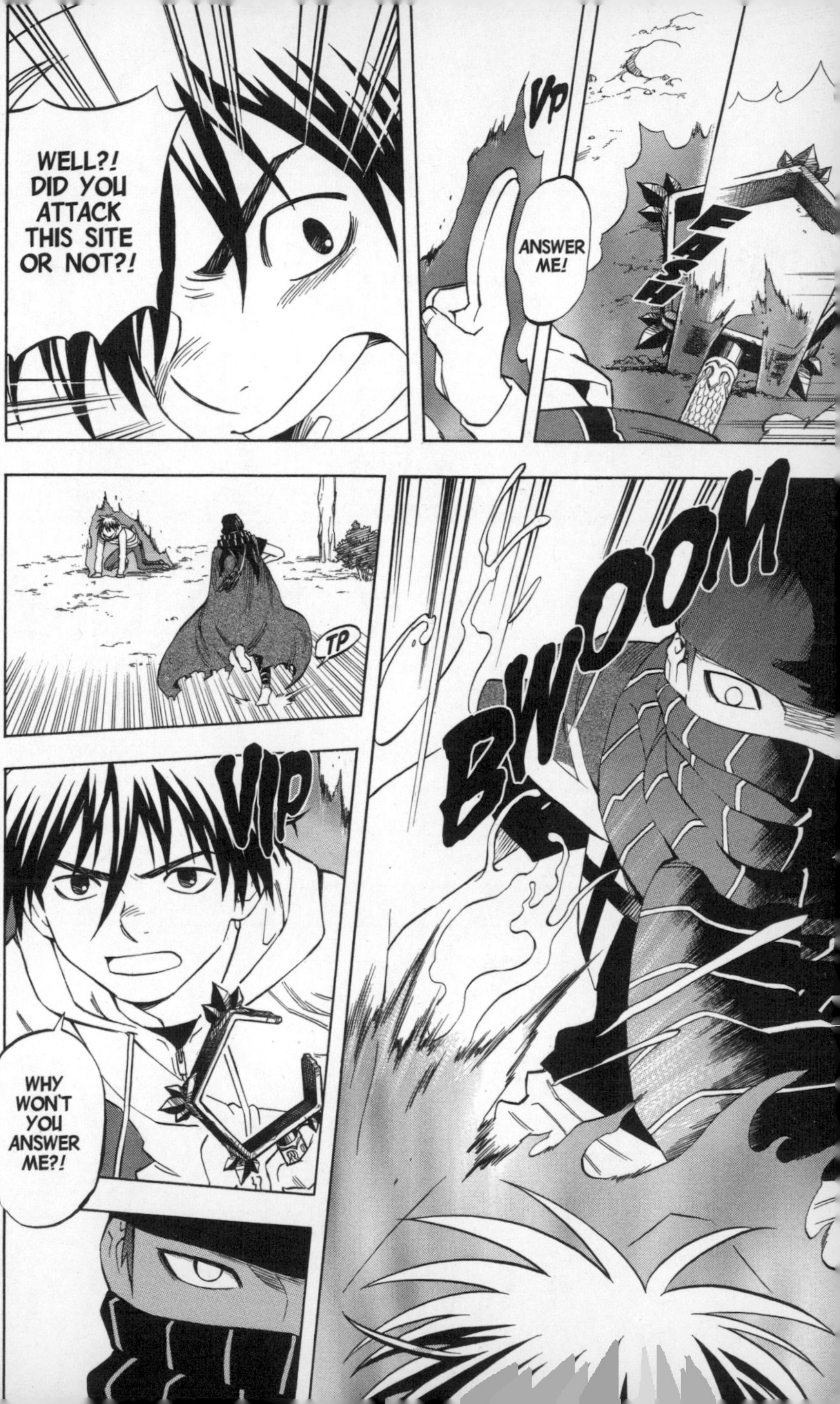
FASH
VP
ANSWER ME!
WELL?! DID YOU ATTACK THIS SITE OR NOT?!
BWOOM
TP
VIP
WHY WON'T YOU ANSWER ME?!

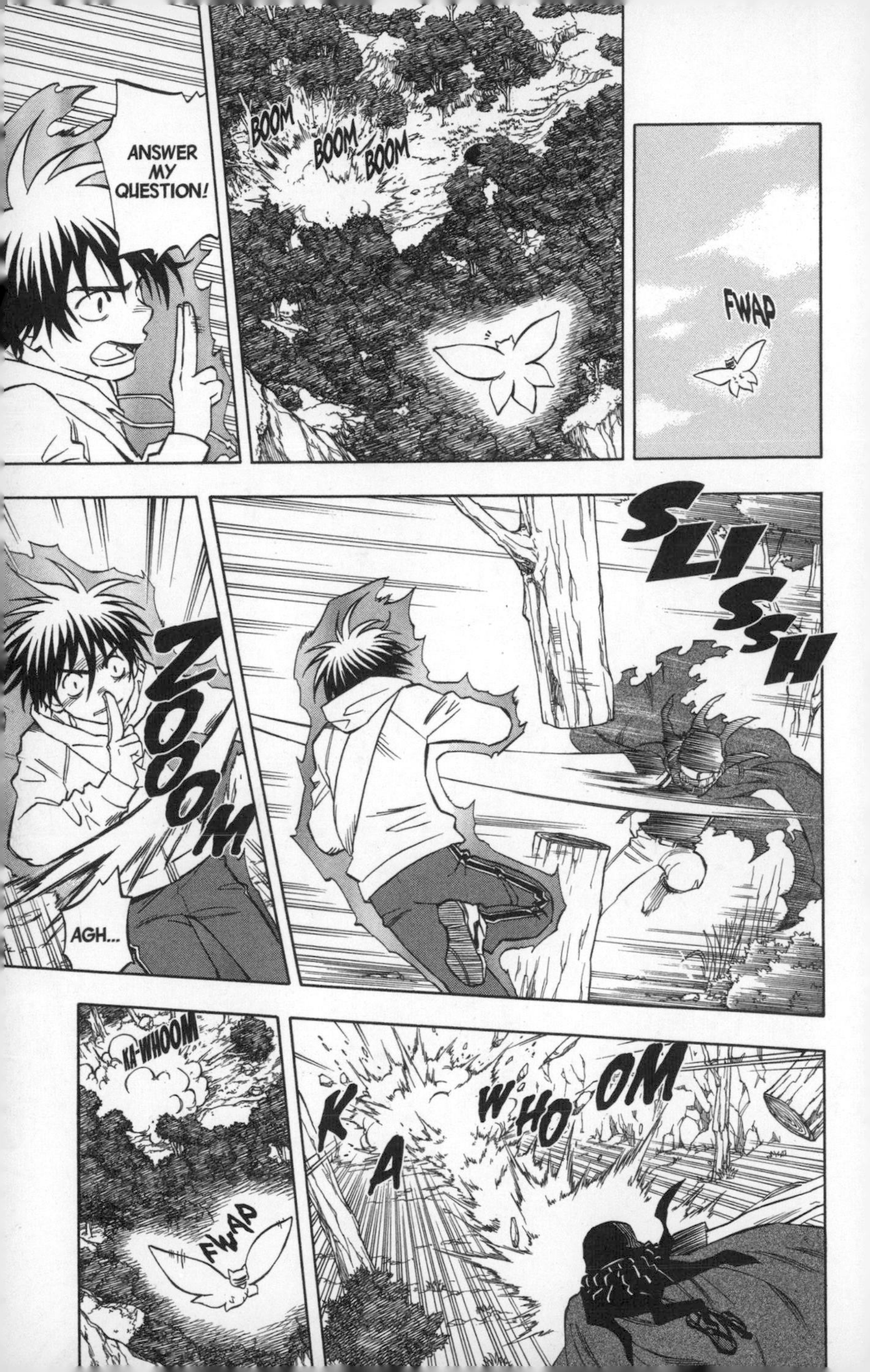
FWAP
BOOM
BOOM
BOOM
ANSWER MY QUESTION!
SLISSH
ZOOOM
AGH...
KAWHOOM
KA-WHOOM
FWAP

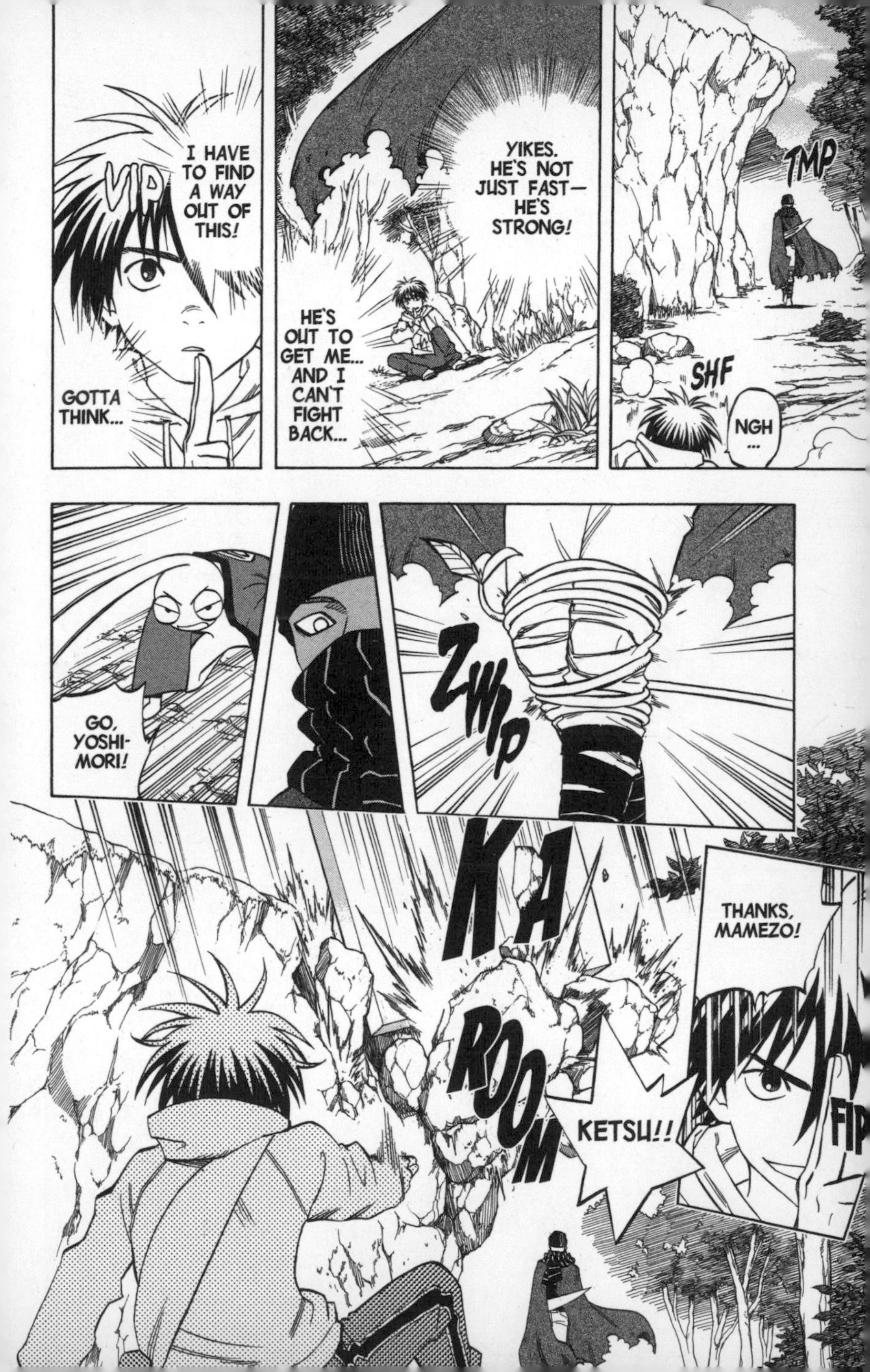
TMP
SHF
NGH
...
YIKES. HE'S NOT JUST FAST— HE'S STRONG!
HE'S OUT TO GET ME... AND I CAN'T FIGHT BACK...
VIP
I HAVE TO FIND A WAY OUT OF THIS!
GOTTA THINK...
ZWIP
GO, YOSHI-MORI!
THANKS, MAMEZO!
FIP
KA ROOM
KETSU!!

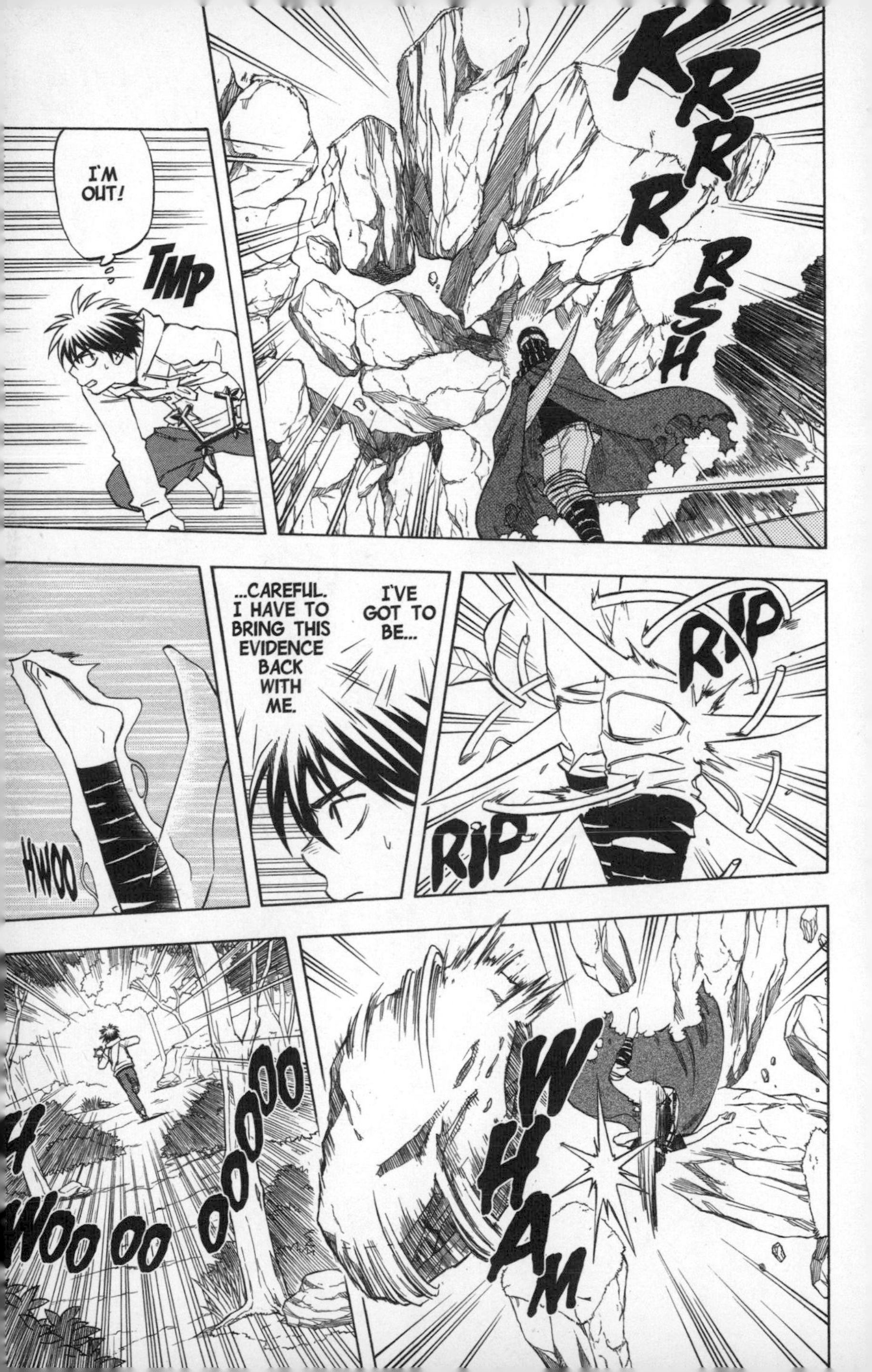
KRRR
RRSH
I'M OUT!
TMP
RIP
RIP
I'VE GOT TO BE...
...CAREFUL. I HAVE TO BRING THIS EVIDENCE BACK WITH ME.
HWOO
WHAM
HWOO OO OOOOOO

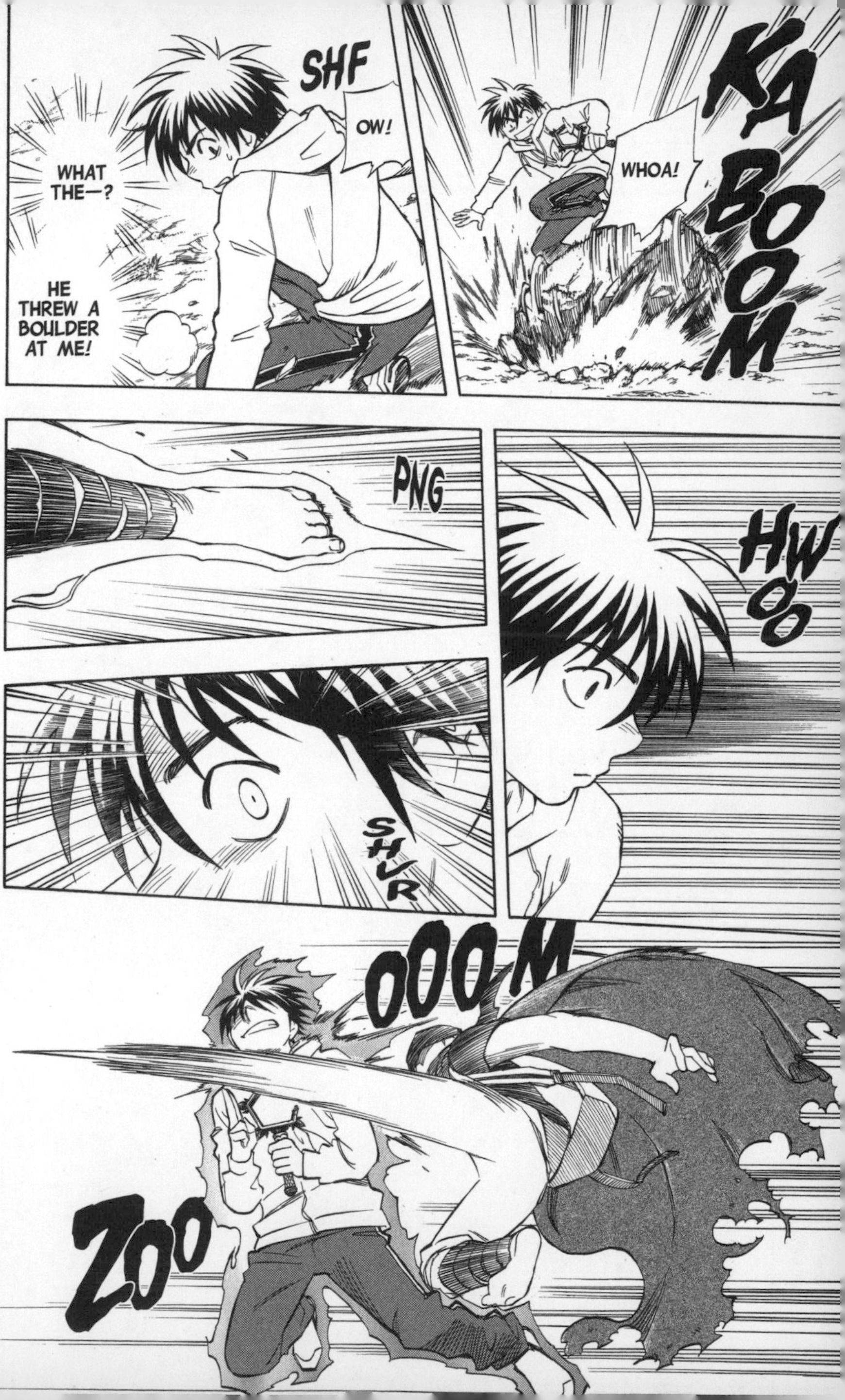
KA BOOM
WHOA!
SHF
OW!
WHAT THE—?
HE THREW A BOULDER AT ME!
HWOO
PNG
SHUR
WOOOM
ZOO

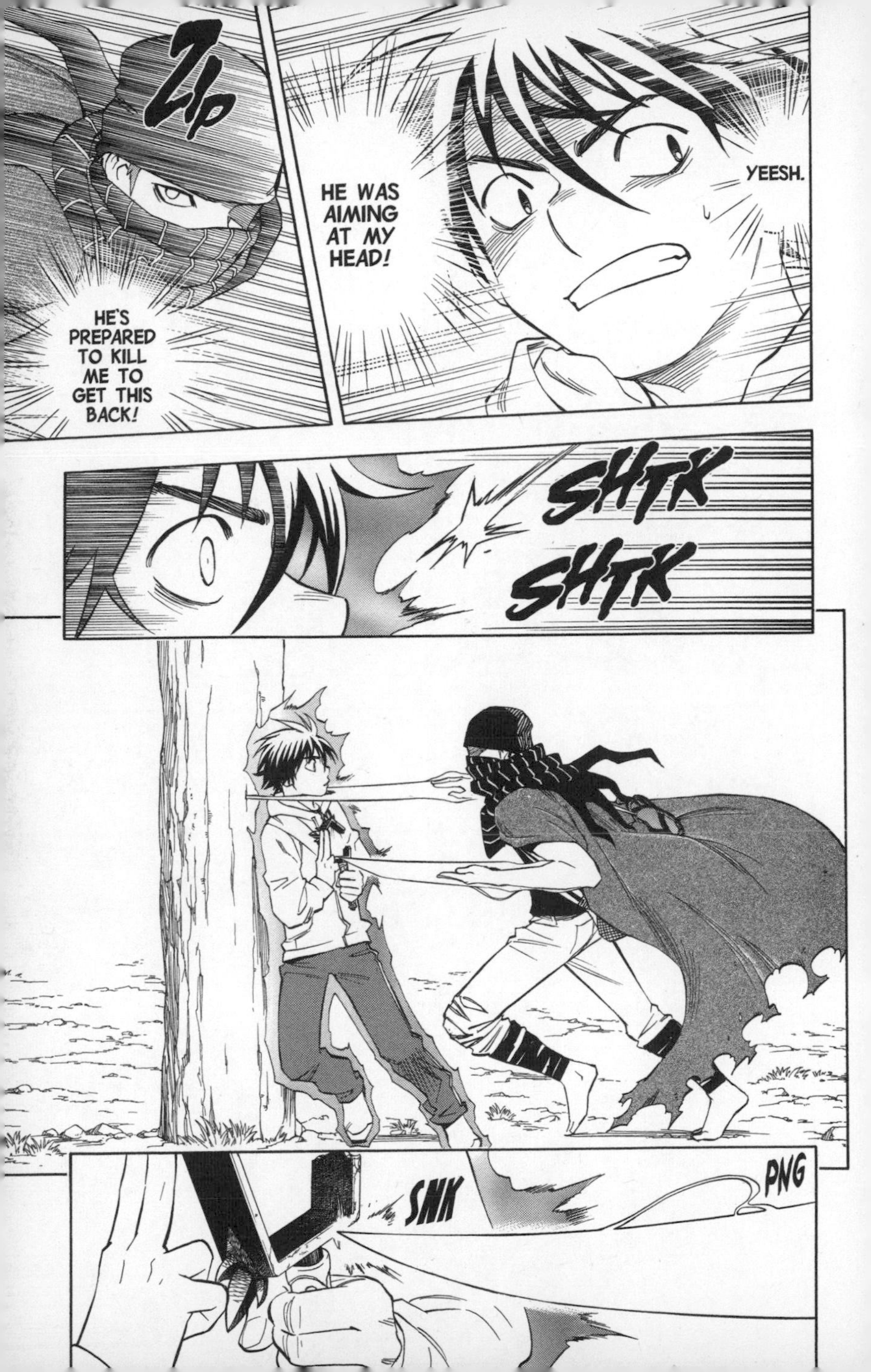
YEESH.
HE WAS AIMING AT MY HEAD!
ZIP
HE'S PREPARED TO KILL ME TO GET THIS BACK!
SHTK
SHTK
PNG
SNK

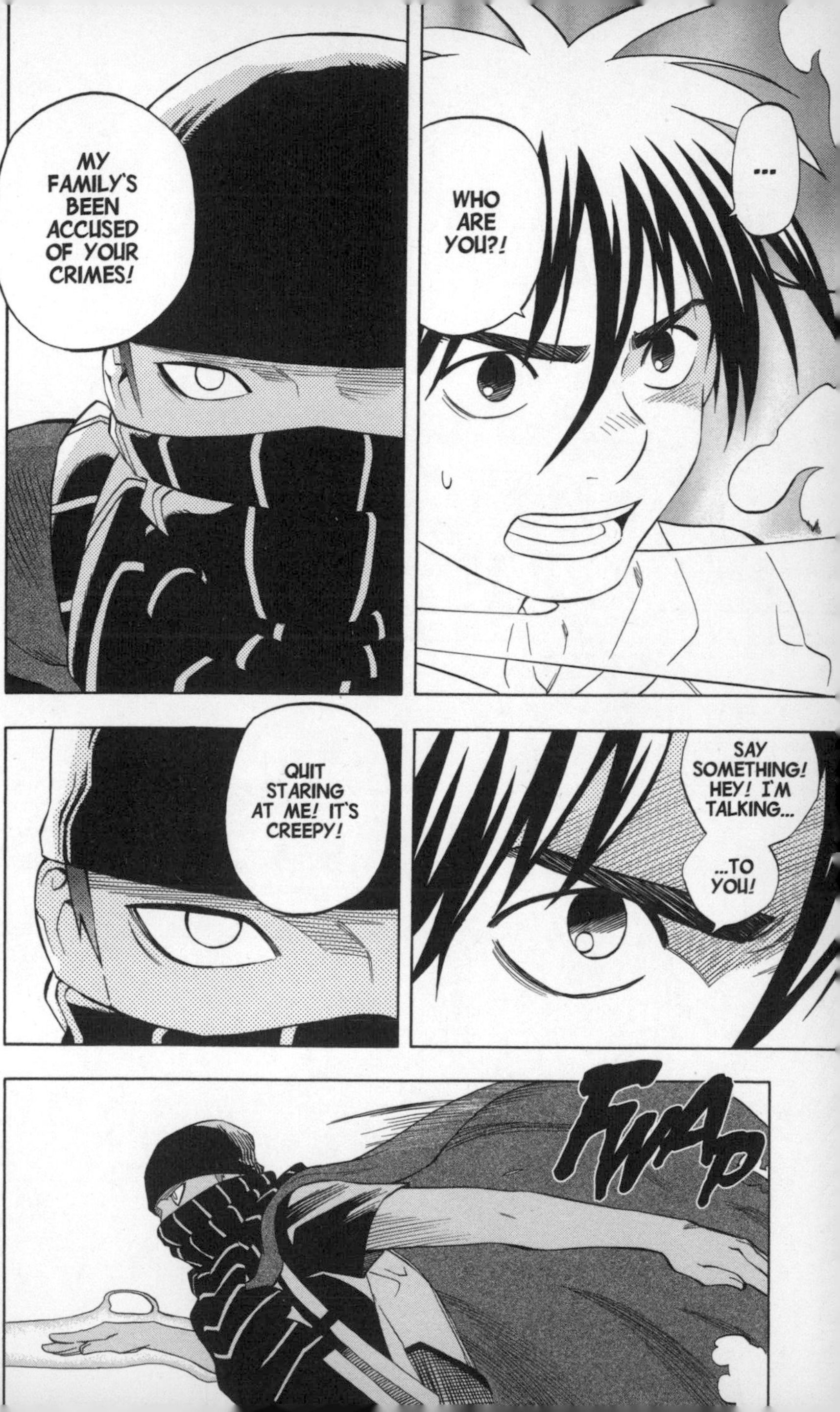
...
WHO ARE YOU?!
MY FAMILY'S BEEN ACCUSED OF YOUR CRIMES!
SAY SOMETHING! HEY! I'M TALKING...
...TO YOU!
QUIT STARING AT ME! IT'S CREEPY!
FWAP

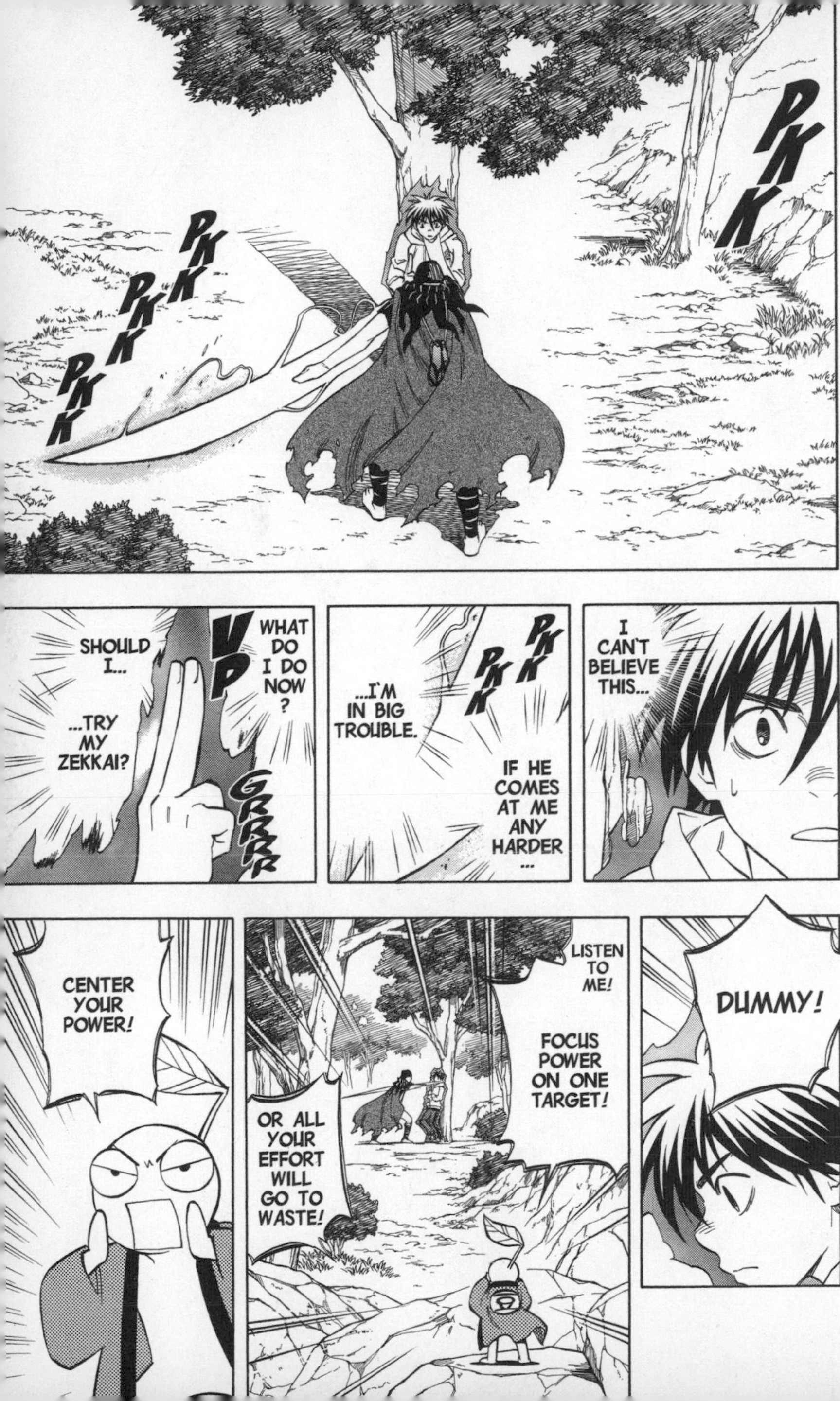
PKK
PKK
PKK
PKK
I CAN'T BELIEVE THIS...
PKK
PKK
...I'M IN BIG TROUBLE.
IF HE COMES AT ME ANY HARDER...
WHAT DO I DO NOW?
VP
SHOULD I...
...TRY MY ZEKKAI?
GRRRR
DUMMY!
LISTEN TO ME!
FOCUS POWER ON ONE TARGET!
OR ALL YOUR EFFORT WILL GO TO WASTE!
CENTER YOUR POWER!

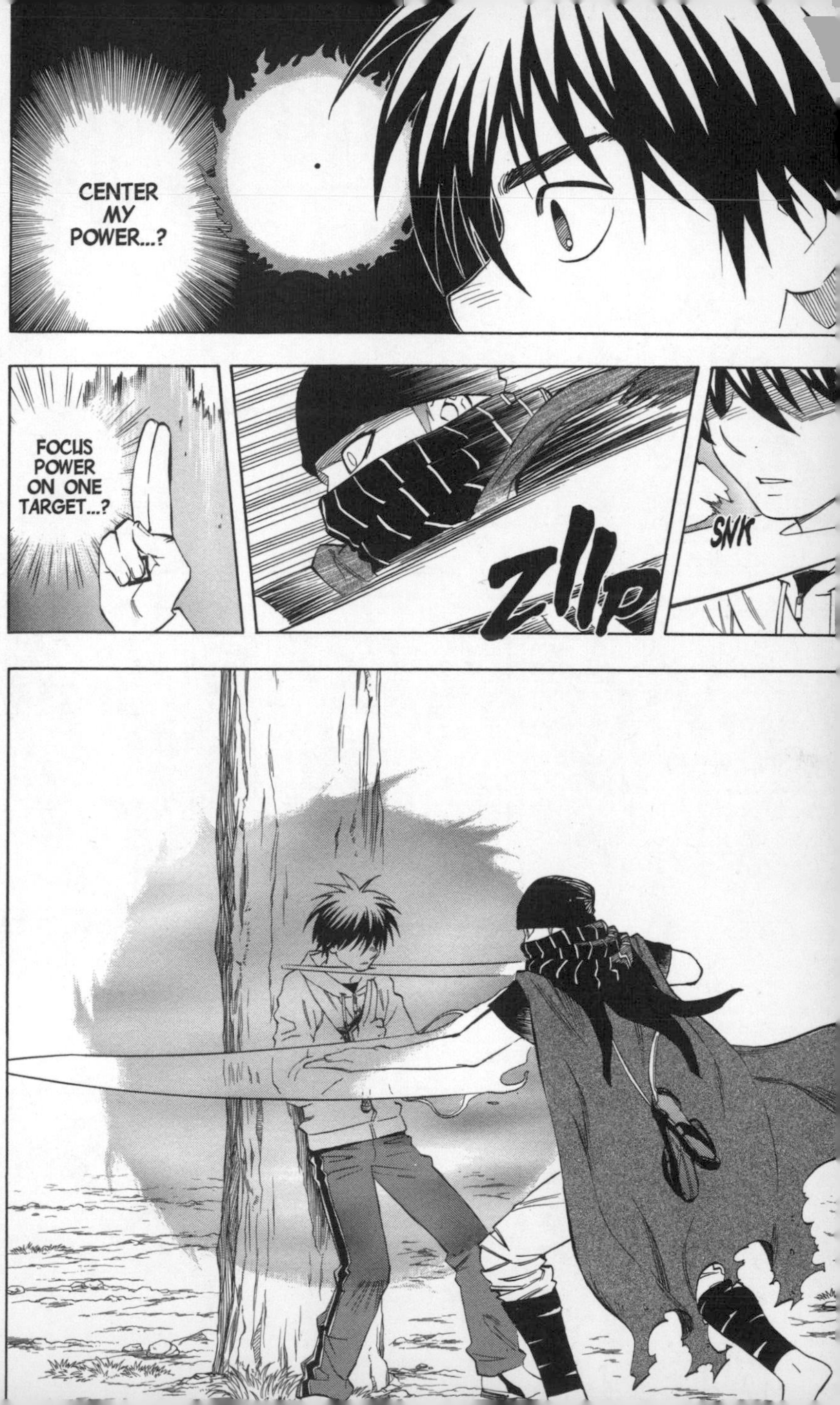
CENTER MY POWER...?
SNK
ZIP
FOCUS POWER ON ONE TARGET...?

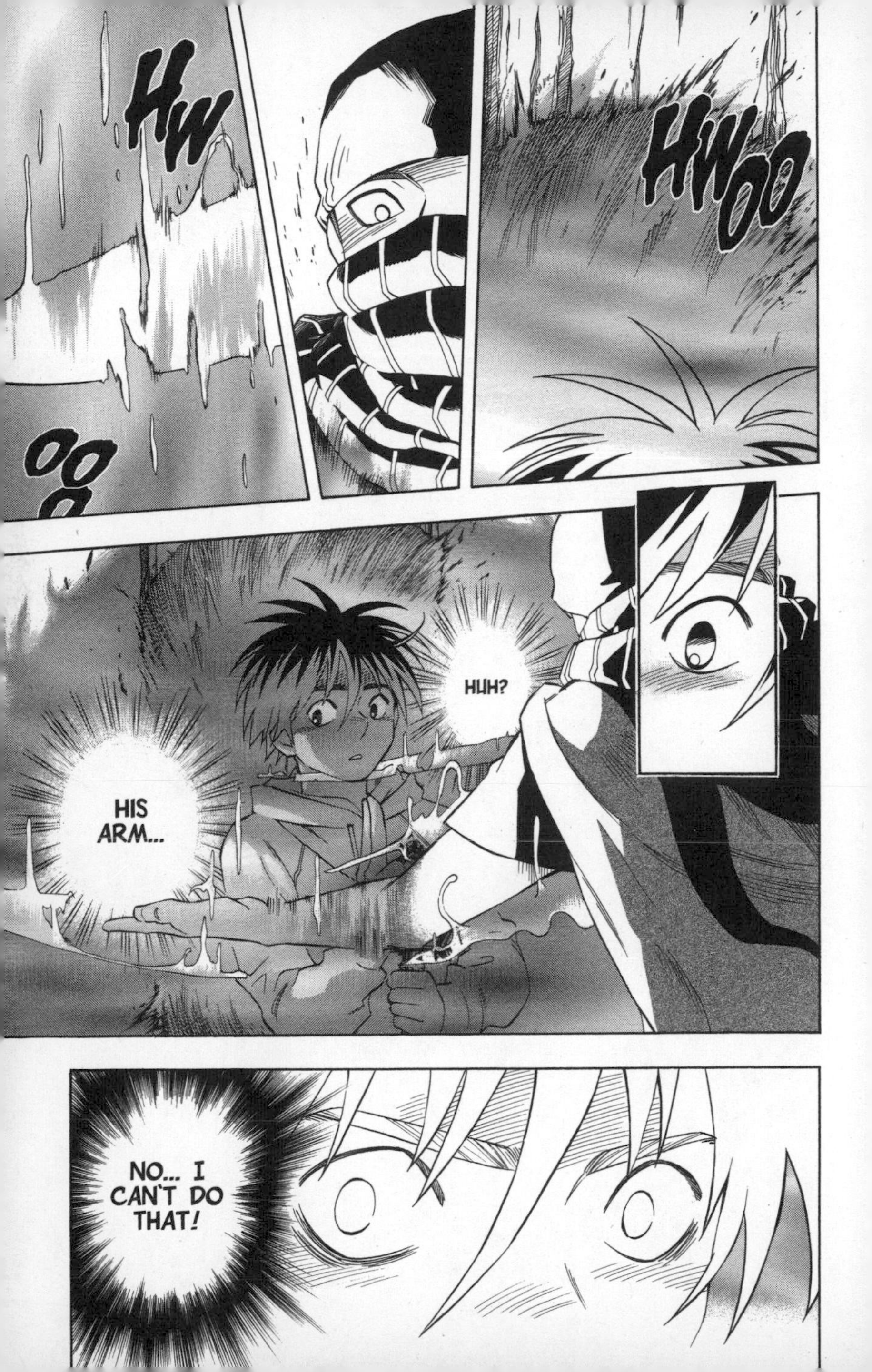
HWOO
HWOO
HUH?
HIS ARM...
NO... I CAN'T DO THAT!

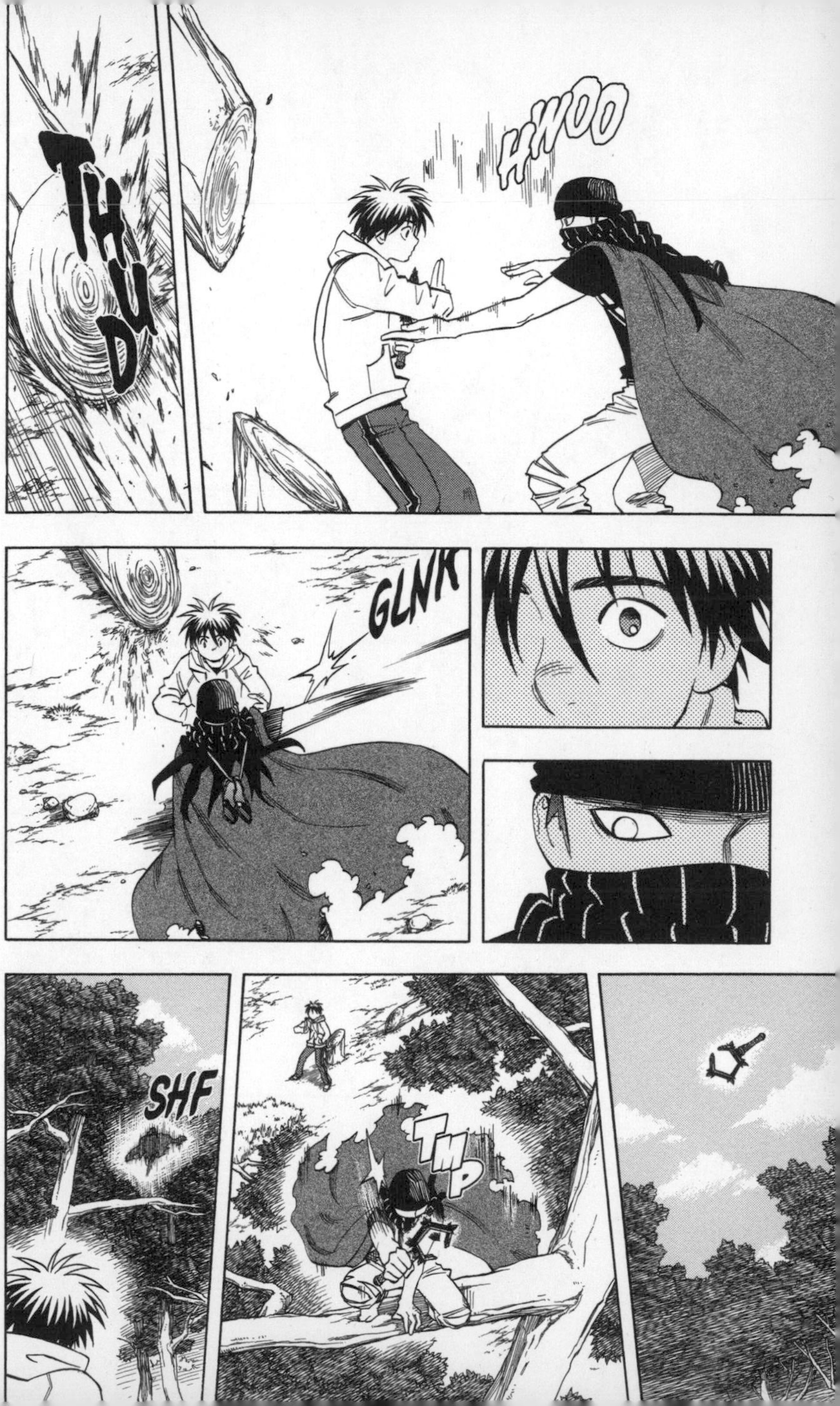
HWOO
THUD
GLNK
TMP
SHF

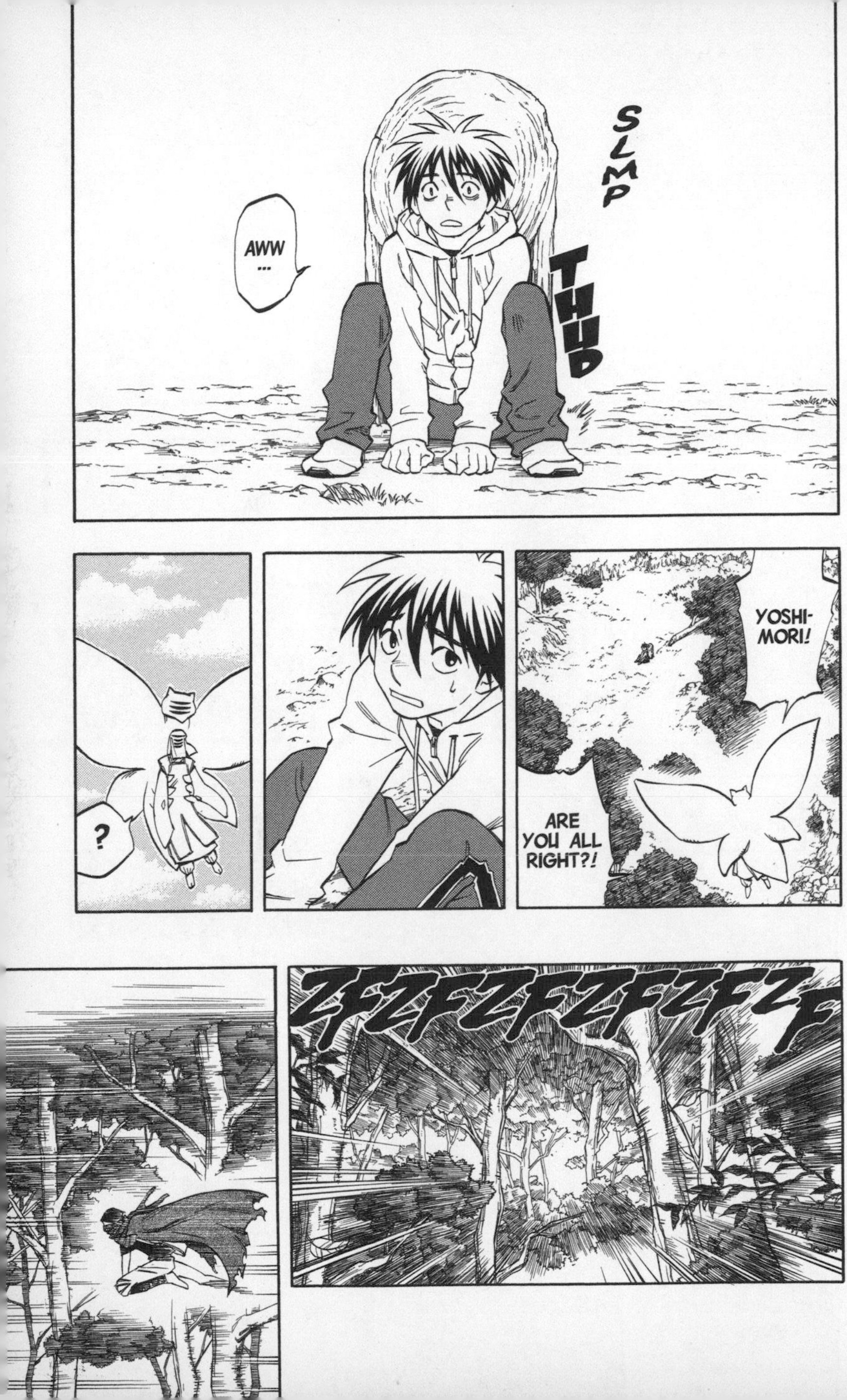
SLMP
THUD
AWW ...
YOSHIMORI!
ARE YOU ALL RIGHT?!
?
ZFZFZFZFZFZFZF

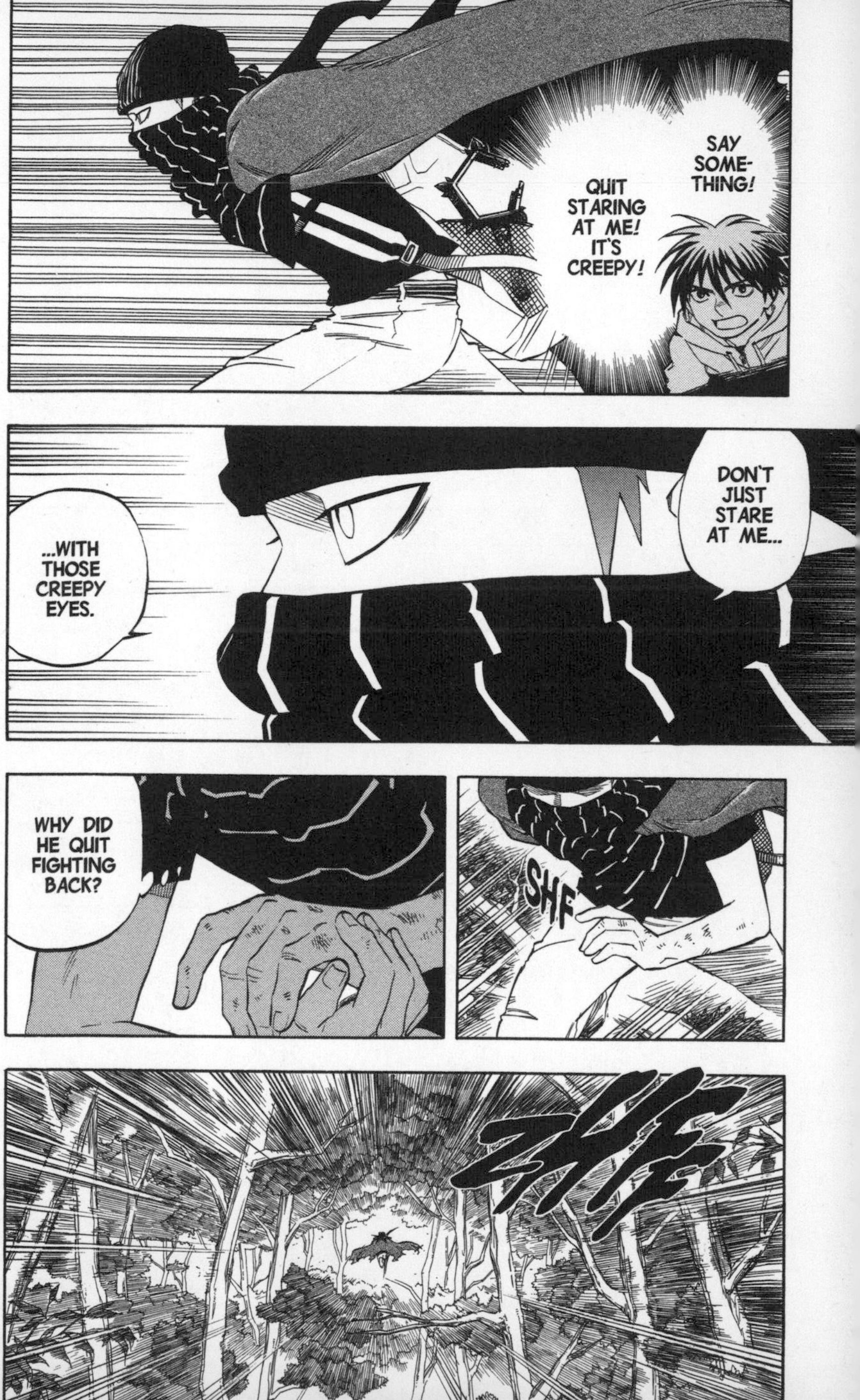
SAY SOMETHING!
QUIT STARING AT ME! IT'S CREEPY!
DON'T JUST STARE AT ME...
...WITH THOSE CREEPY EYES.
SHF
WHY DID HE QUIT FIGHTING BACK?

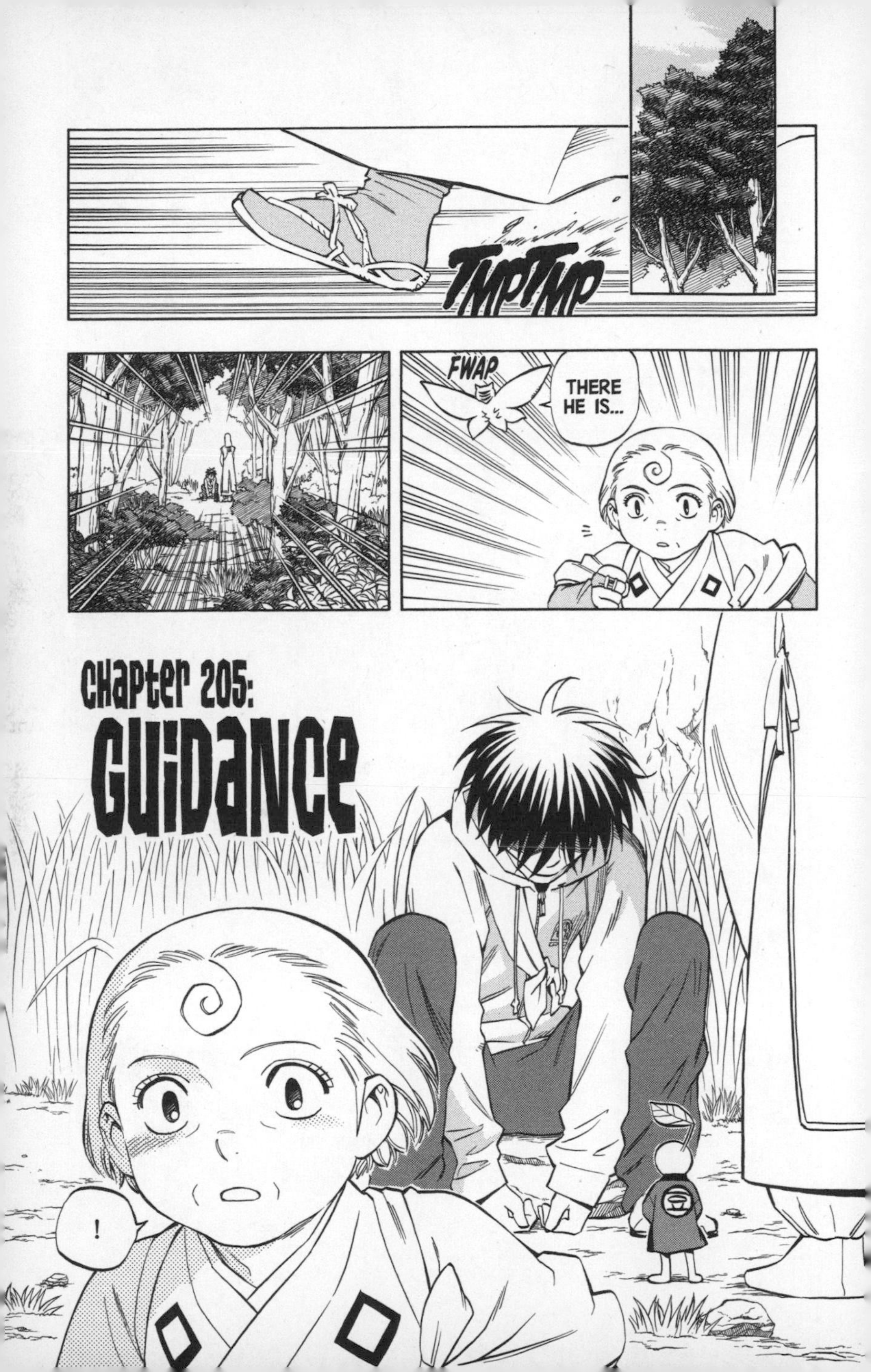
TMPTMP
FWAP
THERE HE IS...
Chapter 205:
Guidance
!

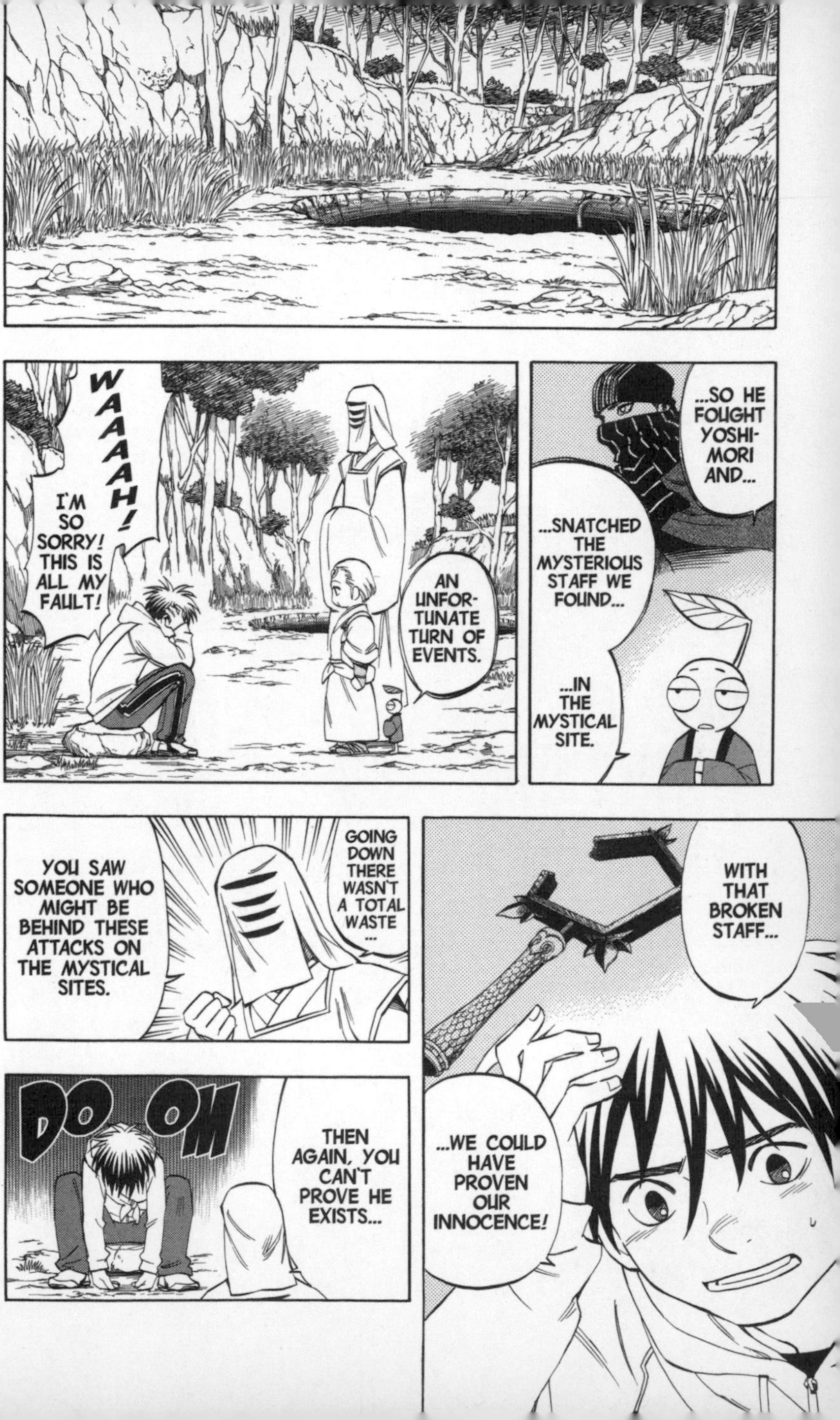
...SO HE FOUGHT YOSHI-MORI AND...
...SNATCHED THE MYSTERIOUS STAFF WE FOUND...
...IN THE MYSTICAL SITE.
AN UNFOR-TUNATE TURN OF EVENTS.
WAAAAAH!
I'M SO SORRY! THIS IS ALL MY FAULT!
WITH THAT BROKEN STAFF...
...WE COULD HAVE PROVEN OUR INNOCENCE!
GOING DOWN THERE WASN'T A TOTAL WASTE ...
YOU SAW SOMEONE WHO MIGHT BE BEHIND THESE ATTACKS ON THE MYSTICAL SITES.
THEN AGAIN, YOU CAN'T PROVE HE EXISTS...
DO OH

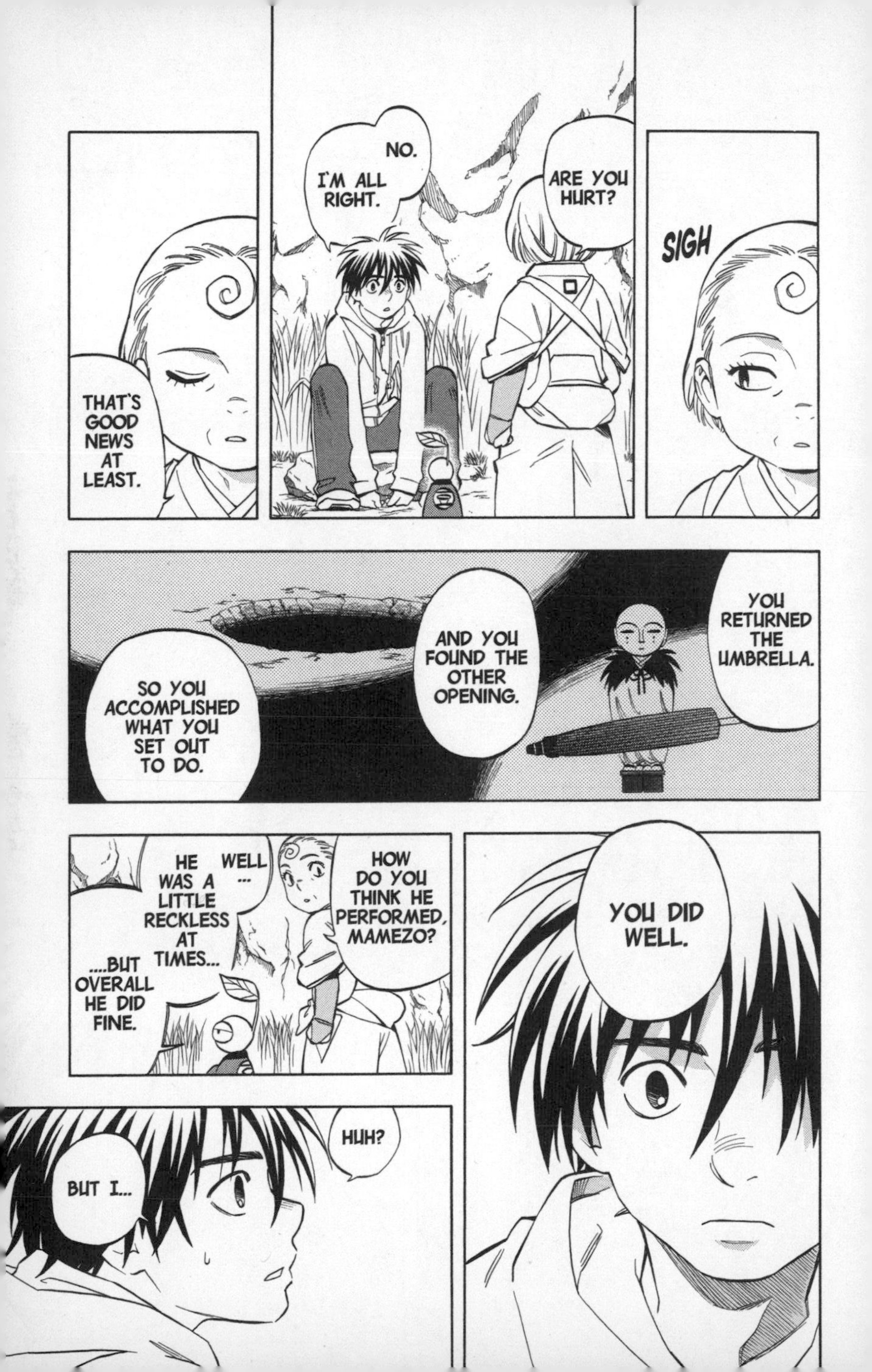
SIGH
ARE YOU HURT?
NO.
I'M ALL RIGHT.
THAT'S GOOD NEWS AT LEAST.
YOU RETURNED THE UMBRELLA.
AND YOU FOUND THE OTHER OPENING.
SO YOU ACCOMPLISHED WHAT YOU SET OUT TO DO.
YOU DID WELL.
HOW DO YOU THINK HE PERFORMED, MAMEZO?
WELL ...
HE WAS A LITTLE RECKLESS AT TIMES...
....BUT OVERALL HE DID FINE.
HUH?
BUT I...

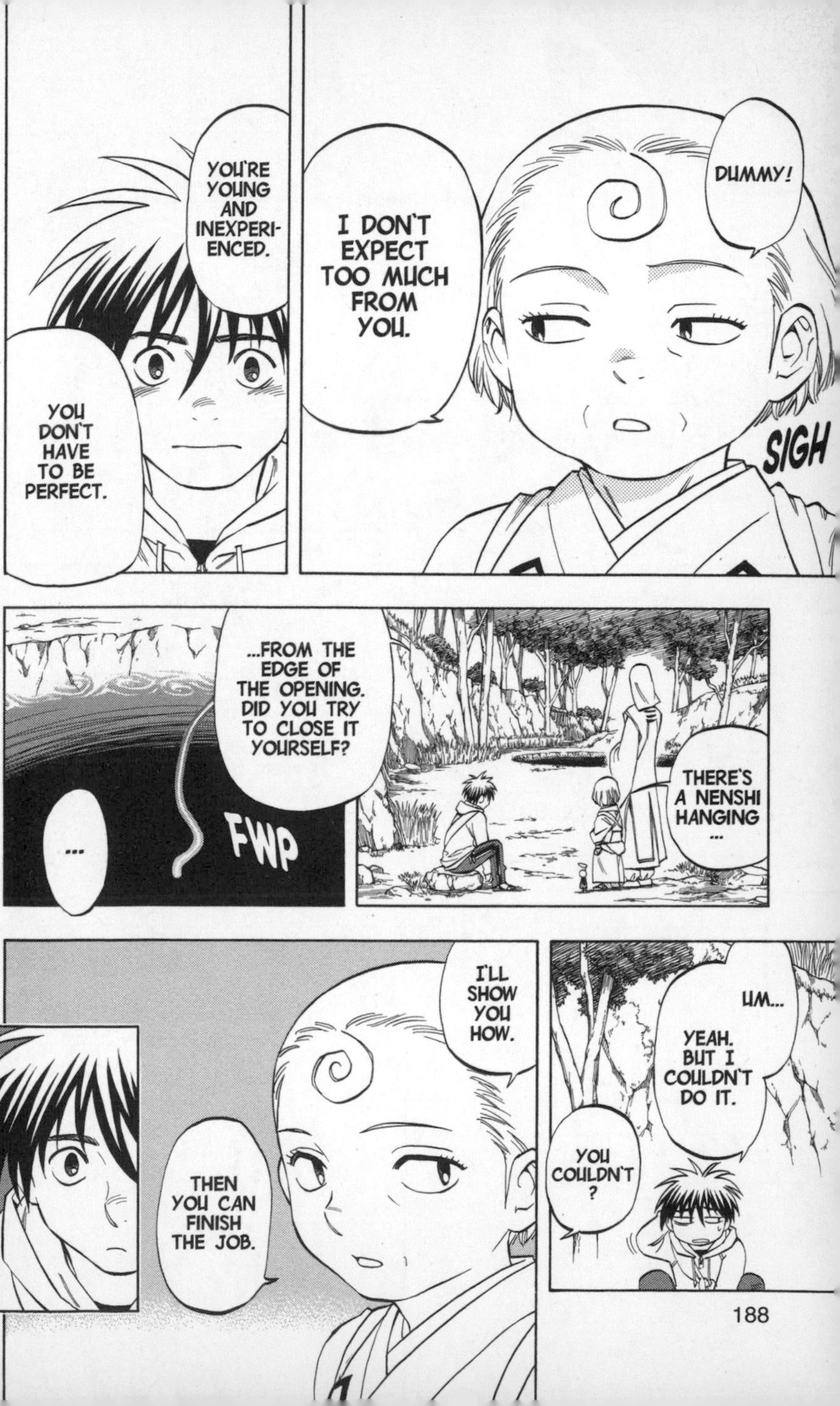
DUMMY!
SIGH
I DON'T EXPECT TOO MUCH FROM YOU.
YOU'RE YOUNG AND INEXPERIENCED.
YOU DON'T HAVE TO BE PERFECT.
THERE'S A NENSHI HANGING ...
...FROM THE EDGE OF THE OPENING. DID YOU TRY TO CLOSE IT YOURSELF?
FWP
...
UM...
YEAH. BUT I COULDN'T DO IT.
YOU COULDN'T ?
I'LL SHOW YOU HOW.
THEN YOU CAN FINISH THE JOB.

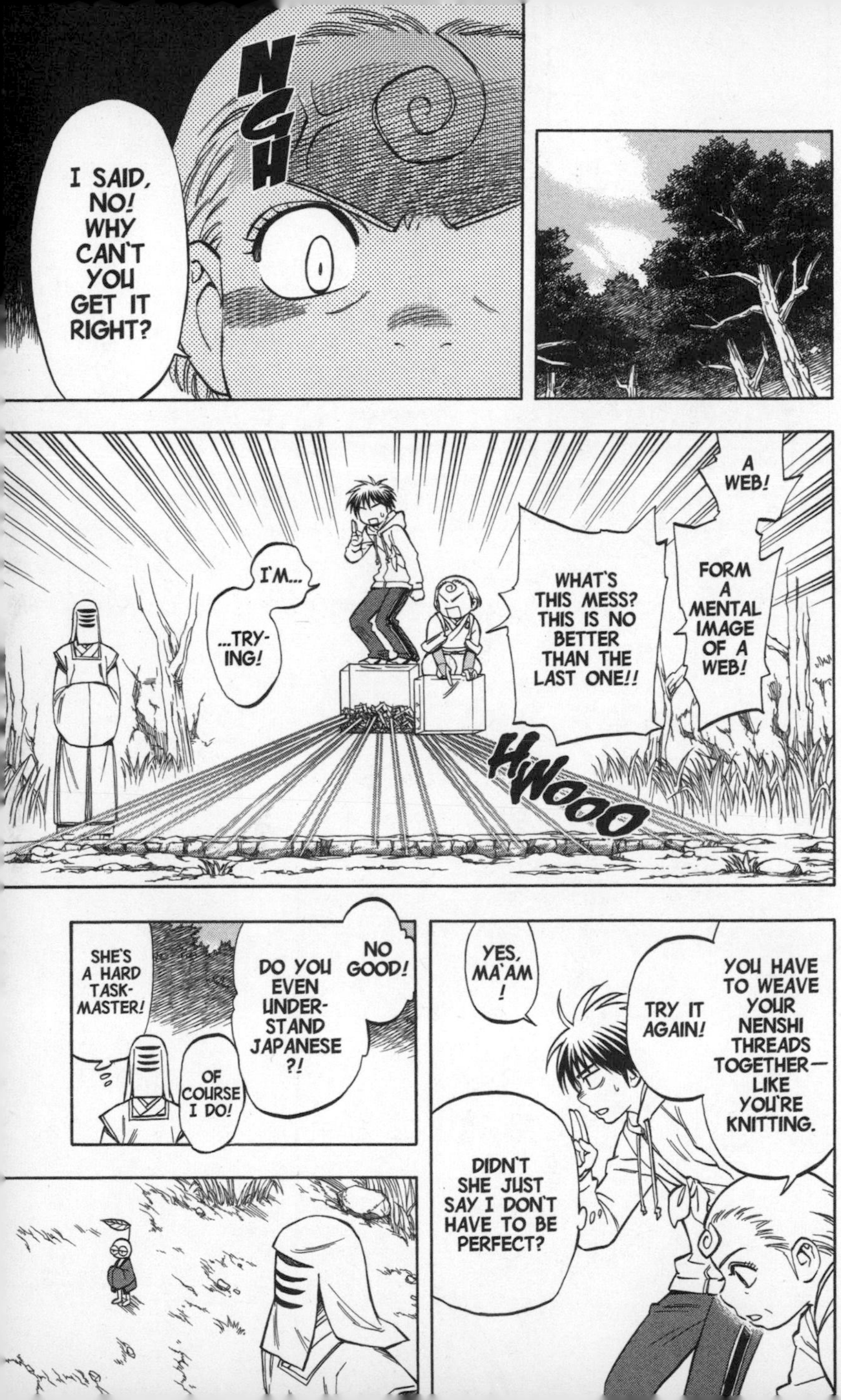
I SAID, NO! WHY CAN'T YOU GET IT RIGHT?
NGH
A WEB!
FORM A MENTAL IMAGE OF A WEB!
WHAT'S THIS MESS? THIS IS NO BETTER THAN THE LAST ONE!!
HWOOO
I'M...
...TRY-ING!
YOU HAVE TO WEAVE YOUR NENSHI THREADS TOGETHER—LIKE YOU'RE KNITTING.
TRY IT AGAIN!
YES, MA'AM!
DIDN'T SHE JUST SAY I DON'T HAVE TO BE PERFECT?
NO GOOD!
DO YOU EVEN UNDER-STAND JAPANESE?!
SHE'S A HARD TASK-MASTER!
OF COURSE I DO!

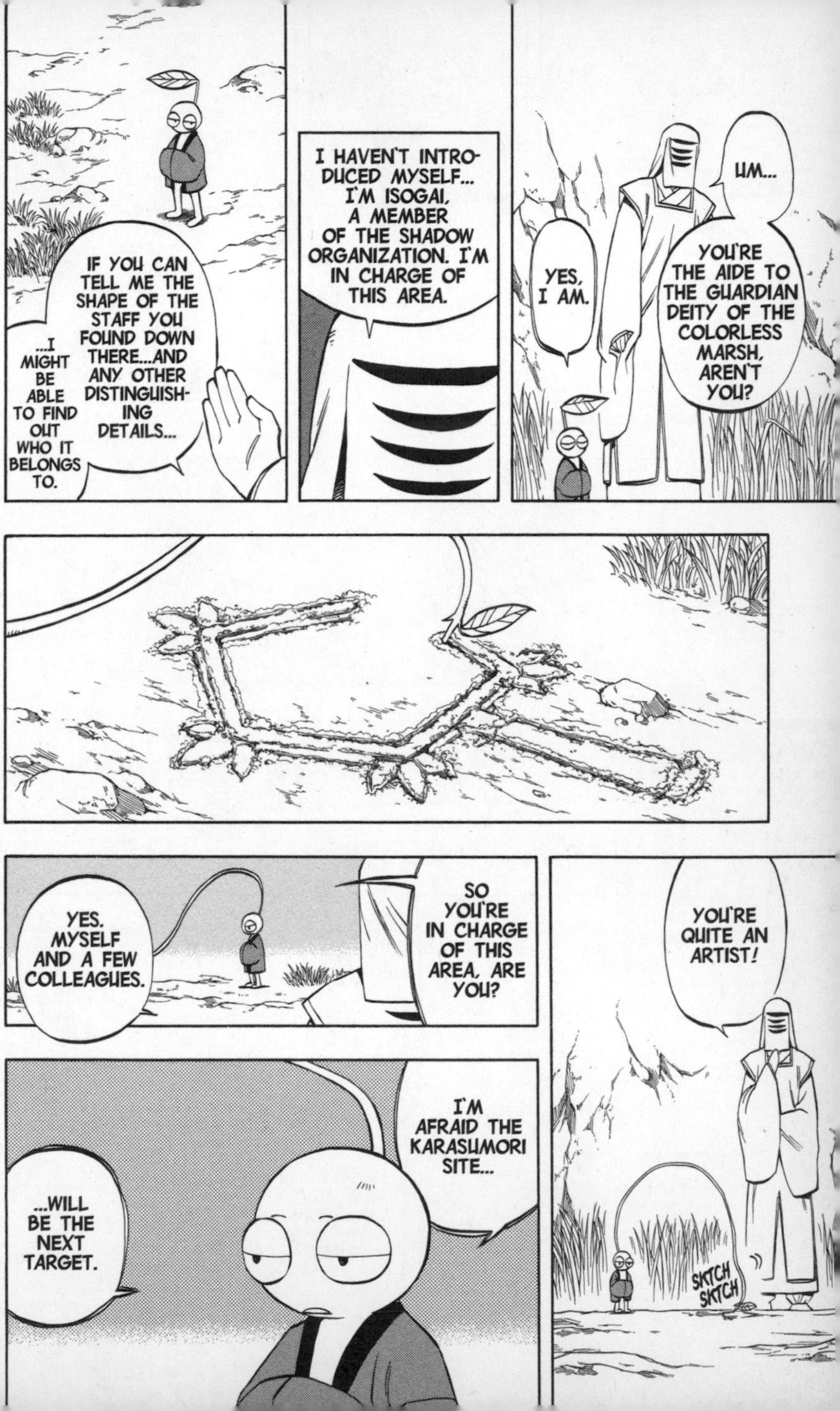
UM...
YOU'RE THE AIDE TO THE GUARDIAN DEITY OF THE COLORLESS MARSH, AREN'T YOU?
YES, I AM.
I HAVEN'T INTRO-DUCED MYSELF... I'M ISOGAI, A MEMBER OF THE SHADOW ORGANIZATION. I'M IN CHARGE OF THIS AREA.
IF YOU CAN TELL ME THE SHAPE OF THE STAFF YOU FOUND DOWN THERE...AND ANY OTHER DISTINGUISH-ING DETAILS...
...I MIGHT BE ABLE TO FIND OUT WHO IT BELONGS TO.
YOU'RE QUITE AN ARTIST!
SKTCH SKTCH
SO YOU'RE IN CHARGE OF THIS AREA, ARE YOU?
YES. MYSELF AND A FEW COLLEAGUES.
I'M AFRAID THE KARASUMORI SITE...
...WILL BE THE NEXT TARGET.

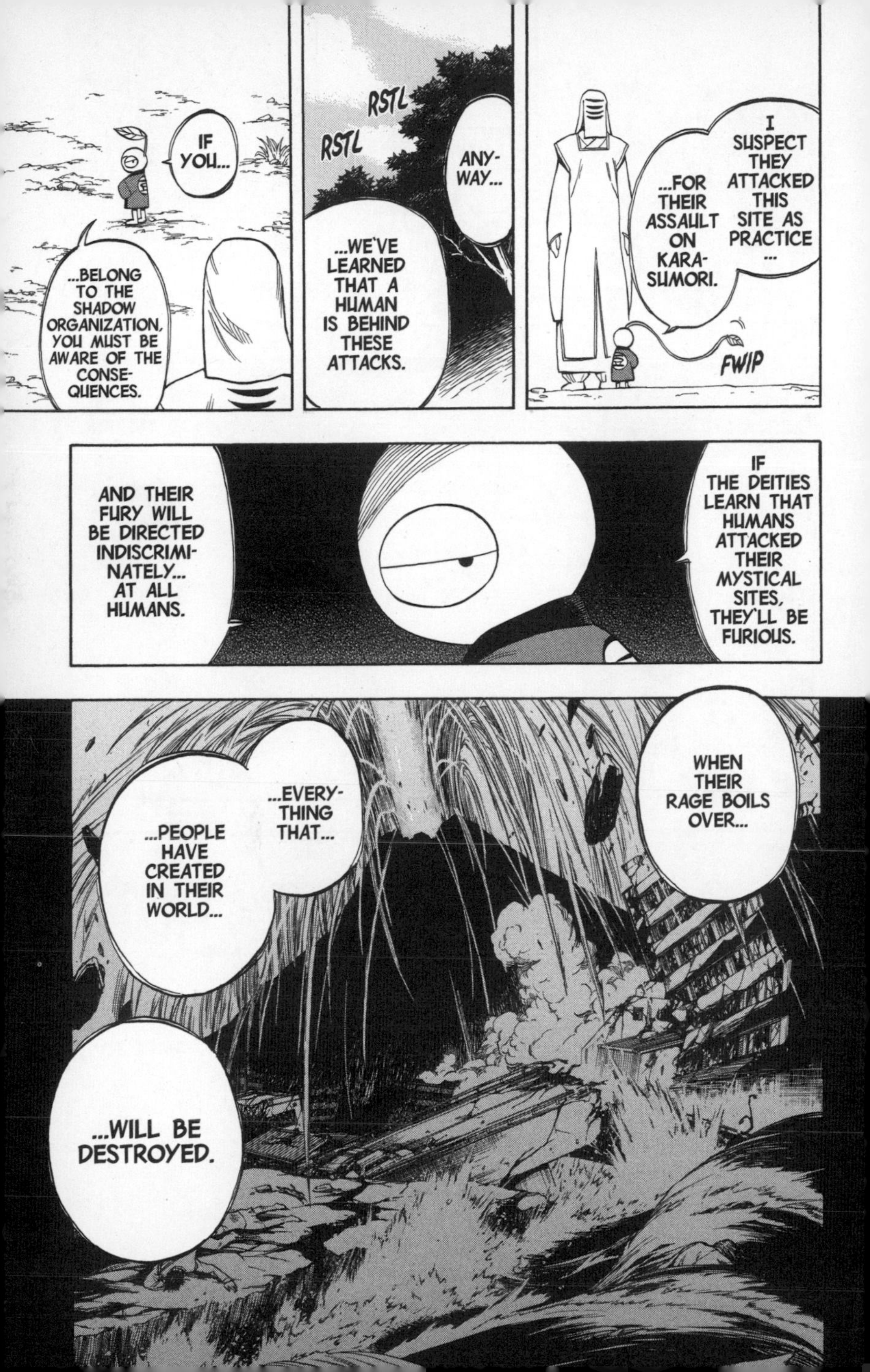
I SUSPECT THEY ATTACKED THIS SITE AS PRACTICE ...
...FOR THEIR ASSAULT ON KARA-SUMORI.
FWIP
ANY-WAY...
RSTL
RSTL
...WE'VE LEARNED THAT A HUMAN IS BEHIND THESE ATTACKS.
IF YOU...
...BELONG TO THE SHADOW ORGANIZATION, YOU MUST BE AWARE OF THE CONSE-QUENCES.
IF THE DEITIES LEARN THAT HUMANS ATTACKED THEIR MYSTICAL SITES, THEY'LL BE FURIOUS.
AND THEIR FURY WILL BE DIRECTED INDISCRIMI-NATELY... AT ALL HUMANS.
WHEN THEIR RAGE BOILS OVER...
...EVERY-THING THAT...
...PEOPLE HAVE CREATED IN THEIR WORLD...
...WILL BE DESTROYED.

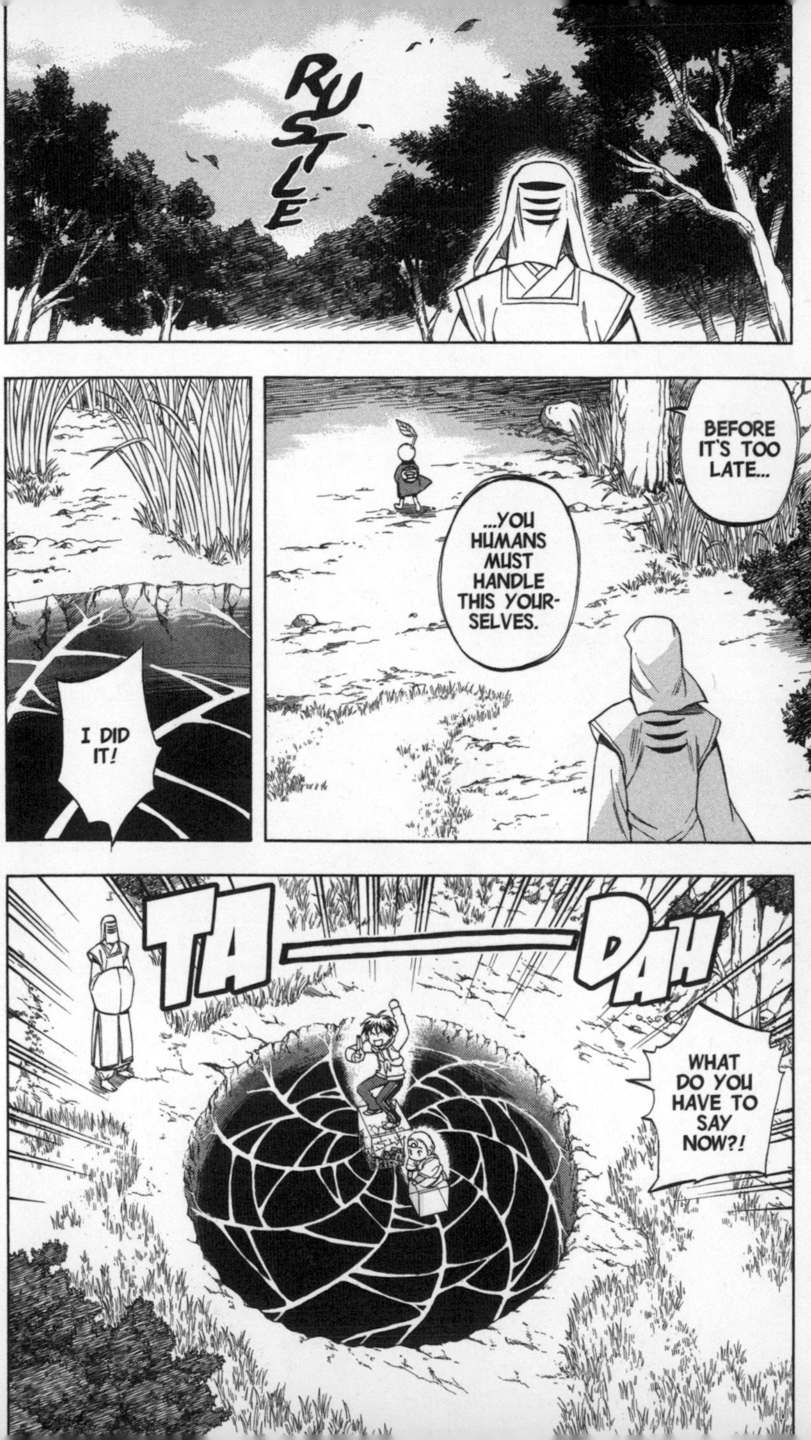
RUSTLE
BEFORE IT'S TOO LATE...
...YOU HUMANS MUST HANDLE THIS YOUR-SELVES.
I DID IT!
TA——DAH
WHAT DO YOU HAVE TO SAY NOW?!

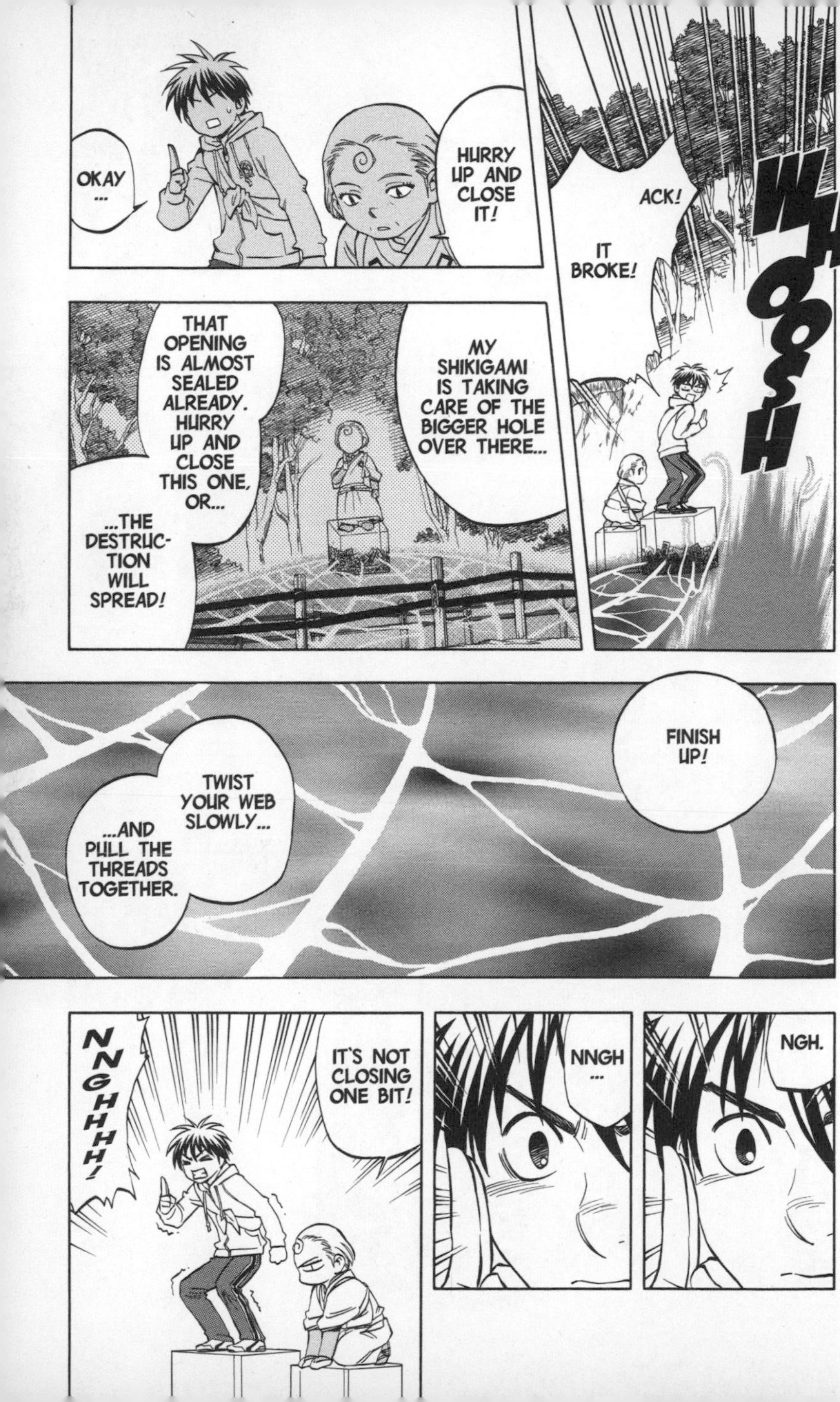
WHOOSH
ACK!
IT BROKE!
HURRY UP AND CLOSE IT!
OKAY ...
MY SHIKIGAMI IS TAKING CARE OF THE BIGGER HOLE OVER THERE...
THAT OPENING IS ALMOST SEALED ALREADY. HURRY UP AND CLOSE THIS ONE, OR...
...THE DESTRUC-TION WILL SPREAD!
FINISH UP!
TWIST YOUR WEB SLOWLY...
...AND PULL THE THREADS TOGETHER.
NGH.
NNGH ...
IT'S NOT CLOSING ONE BIT!
NNGHHHH!

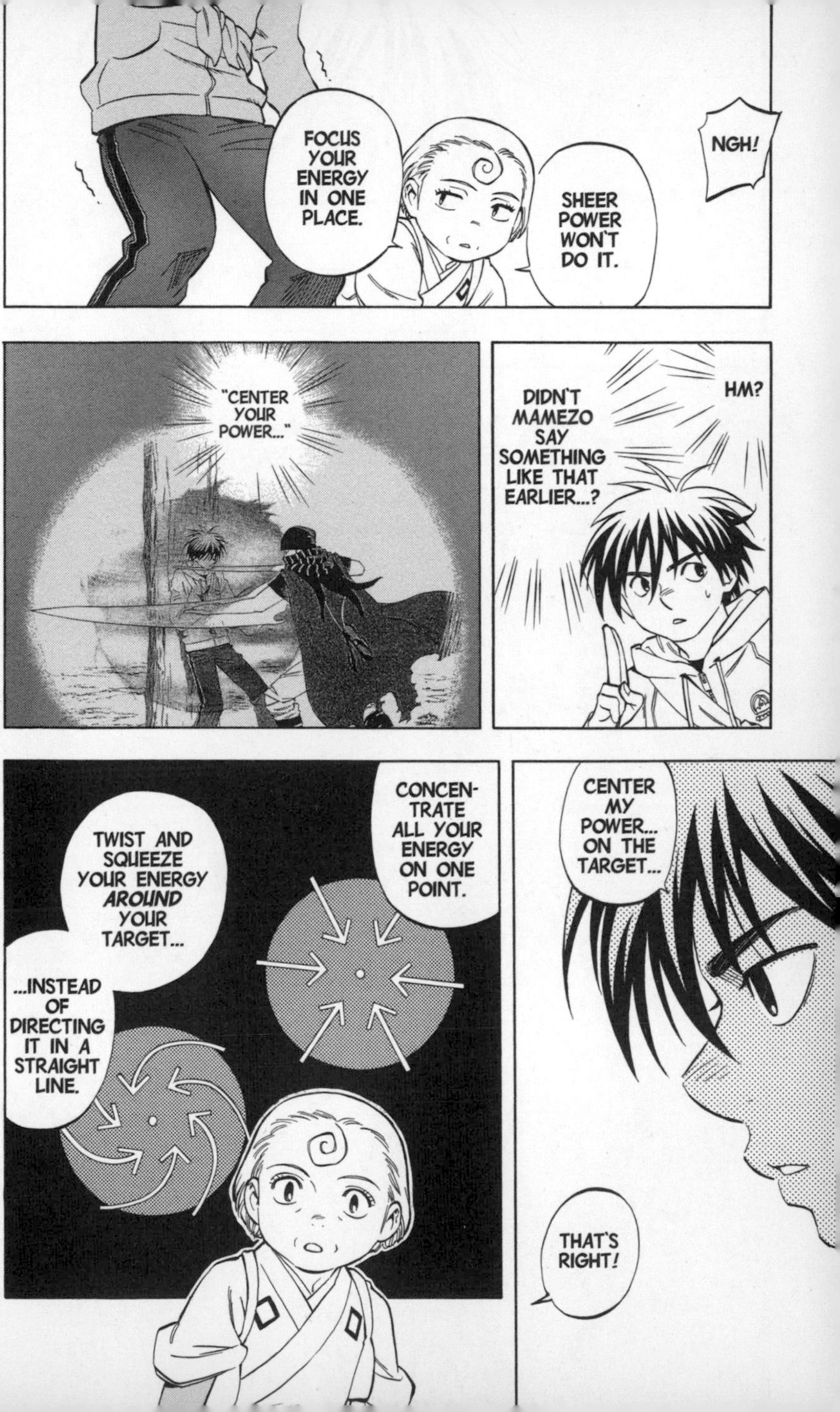
NGH!
SHEER POWER WON'T DO IT.
FOCUS YOUR ENERGY IN ONE PLACE.
HM?
DIDN'T MAMEZO SAY SOMETHING LIKE THAT EARLIER...?
"CENTER YOUR POWER..."
CENTER MY POWER... ON THE TARGET...
THAT'S RIGHT!
CONCEN-TRATE ALL YOUR ENERGY ON ONE POINT.
TWIST AND SQUEEZE YOUR ENERGY *AROUND* YOUR TARGET...
...INSTEAD OF DIRECTING IT IN A STRAIGHT LINE.

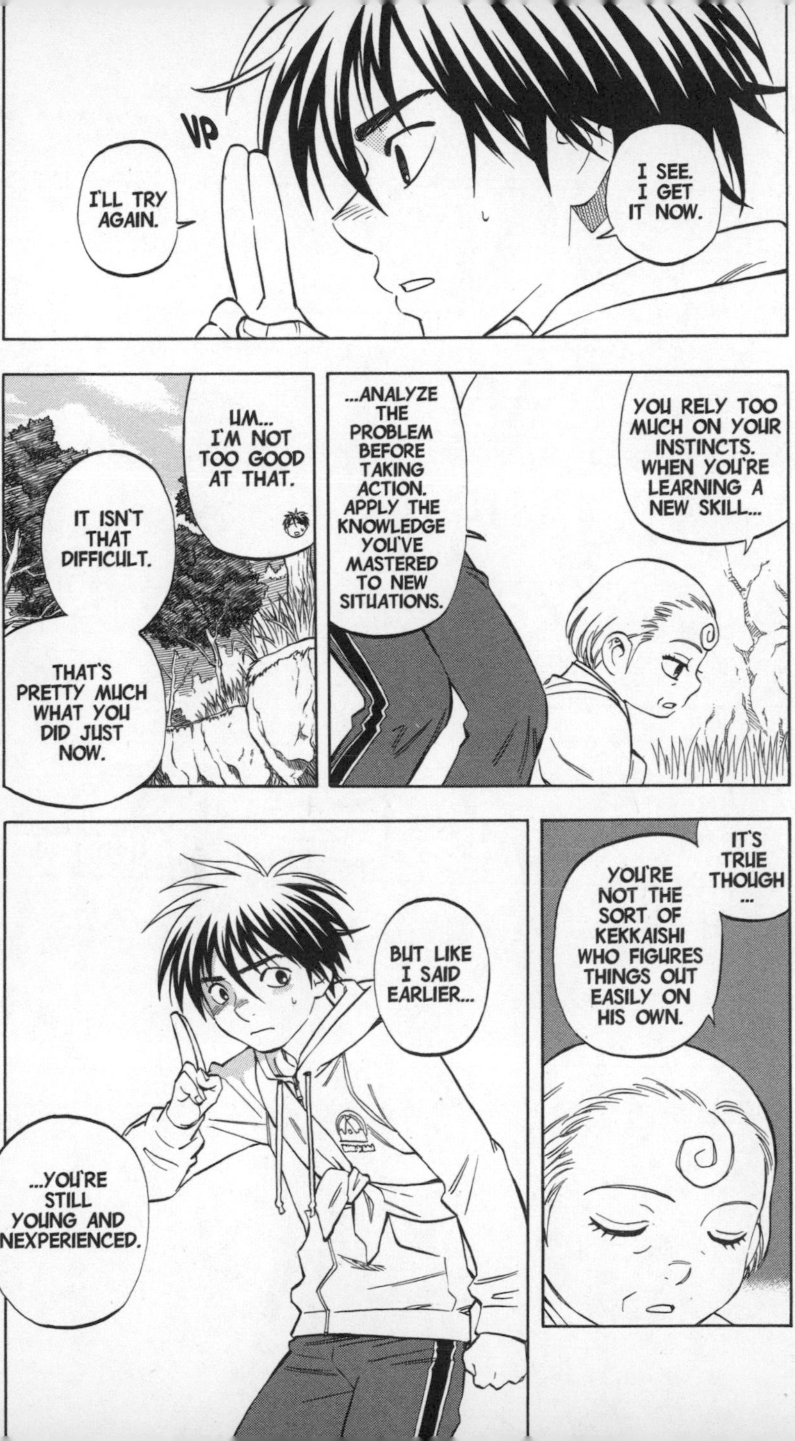

I SEE. I GET IT NOW.
VP
I'LL TRY AGAIN.
YOU RELY TOO MUCH ON YOUR INSTINCTS. WHEN YOU'RE LEARNING A NEW SKILL...
...ANALYZE THE PROBLEM BEFORE TAKING ACTION. APPLY THE KNOWLEDGE YOU'VE MASTERED TO NEW SITUATIONS.
UM... I'M NOT TOO GOOD AT THAT.
IT ISN'T THAT DIFFICULT.
THAT'S PRETTY MUCH WHAT YOU DID JUST NOW.
IT'S TRUE THOUGH ...
YOU'RE NOT THE SORT OF KEKKAISHI WHO FIGURES THINGS OUT EASILY ON HIS OWN.
BUT LIKE I SAID EARLIER...
...YOU'RE STILL YOUNG AND INEXPERIENCED.

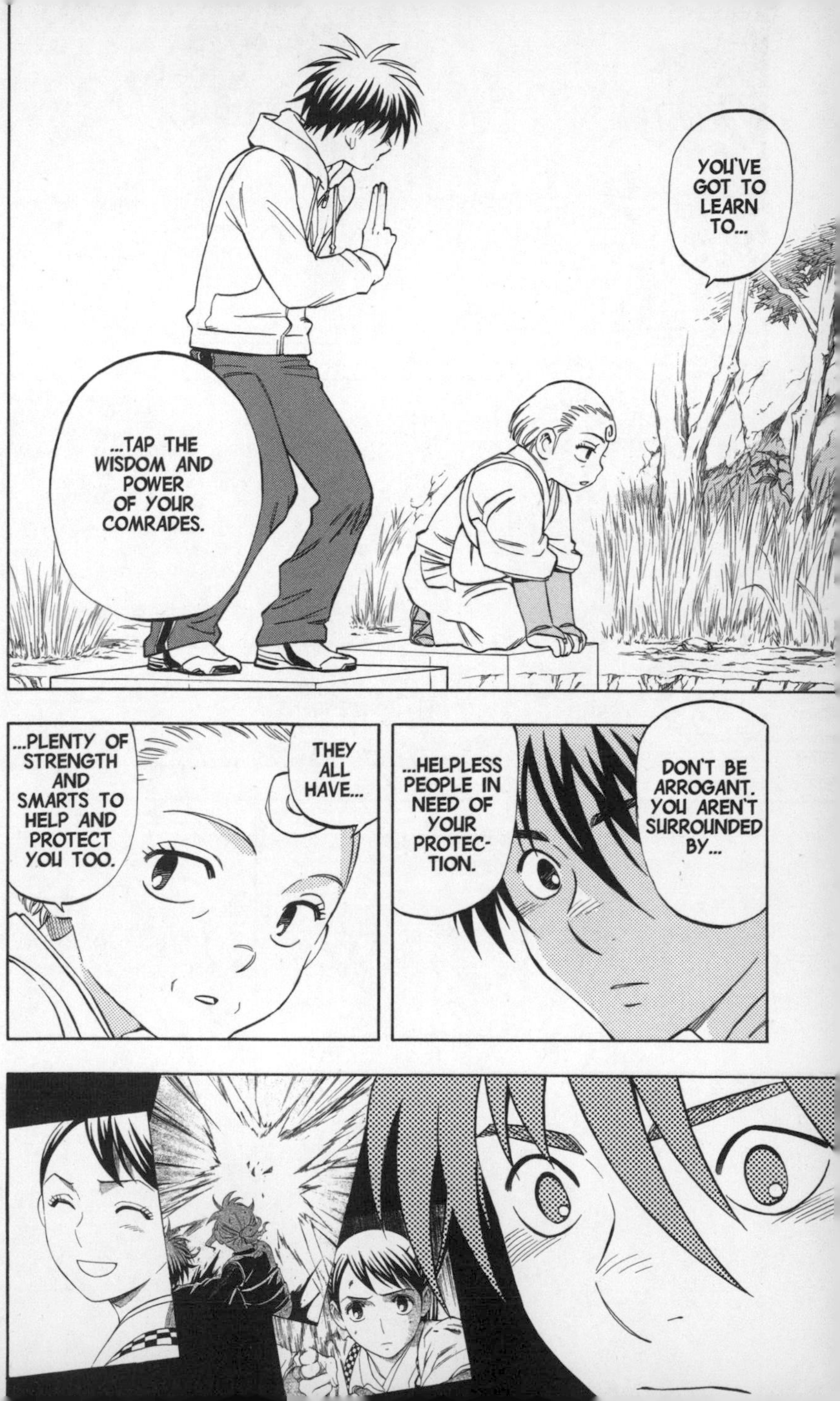
YOU'VE GOT TO LEARN TO...
...TAP THE WISDOM AND POWER OF YOUR COMRADES.
DON'T BE ARROGANT. YOU AREN'T SURROUNDED BY...
...HELPLESS PEOPLE IN NEED OF YOUR PROTECTION.
THEY ALL HAVE...
...PLENTY OF STRENGTH AND SMARTS TO HELP AND PROTECT YOU TOO.

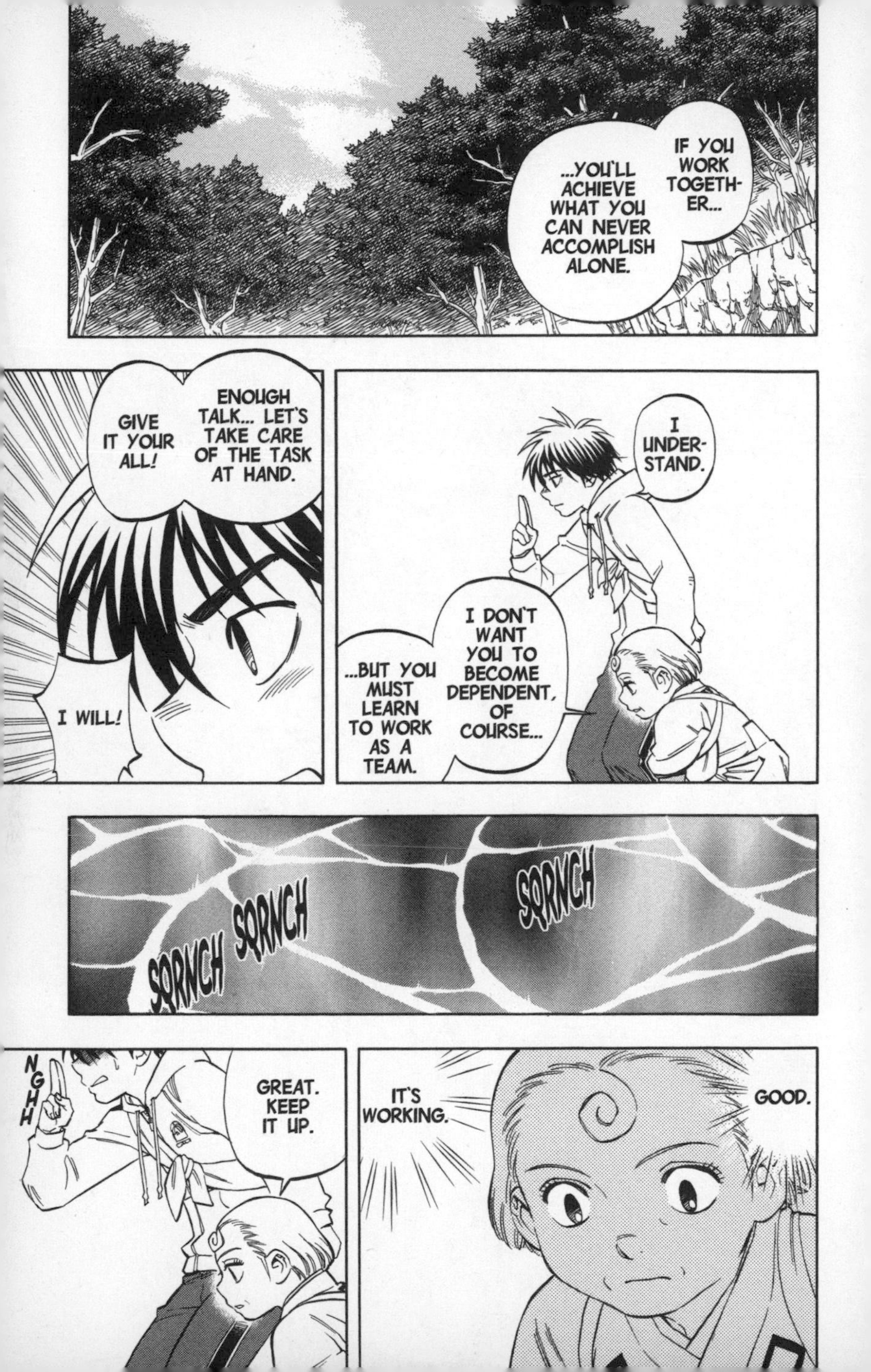
IF YOU WORK TOGETH-ER...
...YOU'LL ACHIEVE WHAT YOU CAN NEVER ACCOMPLISH ALONE.
I UNDER-STAND.
I DON'T WANT YOU TO BECOME DEPENDENT, OF COURSE...
...BUT YOU MUST LEARN TO WORK AS A TEAM.
ENOUGH TALK... LET'S TAKE CARE OF THE TASK AT HAND.
GIVE IT YOUR ALL!
I WILL!
SQRNCH
SQRNCH SQRNCH
GOOD.
IT'S WORKING.
GREAT. KEEP IT UP.
NGHH

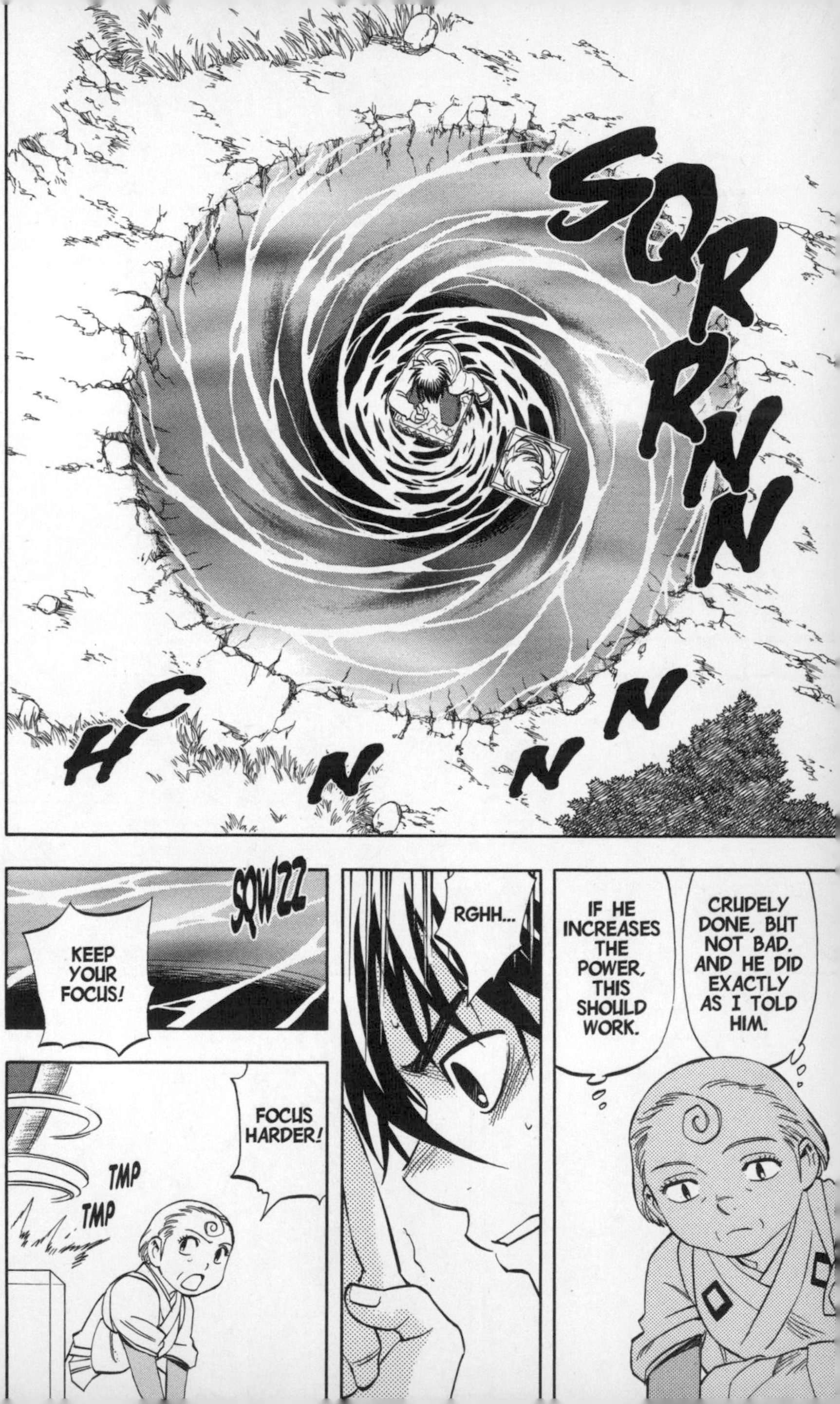
SQRRNN
HCNNN
SQWZZ
KEEP YOUR FOCUS!
CRUDELY DONE, BUT NOT BAD. AND HE DID EXACTLY AS I TOLD HIM.
IF HE INCREASES THE POWER, THIS SHOULD WORK.
RGHH...
FOCUS HARDER!
TMP
TMP

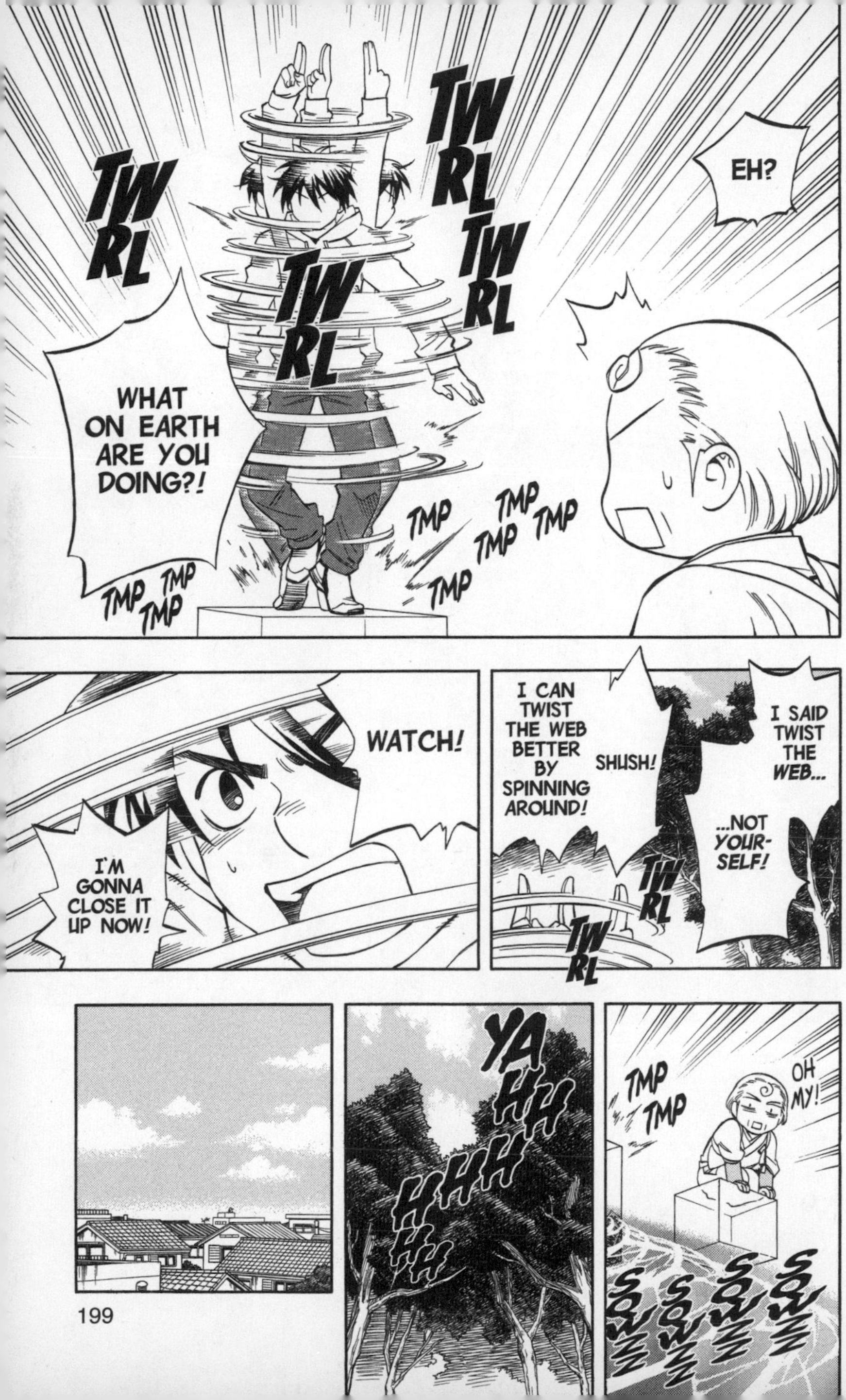
EH?
TWRL TWRL
TWRL
TWRL
WHAT ON EARTH ARE YOU DOING?!
TMP TMP TMP TMP TMP
TMP TMP TMP
I SAID TWIST THE WEB...
...NOT YOURSELF!
SHUSH!
I CAN TWIST THE WEB BETTER BY SPINNING AROUND!
TWRL
TWRL
WATCH!
I'M GONNA CLOSE IT UP NOW!
OH MY!
TMP TMP
SOWWW SOWWW SOWWW SOWWW
YAHHHHHHHHH

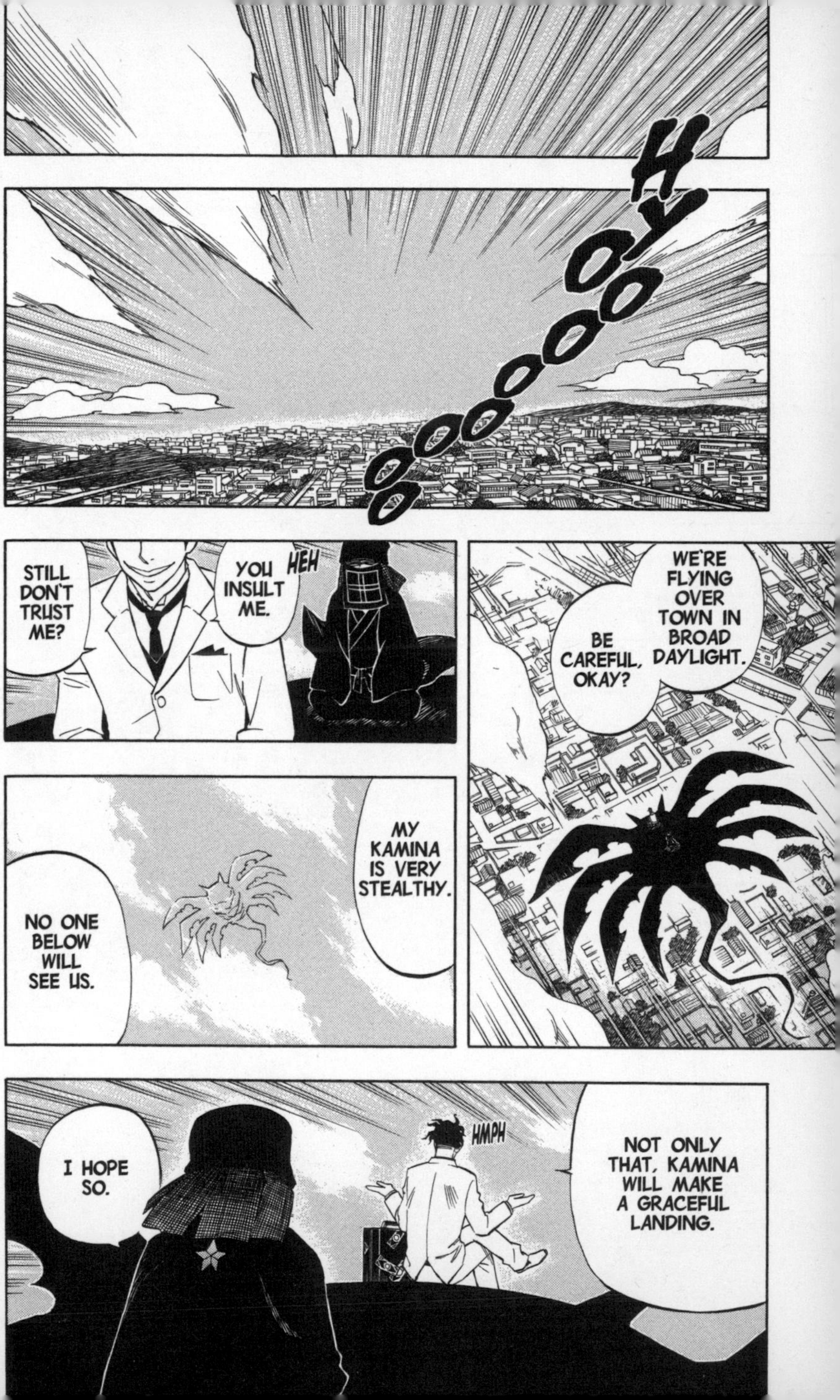
HYOOOOOOOOO
WE'RE FLYING OVER TOWN IN BROAD DAYLIGHT.
BE CAREFUL, OKAY?
HEH
YOU INSULT ME.
STILL DON'T TRUST ME?
MY KAMINA IS VERY STEALTHY.
NO ONE BELOW WILL SEE US.
NOT ONLY THAT, KAMINA WILL MAKE A GRACEFUL LANDING.
HMPH
I HOPE SO.

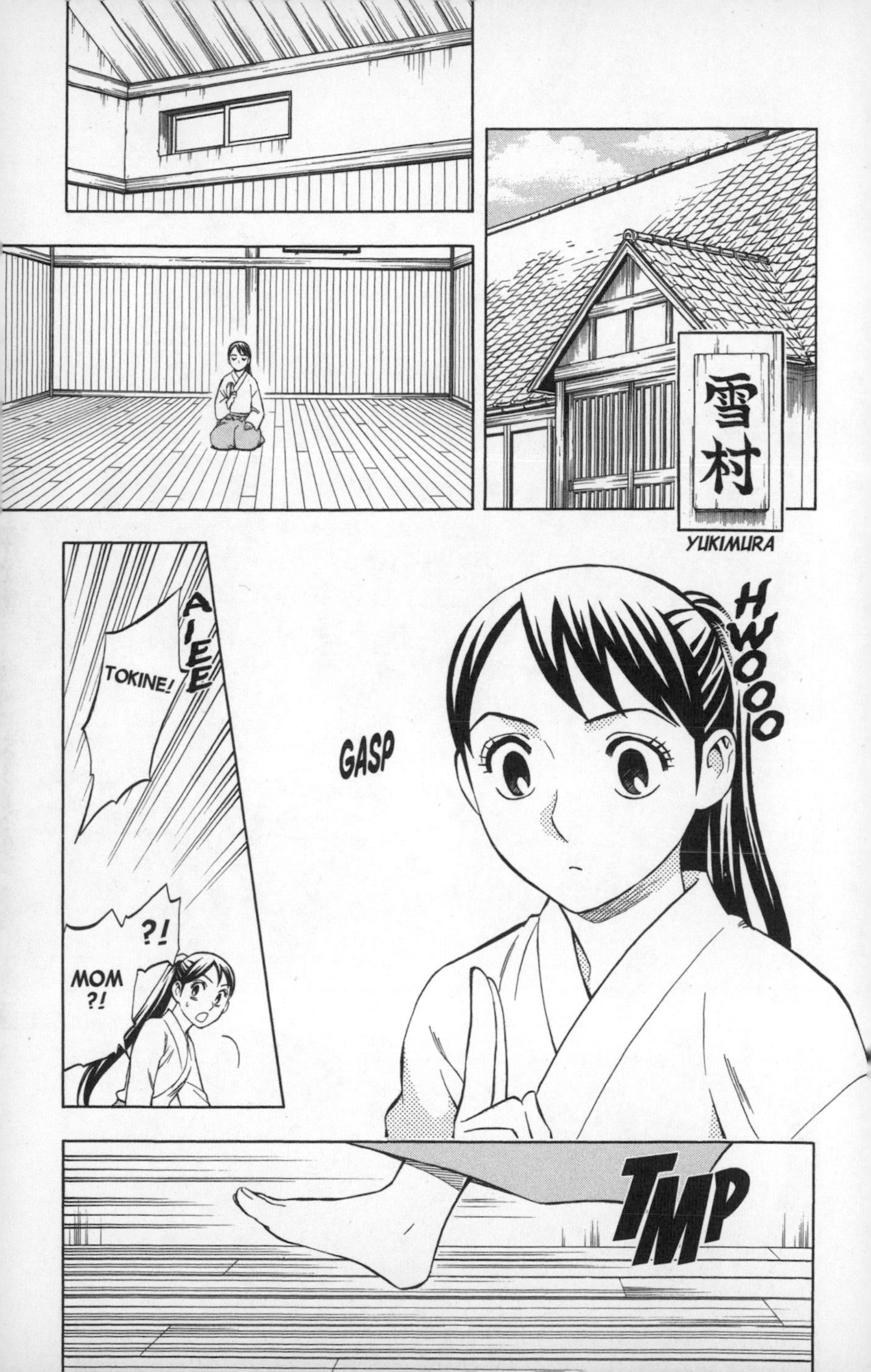
雪村
YUKIMURA
HWOOO
GASP
AIEE
TOKINE!
?!
MOM ?!
TMP

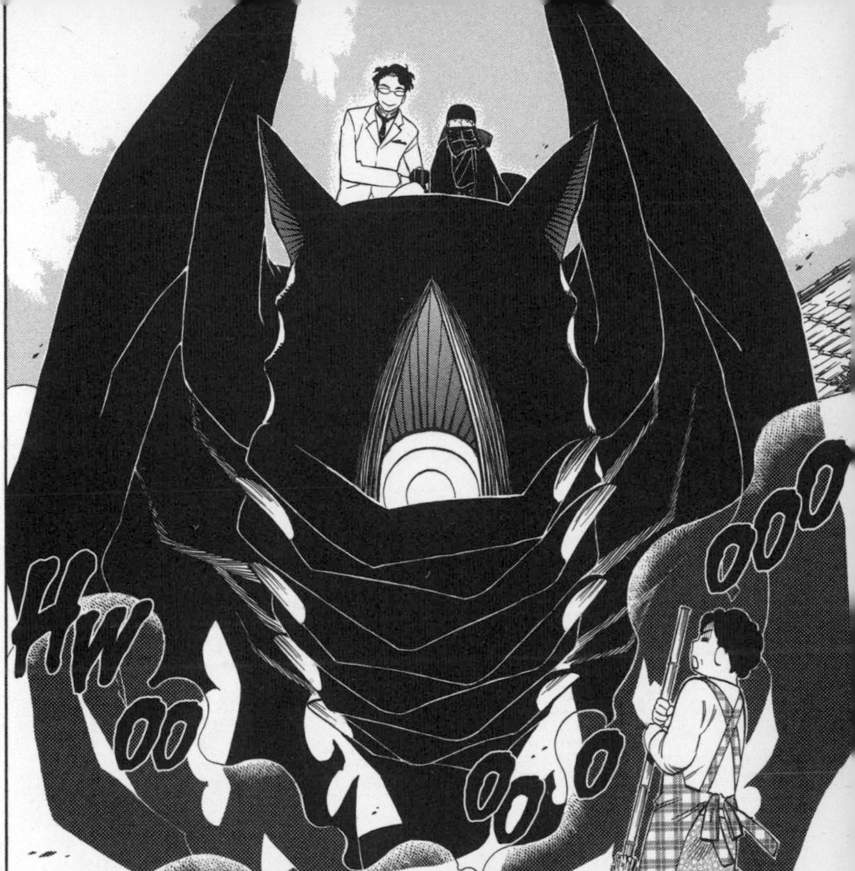
HWOO OOOO OOO
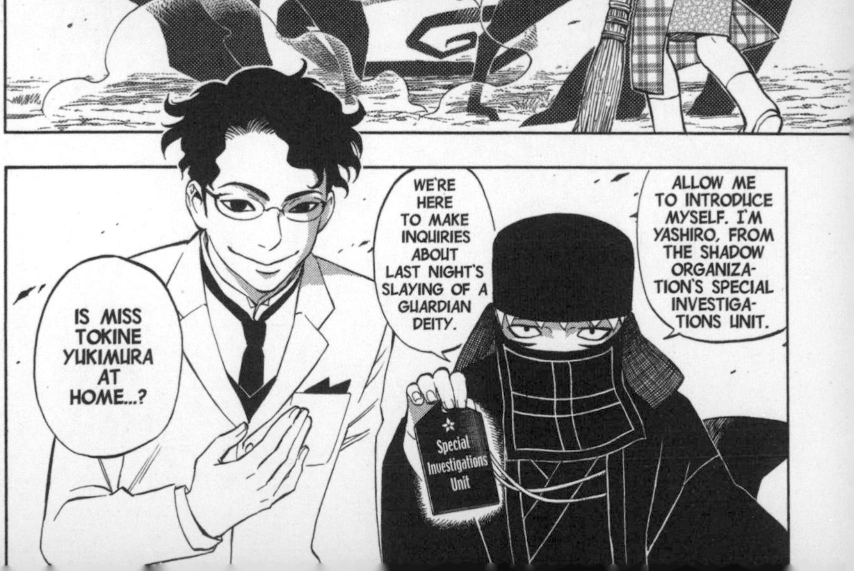
ALLOW ME TO INTRODUCE MYSELF. I'M YASHIRO, FROM THE SHADOW ORGANIZATION'S SPECIAL INVESTIGATIONS UNIT.
WE'RE HERE TO MAKE INQUIRIES ABOUT LAST NIGHT'S SLAYING OF A GUARDIAN DEITY.
IS MISS TOKINE YUKIMURA AT HOME...?
Special Investigations Unit

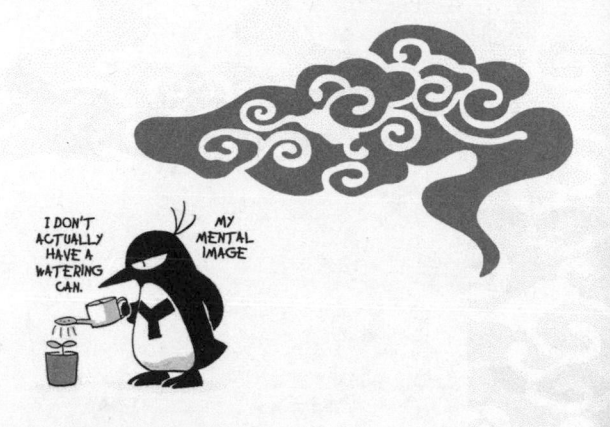

MY MENTAL IMAGE
I DON'T ACTUALLY HAVE A WATERING CAN.

MESSAGE FROM YELLOW TANABE

At the beginning of spring, someone gave me some flower seeds and a gardening kit. I seized the opportunity to try my hand at gardening.

I thought I should place the pots in conspicuous places—otherwise, I'd forget to water them. So I put them right beside my desk.

I'm hoping all the flowers will be in full bloom by the time this volume of *Kekkaishi* hits the bookstores!

KEKKAISHI

VOLUME 21

SHONEN SUNDAY EDITION

STORY AND ART BY YELLOW TANABE

Original Japanese edition "KEKKAISHI" published by SHOGAKUKAN Inc.

Translation/Yuko Sawada
Touch-up Art & Lettering/Stephen Dutro
Cover Design & Graphic Layout/Julie Behn
Editor/Annette Roman

VP, Production/Alvin Lu
VP, Sales & Product Marketing/Gonzalo Ferreyra
VP, Creative/Linda Espinosa
Publisher/Hyoe Narita

Printed in Canada

Published by VIZ Media, LLC
P.O. Box 77010
San Francisco, CA 94107

10 9 8 7 6 5 4 3 2 1
First printing, May 2010

www.viz.com

RATED T FOR TEEN
PARENTAL ADVISORY
KEKKAISHI is rated T for Teen and is recommended for ages 13 and up. It contains fantasy violence.
ratings.viz.com

WWW.SHONENSUNDAY.COM

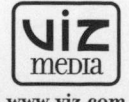

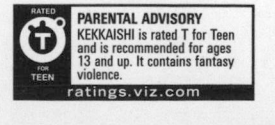

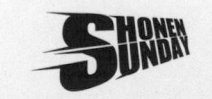

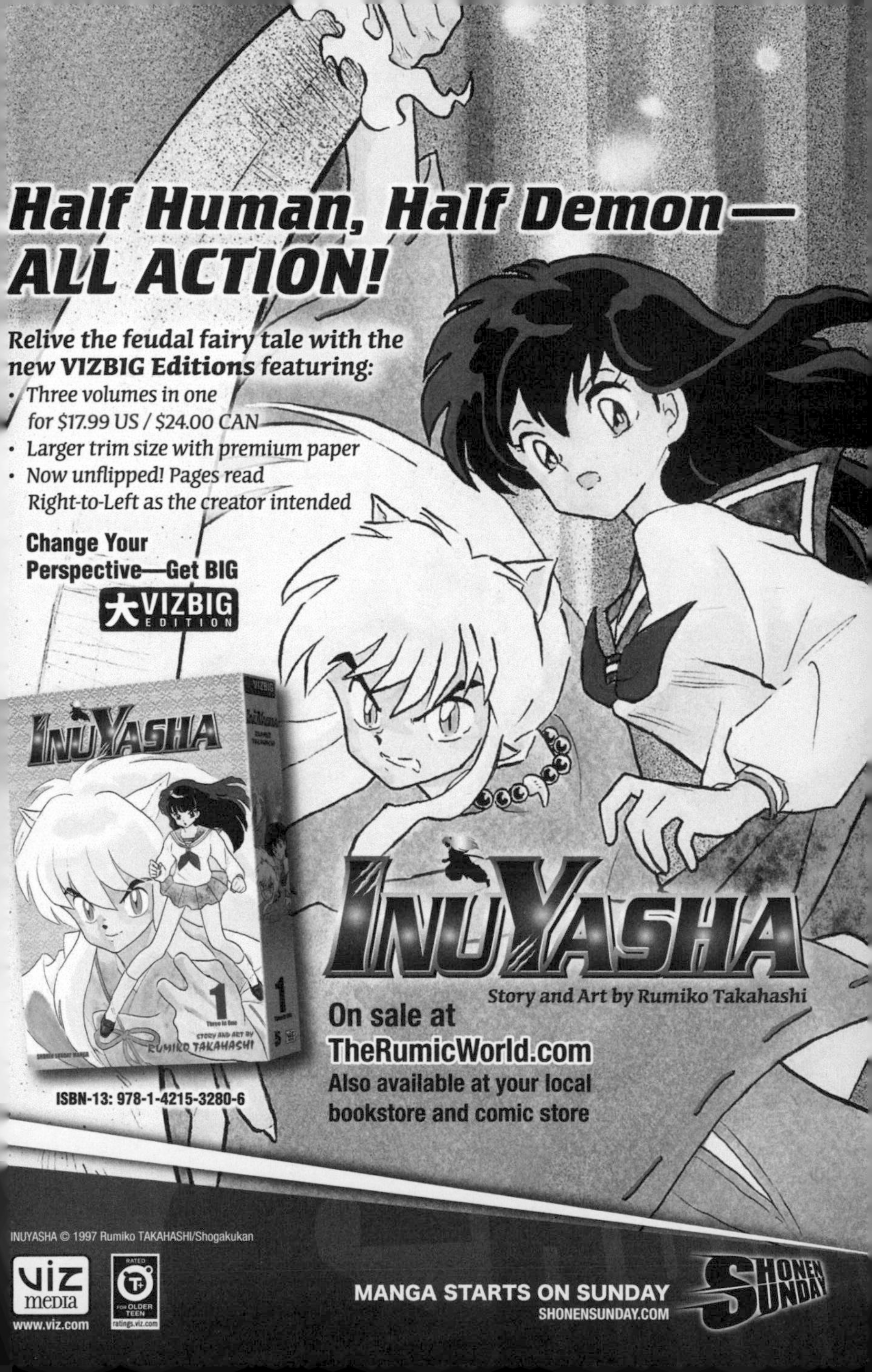
Half Human, Half Demon—
ALL ACTION!
Relive the feudal fairy tale with the new VIZBIG Editions featuring:
• Three volumes in one for $17.99 US / $24.00 CAN
• Larger trim size with premium paper
• Now unflipped! Pages read Right-to-Left as the creator intended
Change Your Perspective—Get BIG
大VIZBIG EDITION
INUYASHA
1
Three in One
STORY AND ART BY RUMIKO TAKAHASHI
ISBN-13: 978-1-4215-3280-6
INUYASHA
Story and Art by Rumiko Takahashi
On sale at
TheRumicWorld.com
Also available at your local bookstore and comic store
INUYASHA © 1997 Rumiko TAKAHASHI/Shogakukan
viz media
www.viz.com
RATED T+ FOR OLDER TEEN
ratings.viz.com
MANGA STARTS ON SUNDAY
SHONENSUNDAY.COM
SHONEN SUNDAY

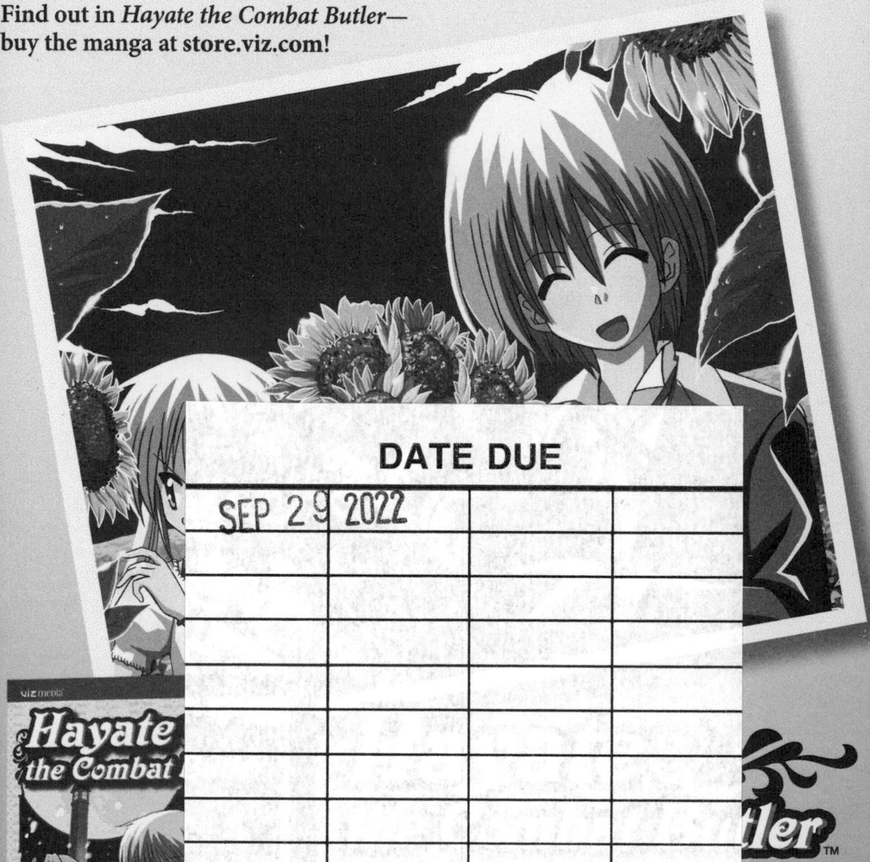

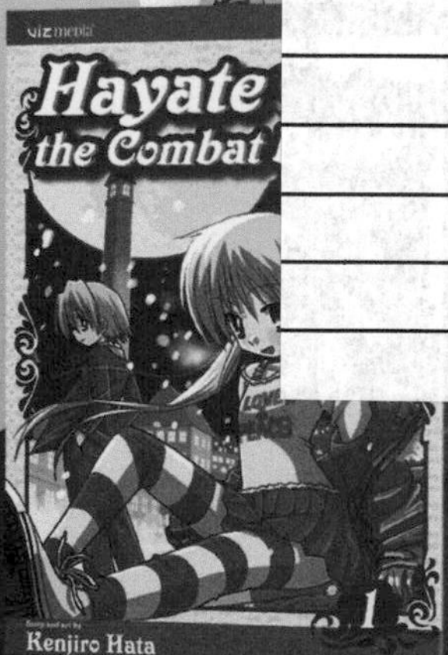
viz media
Hayate the Combat
1
Kenjiro Hata